P9-DTW-222

THE PRINCIPLES OF ECONOMICS COURSE

A HANDBOOK FOR INSTRUCTORS

THE PRINCIPLES OF ECONOMICS COURSE

A HANDBOOK FOR INSTRUCTORS

Phillip Saunders
Professor of Economics
Indiana University-Bloomington

William B. Walstad
Professor of Economics
University of Nebraska-Lincoln

McGraw-Hill, Inc.

New York   St. Louis   San Francisco   Auckland   Bogotá
Caracas   Hamburg   Lisbon   London   Madrid   Mexico
Milan   Montreal   New Delhi   Paris   San Juan
São Paulo   Singapore   Sydney   Tokyo   Toronto

This book was set in Times Roman by Brownstone Research Group, Inc.
The editors were Michael R. Elia, Scott D. Stratford, and Linda Richmond;
the production supervisor was Salvador Gonzales.
The cover was designed by Karen Quigley
Printed and bound by Impresora Donneco Internacional S. A. de C. V.
a division of R. R. Donnelley & Sons Company.
Manufactured in Mexico

THE PRINCIPLES OF ECONOMICS COURSE

A Handbook for Instructors

Copyright © 1990 by McGraw-Hill, Inc. All rights reserved.
Except as permitted under the United States Copyright Act
of 1976, no part of this publication may be reproduced
or distributed in any form or by any means, or stored
in a data base or retrieval system, without the prior written
permission of the publisher.

4 5 6 7 8 9 0 DOR/DOR   9 4 3 2 1

ISBN   0-07-045520-1

Library of Congress Cataloging-in-Publication Data is Available.
LC Card #89-13381.

CONTENTS

FOREWORD

"Poets are the unacknowledged legislators of the World." It was a poet who said that, exercising occupational license. Some sage, it may have been I, declared in similar vein: "I don't care who writes a nation's laws—or crafts its advanced treaties—if I can write its economic textbooks." The first lick is the privileged one, impinging on the beginner's *tabula rasa* at its most impressionable state.

None the less, reality in the university displays a different form. A kind of Gresham's Law prevails in which, left to themselves, professors will compete for the most advanced courses attended by the fewest students. A generation of professors even presided over the liquidation of their own undergraduate schools of business, save where the iron purse of the legislature vetoed the immolation.

It was not always so. And, as I shall argue, there are persuasive reasons for a rise in the prestige of the elementary economics classroom. In the 1890s, President Francis Walker saved for himself the privilege of giving MIT's introductory lectures in economics. And this was a time when General Walker was at the peak of his international fame. Generations of Yale men recalled in later life the economic lectures they heard from President Arthur Hadley. When Yale does something, can Harvard lag behind? Frank Taussig, the spiritual dean of American economics, started the pre-World War I elite off on their understanding of the economic world. At Madison, William Kiekhofer lectured weekly to a thousand sons and daughters of the middle border, not beginning his sermons on supply and demand until self-elected cheer leaders had given him a Wisconsin locomotive. Ira Cross may not have been Berkeley's most prolific scholar, but it was his name that was on the lips of ten thousand alumni returning to twenty-fifth reunions at Old Cal.

Stuart Mill wrote the textbook definition of classical economics. Alfred Marshall, Knut Wicksell, Gustav Cassel, Irving Fisher, and Frank Taussig did the same for neoclassical economics. (Fairchild, Furnis, and Buck, the best-seller in the pre-Samuelson age, textual research will confirm, was Irving Fisher writ large and packaged for administration to students one eye-drop at a time.) William James in psychology, Richard Courant in mathematics, Linus Pauling in chemistry, and Richard Feynman in physics carried on the great tradition in which leaders at the frontiers of science wrote also for the beginning students.

It would be quixotic for me to claim arguments that would successfully persuade teachers to stop lusting for the advanced seminar. My major point is that, along with those advanced courses, there is personal pleasure to be had from the very first level. My old master, Joseph Schumpeter, reveled in lecturing to large audiences—the more the merrier. But he knew he lacked the self-discipline to take on the task of providing basic foundations. Otto Eckstein, of blessed memory, created Harvard's largest undergraduate course and it is in this same vineyard that Martin Feldstein toils. When Jack Gurley appears before St. Peter, the testimonies of the many Stanford students he introduced to economics will speed him on his way.

Taussig and Hadley and Mill had an easier task than we face today in teaching the first economics course. Good sense was all they had to tell. Now economics has become a complicated subject. What not to snow beginners with has become as important as deciding what to emphasize. The present *Handbook*, compiled from experienced authors by wise editors, is particularly prized in these complicated and exciting times.

Paul A Samuelson, MIT
Cambridge, Massachusetts
October 1988

ACKNOWLEDGMENTS

There are several organizations and people who must be recognized for their contribution to the publication of this volume. Credit must first be given to McGraw-Hill for its financial and publication support, and in particular to the help we received from economics editor Scott Stratford and senior editor Michael Elia. This support was provided with no strings attached because McGraw-Hill felt that this instructional volume would be of service to the economics profession. We were given complete control over selection of the chapter authors and content.

We must also acknowledge the advice and support of members of the American Economic Association's Committee on Economic Education. Both W. Lee Hansen and John Siegfried served as chairs of the committee as this project developed and encouraged us in our efforts to prepare the volume. They also displayed their commitment by contributing chapters. Others who have served on the AEA Committee who have contributed chapters include G. L. Bach, William Becker, Michael Boskin, Marianne Ferber, Campbell McConnell, and Michael Salemi.

Both Indiana University-Bloomington and the University of Nebraska-Lincoln have supported our work on this project. Susan White of the Department of Economics at Indiana University-Bloomington helped in the typing of manuscripts, and she did the final preparation of microcomputer disks. Sharon Nemeth at the National Center for Research in Economic Education at the University of Nebraska-Lincoln provided valuable assistance in the preparation of manuscripts.

The Joint Council on Economic Education has long been interested in the improvement of the teaching of college economics. This volume draws a number of ideas from the Teacher Training Program (TTP) that the Joint Council supported during the 1970s and early 1980s. We also have received helpful advice from Stephen Buckles and Robert Highsmith at the Joint Council.

Over the years the *Journal of Economic Education* has published a number of articles on the teaching of economics at the college level. We gratefully acknowledge the permission that we received from Heldref Publications, the *Journal* publisher, to use portions of articles written by Michael Boskin for his chapter and to reprint a table in the chapter by Marianne Ferber. We are also grateful for the permission we received from Holt Rinehart and Winston to reprint Figure 7-1 and from the Macmillan Company to reprint Table 7-1.

Finally, and most importantly, we are most appreciative of the support that we have received from our wives, Nancy and Karen, as we completed work on this project.

Phillip Saunders
William B. Walstad

THE PRINCIPLES OF ECONOMICS COURSE

A HANDBOOK FOR INSTRUCTORS

CHAPTER 1

TEACHING THE PRINCIPLES OF ECONOMICS: AN INTRODUCTION AND SUMMARY

Phillip Saunders
William Walstad

Virtually all colleges and universities and most community colleges offer a course or sequence of courses in the principles of economics. The central importance of economics in today's world has led to a situation in which a principles course is required for students majoring in a wide variety of disciplines and fields in addition to economics, and enrollments in these courses are among the highest of any discipline in post-secondary education. Indeed, most students received their first (and only) formal and substantive exposure to the subject of economics in these principles courses. Instructors' decisions in these courses, therefore, are likely to have a crucial impact on the economic understanding of students and the attitudes they hold toward the subject.

It would be inaccurate to say that the economics profession has not been interested in principles of economics courses, but professional interest in this important area does seem to move in spurts. As Paul Samuelson states in the foreword to this volume, top economists and leaders of the profession have frequently taken an interest in the challenges of teaching or writing textbooks on elementary economics, and there has been periodic renewal of interest in the problems of teaching the principles of economics in every decade since the end of World War II. During the late 1940s, a special committee of the American Economic Association that was headed by Horace Taylor of Columbia University studied the teaching of undergraduate economics and issued an extensive report that was published as a special supplement to the *American Economic Review* (Taylor et al., 1950). In 1957, the economics department at Grinnell College conducted a survey of instructional methods in principles courses. In 1958 they hosted a conference on the teaching of economics that resulted in a proceedings volume on the topic (Knopf and Strauss, 1960). During the 1960s, two conferences on new developments in the teaching of economics, one in 1966 and the other in 1968, were held at Stanford University. The proceedings from those conferences were published in the form of two books edited by Keith Lumsden (1967, 1970). In the 1970s, the Federal Reserve Bank of Minneapolis published a volume on the goals and objectives for the principles course (Larsen and Nappi, 1976) that was widely distributed to colleges and universities and went through a number of printings. The 1970s were also the formative period for the development of the Teaching Training Program (TTP) that was sponsored by the Joint Council on Economic Education and was conducted at major universities throughout the nation (Hansen, Saunders, and Welsh, 1980).

The above works were valuable in their time, but they are now dated. There is no *current* reference on the teaching of the principles of economics. This edited volume, therefore, is designed to fill that void and address the needs of instructors who will be teaching the principles course in the 1990s. Some topics addressed in the past works noted above or in other sources that would still be of interest to instructors have been revised and updated for this volume; most of the content, however, is new and focuses on present educational concerns. The overall objective of this volume is to give instructors a current handbook or guide to teaching, one that is reasonably comprehensive and provides insights into the major dimensions of instruction likely to be important in the next decade.

The *Handbook* is organized around three major themes or questions that are critical to effective instruction in principles of economics courses. The questions will be familiar to instructors who use a "what," "how," and "for whom" approach to introducing their own students to the basic problems in economics.

COURSE GOALS AND OBJECTIVES

Principles instructors must first give thought to *what* they want their students to learn. Accordingly, the first part of the book discusses the goals and objectives of the principles course. This *what* question is vital, for it determines the content that is included in the course, what weight is given to various parts of the course content, and the approaches that are selected for teaching the subject matter in the course. Five different perspectives on the goals and objectives issue are offered by a distinguished group of economists who, in addition to their significant professional accomplishments, also have substantial experience in *teaching* the principles of economics course.

Robert Eisner, the 1988 president of the American Economic Association, has taught the principles of economics course at Northwestern University since the 1950s. In his chapter, he outlines the concepts he uses and the topics he discusses to give his students a basic understanding of the economy in an introductory course in macroeconomics. Eisner likes to begin his course with the fallacy of composition. He uses examples of this fallacy to demonstrate to students that economic thinking gives insights beyond the obvious, and that economics emphasizes social interactions in the economy. He also explains his interesting strategies for teaching about markets, market failures, and the role of government before he turns to macroeconomic questions. As might be expected, Eisner spends a significant amount of time on national income accounting, in part because it is an area of current research work for him but also because he feels that it is important for students to know the underlying components of the gross national product and national income, and how they are measured, so they can understand "what we are talking about." This discussion sets the basis for the study of aggregate demand and monetary and fiscal policy, and then related issues—"real" budget deficits, supply-side economics, and the complications from an open economy. His course concludes with coverage of comparative advantage and with a brief look at comparative economic systems and comparative thought.

Michael Boskin was a popular teacher of a principles course at Stanford University for several years before assuming duties as chairman of the Council of Economic Advisers in 1989. In Chapter 3, he presents his thoughts on teaching current issues in the macroeconomics course and on the current state of principles textbooks. Boskin first focuses on economic policy. He thinks that instructors should discuss the standards of performance for measuring policy achievement and also stress how these standards have changed over time. Another point emphasized throughout his chapter is the need to build an international dimension throughout the course and throughout the textbook so that students do not have to wait until the end of the course or the end of the book to learn about the role of international trade and finance. A large part of Boskin's chapter is devoted to an examination of current textbooks, not any particular textbook, but limitations in the content coverage of the typical textbook, the organizational problems with textbooks, and how textbooks shape the curriculum. Because the textbook has such a major influence on what instructors teach and the content students are expected to learn, many of the problems cited by Boskin are given further attention in Chapter 12.

In Chapter 4, Campbell McConnell offers his reflections on the principles course based on his experience as a distinguished teacher at the University of Nebraska and as the author of a textbook that is now in its eleventh edition. His perspective begins with a look at the evolution of the course and with the observation that it has become much more comprehensive and sophisticated over the years while at the same time student abilities to handle the reading and the quantitative material have probably fallen. Compounding this learning problem is the poor preparation of instructors to teach the course and the lack of interest among many senior staff in teaching principles. McConnell also looks at both sides of the controversy over whether concept coverage in courses should be narrowed to 20 or so basic concepts, as G. L. Bach advocates in Chapter 5, or whether there should be broader coverage of content, as McConnell prefers. A good portion of the chapter is devoted to questions about which course inputs, both student and institutional, and which outputs are most influential in instruction. In fact, some issues raised in this section of the chapter are discussed later in Chapter 7 and Chapter 20. McConnell concludes with the insightful observation that we may expect too much from the principles course: Our dissatisfaction arises from the difference between our aspirations for the course and our accomplishments with it.

G. L. Bach, who has served as a distinguished professor of economics at Stanford University and as chair of the American Economic Association's Committee on Economic Education, asks "What should a principles course in economics be?" in Chapter 5. Bach would like instructors to teach a course that helps students to think critically about economic problems. For guidance, he cites three subgoals for student learning: exhibiting an awareness of major economic problems, demonstrating a firm grasp of basic economic principles and concepts, and applying the analytical tools to think about economic problems. Bach believes these goals can be achieved if the instructor understands and applies some basic propositions of learning theory, a topic that is the subject for further discussion in Chapter 7 of this book. With this background, Bach then turns to the questions of how the principles course should be taught and what principles should be covered. He presents a short list of about 20 concepts that he thinks can be reasonably taught and mastered by students in a well-taught principles sequence.

The goals and objectives section of the book ends with a chapter that focuses on gender and the study of economics. Marianne Ferber, a professor of economics at the University of Illinois and a former member of both the Committee on the Status of Women in the Economics Profession and the Committee on Economic Education, provides a comprehensive look at gender problems and how they affect economics instruction at the principles and other levels. In the first two parts of the chapter, Ferber documents how women are underrepresented in higher education in general and in economics in particular. She also provides a review of the research literature on gender-related differences in economic understanding, a topic which is also covered in Chapter 20. With this background, Ferber then explains three basic problems with the classroom climate in economics for women and with the textbook treatment of women and gender-related issues. The key section of the chapter for principles instructors is the set of recommendations that Ferber makes to improve instructor practices in the classroom and the treatment of women and gender-related issues in class discussions and in textbooks.

INSTRUCTIONAL METHODS

The second section of this *Handbook* covers subjects related to *how* instruction should be conducted. As might be expected, this part of the book is the longest because there are a multitude of instructional methods and teaching practices that can be used to improve teaching in the principles course. This section focuses on eight main topics—(1) applications from learning theory, (2) teaching students effective learning strategies, (3) improving classroom discussion, (4) presenting better lectures, (5) using student writing as a guide to student thinking, (6) the history and content of textbooks, (7) the use of microcomputer programs, and (8) how the use of mathematics and statistics can be made easier for students. Although this section provides instructors with several practical teaching tips, its main purpose is to provide an in-depth discussion of the major educational methods that can be used in principles courses.

In Chapter 7, Phillip Saunders reviews some of the major findings of learning theory that have the most relevance for teaching the principles of economics at the college level. He discusses the limited capacity of the human mind to process information, the importance of prior experience, the importance of motivation, and the dominance of visual over verbal material, along with the implications of these four basic propositions for acquiring, retaining, and transferring knowledge in a principles course. Special attention is paid to the role of instructional objectives and the distinction between the cognitive domain and the affective domain in setting objectives for student learning.

In Chapter 8, Rendigs Fels goes beyond some of the general principles of learning mentioned in Bach's chapter and discussed by Saunders in Chapter 7 to argue that student study methods should be discipline specific. In particular, he advocates a method of studying economics that involves a distinction between feedback courses and skill courses. To help students develop schema to acquire, understand, and use new knowledge, Fels explains and advocates techniques of anchored instruction and of argument reconstruction and evaluation.

W. Lee Hansen and Michael Salemi focus on classroom discussions as an instructional technique in Chapter 9. They emphasize the importance of using two-way talk in the classroom and discuss each of the five elements that underlie effective classroom discussions: (1) making discussions an important part of course planning, (2) selecting discussion material, (3) preparing discussion questions, (4) creating a contract for effective discussion, and (5) the actual conduct of the discussion itself. Many instructors should find their matrix showing a two-way classification of discussion questions, and their specific examples, helpful in improving discussions in their own classes.

In Chapter 10, Phillip Saunders and Arthur L. Welsh discuss lectures as an instructional method. They emphasize the importance of planning, organizing, and evaluating lectures, as well as how to present them. Ways of overcoming two common criticisms of the lecture method are discussed, and seven things to help instructors improve their lecture presentations are suggested.

The close relationship between writing and thinking is explored by Jerry L. Petr in Chapter 11. Emphasizing writing as a way to create learning rather than a way to evaluate it, Petr discusses a variety of different forms of student writing, including notetaking, compiling an economic issues notebook, cartoon analysis, and problem sets and data interpretation in addition to more traditional term papers and essay examinations. Petr offers many specific examples and suggestions from his own experience which should prove useful to instructors interested in helping their students learn economics through writing, as well as those interested in improving student writing skills.

Chapter 12 is devoted to the principles textbook because it is the one pedagogical feature that is used in almost all courses and because there is a major industry providing products for the principles market. In the chapter, William Walstad and Michael Watts first provide a brief history of the use of textbooks for teaching principles from the days of Adam Smith to the publication of Paul Samuelson's influential text. They describe the economic structure of the market for principles textbooks and highlight several criticisms of current texts, some of which were raised in Michael Boskin's chapter. The chapter also reports on a detailed content analysis of some leading principles textbooks across concept clusters. What emerges from the analysis are data to support the conclusion that there is a high degree of standardization in a textbook market that can be characterized as monopolistically competitive or oligopolistic.

Although the textbook is an instructional aid that has been used in most principles courses for centuries, microcomputer programs have begun to be used in principles courses in just the past decade. In Chapter 13, Devon Yoho and William Walstad offer a realistic perspective on this innovation in light of past innovative uses of television and mainframe instruction, before providing descriptions of the available software that accompanies the 1988 and 1989 editions of principles textbooks. The computer software available will, no doubt, change over time; but the chapter provides a detailed review of the main features that should serve principles instructors as a guide for things to consider when reviewing software programs.

In the final chapter of the second part of the volume, William E. Becker discusses the use of mathematics and statistics in the teaching of economics. Because the mathematical shorthand used in economics is not consistent with the symbolism used in other courses, he argues that the mathematical notation usually used by principles instructors is not conducive to helping students learn economics. Using the vocabulary of economics and public policy debate employed in the popular press as a criterion, Becker identifies the limited number of mathematical and statistical concepts that he feels should be included in the principles course, and he suggests specific ways for making notation in these few cases consistent with that which students will learn in other courses.

EVALUATION OF INSTRUCTION

In the final section of the volume, the focus shifts to the evaluation of instruction. To complete the analogy with the fundamental economic questions, you might think about this section as addressing questions related to *for whom* is instruction beneficial, or *whether* instruction is effective. Answering these types of questions first involves measuring student performance to find out what students know and do not know about course content. There is also an element of self-evaluation that needs to be included in studying whether instruction is effective. This self-assessment can be achieved through videotaping of instructors, by studying the responses from student evaluations, and by peer reviews. Finally, research into instruction in economics at the principles level suggests that some practices can be more beneficial than others in facilitating student learning or in increasing the effectiveness of the instructor.

The two basic tools used by most instructors to find out what students learn are the multiple choice test and the essay test. Careful development and use of these assessment instruments is needed if they are to provide accurate measurement of student performance in the principles course. In Chapter 15, William Walstad first makes the case for multiple choice testing by citing reasons why this assessment procedure is considered superior to that of the essay test by test and measurement experts. He then provides a detailed explanation of how to construct multiple choice tests for classroom use and identifies pitfalls to avoid in writing items or selecting items from test banks. The final section of the chapter describes basic statistics for analyzing individual item and overall test results and explains how to interpret the data.

The assessment position is reversed in Chapter 16 where Arthur Welsh and Phillip Saunders make the case for essay questions and tests. They review the strengths and weaknesses of essay examinations and explore situations in which essay questions can be used to advantage. General guidelines to use in preparing questions and tests and suggestions for grading student answers are offered in the belief that careful preparation and grading can overcome some of the weaknesses of essay examinations and improve their strengths—not only in testing student knowledge, but also in influencing student study habits in the directions suggested by Fels in Chapter 8.

In Chapter 17, Michael Salemi discusses the use of videotape for teacher development and self-evaluation. The study of videotapes of their own classroom presentations was rated as one of the most effective features of the 1970s TTP programs sponsored by the Joint Council on Economic Education by the principles instructors who attended these programs. Salemi indicates three other ways in which videotape can help improve instruction in addition to critiquing actual classroom presentations—the use of "trigger tapes" to initiate discussion of selected problems, the use of video to illustrate various teaching techniques, and the use of videotape to master particular skills in "micro teaching" situations—and he offers several suggestions for implementing a successful critiquing program. His chapter concludes with a five-step approach to using videotape for self-evaluation for those instructors who do not want to involve another person in the critiquing process.

James W. Marlin discusses student evaluation of instruction in Chapter 18. He distinguishes clearly between student evaluations aimed at improving instructor performance and those aimed at providing data for making personnel decisions. Questionnaires designed to improve instructor performance can use different types of questions and a larger number of questions than those designed to provide summary evaluation data. Sample evaluation forms and a sample summary table for presenting evaluation results over time or in different courses are provided in appendices. The final section of the chapter offers some advice on using student evaluations in a positive manner, particularly emphasizing what might be done if an instructor finds himself or herself with a poor evaluation.

The use of peer evaluation is discussed by James Niss in Chapter 19. Niss's distinction between formative evaluation and summative evaluation is similar to Marlin's distinction between information aimed at personnel decisions and information aimed at instructor improvement. Summative evaluation focuses on a global decision at a given point in time regarding the worth of an individual with respect to tenure, promotion, or merit pay. Formative evaluation is concerned with improvement and is carried out over a period of time with extensive feedback provided to assist the instructor in modifying his or her performance. Niss discusses how peers can be used to evaluate teaching inputs, the teaching process, and teaching outputs. He discusses team teaching and the construction of common examinations in multisection courses as aspects of peer reviewing, and he also discusses techniques for self-appraisal.

The final chapter of the volume, by John Siegfried and William Walstad, is a review of the research literature on the teaching of college economics. After a brief historical overview of the research in the field of economic education and a discussion of the problems with the measurement of the education product, the main section of the chapter discusses both the relationship between student characteristics and economic teaching and the influence of course format on student learning. It should be noted that this review is not a technical one; it is designed to provide a useful description for principles instructors of what research work has been done over the past thirty years in economics education. The authors have sought to identify major conclusions from the research literature that have implications for instructional practice in the classroom and which should be of interest to administrators.

CONCLUSION

The teaching of the principles of economics is far too important to be left to chance. The material summarized above, and elaborated in detail in the chapters which follow, makes clear that it is possible to improve significantly the quantity and quality of student learning in this important course. Effective course planning and effective teaching are skills that can be learned and developed through study and practice of what is currently known by leaders in the field. It is our hope that this volume will serve as a useful and continuing reference for departments and instructors who want to take seriously their important responsibilities for educating millions of students in a vitally important subject during the 1990s.

REFERENCES

Hansen, W. Lee, Phillip Saunders, and Arthur L. Welsh, "Teacher Training Programs in College Economics: Their Development, Current Status, and Future Prospects," *Journal of Economic Education*, Spring 1980, **11** (2), 1-9.

Knopf, Kenyon, and James H. Strauss, (eds.), *The Teaching of Elementary Economics*, New York: Holt, Rinehart, and Winston, 1960.

Larsen, Allen F., and Andrew T. Nappi, (eds.), *Goals and Objectives of the Introductory College-Level Course in Economics*, Minneapolis: Federal Reserve Bank of Minneapolis, 1976.

Lumsden, Keith (ed.), *New Developments in the Teaching of Economics*, Englewood Cliffs, New Jersey: Prentice-Hall, 1967.

———— (ed.), *Recent Research in Economic Education*, Englewood Cliffs, New Jersey: Prentice-Hall, 1970.

Taylor, Horace, et al., "The Teaching of Undergraduate Economics, Report of the Committee on Undergraduate Teaching of Economics and the Training of Economists," *American Economic Review, Supplement*, December 1950, **40**, 1–226.

PART ONE

GOALS AND OBJECTIVES
OF THE PRINCIPLES
COURSE

CHAPTER 2

LEARNING ABOUT ECONOMICS AND THE ECONOMY

Robert Eisner

I like to start my principles class with the fallacy of composition. A good illustration in the fall is the effort to see better at the football game. If those in one row stand, they see readily over the rows in front. But if everybody stands no one—except possibly in the first row—has any advantage.

Sticking to the ball game, suppose we know it is to be a sellout, with 70,000 trying to get into a stadium for 50,000. One way to get a seat is to get to the gate four hours before game time. Should I then ask the president of the University to authorize spot announcements on all the television channels, urging fans to get to the stadium four hours before game time, so that they can all see the game?

We then get closer to home. I announce the grading will be on a predetermined curve. Can any student hope to do better by studying harder? Of course! Suppose, they all study harder? No dice! One can improve his or her grade at the expense of others. But in the aggregate my students are bounded by the curve.

And finally to economics! How many of you think you can have less money at the end of the week than at the beginning? Giggles! You can always spend it, or even lend it to a classmate without too much trouble. But now I announce that the total quantity of "money" in the country is fixed at, say, $800 billion. (I will explain how when we get to lessons on the creation of money.) Clearly, any individual can get rid of money by palming it off on someone else. But we are powerless in the aggregate to change that quantity. What any one can do, the country cannot.

Then, particularly if we still have some students from agricultural areas, can a farmer earn more by working harder and sending more wheat to market? A resounding yes! But suppose all farmers send more to market. If this drives down the prices by a greater percent than the increase in quantity, they will actually earn less!

Now, what about your uncle, the shirt manufacturer? He is having a hard time making shirts to sell for $10. Sales are down and he has to lay off employees. If only the workers would take a 20 percent pay cut! He could then cut the price to $8 and sell more shirts. All the workers could keep their jobs. Have we discovered the cure for unemployment, cutting wages? But suppose all of your uncle's competitors get their workers to take a similar cut in wages and they cut their shirt prices. And all other workers do likewise so that all prices and all incomes are down by 20 percent. Are we so sure that unemployment will be any less? Complicated, isn't it?

We can go on and even get into the old paradox of thrift and the distinction between individual decisions to save more and the consequences for aggregate saving. What we accomplish, I suggest, is rather neat. First, we give the students a sense that there is something to learn in economics. Things are not exactly what they seem, not all that obvious. Second, we begin to bring out the essential social relations in the economy. The effects of one person's action cannot be understood without recognition of the interaction with others. We are into the beginnings of markets and of macroeconomics, which is the prime focus of the first quarter principles course for many of us. And drawing some hitherto hidden meaning about familiar matters, we have established our own credentials, that we have something to offer.

I usually have a bit of extra fun teaching the Principles in the fall of an election year. It is not that the class gets involved in political discussions. But we do have some background motivation for the issues to which economic theory and analysis can be applied. What about unemployment and inflation? Who suffers most from each? Can different emphases of the two parties be related to differing concerns of their constituencies? Would relatively more moneyed families from wealthy suburbs worry more about inflation than blue collar workers who lose their jobs in a downturn?

And just where do we stand on leaving everything to the market? Are we against all government action to redistribute income? At least a minority of hands go up affirmatively on that one. But what about the poor baby whose parents are killed in an auto accident? What about dependent children in general? The certainty is less.

What are the costs of trying to correct the market? What does the market accomplish, anyway? Here I like to pose a hypothetical. Where would we be without it? Suppose some new nerve gas were set loose on our population, by accident or design, and all economic activity was stopped dead, but we were all able to resume if we knew what to do. You are the dictator, the economic czar or commissar. You have the power to tell everybody where to work, what to produce, what sets of people and material to combine, and who is to get the output. Up to you are the trillions of decisions encompassed in the famous "What, how and for whom?" Where do you begin? Perhaps at least by getting some grasp of the remarkable contribution of even more or less competitive markets and of the virtual impossibility of doing without them in a complex, modern economy. My students get pretty familiar with the delightful aphorism, "If it ain't broke, don't fix it." But suppose there are some problems. We touch on some of them: unemployment, inflation, extremes in the distribution of income, imperfect competition, consumer choice versus consumer sovereignty, the possible endogeneity of tastes and preferences, public goods, externalities and protecting the environment, providing for the future. Where can we expect market failure? Where does it occur and how seriously? And where can we be confident that the cure will not be worse than the disease?

Should we be happy with the dissemination of knowledge on the basis of market incentives? Suppose people have a preference for dirty, trashy books, and so cast their dollar "votes." Should the publishing industry concentrate its resources on them? Suppose the television industry gives us what we "know" to be trash and television news eschews the enlightening for the sensational. But what, again, can we do about it? And what can we say about the curiously indirect way in which commercial television services to the consumer are paid for by business advertising rather than the services' recipients?

Many of these issues strike live nerves in the students' ideologies, and this renders them—the issues and the students—all the more alive. I am fond of telling my audience that I may not change any of those ideologies or political preferences, but I will give them better arguments to defend them. They laugh, and I don't really want to believe that this is altogether true. But I am always pleased and amused when students try to question me on what candidate or party I support and I find that many of them have me pegged some 180 degrees wrong. Perhaps it's just that they don't read the newspapers much, or watch the television news, and they miss my subtleties.

A major goal in the Principles course is to give students an appreciation of the principles. We pride ourselves in economics that we do have a rigorous body of theory. I have been increasingly concerned in recent years—a sign of age?—with the focus of much research and graduate training in the profession. So much of the time and resources of some of the best talent seems to go into more and more remote abstraction, models attractive for their elegance and purity rather than any sensible insights they can give into the economy, let alone sound implications for economic policy. (I am all the more appalled when some of our colleagues seem to think that their abstractions, often built on quite counterfactual, critical assumptions, do have important implications for economic policy. Am I too partisan if I cite policy-ineffectiveness theorems tied to rational expectations with prices that adjust freely and markets that always clear?) But there is beauty and significance in the coherent body of theory at the core of our discipline. It is important that it be the sound foundation of our course in the Principles.

Indeed, I am fond of cracks at the expense of our friends in the "softer" social sciences; as a refugee from an M.A. in Sociology, I feel I have some credentials. The students should learn to join us in pride and pleasure at the role of rigorous theory in economics. Even as we warn of the perils of abstractions which discard the essence with the chaff, we should develop enough facility with our tools so that the potential strength of our analyses can be appreciated.

And so we can be launched. Supply and demand curves, elasticities, production possibility frontiers, opportunity costs, marginal returns, marginal costs, marginal utility, marginal propensities, maximization, multipliers, accelerators, aggregate demand and aggregate supply functions!

In teaching all of this I try to combine the tools and the theory with their applications. There are a few students that can be fully fascinated by the pure mathematics or logic, but for the majority a sense of relevance is essential. On supply and demand curves, I endeavor to show how the concepts fit the notion of the invisible hand, the normal process of adjustment expected to clear markets and satisfy people's wants—if they have the money. Yet we note the complications sometimes ignored. There are of course income effects and price effects, superior and inferior goods, substitutes and complements, stocks and flows, lags and, most important, cross elasticities, not only with other current commodities but intertemporally. Thus, a lower price is generally to be associated with a greater quantity demanded. But a fall in price may generate an expectation of a further future fall (elastic price expectations). In that case, the quantity demanded may fall.

What now does this say about our assurance that markets will always clear? What does it say about our ability to be confident that lower wages and prices, if they could only be attained, would eliminate unemployment? For how can we get lower prices without falling prices?

And while we are on clearing markets, which markets actually do clear? The corner grocer's, the supermarket, admissions to the University? Which sellers ever know the demand curves they face? How much production is for auction markets, how much for inventory and how much to order? Which sellers act as if they face a horizontal demand curve and know their marginal cost curve so that they produce to the point where the two intersect? What if you are producing not one but many products? And are we talking of curves and functions for an instant in time, a day, a week, a life or eternity? We have opened Pandora's Box, but it is necessary. Much as we want to bring out the beauty of our concepts, we cannot be simplistic. We can show the need to add some humility to our normal arrogance.

Having given some notion of the enormous contribution of markets to solving our economic problems, along with the tools and concepts we apply to its analysis, I come back to the issue of market lacks or failures. This leads directly to our first crack at the role of government.

Here I am fond of assigning an old article of Sumner Slichter ("Free Private Enterprise," reprinted in the various editions of Samuelson's "Readings"). Slichter reminds readers that "defenders of free enterprise do not trust competition to do all things. However much they trust it to guard the lives and limbs of workmen against dangerous machinery or to protect consumers against injurious foods, they do not rely upon it to enforce contracts or to prevent fraud." Suppose, I suggest to our students, the worker at the Chrysler plant decides at the end of the week that he is entitled to the car he has driven off the assembly line and takes it home. Does not Mr. Iacocca expect the police to intervene so that he can get back *the company's* car? For that matter do not the workers expect to have the law behind them if Mr. Iacocca or any other employer fails to pay wages which are due?

And while acknowledging the problems with our Pure Food and Drug Administration, I like to tease a bit about the checks of the market on the druggist who gets into the habit of selling mortal drugs. He might eventually be driven out of business as he loses his customers to the other world.

So we do begin to see roles for government as a protector of basic property rights and the rules of the game, as a purveyor of essential market information, or as the regulator who demands that information be provided, as the producer (or purchaser) of public goods and the corrector for externalities. And then we move to some more difficult ones: guarantor of competition, redistributor of income, controller of the money supply and taxer and spender. Macroeconomic policy is generally put off until after the development of the basic tools of analysis for the determination of income and employment and the banking system and the nature and creation of money.

There is much else to do on government first, pointing out some of the empirical and institutional facts of our Federal system, how little of the Federal budget actually goes to non-defense goods and services and how much to defense and to transfer payments, how much of state and local expenditures relate to education, to roads and to police. Then a good thought provoker! How many of you want to cut government spending? Many hands go up. What then do you want to cut? Waste! Yes, but where? With our students as in the general population it is usually much easier to get agreement on the aggregate than on any of the components that make it up. And we will have more to say on the aggregate when we get to macroeconomic policy.

Taxation can be fun, at least in class. Students are usually surprised to learn, if only on an exam, that taxes on Cadillacs are likely to prove regressive; as incomes get higher and higher there are usually just so many Cadillacs that a family will buy. Regressivity and progressivity, the tricky problems of tax incidence, use taxes, general excise and "sin" taxes, income, sales, payroll and property taxes, taxable income, capital gains, credits, deductions, exemptions and loopholes offer a rich field for relating tools, analysis and policy issues that strike very close to home.

Before I finally get to macroeconomic theory, I like to get pretty deeply into national income accounting. It is important, I insist to my students, as I do to a wider public, that we literally know what we are talking about. What then are gross national product and national income? What are the underlying concepts? What are the various components and how do they interrelate? I am usually nasty enough to give exam questions that require putting some jumbled accounts back together to get the correct numerical answers. I can use the accounts to bring out the basic saving-investment identity, while preparing the warning as to the distinction between identities and behavior. Gross investment is identically equal to gross saving, which is the total of personal saving, corporate saving and government saving. But does that mean that efforts to raise any one component, such as raising taxes to increase government saving (reduce the budget deficit) will raise gross or national saving or gross investment? Not so clear, I point out, at the risk of upsetting some of our colleagues.

But then, pursuing my own interests—which I do think important—I get into extensions of conventional measures, the "Total Incomes System of Accounts."[1] Conventional GNP does not include most non-market activity. What about services produced in the home? The value of housekeeping and child care, still undertaken overwhelmingly by "the weaker sex," would add over 40 percent to our conventional measure of GNP, if we counted it. And the value of government production corresponding to the services of government capital? And the services of consumer durables such as autos? And an imputation for the opportunity cost of the time students might otherwise spend in the labor force?

And what about the boundary between intermediate and final product? Is much of government output, and particularly police and defense, better viewed as intermediate, perhaps necessary to protect the capital and labor used in production but no more final than the services of the private guards or watchmen hired by the steel mill? Should the identity of the purchaser and how the purchaser disposes of the product, by market sale or not, determine whether it is "final" and hence not subject to the indictment of "double-counting"? Are the television programs we watch and the articles we read in newspapers not properly part of real consumption and GNP just because they are paid for by business advertising and then largely if not entirely given away rather than sold to viewers and readers?

Most important, what are real saving and investment? Is a new car properly consumption if purchased by a household, government expenditures if acquired by the City of Chicago and investment only if it is bought by Hertz or Avis or some other private business? Is government construction of roads for cars, trucks, and busses no less investment than private construction of railroad tracks? Are business, nonprofit institution or government expenditures for research and development no less investment than business purchase of plant and equipment? What about investment in education and training, health and human capital generally? If saving is the addition to our wealth, is it proper to exclude from saving, and from income, our real gains (after adjusting for inflation) in the stock market or in the values of our foreign assets or of our homes?

But if all or most of these are, in an economically relevant sense, capital accumulation, what are we to make of much of the current, heated discussion about our purported lack of "national saving"? Will we increase national saving, I ask the students, by cutting the budget deficit, thus reducing the official measure of government dis-saving, if that is accomplished by reducing government spending for infrastructure, research and education? Our students may well now be alerted to some important concepts and issues in economics and the economy.

And on at last to macroeconomic theory. We begin with some stylized facts we wish to explain. Perhaps to the consternation of some of our colleagues, I do not see these as encompassing an economy generally at its "natural rate" (perish the phrase!) of unemployment where those out of work are exclusively voluntarily between jobs or prefer to work at some future time when they expect the real wage to be higher. Rather I develop an historical picture with huge variations in unemployment from the quarter of the labor force in the Great Depression to the single percentage point during the Great War (II) and 3 percent range during the Vietnam war, up to 10.7 percent in the 1982-83 recession and down again to 5 1/2 percent in the fall of 1988. Why? Did peaks in unemployment signify in Modligiani's sarcastic phrase, waves of "contagious laziness"? Were the associated declines in GNP subject to "supply side" explanations—droughts, pestilence, war destruction?

We of course look elsewhere, to the determinants of aggregate demand. I begin by asking students about their own consumption and quickly draw from them the key role of income. I get from them, too, a marginal propensity to consume greater than zero but less than unity, with some good-natured thanks, with regard to the latter, for sparing me the dynamic instability which would ruin our analysis. We explain the important complications regarding wealth and transitory and permanent components of income. We then assure all and sundry that in this case, assuming slack resources, we are free of my much trumpeted fallacy of composition and can safely aggregate.

That leads us merrily to investment *demand* functions. (I stubbornly stick to the old Keynesian term, which ties in neatly to the concept of aggregate demand and avoids manifold sloppiness and confusion with concepts such as "planned," "desired," and, God forbid!, "*ex ante*.") I first assume a schedule of ID with respect to income (Y) as we get into parallel graphic, tabular and mathematical presentations, and note how exogenous variations in that schedule will affect the equilibrium level of output, here of course developing the multiplier, playing with that paradox of thrift and hinting at the accelerator to come. And then we can go hot and heavy into those determinants of investment—changing demand for output, interest rates and rental prices of capital, replacement and technological change—that were for some time my research habitat.

I next usually follow my text into the banking system and the role of money, noting both the small space of the latter in the large spectrum of financial assets and liabilities and its somewhat special importance. We have occasion to see how far the money of M1, M2 and M3 differ from the M of that old quantity theory. And we prepare the tie-in back to investment and aggregate demand by suggesting, I confess, that the monetary authority, while far from omnipotent, is not without power to affect interest rates, real as well as nominal (sorry about that, Milton), and with it such real variables as investment, output and employment.

We are now ready for the grand synthesis of determinants of aggregate demand and monetary and fiscal policy. The effects of changes in the quantity of money, government spending and tax rates are explored. We may even get into relations involving imports and exports, although that is usually better postponed to a later week on the open economy and international economic issues.

But we do plunge into the issues of the Federal debt and how it matters, in ways quite different from popular conceptions. I offer only a somewhat disdainful nod to "Ricardian equivalence" and supply-side considerations, insist upon the role of public debt as a private asset entering into consumption functions, and recognize (but belittle) its possible effect on interest rates.

And of course I expose the students to my own not entirely accepted, but nevertheless profoundly sound, perceptions of the nature and impact of budget deficits. I explain the concept of a "real" deficit, adjusted for the inflation tax or, generally, changes in the real value of outstanding government debt. And I point out the observed relations, consistent with our theory, between real, structural or high-employment budget deficits and increases in consumption, investment and GNP.[2] These relations are all positive, and real, high-employment deficits have also been associated with decreases, or lesser increases in unemployment. Whatever our view of the future, budget deficits have been good for us! All this keeps the students interested.

We do consider the presumed twin—most unidentical—of unemployment. I surprise students by pointing out the very limited welfare loss, aside from distribution effects, that economists can find in inflation. I point to the danger of inflation from excess demand in an economy at or approaching full employment, but that this is *not* a purely monetary phenomenon. The excess demand can stem from excessive government spending as well as too much money. I stress, though, that excess demand inflation in at least a century or so of American history has been exclusively a war or post-war event. I then emphasize that our inflation of the 1970s and early 1980s was essentially due to supply shocks, the explosion in petroleum prices along with crop failures raising world market agricultural prices.

I have a crack, not entirely original, for those who ask about "supply-side economics." "God," I announce haughtily, "gave all economists two eyes, one to watch demand and one to watch supply." Economists ignore either at their peril. I proceed to point out that while aggregate demand can affect output up to the amount of available resources, we must increase those resources, or the efficiency with which we apply them, for long run growth.

Of course, aggregate demand can itself affect the supply of resources as it influences the rate of investment. But it is to that investment, broadly defined, that we must look to increasing supply, and to incentives and motivation for bringing that supply into production. I explain to students why low marginal tax rates are desirable, while alerting them to the possible conflict with egalitarian aims for income distribution, but caution them against gullibility regarding their consequences for the supply of capital or labor.

Will you really save more for retirement if the after-tax rate of interest is more, or will you find less need to contribute out of your earned income as higher interest returns add to your nest egg? And how many of you will turn down that $50,000 job offered on graduation because you learn that the take-home pay will be only $35,000? All this is of course not to deny the role of supply factors—I too have two eyes—but to suggest that, particularly in comparison to variations in demand, they be kept in perspective.

When we finally open up the economy to the rest of the world we can extend our macroeconomic theory. We consider the complications imports and exports bring to the multiplier and plunge into the nature and determinants of exchange rates and revel in the new identity: the current account deficit is identically equal to the capital account surplus. Like in that old song about love and marriage, but perhaps more so, you can't have one without the other. This may lead me to a few choice words on the widely repeated nonsense about the calamity in store for us if foreigners refuse to continue to finance our trade deficit. The fact, I can explain to students, bringing our new accounting insight to this prominent contemporary issue, is that when we buy Toyotas, the Japanese accumulate dollars. The capital surplus is the other side of the coin of current account deficit. Foreigners wishing to end their financing of U.S. current account deficits cannot do so as long as the deficits persist. They can only drive down the value of the dollar by trying to pull out of their dollar investments. If and when this ends the current account deficit, their financing of it, which is their net investment in the United States, will also end.

A solid lesson on the law of comparative advantage is always satisfying. Once more it offers a choice opportunity to show the power of economic theory and our ability to prove that things are not what they seem. We can bring front and center the rationale for a conspicuous and important example of our proud battles against special interests and for the General Good. By way of explaining our lack of universal success in this battle, we can tie in again to some real world problems of failures or inability of winners to compensate losers, non-clearing labor markets and imperfect human capital markets, and other more subtle qualifications.

I usually end my Principles course with a couple of lectures on comparative systems and comparative thought. The first topic is a particular delight in these days of Soviet perestroika and economic reform in Eastern Europe and China. It brings us back to the overwhelming importance and value of competitive markets and the cost of ignoring economic principles which, if not natural or God-given, and not necessarily universal, are costly to defy in the world that we know. It should open the students, nevertheless, to some of the many possible variations in economic organization and systems and generate some freedom from mind-closing dogma. I try to accomplish a similar purpose in final attention to divergent economic thoughts from a range of dissidents extending from Marx to Libertarians.

My goals and objectives in teaching the Principles then are to initiate students in a basic understanding of the economy and the tools of economics that make this possible. Once more, I would insist, you can't have one without the other.

NOTES

1 In Eisner (1985, 1988, and 1989b).
2 See Eisner and Pieper (1984, 1985) and Eisner (1986a, 1986b, 1989a), for starters.

REFERENCES

Eisner, Robert. "The Total Incomes System of Accounts," *Surv. Curr. Bus.*, Jan. 1985, 65(1), pp. 20-25.

———. *How Real Is the Federal Deficit?* NY: The Free Press, A Division of Macmillan, 1986a.

———. "Will the Real Federal Deficit Stand Up?", *Challenge*, May/June 1986b, pp. 13-21.

———. "Extended Accounts for National Income and Product," *Journal of Economic Literature*, December 1988, pp. 1611-1684.

———. "Budget Deficits: Rhetoric and Reality," *Journal of Economic Perspectives*, 1989a.

———. *The Total Incomes System of Accounts*. Chicago: The University of Chicago Press, 1989b.

Eisner, Robert, and Paul J. Pieper. "A New View of the Federal Debt and Budget Deficit," *The American Economic Review*, Mar. 1984, 74(1), pp. 11-29.

———. "How To Make Sense of the Deficit," *The Public Interest*, Winter 1985, pp. 101-118.

CHAPTER 3

SOME THOUGHTS ON TEACHING PRINCIPLES OF MACROECONOMICS

Michael J. Boskin[*]

In this chapter I will discuss my views on teaching principles of macroeconomics with particular attention to the role of textbooks in this process.

In teaching at the principles level, the procedure we should follow in evaluating current macroeconomic policy is to define the current policy; define the state of the economy; measure our macroeconomic performance against what we believe to be appropriate norms; and then ask, "Can the government contribute to an improved performance? If it can, how? If it is hindering performance by its policy, what should it stop doing? What are the levers that government has for quick and decisive action when policy makers believe there is going to be a long and severe recession or a pronounced rampant inflation? How do we decide when to activate policies?" Monetary and fiscal *fine-tuning* measures are of little value, and cumulatively are probably harmful. But *if* the economy is *way* out of kilter, how can we tell when the circumstances are right for *gross* tuning?

It is within this framework that I wish to comment on what I think deserves increasing emphasis in our principles courses. First, I should observe that it is remarkable how much our performance standards for the economy have changed. In the mid 1980s it was not uncommon to view an unemployment rate between 6 percent and 7 percent as acceptable if accompanied by "modest" growth and a "low" inflation rate of about 4 percent. Viewed in an historical perspective, one is prompted to ask, "Are those standards and goals the right ones?" What happened to the 4-4-1 we used to hear—4 percent growth, 4 percent unemployment, and 1 percent inflation—as our goals? A variety of reasons, including structural and demographic changes in the labor market and a long and sustained slowdown in productivity, probably make those goals unattainable today. One might also recall that it was only recently that a large number of economists, of a certain persuasion, suggested that high single-digit, or even low double-digit, inflation was not harmful to the economy, particularly if various contracts were indexed. To their credit, many economists fought hard against acceptance of high inflation rates as harmless. They pointed out that high inflation almost certainly means fluctuations in the inflation rate because it is very hard to sustain a stable 10 percent or 15 percent inflation rate. Inflation interacts insidiously with our tax system to erode incentives, and it distorts relative prices, as well as increasing their uncertainty. Some of the policy responses have been shown to be costly in themselves. Alan Blinder has suggested that the wage and price controls of the Nixon administration actually worsened the permanent inflation rate by about 1 1/2 percent. Most economists, myself included, believe that incomes policies would be no more successful.

The disinflation that began in 1981 was, indeed, very costly, although perhaps much less so than was anticipated. A common prediction in 1980 was that for each percentage-point reduction in inflation, we would bear a $220 billion loss (1980 dollars) in real output. That is at least double what the actual cumulative real output loss appears to have been. The rise in unemployment was severe in the 1981-82 recession, but the loss of output was much less than a rise of that size normally entails.

A most important and remarkable feature of the 1981-82 recession was the fact that *almost half* of the decline in real GNP was in our net exports. This is probably the single most important fact to stress, for it reflects the internationalization of our economy, its trade and capital flows. I cannot overemphasize the implications of this development for what we teach in our principles courses. We can no longer teach them in the traditional way, that is, assuming a closed economy and leaving international trade and finance to the end, without sufficient time for serious treatment or integration into the macroeconomics. Although only a tenth of our economy is in exports and imports, most goods are traded on world markets *at the margin.*

Even more significant for macroeconomics are the until-recently unimaginable federal budget deficits, and the financing of about half of these deficits through capital imports. We are now obliged to place higher priority on our international economic activity, integrating it in to the mainline teaching of macroeconomics theory and policy. Macroeconomic monetary policy can no longer be properly understood by our students without some familiarity with international trade and finance.

Let me turn now to a few further comments on how and what to teach in the elementary macroeconomics course and the role of textbooks in our teaching. I do not think Keynesian economics is totally dead. The new classical macroeconomics, rational expectations, equilibrium models of the business cycle, Ricardian equivalence theorems, and the new theoretical refinements have some important grains of truth in them. But I do not think that we have a perfect set of markets with perfect information that adjust instantaneously, that there are no price rigidities or wage rigidities or other types of problems that preclude the potential for some Keynesianesque fiscal policy action. Nevertheless, I think that the types of stimuli we can expect are sharply curtailed because of the internationalization of our economy. We should be more cautious and modest in teaching about the range and efficacy of macropolicies.

We must also take pains to incorporate the rest of the world into our description of the process by which domestic macroeconomic policies affect the domestic and world economies. And we must be more realistic and cautious in our use of the traditional diagrams. We typically draw the Keynesian cross on the blackboard or on a transparency with the 45-degree line and the C + I + G functions. We then say, "Now let's suppose we have a tax cut," and we shift the C + I + G line up by 20 percent. We assume a particular marginal propensity to save and a huge multiplier, and lo and behold, GNP is doubled! Deep down in our hearts, most of us would undoubtedly be delighted if the overwhelming majority of our students could simply identify the right sign, the right direction of change. But consider the subconscious misconceptions we introduce when we shift GNP so casually by, say, 50 percent without assigning and emphasizing realistic slopes and values and correct positions for the curves. It denigrates the seriousness of economic policy and does a great disservice. I have resolved that the next time I teach principles of economics I am going to redraw the curves more realistically.

In this quest for greater realism, how do we get our students to start thinking beyond the simple cash-flow analysis typical of the explanations of what drives consumption and investment spending, as depicted in the simple Keynesian cross? I find it convenient to focus on three things: expectations, incentives, and time horizons. Students seem to find it intuitively plausible to relate consumption decisions to expectations. As aspiring medical students or engineers or lawyers, the students find the ideas of consuming out of permanent income or some longer-term average income plausible. They can readily understand the significance of expectations about future income, future interest rates, and future rates of inflation as determinants of consumption spending. I also find it tremendously convenient and effective to introduce some microeconomic concepts about incentives in order to develop their role in macroeconomics. The role of incentives helps to explain the macroeconomic composition of output between net exports and investment—the interest-sensitive parts of our economy—and consumer and government purchases; also, it helps us to understand the uses of income among saving and consumption of nondurables and durables. The three concepts—expectations, incentives, and time horizon—can be integrated as we gradually lengthen the time horizon of expectations about inflation or future income and explain how incentives translate our expectations into behavioral decisions. This permits us to build in and apply these concepts into explanations of how the private sector reacts to what they expect the public sector to do through monetary and fiscal actions. We may then raise the warranted questions about the efficacy of monetary and fiscal policy in this framework.

Before turning to the role of textbooks, let me sum up this part of the chapter by stating that I, like most economists, have rejected fine tuning. I won't pretend to know exactly where the distinction between fine and gross tuning should be drawn. However, I do want to indicate that it is my view that there is a modern eclectic macroeconomics in practice. In our teaching, we must try to give students an idea of what is at stake in different points of view, and upon what empirical information these views ultimately depend. We must also recognize that we are not at all certain of the full consequences of a large tax cut or major monetary expansion in any particular environment. They may very well depend on things that we do not control, and this has become especially true as our own macroeconomy has become internationalized.

We also should be teaching the most basic analysis, facts, historical episodes, and current events concerning the United States and world economies. We need to focus on why trade occurs, opportunity costs, arbitrage, supply and demand, the equaling of national income to the sum of its components, a brief factual overview of the economy such as the composition of spending on major categories of goods, the share of resources devoted to investment versus consumption, the differences between the average and marginal propensities to consume and import, marginal analysis, the distribution of income, measurement of economic well-being, the role of the price system as the primary and usually most efficient method of allocating resources, the role of profit rates as opposed to the absolute nominal dollar amount of profit in determining the allocation of the capital stock among uses, and so on.

In brief, I set as my goal helping my students to achieve mastery of enough simple analysis and descriptive overview that they can read the newspaper intelligently and critically. In addition, I hope they enjoy the process enough so that they will—or at least a substantial fraction of them will—keep up their interest in economics and economic events. If so, they can offset, at least partially, the decay of the knowledge they crammed into their brains in the short period of time they were in my course. An auxiliary goal is to paint a mural of the economy etched well enough in their minds to assist them in rejecting spurious analysis and claims, with due respect for the fact that the mural changes, sometimes rapidly.

A FRAMEWORK FOR THINKING ABOUT PRINCIPLES TEXTBOOKS

I believe that the single most important place to start thinking about the role of textbooks in principles courses is to realize that the textbook is part of a portfolio of inputs used to produce whatever output we produce. Other inputs in the portfolio include the supplementary study guide and similar materials that usually accompany textbooks, lectures, section meetings, examinations, and, increasingly, computer-assisted tutorials. Given the mix of these inputs (some universities offer them all, or each in varying proportions), the role of the textbook may acquire increasing or decreasing importance. I believe the textbook is important and will remain important for a substantial length of time. First, even the best students—and Stanford certainly has its share of them—need a ready reference beyond daily lectures. Second, the textbook should be an invaluable resource and reference for at least several years beyond the principles course. Third, many students absorb information better by reading than by listening or by interacting with a computer or a teaching assistant. Finally, the increasing preponderance of foreign graduate students with limited English language skills is straining the traditional role of the teaching assistant. For all of these reasons, modern technology is not likely to relegate the principles of economics textbook to the scrap heap.

It is also important to note that there is a huge number of principles of economics textbooks from which to choose. Although a large fraction of them follow in what has come to be called the Samuelson tradition, that is, an encyclopedia of at least first cuts at providing coverage of virtually all topics in economics, not all attempt to be so encyclopedic. They differ in length, topic coverage, level, quality of writing, visual effects, and a variety of other attributes. The overwhelming bulk adequately cover the 70 percent of common material we all tend to cover in our principles courses. Thus, although I have opinions about individual books, I believe that the segmentation of the market is socially desirable and that *matching* the type of textbook with the desired emphasis or complementary focus of the instructor, and the nature of the students in the course, is extremely important.

With this general perspective concerning the textbook and the principles course in mind, I turn now to several potential problems with principles textbooks as one of the inputs used in principles of economics courses.[1]

POTENTIAL PROBLEMS

At virtually every university, enormous heterogeneity exists in the class of students taking principles of economics. This heterogeneity occurs because of student differences with respect to interest in economics, intelligence, motivation, classroom experience, time input (which may be driven by other academic and nonacademic demands), and, as mentioned above, the ability to learn via alternative media (listening to lectures, reading, etc.). The heterogeneity poses a fundamental dilemma to anyone teaching principles, particularly those teaching at the introductory level (presumably, when one moves further along in the economics major, selection and other processes are at work in rendering classes less heterogeneous). The same issues that arise with respect to the level at which one pitches the lecture—lowest common denominator, median student, best students, and so on—and the costs and benefits of each also apply to the method by which each principles textbook is used, and indeed, written. Many principles textbooks have optional, more advanced appendixes, special exercises, and so on, for students who are doing well and who are well motivated. Some even have remedial chapters or sections within chapters. The ability to write textbook material that is simultaneously intelligible to the bulk of the students yet challenging to the brightest of them is probably the single most important characteristic by which we all evaluate, or at least pretend to evaluate, textbooks. I have no magic answers as to how to do better, but I can assure you that from the standpoint of a teacher who has used many textbooks, the ability to deal with this heterogeneity in the textbook is the driving force behind the use of other resources, such as computer-assisted tutorials and extensive and expensive faculty and graduate assistant time.

I personally believe that current textbooks do a better job segmenting the market by reading ability, mathematical ability, and so on, into a high, middle, and lower end than they do in dealing with heterogeneity within each group.

Second, by the *n*th edition of their textbook, most successful textbook authors have added various topical and timely material but have usually deleted precious little. Some resemble my notoriously cluttered office or bedroom closet. The fundamental economics concepts such as choice subject to constraints appears to be insufficiently enforced by authors and editors.

Third, keeping a textbook current not only by topic but by useful information is a major problem with textbooks. Typically published on a three-year cycle, an edition will have data that may be four or five years old. This can be partly redressed by having professors provide the data and update particular tables, charts, or trend graphs in the textbook for their own lectures, but to be honest, I believe that I spent way too much of my time having to do so. Perhaps teaching graduate students with some information from several years ago and commenting in your lectures about what has happened in the interim is sufficient, but the visual impact in the textbook is often of paramount importance to a freshman or sophomore. Worse yet, examples are often historically dated. Most students taking principles this academic year were not yet born at the time of the Kennedy tax cuts, were not yet in school during the Arab oil embargo, and were in the fourth or fifth grade during the 1981-82 recession. We are increasingly less likely to be teaching children whose parents lived through the Great Depression and who have had substantial family discussion of this major economic disruption.

In the electronic age, there ought to be much more advantage taken of the opportunity to provide updated information. Often, instructors like to incorporate current events into the course. Although there is no substitute for this practice, students are sometimes confused by differences in data presented in class and in the textbook.

Fourth, too many instructors allow a textbook to set an agenda *beyond* the basic economics upon which we all can agree. This problem is partially ameliorated by the wide variety of textbooks and by the latitude instructors have in combining the textbook with other inputs. Instructors can supplement or deemphasize the particular topic, approach, and agenda of a given textbook by using alternative material (e.g., historical analysis). Nevertheless, the topics and approaches of textbooks are often followed very closely by instructors. This practice may be easy on the instructors and students, but many opportunities for value-added are missed.

Fifth, the encyclopedia-like structure of most principles textbooks tends almost de facto to underemphasize basic economic concepts such as scarcity, opportunity cost, and marginality. This style of textbook may have been less of a problem in the late 1940s and 1950s when Samuelson's pathbreaking textbook, along with others, set the tone for what was to follow. At that time, it was more reasonable to presume that a fairly large fraction of instructors in principles of economics courses knew a fairly substantial fraction of close-to-the-frontier economic knowledge. But since then, there has been an unprecedented explosion and extension of economic theory and data and, therefore, empirical analyses of the economy. The recent increase in specialization of knowledge by subdiscipline also means that a much smaller percentage of economists are likely to possess a large percentage of close-to-the-frontier knowledge in any but their own subdiscipline. In today's job market for Ph.D. candidates, for example, it is not unlikely that one will interview a prospective assistant professor whose main field of expertise is the economics of information. With all due respect to the importance of this body of knowledge, a decade ago that same person would have described himself or herself as an applied micro theorist or an industrial organization specialist. The incredible expansion and specialization of knowledge within subfields in economics means that a very small fraction of instructors of economics can be close to the frontier of knowledge in any but their own subdiscipline. This occurs because of both advances in economic knowledge and the fundamental changes in the economy, only some of which can be closely followed by today's specialist. Consider just the changes in the tax laws or the conduct of monetary policy and how quickly a teacher who is not a public finance specialist or monetary economist can lose command of the essentials.

To take another example mentioned above, the role of expectations is fundamental to discussion of macroeconomic events, theory, and policy. Two decades ago, most introductory macroeconomics lectures could mention expectations only anecdotally. Today, that would be wholly inadequate. What fraction of principles of economics students have had an introductory probability/statistics course? Thus, we are forced to develop some simple concepts from another discipline that are used as inputs into economic analysis, and thereby crowd out some other material. Yet, as mentioned above, in most textbooks, little has been crowded out. Material has just been slapped on in additional chapters, paragraphs, or subsections. Although the structure of these encyclopedia-like textbooks generally provides discussion relating to virtually all of the issues presented by instructors in lectures, the extensive scope of textbooks can limit their effectiveness as a teaching aid, unless very carefully monitored by instructors, section leaders, and students.

Chapters in textbooks are often assigned to supplement the instructor's lectures, when they do not closely coincide. However, the coverage of material in each chapter is often so extensive in the encyclopedia-like format that students have difficulty in determining which parts of the chapters are most important. In many cases, the side issues can be distracting or confusing for a large subset of the students.

Finally, let me add that, in my opinion, a variety of topics are underemphasized in principles of economics books in addition to the internationalization of trade and capital flows emphasized above. I am certain that future editions of existing books will attempt to redress some of these shortcomings. Let me just mention the following six examples:

1 The post-World War II Keynesian emphasis on short-run demand management has relegated long-run growth problems, technical change, and productivity to the last part of introductory textbooks (usually not reached because we fall behind the class schedule). They deserve better.

2 Generally, there is very little said about what it means for economic agents to be rational. Because a form of rationality is often assumed in economics, it would be helpful to discuss the importance of maximizing behavior and the limitations of the assumption of rationality for households, firms, or governments. The public choice approach has provided a useful counterpoint to the assumption that government is always working in the national interest. A related problem is that, although many students understand the concept of marginality, a large fraction fail to grasp the similarity in the optimizing procedures used in many different economic problems.

3 Discussion of alternative mechanisms for allocating resources (e.g., central planning and rationing) prior to the detailed discussion of the market system would be helpful from a conceptual point of view. Too often, these alternatives are discussed very briefly in a concluding chapter of the textbook. Yet the students should keep the market mechanism in perspective as one of a range of allocation schemes, others of which are, and have been, used extensively in other countries as well as historically in the United States.

4 I find it distressing that micro- and macroeconomics are often still treated as two distinct types of economic analysis. While I do not believe, as some extremists do, that macroeconomics is simply a question of appropriate aggregation of micro behavior, the similarities and relationships between the two branches of economic analysis are often not well developed. It would help to unify the subject matter in the introductory course if the common elements of micro and macro, as well as their differences, were developed more fully.

5 Although most textbooks highlight various points of view, especially in macroeconomics, and although this is a useful pedagogical device, too much attention is paid to the disputes themselves rather than to the reasons for them (e.g., assumptions concerning behavior, empirical estimates of various parameters, etc.). A related point is that even the grossest historical evidence is often ignored in coming to a *conclusion* about such debates. For example, (a) the deficit experiments of the 1980s that coincided with a fall in the saving rate would seem to be an indictment of the Ricardian equivalence conjecture; (b) the collapse of velocity was not too kind to mechanical monetarism; and (c) the real GNP loss accompanying the post 1981 disinflation apparently was much less than most neo-Keynesian Phillips-curve-augmented macro models were predicting.

6 Finally, although different points of view are legitimate, and a modern eclectic macroeconomics combining elements of Keynesian fixed-price models with some insights from monetarism, rational expectations, and the legitimate part of supply-side economics is emerging, there is need for neither nihilism nor apology. We should not expect the precision of the natural sciences, but we *must* establish reasonable or plausible bounds within which to operate. Although a blend of various macro theories is emerging, it is not permissible to choose parts of each approach and combine them in one's own experimental recipe (the original 1981 "Claremont" forecast, for example, required an astounding increase in velocity to be consistent; although this was not absolutely impossible, it was implausible).

Yet it is increasingly clear that these topics are far more important than the attention they receive in introductory textbooks.

My conclusion is simple: Although our attempts at objective measurement leave much room for interpretation, the net marginal social benefit of improved economic understanding may well be enormous. The extent to which the principles of economics course has somehow failed to imbue successive cohorts of students with these principles is open to question. I personally do not believe that we have failed in that undertaking, but I do believe we can and should do better. The textbook is but one item in the portfolio of inputs, and although over some range it substitutes for lectures, sections, and computer-assisted tutorials, for many students those substitution possibilities are limited. Thus, in the design and presentation of the economics textbook, my major concern is *emphasis of basics*: that most of the students leave the course with some real understanding of marginal cost, opportunity cost, basic material on the current economy, and so forth. Further I hope the instructor has stimulated in them enough of an interest in economic events that they will keep the textbook as a potentially valuable reference later on. Finally, we should take advantage of rapidly changing technology in microelectronics to make the material in the textbook more up to date, provide alternative learning environments in electronic classrooms for our students, and better integrate this material with traditional textbooks to increase our productivity—to enable more students to learn and retain more principles of economics.

NOTES

*This chapter is an edited combination of two articles that appeared in the *Journal of Economic Education*: "Some Thoughts on Teaching Principles of Macroeconomics," Fall 1986, **17**, 283-287 and "Observations on the Use of Textbooks in the Teaching of Principles of Economics," Spring 1988, **19**, 157-164. Reprinted with permission of the Helen Dwight Reid Educational Foundation. Published by Heldref Publications, 4000 Albermarle Street., N. W., Washington, D. C. 20016. Copyright © 1986 and 1988.

1 Throughout this part of the chapter, I refer to the collection of principles of economics textbooks and what I perceive to be central tendencies in the collection. Virtually every criticism levied or praise heaped upon the collection will be inaccurate with respect to some members of the set.

CHAPTER 4

SOME REFLECTIONS ON THE PRINCIPLES COURSE

Campbell R. McConnell[*]

An invitation to reflect upon the character of, and some of the problems associated with, the principles of economics course is irresistible. But the breadth of the topic also obligates one to ponder his or her qualifications in responding. Mine, I find, are far from impeccable. However, they do include (1) almost four decades of university teaching, much of it at the principles level; (2) some very modest research contributions to the field of economic education; and (3) the authorship of a principles text which has remained viable over three decades. The latter—the writing and revision of an introductory text over an extended period—has had a considerable impact upon my thinking about the principles course as will become quite evident in the ensuing commentary.

It is not my goal to summarize research findings relevant to the principles course; that task has been admirably accomplished elsewhere (see Siegfried and Fels, 1979, and Chapter 20 of this volume). Nor do I propose to offer a comprehensive evaluation or critique of the course. Rather, taking full advantage of the latitude explicit in my assigned topic, I intend to offer a subjective and impressionistic series of observations and questions which I associate with the introductory course. These will focus upon the evolution of the principles course; the effectiveness with which the course is taught; its appropriate scope; the potential roles of student and institutional inputs in determining student achievement; and, finally, a consideration of the goals or outputs which might be associated with the course.

COMPREHENSIVENESS AND SOPHISTICATION

Perhaps the most obvious point to be made is that over the years principles of economics has become much more comprehensive in terms of content and more sophisticated with respect to level of analysis. There is more in the course and the concepts are more demanding. The unprecedented knowledge explosion in economics since World War II has simply added a plethora of new concepts, theories, and empirical analyses which call out for inclusion in the introductory course. If one is willing to accept the assumption that course content is fairly accurately mirrored in textbooks, it becomes a fascinating exercise to compare current texts with pre-Samuelson texts. The quantum leap in content, of course, was the addition of formal macroeconomics achieved successfully by Samuelson in 1948. Since then such topics as economic growth, monetarism, the new classical economics and public choice theory, to mention only a few, have been added to the list of core topics. And, with the great expansion of international trade and finance, the trend toward internationalization of the course has spurred increased emphasis on topics and concepts which previously were assigned a more secondary role. The amount of "crowding out" has not been great, with the result that the array of subjects confronting students has expanded significantly.

Although levels of analytical difficulty are not easily compared, it is my impression that it has increased significantly. It is striking that geometric analysis was extremely limited in pre-Samuelson texts. For example, the two-volume, 1150 page Taussig text (Taussig, 1946) contained about a dozen diagrams as compared to perhaps 150 or 200 in a present-day mainstream text. In my judgement one finds nothing as demanding in the pre-Samuelson texts as, for example, the long-run aggregate supply analysis or the international repercussions of budgetary deficits and macro policies which are now becoming common to modern texts. Furthermore, a casual perusal of pre-Samuelson texts makes it clear that easy-to-understand historical, institutional, and anecdotal material was much more in evidence than it is today. My impression is that the limited amount of crowding-out which has occurred in principles texts and courses has been in these "soft" areas. I confess that the thought has crossed my mind that the compression of such non-theory material has perhaps gone too far.

Has student understanding grown apace with the content and sophistication of the principles course? At the conclusion of the course does the student of 1990 know more about the economic system than did the student of, say, 1940 or 1960? I do not profess to know the answer to this question, but I am doubtful. We know that during much of the 1970s and into the early 1980s the communicative and quantitative skills of high school students, as measured by college-entrance examinations, declined. Furthermore, demographic considerations brought about a diminished pool of potential college students and perhaps eroded admission standards. Hence, we may be confronting the challenge of teaching an increasingly difficult subject matter to students who, on the average, may possess diminished capability for college-level work. If this "sophistication-ability squeeze" does in fact exist, it may help explain why the principles course is often a source of frustration for both students and instructors.

IS THE COURSE WELL TAUGHT?

There can be no question that there are many superb teachers—including internationally known research scholars—who are deeply committed to the introductory course.

Yet it is reasonable to question whether principles students in general are well-served in the classroom. This is a disturbing assertion, but consider the following supporting points.

First, most economics departments tend to assign their least-experienced staff to the principles course. Indeed, at most Ph.D.-granting institutions, the principles course is heavily staffed by inexperienced teaching assistants (TAs). Inexperience inevitably is conducive to mistakes, an absence of depth of subject matter understanding, a restricted range of knowledge, and a constrained grasp of effective pedagogical techniques. It should be added that TAs are undergoing a very demanding and stressful educational process at unenviable rates of pay. Neither consideration is conducive to placing a high priority on classroom performance. Furthermore, approximately one-third of all graduate students—and I would presume TAs—in the United States are foreign born. This has often posed communication problems that have become a serious source of dissatisfaction among principles students at many Ph.D.-granting universities.

Second, the propensity of most permanent staff to opt for the principles course is probably not high. Suppose you are an associate or full professor and your department chair poses these teaching options for you. "Option one: teach principles of economics. You will be confronted with a relatively large number of students whose backgrounds, interests, and motivations are highly diverse. Many students take the course simply because it is required. The subject matter is varied and far-reaching, covering many topics in which you have minimal background and preparation. Hence, rather than being complementary with your research agenda, your teaching will tend to be competitive. Your student evaluation at the end of the semester will tend to be low because evidence indicates that, *ceteris paribus*, student ratings vary directly with course level." Now consider a second option: "Teach an intermediate or advanced course in one of your areas of specialty. Because of self-selection and student attrition, you will have fewer students and they will be more interested in the subject matter and motivated to perform well. The subject matter is your specialty and therefore complementary to your research interests. Your student evaluations will benefit from the aforementioned direct relationship between such ratings and class level." While my statement of options is overdrawn and somewhat facetious, it is clear that option two will clearly be preferable to most instructors. In short, I would surmise that comparatively few senior staff will be found in the principles classroom.

Furthermore, the increased specialization which has occurred in graduate training may not bode well for teaching in the principles course. As Michael Boskin mentions in Chapter 3, a new assistant professor, who a decade ago would describe herself as a specialist in applied microeconomics or industrial organization, is now a specialist in the economics of information (p. 24). This increased fractionalization of the discipline suggests that most new college and university teachers are less and less likely to be near the frontiers of knowledge of the array of specialties which comprise the principles course.

I have one modest suggestion which *might* improve instruction in the principles course and undergraduate teaching in general. And that is to accept the notion of specialization in accordance with comparative advantage as it might apply to our academic endeavors. It is a curious spectacle to observe economists preaching the virtues of specialization based upon comparative advantage in their classrooms and then, in formulating faculty policies, insist that staff members be nonspecialists. That is, we demand that all staff members, with rare exceptions, allocate significant portions of their efforts to teaching, research, and service. This insistence is not arbitrary; it is based upon a plausible rationale. But it also seems eminently sensible to let the superb teachers devote the bulk, if not all, of their time to teaching and the exemplary researchers to spend most of their time in research. If our profession practiced the specialization it preaches, might it not be possible to obtain both a higher level of economic literacy for students and the generation of more new knowledge from a given quantity of academic inputs? In short, might we not collectively be more productive?

Aside from issues of staffing, there is perhaps a more pervasive consideration which makes effective teaching of the principles course difficult to achieve. To the extent that they exist, the aspirations of students are often such that they expect the course will provide them with clear-cut and unassailable answers to current socioeconomic problems. Given the inherent nature of the course—it is merely an introduction, after all—it quickly becomes apparent to students that their aspirations will not be fulfilled. Students frequently encounter a sense of disappointment during the course, even though they may be learning a great deal.

Why can't we provide the definitive answers which students seek? In the first place, in many critical instances we simply don't have the answers. For example, despite a substantial research effort, the profession has not as yet provided a convincing and generally accepted explanation of the productivity slowdown of the past two decades. Second, good answers to many current socioeconomic problems frequently require a substantial box of analytical tools which exceeds that provided by the introductory course. Finally, answers frequently transcend the discipline of economics. Economic analysis alone is inadequate to explain the persistence of poverty in an affluent society or why certain less-developed countries have achieved remarkable growth while others confront declining living standards.

COURSE SCOPE: SHORT-LIST OR LONG-LIST?

There has been a great deal of controversy—dating at least back to the early 1950s—as to the proper scope of the principles course. Should students examine intensively a relatively few topics or devote less time to each of a longer list of topics? Certainly complaints persist that the principles course is too ambitious, too comprehensive, too encyclopedic. Those who feel this is the case advocate a "short list" of core topics which are to be taught carefully and in depth. Supporters of the short-list view contend that a "long list" of topics dooms the course to comparative failure. They argue that the long list is simply too much for students to handle. As a consequence of receiving fleeting exposure to a wide variety of concepts, theories, problems, and institutional considerations, students come away from the course with no real understanding of economic logic. Hence, students will be ill-equipped to analyze economic problems they will encounter as citizens or in business some five or ten years after the final examination. In brief, the short-list position, which is eloquently stated by G. L. Bach in the next chapter of this volume, is that a concept or theory must be learned well or students will simply not retain it. The long-list approach attempts to accomplish too much and, as a consequence, those who use it achieve too little.

The counterview is that the short-list approach provides no assurance that student understanding will be enhanced. Perhaps the learning process for individual concepts or theories may be subject to rapidly diminishing returns. If, for example, a student cannot grasp the concept of comparative advantage on the basis of a one-hour lecture-discussion, then he or she is not likely to be further enlightened if the time devoted to the topic is extended. One might even contend, for example, that if a student does not fully grasp the MR = MC profit-maximization rule in a reasonable period of time, it might be advisable to turn to other topics in the hope that, when the MRP = MRC input rule is encountered later, the student will comprehend the latter and come to understand that the logic underlying both rules is identical.

Another potential problem with the short-list approach is that the list itself is typically comprised of all the theoretical concepts associated with the course and little else. If one of the objectives of the course is to create and sustain interest in the discipline, one may question whether an uninterrupted diet of economic theory will foster this goal. It may be injudicious to lead students through the desert of analysis up to the oasis of real-world applications and issues and then not allow them to drink.

Finally, one may argue that it simply may be equally or more desirable to fulfill rather ambitious goals partially than to achieve modest ones more fully. To my knowledge the hypothesis that the principles course is "overloaded" has never been substantiated (Fels, 1969, p. 7). In any event, this remains an important issue. As an aside, given the surfeit of "encyclopedic" principles texts and the paucity of "bare bones" books, it would seem clear that publishers and authors have favored—or at least supported—the long-list approach. The extent to which this reflects marketing considerations as opposed to consumer (instructor) preferences is open to debate.

I must admit to considerable ambivalence on the short-list versus long-list controversy. Specifically, I am sympathetic to the short-list position in the sense that I question the *level* of analytical sophistication upon which some instructors and departments insist. Some years ago an exemplary teacher (Mandelstamm, 1971, p. 43) pinpointed this problem and its implications as follows:

> Most of us are simply giving the students too many "principles." Every year, it seems, more and more concepts, which previously had been reserved for the intermediate theory or even the advanced theory sequences, are being taught in principles courses. In fact, I have an uneasy feeling that there is enough in several of today's principles texts to warrant their use in certain graduate courses. For example, indifference curves and isoquants, with all their ramifications, are frequently taught as part of elementary economics. We find ourselves enmeshed by envelope curves and saddle points. We are caught up by accelerators and even LaGrange multipliers and set theory. Then we spend the rest of the undergraduate program, and a good deal of the graduate program, repeating the same material. The results are predictable. The poor students are hopelessly swamped in the principles course, and the best students are turned off in later courses, when they find that they are getting very little new material.

On the other hand, I wonder whether the notion that the problems associated with the principles course stem largely from its encyclopedic character is not overdrawn. I find some merit in the aforestated arguments on behalf of the long-list approach. "Smorgasbord" should not necessarily be deemed a pejorative term. In short, the central question may not be the *length* of the list of topics included in the introductory course, but rather the *depth* at which we choose to pursue each of those topics.

WHICH INPUTS MATTER MOST?

It is an intriguing mental exercise to reflect upon the many inputs which might affect a student's achievement in the principles course. It would be fascinating if we were able somehow to construct a complex educational production function for the principles course wherein we could assess the marginal contributions of a multitude of inputs to an output somehow accurately measured as, say, "enhanced student understanding" of the discipline. A useful taxonomy is to classify inputs as (1) student inputs and (2) institutional inputs. The former refers to the bundle of characteristics—such as genetic endowment, gender, age, previous educational experience, socioeconomic background, motivation, and so forth—which a student brings to the principles course. Institutional inputs, as we shall see momentarily, designate a variety of inputs which are determined or controlled by the college or university.

Student Inputs

The most obvious question is: What is the relative importance of the two types of inputs in determining output? There is some evidence which implies that student inputs may be more important than institutional inputs. For example, some of the literature on human development suggests that an individual's future academic achievement may be determined in the first several years of one's life. You may also recall Coleman's admittedly controversial conclusion that family background is the critical determinant of achievement and that school inputs are of relatively little importance (Coleman, 1966). Similarly, studies of earnings differences by level of education suggest that a significant portion of observed earnings differences are attributable to differences in "ability" and family environment, rather than formal education (Taubman, 1978, p. 102). If this reasoning is accurate, then as teachers we face considerable constraints as to what we might accomplish.

Institutional Inputs

As noted, institutional inputs are those which—subject to obvious budget constraints—can be manipulated by the educational institution or the individual instructor. Here a wide spectrum of questions come to mind. Do instructional techniques have a significant impact upon student achievement? Does it make much difference whether students are taught by a conventional lecture-discussion technique, by closed-circuit television, by video cassettes, by computer, by the Keller Plan, or by some other method? It is to the credit of economic educators that the past several decades have been characterized by considerable experimentation with new techniques and approaches to instruction in the principles course. From the students' vantage point these attempts at "product differentiation" would seem to be desirable. After all, the economist's own theory of consumer behavior suggests that, within limits, a wider range of consumer choice tends to increase consumer welfare. Hence, it would seem worthwhile for a department to offer its principles course through several options.

But there may be attendant problems. First, student-consumers are only in the "market" once for the course in its various guises. They therefore lack information *ex ante* with respect to the satisfaction (accomplishment) which they may derive from each of the various options. How can we achieve the most efficient allocation of students among the various pedagogical options being offered? Second, it is fair to ask whether the availability of instructional options is the result of a department's interest in the welfare of its student clientele or rather a reflection of its desire to utilize its available resources to maximize the profession's perception of its quality. Does an economics department offer its introductory course via television or the Keller Plan because those are pedagogically superior approaches for some students? Or are these means for reducing teaching loads to provide more time for highly visible research?

What about class size? Are large classes *per se* an impediment to learning as the conventional wisdom suggests? Should institutions with large enrollments establish an array of introductory courses for various clienteles? Should potential majors and business students be sorted into one course and all other students into a separate and distinct course? Should special courses be offered for engineers or journalism students? Is it a valid hypothesis that the more a course is fashioned to the interests and background of a particular clientele, the greater will be student motivation and hence achievement? Should we make an attempt to allocate students into sections on the basis of ability as measured by SAT scores or GPAs? Will homogeneity stimulate competition and enhance student performance? Or in a heterogeneous class will the recognition of superiority provide a positive reinforcement for the better students, while the less capable students strive to emulate the top students?

What is the optimal sequencing of material? In particular, should macroeconomics precede microeconomics or vice versa? Advocates of a macro-micro sequence point to the apparent logic of providing a "big picture" overview of the level of national output before analyzing and explaining its composition. There is also the more pragmatic argument that many students take only one semester of a two-semester principles sequence and macroeconomics is perhaps more helpful to students in understanding current events. The opposing view is that the increasing importance of the micro-foundations of macroeconomics calls for a micro-macro sequence. Furthermore, students need to understand marginal analysis before they can appreciate the incessant controversies over the legitimacy and scope of macroeconomic policies. Or is sequencing a matter of little consequence?

To what degree, if any, do instructor characteristics influence student achievement? Does it make a difference whether an instructor has his or her degree from a more- or less-prestigious institution? Is there a positive relationship between the years of experience of the instructor and student achievement? Or do newer faculty bring greater enthusiasm and approachability to the classroom which more than compensates for inexperience? On balance, are teaching effectiveness and research productivity complementary or competing endeavors?

The sometimes lengthy deliberations and machinations of textbook selection committees imply that choice of textbook has an important influence upon student performance. But there seems to be little evidence on the matter. The more widely used texts are accompanied by student workbooks, programmed materials, and computer software. What contributions, if any, do these make to student understanding? And, more particularly, do the added benefits exceed the associated costs?

Student Motivation

Student motivation is a peculiar consideration in that it is both a student and an institutional input. Learning theory clearly suggests that a student's motivation and effort are important determinants of the amount of learning achieved. In the absence of effective student motivation, little learning will occur. Lydall (1976, p. 35) has suggested that intelligence might interact multiplicatively with what he calls the "D-factor" (representing drive, dynamism, and determination) to explain the skewness found in the distribution of earnings. One cannot help but wonder if an analogous explanation might be applied to the distribution of achievement among principles students.

Given the critical role which motivation may play in determining student achievement, it is interesting to ponder whether the traditional orientation of the principles course is conducive to student motivation. The principles course typically focuses upon "economics for citizenship" and treats broad social questions rooted in efficiency, stability, growth, and so forth. The benefits of such knowledge are largely social, rather than private or personal. In comparison, students might be more motivated in vocationally oriented courses wherein benefits are primarily private rather than social. Bluntly put, a student might be more highly motivated in an accounting or finance course wherein the subject matter directly enhances career opportunities and expected future earnings than in an economics course which seeks to render the student a more intelligent citizen.

WHAT OUTPUTS DO WE SEEK?

What are the objectives or goals of the principles course? At the most general level, we would perhaps all agree that we seek to achieve (1) a usable level of economic literacy for those students who do not go beyond the principles course and (2) a viable foundation of economic understanding for those who will pursue upper-division courses.

But there are also a number of more elusive noncognitive outcomes which are necessarily involved. At the most mundane level, we seek to generate continuing interest in economic issues and problems. At a more nebulous level, we might hope that the principles course will contribute significantly to the overall scholarly maturation of students and also impact upon their value systems. For example, one can plausibly argue that a highly significant outcome of the principles course is enhanced student ability to grasp and manipulate abstractions. Piaget's theory of human intellectual development distinguishes between the lower "concrete level" of mental achievement which involves specific facts or experiences and the higher "formal level" of achievement which entails analytical reasoning about hypotheses, the mental manipulation of abstractions, and the understanding of contrary-to-fact situations. The distinction may be particularly relevant for the principles course because the most baffling concepts of economics tend to be those which are the most abstract. Instructors often respond to student complaints about the abstractness of economics by pointing out that economics is formalized common sense. But this is only partly true. The concept of comparative advantage and the multiple-lending capacity of the banking system are contrary to common sense and intuitively incorrect in the minds of students.

If the principles course is instrumental in upgrading the mental capacities of students from the concrete to the formal (abstract) level, we might expect a number of desirable payoffs. First, cognitive achievement should be enhanced. Second, the teaching-learning process should become more efficient. For example, students will come to recognize that markets for products, labor, money, foreign exchange, and property rights are not distinct analytical constructs to be learned separately, but are rather variations of a common analytical framework. They will also understand that the rule for maximizing consumer utility and the rule for realizing the least-cost combination of inputs entail a common logic. Third, if students are more able to grasp abstractions, their affinity for economics should be enhanced. Finally, an important spillover benefit for students is that they can apply their greater capacity to reason formally to other disciplines and to the real world.

Perry's[1] theory of intellectual development envisions a first stage which is "dualistic" in that students think in terms of polarities. Answers are either "right" or "wrong"; value statements are either "good" or "bad." Furthermore, the "right" answers and the "good" values are determined by authority. At a second and higher stage, dualistic thinking and the role of authority are replaced by relativism, that is, by the legitimization of uncertainty and diversity. It is also recognized that authorities embrace conflicting views as to what is "right" and "good." Knowledge and values come to be relativistic and contextual. In a third and final stage students become committed to social and moral values and to political, religious, and intellectual viewpoints. Decisions are made as to vocational choice, interpersonal relationships, and overall lifestyle. Do the pedagogical inputs which comprise the principles of economics course contribute to this maturation process?

The point to be made is that the principles course contributes to affective as well as to cognitive outcomes. The ability to grasp and manipulate abstractions, shifts in student attitudes from closed- to open-mindedness, and the maturation of student values are equally or perhaps more important than gains in TUCE scores in judging the success of the course.

I would be remiss not to mention that the role of textbook authors and publishers in promoting the overall maturation of students has not been without blemishes. I refer in particular to the issue of textbook readability. Perhaps in response to low and declining student reading levels, there has been a corresponding tendency of some authors and publishers to lower the reading level of their products. You may have endured the curious phenomenon of a publisher's representative praising a text because it embodied a ninth- or tenth-grade reading level. My point, of course, is that the provision of texts at or below the students' actual reading levels may be insufficiently challenging and students may miss an opportunity to improve their reading and linguistic abilities. Furthermore, one cannot help but wonder about cause and effect; some authorities feel that the diminished reading levels of widely used elementary and high school texts are a cause of declining student verbal scores.

A similar point might be made with respect to the widespread use of behavioral objectives. The presumption underlying the use of behavioral objectives seems to be that it is inefficient for instructors and students to engage in a cat-and-mouse game of determining what is important in a course. The argument is that students should be clearly and explicitly told what must be accomplished and provided with a mechanism for determining whether they have achieved that objective. For example, we should tell students that they must understand the average and marginal propensity to consume concepts and indicate that this knowledge can be demonstrated by computing the APC and MPC from given income-consumption data. Equipped with such guidance, it is hoped that a given amount of student study time will generate more educational output. My concern is that, if the development of a student's ability to discern the important from the inconsequential is a vital component of the learning process, the use of behavioral objectives may undermine that process. I also wonder if the use of behavioral objectives entails a subtle bias wherein we emphasize quantifiable relationships which permit unambiguous responses at the expense of less-explicit concepts and more debatable issues. For example, it may be easier to construct a behavioral objective concerning the nature of the Lorenz curve than one pertaining to the shortcomings of income distribution data. The latter point may be of as much consequence as the former. Do learning objectives dilute the learning process and give us a somewhat distorted picture of what is important?

UNREALISTIC EXPECTATIONS?

The preceding comments touch on a number of problems associated with the principles course. For example, the content of the course has increased in scope and perhaps in level of difficulty at a time when student capabilities may be eroding. The processes of teacher assignment and selection may not be conducive to high quality instruction in the course. Furthermore, some observers feel that the encyclopedic character of the course necessitates that it will impart little of lasting value to students. The reader, I am certain, could readily add to this list.

While there can be little question that these and a host of other problems are causes for concern, I feel that much of our lingering frustration concerning the introductory course has different roots. As I have argued elsewhere (McConnell, 1980, p. 21), we may simply expect too much of our students. Marginalism, elasticity concepts, comparative advantage, allocative efficiency, externalities, and the other baggage which constitutes the course may all be commonplace and self-evident to professional economists who are imparting this wisdom to their charges for the tenth or twentieth time. But we must always be cognizant that these concepts are abstract, esoteric, and quite mystifying to most freshmen and sophomores. It is not reasonable to expect the basic tool kit of economics to be swallowed and digested in two semesters.

It is sometimes pointed out that the difference between aspirations and accomplishment is dissatisfaction. One cannot help but wonder whether some portion of our dissatisfaction with the principles course is due to our aspirations being unrealistically lofty rather than our level of accomplishment being low. All in all, we may be doing a quite commendable job in the principles course. Our more-or-less chronic discontent may stem from the possibility that we expect too much.

NOTES

*I want to express my indebtedness to Professors Jerry Petr and William Walstad for their helpful comments.

1 See Perry, 1970, and Heffernan, 1975, p. 493.

REFERENCES

Coleman, James S., *Equality of Educational Opportunity* (Washington: U. S. Department of Health, Education, and Welfare, 1966).

Fels, Rendigs, "Hard Research on a Soft Subject: Hypothesis-Testing in Economic Education," *Southern Economic Journal*, July 1969, **36**, 1-9.

Heffernan, James M., "An Analytical Framework for Planning and Research in Higher Education," *Liberal Education*, December 1975, **61**, 493-503.

Lydall, Howard F., "Theories of the Distribution of Earnings," in A. B. Atkinson (ed.), *The Personal Distribution of Income* (Boulder, Colorado: Westview Press, 1976).

Mandelstamm, Allan B., "The Principles Course Revisited," *Journal of Economic Education*, Fall 1971, **3**, 41-44.

McConnell, Campbell R., "Economics 101: Where Do We Stand?," *Journal of Economic Education*, Winter 1980, **12**, 15-22.

Perry, William G., Jr., *Forms of Intellectual and Ethical Development in the College Years: A Scheme* (New York: Holt, Rinehart, Winston, 1970).

Siegfried, John J., and Rendigs Fels, "Research on Teaching College Economics," *Journal of Economic Literature*, September 1979, **17**, 923-969.

Taubman, Paul, *Income Distribution and Redistribution* (Reading, Mass.: Addison-Wesley Publishing Company, 1978).

Taussig, Frank W., *Principles of Economics* (New York: The Macmillan Company, 1946).

CHAPTER 5

WHAT SHOULD A PRINCIPLES COURSE IN ECONOMICS BE?

G. L. Bach[*]

The principles course clearly is our most important teaching assignment. Here is our one big chance to teach economics to most of the people who go through colleges and universities. Two-thirds to three-fourths of all students we teach take only the elementary course; yet most evidence suggests that we are not doing as well as we might in teaching the course.

Ask your neighbors whether they took a course in economics and what they thought of it. The answer will probably have a dusty flavor, include lots of abstract curves that don't seem to apply to much, and have little useful application. The recent level of political discourse on such policies as government spending and fiscal policies confirms this conclusion.

GOALS, CONTENT, AND METHODS

The main goal of the principles course should be to help students learn to think effectively for themselves about economics problems. We should be concerned primarily with the *process* of straight thinking in economics, rather than emphasis on facts and descriptions of institutions. If we want to produce students who can and will think intelligently for themselves about economic issues five and ten years after they have taken the final exam and have left the campus, we must emphasize that *economics is a way of thinking about problems*, not a set of answers ready to be taken off the shelf.

To flesh out this overall goal, let me specify some subgoals for the principles course. Each of these subgoals is stated in terms of what the *student* should be able to do, not in terms of what the instructor should say or do. Students completing a good principles course should:

- Exhibit an awareness of, and a continuing interest in, the major economic problems of modern society.
- Demonstrate a firm grasp of the few basic principles and analytical concepts necessary to think intelligently about economic problems for themselves. (Technical theoretical detail should be sacrificed in order to obtain proficiency in the use of the basic analytical tool kit.)
- Develop an independent ability to apply these analytical tools in thinking independently about economic problems. (This involves placing major stress on the *process* of *applying* economic concepts and principles in thinking about economic issues.)

While these objectives may appear commonplace, they are really quite untraditional in the way they focus specifically on student behavior and student learning, rather than on the detailed economic subject matter of the course per se.

FOUNDATIONS FROM LEARNING THEORY

How can we achieve the basic goal of developing students' interests and abilities so that they can do their own thinking about economic issues years after they leave the classroom? I argue that we should state instructional goals in behavioral terms—in terms of what we want the student to do now and later. To make sense of this proposition, we must have a foundation of how people learn, of what psychologists call learning theory.

Experts on learning agree that there is no one satisfactory general theory of human learning. Yet a considerable body of evidence, much of it highly convincing, has been accumulated on what kinds of learning generally occur best under what kinds of circumstances or, conversely, what conditions are unconducive to learning. I do not presume to pose as an expert on learning theory. I do want to suggest a series of propositions which, from a review of the psychological literature, appear to be generally valid and which can be used as important foundations for course planning, given the general goals I have stated above.

IMPORTANCE OF MOTIVATION

Most psychological evidence suggests that the learner's motivation is the most important variable controlling the amount of learning that occurs. A related proposition is that reward is generally a stronger inducement to learning than punishment. People who are highly motivated to learn generally do learn; those who are not motivated seldom do. This has proven true in experiments with rats and with people, and in just about every circumstance one can imagine. It holds true for all ages, from small children to adults, although, of course, the motivating factors may be different at different ages and for different groups. If we accept this proposition, it has sweeping consequences for the way we design our courses and the way we teach: Without effective student motivation, nothing else matters much.

THE COGNITIVE PROCESS: LEARNING, RETENTION, AND TRANSFER

Turning then, to what psychologists call cognitive processes—the intellectual kinds of learning as distinct from attitudinal and motivational issues—it is convenient to look at the facts which appear to govern learning, those which govern retention, and those which govern learning transfer.

Learning

Prompt, accurate feedback appears to be of critical importance to the learning process. That is, students must receive knowledge of how they are doing if they are to learn effectively. This is the central proposition underlying so-called "programmed learning," but it can apply to all kinds of learning processes. The proposition seems to hold firm with rats in mazes and with children and adults in a wide variety of situations.

Moreover, the acquisition of knowledge is faster and easier if the learning is meaningful (relevant) to the student. This, of course, appears closely related to the motivation point mentioned above.

Most experts suggest that effective learning involves active response. The student must *do something*—whether verbally in class or in out-of-class discussion. Learning is not a passive process in which the student merely sits and "receives" information from a lecturer.

Finally, on the degree of guidance conducive to effective acquisition of knowledge, there appear to be several reasonable and well-established propositions. These include:

- The more highly the learner is motivated, the less teacher guidance is required.
- The more complex the learning situation, the more valuable is instructor guidance.
- More teacher guidance is generally valuable in the early stages of complex learning processes but is decreasingly valuable in later stages as students are able to do more independent learning.
- Excessive teacher guidance, in the form of lecturing or otherwise telling people what to do, tends to violate the principles of feedback, which involves having students do something for themselves and then telling them how they have done in terms of results.

Broadly, a case emerges for a mixture, and for a changing mixture, between induction on the part of the student and guidance on the part of the instructor in most learning situations.

Retention

Psychological studies on learning retention indicate that people tend to retain more of what they study when the subject matter is organized and meaningful. In contrast, retention levels diminish when the subject matter being learned is unmeaningful and unrelated. Anything that is learned by rote is likely to have a short half-life. Similarly, the retention rate goes up rapidly as material is "overlearned." That is, learning the same material several times, even though it may appear wasteful at the time, produces more lasting learning in most circumstances. Conversely, the retention rate is low on barely learned materials.

Transfer

While evidence on learning transfer is both conflicting and unsatisfactory, there is substantial evidence that transfer occurs most effectively when the process of problem solving is stressed, in contrast to stressing a particular technique. But evidence also suggests that people who take courses in formal logic or mathematics show no increase in "logical thinking" in applied situations over those without such formal training. There is also some evidence that verbalization of principles facilitates transfer.

This is by no means a complete list of what the experts know and are discovering about the learning process in human beings. But it seems to provide a significant psychological foundation for developing a course that would put its major stress on what the student learns; therefore, what the teacher does becomes secondary to that basic purpose.

PLANNING THE COURSE

Given our general goal for teaching economics and these propositions about learning, some fundamental things can be said about how to plan a principles course. First, the crucial focus should be on the students and what they will be expected to do on completion of the course. What a teacher says or does should be governed by the test of how much the student is learning. Second, the course content should meet one central test: Will it help the student to think independently about economic issues five years later? This can be broken down into two questions: (1) Is learning of general applicability to different problems which the student will face in the future? (2) As a practical matter, is it simple and important enough for the student to remember and use independently?

Since we know students learn and retain only a limited amount (in economics as well as in other areas) in any day's work and in any class, it is essential that we pare down the content of the course to the core. For most economists, this will involve the painful process of giving up a lot of details that they think are intriguing and important. But if the student won't learn them and remember them for the five-year-after test, there is little point in trying to teach them. The half-life of uninteresting and irrelevant niceties of economic theory is about as long as the half-life of the nonsense syllables which psychologists are fond of using in their tests.

Finally, it is essential that as teachers we know precisely what it is we want the student to learn. Unless we are clear about exactly what this is, it is very unlikely that students will somehow determine this essential core on their own.

THE COURSE

There is, of course, no one ideal principles course in economics. Let me suggest, however, a general pattern that meets the general criteria I have just laid out. First, it seems essential to list the central economic concepts that we want students to learn—the tool kit of analytical concepts that students should be able to use for themselves five years out. It is the combination of concepts, principles, simple models, and institutional background on the economic system that comprise the framework of a good elementary course. Listed below are twenty central concepts for the entire course. Perhaps you would prefer to put some of them in the form of principles or simple models; either way, these central concepts should be clear to economists.

1 Scarcity (limited resources) and need for choice (economizing)
2 Opportunity (alternative) cost—at individual, organization, and national levels
3 Marginalism
4 Self-interest (including profits) as a motivating force
5 Voluntary exchange
6 Markets and market prices
7 Supply and demand
8 Competition
9 Principles of comparative advantage
10 Interdependence
11 "Optimal" allocation of resources—economic efficiency
12 "Market failures" (market imperfections, income distribution, etc.)
13 Externalities and public goods
14 Aggregate demand (and main components)
15 Aggregate supply (and potential productive capacity of the system)
16 Real and money income—price level changes
17 Money and monetary policy
18 Fiscal policy
19 Saving and investment
20 Economic growth

If the problem is to teach a one-semester or one-quarter course, I would probably give up some of these—for example, items 11 and 12. These are important ideas, but something probably needs to go if we are to face the five-year-after test in such a short course. Remember that unless something is learned very well, it will probably not last. To teach the "optimal" allocation of resources and "market failures" in the usual fashion requires a large block of time that probably cannot be justified in the one-semester or one-quarter course. But as an economist, you will have your own notions about which of these concepts are most dispensable.

NOTES

*This chapter is an edited version of a paper that appeared in Allen F. Larsen and Andrew T. Nappi, (eds.) *Goals and Objectives of the College-Level Course in Economics*, Federal Reserve Bank of Minneapolis, August 1976, pp. 15-18.

CHAPTER 6

GENDER AND THE STUDY OF ECONOMICS

Marianne A. Ferber [*]

The introductory economics course has two primary goals. One is to generate and maintain interest in the subject among students who will go on to become economists. The other is to teach a far larger aggregation of students the rudiments of economics, which will provide a sound foundation for those who go on to take additional courses, and increase economic literacy among those who do not. A great deal of attention has been focussed on the extent to which the profession has fallen short of achieving these aims.[1] Increasingly it is also recognized that this is particularly true with respect to women and minorities. Gender issues are the ones specifically addressed here, but many are similar for both these groups.

In the first section of this chapter we provide information about the representation of women among students of economics. This is followed by a review of the evidence on differences between male and female undergraduates in understanding economics. We next go on to consider possible reasons for these outcomes, then offer suggestions for remedies. Last, there is a brief section summarizing our conclusions and recommendations.

REPRESENTATION OF WOMEN AMONG ECONOMICS STUDENTS

Women in this country have traditionally been underrepresented in higher education, the more so at the most advanced levels. The proportion of bachelor's degrees awarded to women increased from 15 percent in 1870 to 41 percent 70 years later, just before World War II, while the proportion of doctor's degrees remained at around 15 percent between 1920[2] and 1940. After that, as a result of the GI bill and the consequent influx of men, the proportion of women among students in universities and colleges declined precipitously. In 1950, only 21 percent of bachelor's and 10 percent of doctor's degrees were awarded to women, and it was 20 years before they

TABLE 6-1   PROPORTION OF DEGREES AWARDED TO WOMEN IN ECONOMICS AND OTHER SELECTED FIELDS, 1983-84

	B.A.	**M.A.**	**Ph.D.**
Economics	34.1	23.5	15.0
Anthropology	63.1	57.8	49.8
Political Science and Government	39.1	30.4	23.0
Psychology	67.9	63.0	49.0
Sociology	67.9	54.8	44.4
Business and Management	42.8	30.1	20.6
Mathematics	34.1	34.7	18.1

Source: *Digest of Education Statistics*, U.S. Department of Education, Center for Education Statistics, 1987, Washington, D.C.: U.S. Government Printing Office.

recovered to the earlier levels. By 1984, however, women received fully half of bachelor's and one-third of doctor's degrees.

The story is substantially different for women in economics. They obtained only 8 percent of B.A.s and 4 percent of Ph.D.s in 1950, and no more than 34 percent and 15 percent respectively in 1984. As can be seen in Table 6-1, women are doing substantially better in all the other major social and behavioral sciences. Because it is often argued that the reason for this difference is either the close link between economics and business, or its use of quantitative methods, we also show data for business and management, and for mathematics. It will be noted that women are more highly represented at all levels in the former, and at the two higher levels in the latter, raising serious doubts about the above explanations.

Another interpretation frequently encountered is that women tend to avoid economics because they have been socialized to avoid male fields. Such occupations as law and medicine requiring "professional degrees" certainly were representative of this category. As recently as 1961 (the first year for which data are available), women received only 3 percent of first professional degrees. Nonetheless, this figure had increased to 31 percent, substantially greater than for advanced degrees in economics. This evidence, therefore, once again suggests that we must look for an explanation elsewhere. The fact that women undergraduates, who overall earn higher GPAs than men,[3] appear to perform less well in economics may be relevant to this issue. We shall briefly report on the available research evidence below.

GENDER-RELATED DIFFERENCES IN UNDERSTANDING ECONOMICS

As long as a decade ago, Siegfried (1979) found a substantial amount of information on gender differences in performance among undergraduates. It was almost invariably obtained as a by-product of research concerned with the evaluation of economics teaching. Gender was merely added as a control variable. The evidence was somewhat mixed, but nonetheless pointed toward the conclusion that if there is a difference, it is in favor of men.[4]

Siegfried distinguishes between those studies that examine the level of knowledge—a stock—and the rate of learning—a flow. He accepts as conclusive the findings of a number of studies that showed a difference in understanding of economics at the time students graduate from high school.[5] As for college students, two-thirds of the papers reviewed reported that men were significantly ahead of women,[6] and these generally used more sophisticated methods and larger samples[7] than those that failed to find such divergence. When it comes to the rate of learning, however, only about one-third of the investigations that examined the flow found that men's performance was better to an extent that was statistically significant,[8] while others did not obtain such results.[9] Equally sound research is represented on both sides of this issue.

Two later studies determined that women do relatively better when essay questions are used rather than the multiple choice tests generally used in research. Even so, Ferber, Birnbaum and Green (1983) also found that men's scores on essay exams were somewhat higher, though the difference was not statistically significant, and Lumsden and Scott (1987) found that women had lower learning rates.

In view of the fact that the main purpose of most of the research reviewed above was not to determine male-female differences, it is perhaps not too surprising that there is little concern expressed why such differences exist. One exception to this is MacDowell, Senn and Soper (1977), but even they offer little more than brief speculation. The explanations they consider tend to center on potential inadequacies of women, from early socialization and insufficient career motivation, to inferior quantitative and spatial abilities.[10] The only possibility mentioned with respect to the way courses are taught is that large classes and poorly trained teaching assistants may cause more serious problems for women because they penalize dependency.[11] Further, the only implications offered are that eliminating the differences may be difficult, and that policies intended to remedy sex bias in the world of work may be doomed to failure.

In contrast, two other studies (Ladd, 1977; Jackstadt and Grootaert, 1980) directly address the question how women differ from men in knowledge and learning of economics, and the continued sex stereotyping in the presentation of economic principles. Though only pre-college students are examined, these researchers make useful contributions to our understanding of the issues involved. We shall return to their concerns in the subsequent sections of this chapter.

Unlike MacDowell, Senn, and Soper (1977), these do not suggest that women, unfortunately, are not as capable as men are, but rather focus on the extent to which the male bias in point of view, teaching and subject matter may disadvantage women. They also discuss what might be done about it.[12]

THE CLASSROOM CLIMATE: PROBLEMS[13]

Faculty—men and women alike—often inadvertently—treat men and women students *differently* and thereby subtly undermine women's confidence in their academic ability, lower their academic and occupational aspirations, inhibit their learning and generally lower their self-esteem (Sandler, 1987, p. 113).[14]

Three issues deserve careful consideration as possibly contributing to women's problems in higher education in general and economics in particular. First, there tend to be differences in teacher attitudes toward male and female students; second, there continues to be sex stereotyping; third, there is a lack of balance in the content of economics courses.

1 Much of the research on interaction of instructor and students comes from primary and secondary educational levels on the one hand, and from the graduate level on the other. It is, however, reasonable to suppose that difficulties encountered there are likely to exist at the college level as well.

   Studies in elementary and high schools showed that teachers give more reprimands, but also more encouragement, to boys than to girls. They interact more with boys, and give them more detailed instructions on how to do things for themselves, while tending to do things for girls (Sadker and Sadker, 1979). Others found that professors are more attentive to and interact more with male than female college students (Sandler, 1987).

   Among college and graduate students, women are viewed by the primarily male faculty as less dedicated and less promising (Feldman, 1974), even though they tend to have higher grades than men (Roby, 1972; Solmon, 1976). Further, faculty tend to be more supportive of students of the same sex (Berg and Ferber, 1983; Tidball, 1976).[15] This too is a disadvantage for female students as long as there are few women on faculties and all the more so when these are clustered at lower ranks.[16] These issues are especially serious because young women in any case are generally less confident about their intellectual capabilities, and hence could benefit more from moral support (Katz, 1980; Hearn and Oizak, 1982). As it is, educational programs often seem to reinforce stereotypical differences in personality and aspirations, all the more so in predominantly male fields, such as economics.

2 Sex stereotyping shows up in a variety of ways. All too often in classroom and textbook stories physicians, lawyers and researchers are men; nurses, secretaries and grade school teachers are women. Further, women are portrayed only in a very narrow range of occupations. Even when both husband and wife are working, he is viewed as the breadwinner who helps around the house, she as the homemaker who is also a secondary wage earner. Inevitably, such images help to perpetuate the status quo and fail to raise women's sights toward higher professional goals.

   Such textbook illustrations as the wise governor of New Jersey persuading his misguided wife that it would not be a good idea to subsidize grapefruit growers in their state (Heilbroner and Thurow, 1975) may be even more damaging to the female ego. The same is true of examples cited in Feiner and Morgan (1987), such as the widow who hides her life savings in her mattress, "Minnie the Moocher" who struggles to decide how to spend 60 cents (Lipsey and Steiner, 1975), and the female economics graduate student who needs to learn about supply and demand from an old woman who sells vegetables from a roadside stand (Leftwich, 1984). Even the generic use of gender-specific words such as "man" or "his," and biased phrases such as "pioneers and their wives," "writers and women writers," or "old wives' tales" are not conducive to providing a favorable classroom climate for women. References to males as "men" but to their female peers as "girls" have comparably negative implications. Similarly, prejudiced perceptions are likely to damage self-esteem. This may take the form of ascribing a positive or negative connotation to the same characteristic, depending on the gender of the person. A good example is the aggressive young man who becomes a successful executive, and the woman candidate who loses the election because she is viewed as aggressive. Or again, men who are putting their heads together are seen as discussing private matters, while women are gossiping.

Another example of stereotyping involves treatment of men or women who act outside of prescribed sex roles as deviants, while cases of conformity are accepted as non-problematic (Feiner and Morgan, 1987).

3 Economics texts and classroom instructors frequently refer to "economic man." The content of the books and courses typically reflect a "man's" world, with women and their concerns too often remaining invisible or, at best, of marginal interest.[17] This is related to the problem that the American Sociological Association Committee on the Status of Women in Sociology (1979) terms gender-blind social theory, which often ignores that "gender may be a significant variable in a social setting, institution, or society," and fails to incorporate it "into a theory, interpretation, or analysis of the system."[18] Admittedly, this is less true in economics than in other social sciences, where feminist scholars have been more inclined to challenge standard paradigms and at times even develop alternative paradigms (Blank, 1988). A number of examples serve to illustrate these points.

a "The unit of analysis in economics is the individual . . . [though] individuals group together to form collective organizations such as corporations, labor unions, and governments" (Gwartney, Stroup and Clark, 1985, p. 3). There is no mention of the family, still the center of most women's lives, nor of voluntary groups, which perform so many important functions not provided for by either the market or the public sector.

b The "assumption is that man is a rational maximizer" (Heilbroner and Thurow, 1983, p. 86). The extent to which behavior is constrained by such factors as, for instance, tradition is ignored. It is somewhat more realistic to assume rationality on the part of a young man who makes the choice to become a carpenter, a computer operator, an accountant, or a short-order cook largely in terms of his talents, preferences and expected rewards, than for a young woman who even today tends to plan her life around the fact that, whatever else she may do, she will spend much of her time and energy on being a homemaker, as her mother did. This is quite different from simply recognizing that choices are made under constraint. It is rather that the heavy hand of tradition continues to dictate what is proper behavior; there is no choice.[19]

c "The accepted measure of total output is *gross national product*. . . . An important kind of output not counted in GNP is that produced in the household.

. . . Many people, particularly leaders of the women's movement, argue that household work should be given a value and included in GNP. This is worth thinking about. Would it be a reasonable thing to do? If so, how would one go about valuing household production?" (Reynolds, 1988, pp. 60-62). That is the end of the discussion. We are not told that estimates of the value of housework have been made, how this was done, or what their magnitude is as compared to measured GNP.

d Even when a topic that is particularly relevant for women is discussed, this aspect of the question is at times ignored. In four pages concerned with "the poverty problem," Reynolds (1988) says, "People are poor for a variety of reasons. Old age, broken families, low employability, and color are the main ingredients of the problem" (p. 609). There is no explicit mention of the fact that households headed by females are twice as likely to fall under the officially defined poverty line as those headed by men. Equally surprising is that in discussing the official definition of poverty, based on number of people in the household and money income, question is raised about not counting such noncash transfers as food stamps, Medicaid benefits, etc., but not about ignoring the value of the contribution of homemakers.

These illustrations should suffice to show that there is justification for the claim that issues especially related to women still tend to receive short shrift. Adequate attention to such topics does not constitute sex stereotyping, nor does it mean that girls are especially catered to. On the contrary, it is important for both boys and girls to learn about households as well as markets, to appreciate the extent to which there are differences as well as similarities in achievements of and rewards for women and men.

It would be unfair to overstate the case. The situation has improved substantially in recent years. We have come a long way since Samuelson's *Economics* (1948), a text rightly regarded as revolutionary in other respects, had only two references to "Females" (none to women) in the index, both included in a segment on "The Position of Minorities." It is now increasingly easier to find instances where authors have incorporated information on women and topics especially relevant to them, and have done so in a sensitive way. We shall draw upon such examples in the following section. Nonetheless, Table 6-2, compiled only five years ago, shows that there is considerable room for further progress.

THE CLASSROOM CLIMATE: SOLUTIONS

Each of the three problem areas discussed above needs to be addressed if women are to be attracted to economics in greater numbers, and are to be offered an environment more conducive to learning the subject and to succeeding in the field. It is often suggested that there is little that the economist qua economist can contribute to improving teacher-student relations. They can, however, help to make sure that women are not discriminated against when their department has faculty positions, and are made to feel welcome after they are hired. They can also reduce stereotyping in the classroom and, to the extent that they are authors, in texts and other publications. Follow-

TABLE 6-2   NUMBER OF PAGES REFERRING TO MINORITIES OR WOMEN IN TEXTBOOKS CURRENT IN 1984

Author	Edition	Year	RGPGS	Total pages	RGPGS as a percentage of total
Amacher	1st	1983	5	725	0.69
Atkinson	1st	1982	5	723	0.69
Baumol and Blinder	2nd	1982	16	836	1.91
Bronfenbrenner, Sichel, and Gardiner	1st	1984	15	915	1.64
Dolan	2nd	1983	4	773	0.52
Fischer and Dornbusch	1st	1983	21	955	2.20
Fusfeld	1st	1982	6	718	0.84
Gwartney and Stroup	3rd	1982	5	766	0.65
Heilbroner and Thurow	6th	1981	12	670	1.79
Leftwich	2nd	1984	0	399	0.00
Lipsey and Steiner	6th	1981	15	958	1.57
McConnell	9th	1984	16	850	1.88
Mansfield	4th	1983	13	887	1.47
Miller	4th	1982	17	830	2.05
Ruffin and Gregory	1st	1983	6	798	0.75
Samuelson	11th	1980	22	861	2.56
Scott and Nigro	1st	1982	18	909	1.98
Spencer	5th	1983	4	868	0.46
Truett and Truett	1st	1982	7	848	0.83
Waud	2nd	1983	2	856	0.23
Wonnacott and Wonnacott	2nd	1982	9	858	1.05
All books current in 1984 (mean)			10.38	810	1.28
First editions current in 1984 (mean)			10.38	823	1.26
Revised editions (mean)			10.38	743	1.40

Note: The abbreviation RGPGS represents the number of pages referring to minorities or women.
Source: Susan F. Feiner and Barbara A. Morgan, "Women and Minorities in Introductory Economics Textbooks: 1974," *Journal of Economic Education*, vol. 18, No. 4 (Fall 1987), p. 379. Reprinted with permission of the Helen Dwight Reid Education Foundation. Published by Heldref Publications, 4000 Albermarle St., N.W., Washington, D.C. 20016. Copyright © 1987.

ing are some comments on these subjects. The main emphasis will be on changing the content of the economics course so as to make it more relevant to a world in which more than half of the population and more than 40 percent of the labor force is female.

1 One factor which in a variety of ways influences the classroom atmosphere is the ratio of women to men on the faculty. It is not merely that teachers tend to have better rapport with students of the same sex.[20] The presence of women instructors is also persuasive evidence to students that this is not an entirely male field. Further, interacting with women colleagues may be expected to have a similar effect on male faculty, and would enable them to see young women more readily as future scholars.[21]

There may be objection that it is not possible to have more women faculty as long as so few women get advanced degrees in economics. It should, however, be noted that according to the 1987 Report of the Committee on the Status of Women in the Economics Profession only 49 percent of new women Ph.D.s in Economics were planning to enter academia in 1985, as compared to 79 percent of women in 1975, and 63 percent of men in 1985. This suggests that colleges and universities might be able to attract more women if they chose to do so.

2 Turning to stereotypes, authors and teachers can make a contribution to combatting them by pointing out when they represent past rather than present reality, when trends are moving away from long-established patterns, and when established norms in this country are different from those in some other countries. Some examples of each come readily to mind.

It is still common to speak of "women" as being supported by their husbands. This ignores the relatively small number who remain single, the much larger number who are divorced, and the vast number who are members of two-earner families. Pointing out that only 7 percent of families consist of father/breadwinner, mother/homemaker and children will give pause to those who continue to view this as "the" family structure today. Once this situation is recognized, it is also less likely that the importance of homemaking in men's lives will be overlooked. That this is still the case today is clear when one reads "Scarcity calls the tune in economics. We cannot have as much of everything as we would like. Most of us would like to have more time for leisure, recreation, vacations, hobbies, education and skill development" (Gwartney, Stroup and Clark, 1985, p. 19). Clearly, this is, implicitly, a model of a man who has a wife to take care of children and housework. Changes in the economy also need to be noted. Showing the growing proportion of women in business and professional schools will make it clear that these fields may be expected to be less dominated by men in the future than they are today. Looking beyond our borders to countries where physicians are predominantly female and others where clerical workers are predominantly male, should cause those who believe that men naturally make better doctors and women better secretaries to reconsider their views.

3 As suggested in the previous section, newly gained insights about important gender similarities and differences in economic behavior, and in the impact of policies on women and men, are more likely to be presented. It is, however, not always done in a spirit of recognition that matters concerning, say, occupational segregation, division of labor in the household, investment in children, and economic effects of divorce, affect men and women alike, as well as the economy as a whole. Ghettoizing them as "women's issues" may quite likely be counterproductive. Also, there is often a tendency to blame the victims, rather than to examine to what extent women are at a disadvantage because of factors beyond their control, and explore what could be done to improve this situation. Some progress has been made in these respects, though it has been somewhat slow and uneven, but more needs to be done.

One example of a subject no self-respecting text would fail to mention today is discrimination, and it is not uncommon to have a brief section dealing specifically with discrimination against women, because it is different in nature from, say, race, ethnic and class discrimination. Similarly, it would be difficult to find a discussion of labor force participation that does not single out for attention the rapid influx of women into the labor force. Most, though not all, texts also point out the fact that the usual measure of GNP is deficient because it does not include the value of goods and services produced in the household. Many mention female-headed families when discussing income distribution and poverty. At the same time, such topics tend to be mentioned briefly and generally little effort is made to integrate them into a broader theoretical framework. This makes them appear more like asides than a part of the major thrust of the discipline. Yet, it would not be difficult to change that.

The discussion of discrimination, against women and others, could be part of the consideration of the functioning of labor markets, focusing on the evidence it provides for the existence of competition on the one hand and the prevalence of barriers on the other hand. It would also be useful to emphasize that discrimination not only places a burden on those against whom it is directed but conflicts with efficiency for the economy as a whole. The rapid entry of women into the labor market might be explored as part of the larger issue of what factors determine the supply of labor, to what extent relevant decisions are influenced by purely economic factors, and to what extent they are constrained by tradition.[22] What we learn in this respect will help to shed light on how people make choices, and whether the assumption of rational behavior tends to be a useful approximation.

Mentioning the failure to include the value of housework—and volunteer work—in GNP is not very meaningful without suggesting some estimate of its magnitude. Efforts along these lines have been made, using either the "market cost approach," which essentially sets the value of nonmarket production equal to the cost of hiring someone to do it, or the "opportunity cost approach," which sets the value equal to the income the person could earn in the labor market. The importance of this subject becomes clear when it is noted that existing research suggests that GNP in this country is underestimated by about 25 percent (Blau and Ferber, 1987, p. 97), and that the figure is undoubtedly greater in developing countries (Goldschmidt-Clermont, 1987). Doing this would also provide an excellent introduction to the crucial topic of opportunity cost, for it would do so in the context of the household, a setting students are familiar with.

A related issue similarly offers an excellent opportunity for illuminating another basic tool of economics. There is no better introduction to comparative advantage, with all its strengths and weaknesses, than a discussion of the gains and losses to the family when each spouse concentrates on what s/he does best. Income will be greater, but there will be less opportunity for developing different skills, pursuing a variety of interests. Interdependence, always a potential problem, especially to the partner with less bargaining power, and painful to both in case hostilities should break out, is inevitable. The long-term costs of concentrating on developing skills that are highly rewarding now, but soon become obsolete, may be substantial. All these points should be easier for young people to grasp than the same issues presented, as they usually are, in the context of international trade.

A number of important policy issues arise in this context. Taxing money income but not real income produced in the household favors families with a full-time homemaker over those with two wage earners. This is also true of the Social Security System which provides benefits for spouses who are not in the labor market, without requiring additional payments from the employed spouse. These practices have a far greater impact than the more often discussed "marriage penalty," which refers to the fact that two people with relatively equal earnings pay a larger amount in taxes as a married couple than they would as single individuals. Interesting questions of efficiency and equity arise because of such practices, which in effect subsidize "traditional families." Tax deductions or subsidies for child care, widely viewed as subsidies to employed mothers, might therefore rather be seen as a means of levelling the playing field between one-earner and two-earner couples.

One reason for concern with these questions is the rapidly growing number of female heads of families confronted with the need to support themselves and their children, after being out of the labor market for a long time. These "displaced homemakers" face serious problems, and though government programs for them have not been overly generous, they also constitute a drain on the public purse. Recently we have seen major reforms in the welfare system which for the first time not only removed obstacles to and provided incentives for their entry into the labor market, but even introduced some elements of compulsion. All these policies have been the subject of lively debates which involve social as well as economic issues, and would provide the basis for illustrating the frequent interaction between the two. Family composition, and the division of responsibilities among family members may, superficially, not seem to be matters of particular interest to economists. But, as we have seen, they influence labor force participation, earnings, and government budgets, topics central to the discipline.

More generally, the problems of female-headed families, as much as those of any group in poverty, could be used as an easily grasped example of the limitations of positive economics. As Samuelson (1987, p. 109) says, "Pareto efficiency is today all the rage. Since it is not easy to say things uncontroversial about distributional equity, let equity go hang." This approach is clearly not helpful in a situation where any solution will almost inevitably have to involve redistribution, and where almost nothing useful can be said without overstepping the boundary between detached analysis and normative judgments.

These are only a few of the more numerous examples that might be provided to show how subjects of particular importance for and interest to women could be introduced in the elementary economics course, and could be done in a way that would also lead to a fuller understanding of the economy. As Bergmann (1987) says, "The ongoing revolution in sex roles has created some new issues and some lively controversies that deserve a place in the economics curriculum. Both female and male students will find them interesting and important. Students recognize that these issues have affected their parents' lives and will affect their own—their career prospects, their chances to enjoy affluence, and their everyday domestic arrangements" (p. 393).[23] Among the topics, not mentioned above, that might be discussed are family policies, such as parental leave, flextime and part-time work, facilitating care of children and elderly parents, and labor market policies, such as protective labor legislation, affirmative action, and equal pay for work of comparable worth.[24] It is rather striking how much less attention these topics tend to receive than, for instance, the problems of farmers who currently comprise less than five percent of the population.

SUMMARY AND CONCLUSIONS

The proportion of economics students who are women has been increasing very slowly, especially at the advanced level. Further, there is substantial evidence that both at the pre-college and college level women students do not do as well in economics courses as their male peers. In view of the general concern with the need to improve the level of knowledge of economics, this poor performance is of particular concern.

There is considerable evidence that women tend to be at a disadvantage because of unequal treatment of students and the continued perpetuation of gender stereotypes in the classroom, as well as the continued male bias in the content of economics courses. The profession as a whole, but particularly authors of textbooks and teachers, can help to change this situation, and to some extent has already begun to do so. The primary purpose of this chapter is to facilitate further progress in this respect. Because some of the problems of women are similar to those of other disadvantaged groups, it is hoped that the suggestions provided here will be useful for them as well, and might even, to some extent, address questions that are being raised by dissenters in the ranks of the profession.

It is frequently suggested by critics that there has been far too little recognition within economics of the social, political and moral aspects of the issues, and too little acknowledgement of the fact that economic analysis is not, and cannot be, entirely value free (Highsmith and Kasper, 1987). Feminists, particularly, often charge that there is too much emphasis on competition, not enough on cooperation, too much emphasis on efficiency and not enough on equity. Replacing "homoeconomicus" with a less single-minded human being might not only provide an atmosphere more congenial to women and other "outsiders," but also broaden and enrich the whole field of economics.

NOTES

[*]I would like to thank Barbara R. Bergmann, Rebecca M. Blank, Susan F. Feiner, Paulette Graziano, Julie A. Nelson, and Donald W. Paden for their helpful comments.

1 It is widely believed that the low status in the economics profession of undergraduate teaching, and, in particular, teaching the beginning undergraduate course, may be one of the causes. This broad topic is, however, beyond the scope of this chapter.
2 Before then the total numbers were too small to be meaningful.
3 See, for instance, Roby (1973) and Solmon (1976).
4 Only one of the studies surveyed, Bach and Saunders (1966), found a statistically significant advantage for women in level of knowledge achieved, and one, Rothman and Scott (1973), in rate of learning.
5 Among these are Highsmith (1974), and Mayer and Paden (1968). Ladd (1977) believes that this is the only deficiency for which there is convincing evidence, and hence concludes that our attention should be focused on the pre-college level. She also points out that not too much should be made of the modest differences found in mean knowledge in any case, because there is clearly a very large overlap of the distributions for boys and girls.

6 Such evidence is found in Allison (1976), Attiyeh and Lumsden (1971, 1972), Bach and Saunders (1965), Bolch and Fels (1974), Chizmar, Hiebert, and McCarney (1977), Clauretie and Johnson (1975), Lewis and Orris (1973), Marston and Lyon (1975), Saunders (1975), Siegfried and Straud (1975), Soper (1973), and Soper and Thornton (1976). A number of recent studies showed similar results, viz, Buckles and Freeman (1983), Saunders (1980), and Watts (1985).

7 Danielsen and Stauffer (1972), Emery and Enger (1972), Harbury and Szreter (1970), Lewis and Dahl (1972), Marston, Lyon, and Knight (1972), Morgan and Vasche (1978), and Paden, Dalgaard, and Barr (1977) found no difference by gender in the level of performance, as did later studies, such as Reid (1983).

8 These include Attiyeh and Lumsden (1971, 1972), Crowley and Wilton (1979), Sloane (1972), Soper (1973, 1976), Soper and Thornton (1976), and Tuckman (1975). An early claim by Fels and Bolch (1974) that we "now know beyond a reasonable doubt that performance in elementary college economics is sex linked" proved not to be well founded.

9 Buckles and McMahon (1971), Elliott, Ireland, and Cannon (1978), Gery (1972), Kelley (1975), Lewis and Dahl (1973), Lewis, Wentworth, and Orris (1973), Paden and Mayer (1969), Palmer, Carliner, and Romer (1979), Ramsett, Johnson, and Adams (1973), Siegfried and Straud (1977), Weidenaar and Dodson (1972), and Wentworth and Lewis (1975) belong to this group.

10 It is interesting to note that women do not appear to be disadvantaged in this respect in all societies. The Minister of Education of Finland, disturbed by the substantially higher admissions of women, based on entrance exams, to their college-preparatory gymnasia, commented "boys tend to be afraid of languages and even of mathematics, while girls are not nervous about those subjects" (*On Campus with Women*, No. 30, Spring 1981, p. 14). It should also be noted that careful studies by psychologists found no significant gender differences in analytical ability and concept mastery, two specific skills generally assumed to be particularly important for understanding economics. The common perception that the opposite is the case is ascribed to the male superiority in the far narrower area of visual spatial skills (Maccaby and Jacklin, 1974).

11 This is also suggested by Allison (1977), and by Siegfried and Straud (1977), who found that women did relatively better in self-paced courses. An alternative interpretation is that it is students who are self-starters, conscientious, and resistant to regimentation who would have a relative advantage in such courses. Allison also suggests that women need more help because they begin with fewer analytical skills.

12 One possibility, suggested by a colleague who has for many years taught large undergraduate economics courses, is that students with more rigorous majors, and particularly those requiring a good deal of mathematics, are likely to do better. Women continue to be underrepresented in such curricula.

13 Some of the information in this and the following section is based on an earlier paper (Ferber, 1984), which in turn was based to a considerable extent on *Sex and Gender in the Social Sciences: Reassessing the Introductory Course* produced under the Women's Educational Equity Program, and brought together by the Curriculum Analysis Project for Social Sciences at Utah State University.

14 Such behavior occurs not only in the classroom, but also in office consultations, academic advising situations, etc.

15 It has also been found that even male graduate students perceive their female peers differently, and interact less with them (Herman and Sedlacek, 1973).

16 There is evidence that women are more useful as role models when they themselves have been successful (Shapiro, Haseltine, and Rowe, 1980).

17   The main difficulty here is that there is a tendency on the part of many economists to define their field rather narrowly in terms of markets, rather than more broadly as concerned with using resources efficiently to satisfy human wants, whether in the market or the household sector.

18   According to Feiner and Roberts (1988) the Organization of American Historians, the American Political Science Association, the American Psychological Association, and the Speech Communication Association, as well as the American Sociological Association, all have adopted a position that there is need for greater balance in their curricular materials, or have supported research designed to remedy existing imbalances.

19   It has also been suggested, perhaps somewhat unkindly, that the neoclassical paradigm has, in any case, difficulty dealing with issues of power and acculturation which creates important differences between human beings. "Neoclassical thought treats all consumers and workers alike—regardless of family background, culture, social class, sex, or household structure" (Greenwood, 1984).

20   Viz the findings of Berg and Ferber (1983) and Tidball (1976) cited earlier. Also, Ferber, Birnbaum, and Berg (1983) found that when the same exams were graded both by graduate students teaching discussion sections and by a hired grader who did not know the students, the teaching assistants tended to assign somewhat higher grades to students of the same sex.

21   Ferber, Huber, and Spitze (1979) found that both men and women who had known women in a predominantly male profession were more inclined to be accepting of women in that profession than those who had not. Further, Rosabeth Kanter (1977) found that members of an identifiable group of "outsiders" tend to be more readily accepted when their number increases beyond mere tokens.

22   This, again, is a subject that is often ignored because of an unduly rigid delimination of the subject of economics.

23   Reynolds (1988) also uses the device of asking some policy oriented questions specifically of men and others of women. This may be a useful device, but needs to be used carefully so that it does not ghettoize certain subjects.

24   A substantial literature exists today on all these topics. Excellent references are, Kamerman and Kahn (1987) on family policies and Treiman and Hartmann (1981) on comparable worth.

REFERENCES

Allison, Elisabeth K., "Three Years of Self-Paced Teaching in Introductory Economics at Harvard," *American Economic Review*, Vol. 66, No. 2 (May 1976): 222-228.

American Sociological Association Committee on the Status of Women in Sociology, "How to Recognize and Avoid Sexist Biases in Sociological Research: Some Problems and Issues," (June 1979).

Attiyeh, Richard, and Keith G. Lumsden, "Some Modern Myths in Teaching Economics: The U.K. Experience," *American Economic Review*, Vol. 62, No. 2 (May 1972): 429-433.

———, and ———, "University Students' Initial Understanding of Economics: The Contribution of the A Level Economics Course and Other Factors," *Economica*, Vol. 38, No. 149 (February 1971): 81-97.

Bach, George L., and Phillip Saunders, "Economic Education: Aspirations and Achievements," *American Economic Review*, Vol. 55, No. 3 (June 1965): 329-356.

Berg, Helen M., and Marianne A. Ferber, "Men and Women Graduate Students: Who Succeeds and Why?," *Journal of Higher Education*, Vol. 54, No. 6 (Nov./Dec. 1983): 629-648.

Bergmann, Barbara R., "Women's Roles in the Economy: Teaching the Issues," *Journal of Economic Education*, Vol. 18, No. 4 (Fall 1987): 393-407.

Blank, Rebecca M., "A Female Perspective on Economic Man?" in Sue Rosenberg Zalk and Janice Gordon-Kelter, eds., *Revolutions in Knowledge: Feminism in the Social Sciences*.

Blau, Francine D., and Marianne A. Ferber, *The Economics of Women, Men, and Work*, Englewood Cliffs, NJ: Prentice-Hall, 1986.

Bolch, Ben W., and Rendigs Fels, "A Note on Sex and Economic Education," *Journal of Economic Education*, Vol. 6, No. 4 (Fall 1976): 64-67.

Buckles, Stephen G., and Vera Freeman, "Male-Female Differences in the Stock and Flow of Economic Knowledge," *Review of Economics and Statistics*, Vol. 65, No. 2 (May 1983): 355-358.

————, and Marshall E. McMahon, "Further Evidence on the Value of Lectures in Elementary Economics," *Journal of Economic Education*, Vol. 3, No. 2 (Spring 1971): 138-141.

Chizmar, John F., L. Dean Hiebert, and Bernard J. McCarney, "Assessing the Impact of an Instructional Innovation on Achievement Differentials: The Case of Computer-Assisted Instruction," *Journal of Economic Education*, Vol. 9, No. 4 (Fall 1977): 42-46.

Clauretie, Terrence M., and William E. Johnson, "Factors Affecting Student Performance in Principles of Economics," *Journal of Economic Education*, Vol. 6, No. 2 (Spring 1975): 132-134.

Committee on the Status of Women in the Economics Profession, Report, *American Economic Review*, Vol. 77, No. 2 (May 1987): 401-403.

Crowley, Ronald W., and David A. Wilton, "A Preliminary Report on the Efficiency of Introductory Economics Courses," *Journal of Economic Education*, Vol. 5, No. 2 (Spring 1974): 103-108.

Danielsen, Albert L., and A. J. Stauffer, "A Television Experiment in College Economics," *Journal of Economic Education*, Vol. 3, No. 2 (Spring 1972): 101-105.

Elliott, Ralph D., M. Edwin Ireland, and Teresa S. Cannon, "An Analysis of the Marginal Products of the One- and Two-Semester Introductory Economics Courses," *Journal of Economic Education*, Vol. 10, No. 4 (Fall 1978): 18-25.

Emery, E. David, and Thomas P. Enger, "Computer Gaming and Learning in an Introductory Economics Course," *Journal of Economic Education*, Vol. 3, No. 2 (Spring 1972): 77-85.

Feiner, Susan F., and Barbara A. Morgan, "Women and Minorities in Introductory Economics Textbooks: 1974-1984," *Journal of Economic Education*, Vol. 18, No. 4 (Fall 1987): 376-92.

————, and Bruce B. Roberts, "Hidden by the INVISIBLE HAND: Race and Gender in Introductory Economics Textbooks," (unpublished paper, 1988).

Feldman, Saul D., *Escape from the Doll's House: Women in Graduate and Professional School Education*. Report prepared for the Carnegie Commission on Higher Education. New York: McGraw-Hill, 1974.

Fels, Rendigs, and Ben Bolch, "A Note on Sex and Economic Education," *Journal of Economic Education*, Vol. 6, No. 1 (Fall 1974): 64-67.

Ferber, Marianne A., "Suggestions for Improving the Classroom Climate for Women in the Introductory Economics Course," *Journal of Economic Education*, Vol. 15, No. 2 (Spring 1984): 160-168.

————, Bonnie G. Birnbaum, and Carole A. Green, "Gender Differences in Economic Knowledge: A Reevaluation of the Evidence," *Journal of Economic Education*, Vol. 14, No. 2 (Spring 1983): 24-37.

————, Joan A. Huber, and Glenna Spitze, "Preferences of Men as Bosses and Professionals," *Social Forces*, Vol. 58, No. 2 (Dec. 1979): 466-476.

Gery, Frank W., "Is There a Ceiling Effect to the Test of Understanding in College Economics?" In Arthur L. Welsh, ed., *Research Papers in Economic Education*. New York: Joint Council on Economic Education, 1972.

Goldschmidt-Clermont, Luisella, *Economic Evaluations of Unpaid Household Work: Africa, Asia, Latin America and Oceania*, Geneva: International Labour Office, 1987.

Greenwood, Daphne, "The Economic Significance of 'Women's Place' in Society: A New-Institutionalist View," *Journal of Economic Issues*, Vol. 18, No. 3 (Sept. 1984): 663-680.

Gwartney, James D., Richard Stroup and J. R. Clark, *Essentials of Economics*, New York: Academic Press, Inc., 1985.

Harbury, C. D., and R. Szreter, "The Value of Prior Experience of Economics for University Students," *Journal of Economic Education*, Vol. 2, No. 4 (Fall 1970): 56-62.

Hearn, James C., and Susan Oizak, "The Role of College Major Departments in the Reproduction of Sexual Equality." Unpublished paper, 1982.

Heilbroner, Robert L., and Lester C. Thurow, *The Economic Problem*, Englewood Cliffs, NJ: Prentice-Hall, Inc., 1983.

————, and ————, *The Economic Problem*, 4th Ed., Englewood Cliffs, NJ: Prentice-Hall, 1975.

Herman, Michele H., and William E. Sedlacek, "Sexist Attitudes Among Male University Students," *Journal of College Student Personnel*, Vol. 14, No. 6 (Nov. 1973): 544-548.

Highsmith, Robert, "A Study to Measure the Impact of In-Service Institutes on the Students of Teachers Who Have Participated," *Journal of Economic Education*, Vol. 5, No. 2 (Spring 1974): 77-81.

————, and Hirschel Kasper, "Rethinking the Scope of Economics," *Journal of Economic Education*, Vol. 18, No. 2 (Spring 1987): 101-105.

Jackstadt, Stephen L., and Christiaan Grootaert, "Gender, Gender Stereotyping, and Socioeconomic Background as Determinants of Economic Knowledge and Learning," *Journal of Economic Education*, Vol. 12, No. 1 (Winter 1980): 34-40.

Kamerman, Sheila B., and Alfred J. Kahn, *The Responsive Workplace. Employers and a Changing Labor Force*, N.Y.: Columbia University Press, 1987.

Kanter, Rosabeth, *Men and Women of the Corporation*, New York: Basic Books, Inc., 1977.

Katz, Joseph, in *Men and Women Learning Together: A Study of College Students in the Late 1970s*, Office of the Provost, Brown University, April 1980.

Kelley, Allen C., "Uses and Abuses of Course Evaluations as Measures of Educational Output," *Journal of Economic Education*, Vol. 4, No. 4 (Fall 1972): 13-18.

Ladd, Helen F., "Male-Female Differences in Precollege Economic Education." In Donald R. Wentworth, W. Lee Hansen, and S. H. Hawke, eds., *Perspectives on Economic Education*, New York: Joint Council on Economic Education, Washington, DC: National Council for Social Studies: Boulder, CO: Social Sciences Education Consortium, 1977.

Leftwich, Richard, *A Basic Framework for Economics*, TX: Business Publications, 1984.

Lewis, Darrell R., and Tor Dahl, "Critical Thinking Skills in the Principles Course: An Experiment." In Arthur L. Welsh, ed., *Research Papers in Economic Education*. New York: Joint Council on Economic Education, 1972.

————, and ————, "Factors Influencing Performance in the Principles Course Revisited." In Arthur L. Welsh, ed., *Research Papers in Economic Education*. New York: Joint Council on Economic Education, 1972.

————, and Charles C. Orris, "A Training System for Graduate Student Instructors of Introductory Economics at the University of Minnesota," *Journal of Economic Education*, Vol. 5, No. 4 (Fall 1973): 38-46.

————, Donald R. Wentworth, and Charles C. Orris, "Economics in the Junior Colleges: Terminal or Transfer?," *Journal of Economic Education*, Vol. 4, No. 2 (Spring 1973): 100-110.

Lipsey, Richard G., and Peter Steiner, *Economics*, NY: Harper and Row,1975.

Maccoby, Eleanore E., and Carol N. Jacklin, *The Psychology of Sex Differences*, Stanford, CA: Stanford University Press, 1974.

MacDowell, Michael A., Peter R. Senn, and John C. Soper, "Does Sex Really Matter?," *Journal of Economic Education*, Vol. 9, No. 4 (Fall 1977): 28-33.

Marston, Glenn F., and Kenneth S. Lyon, "Learning and Attitude Change of Students Subjected to a National Income Simulation Game: Some Further Evidence," *Journal of Economic Education*, Vol. 7, No. 4 (Fall 1975): 20-27.

———, ———, and Richard Knight, "Learning and Attitude Change of Students Subjected to a National Income Simulation Game." In Arthur L. Welsh, ed., *Research Papers in Economic Education*. New York: Joint Council on Economic Education, 1972.

Mayer, M. Eugene, and Donald W. Paden, "On the Efficiency of the High School Economics Course," *American Economic Review*, Vol. 58, No. 4 (Sept. 1968): 820-877.

Morgan, W. Douglas, and Jon David Vasche, "An Education Production Function Approach to Teaching Effectiveness and Evaluation," *Journal of Economic Education*, Vol. 8, No. 2 (Spring 1978): 123-136.

Paden, Donald W., Bruce R. Dalgaard, and Michael D. Barr, "A Decade of Computer-Assisted Instruction," *Journal of Economic Education*,Vol. 9, No. 4 (Fall 1977): 14-20.

———, and M. Eugene Mayer, "The Relative Effectiveness of Three Methods of Teaching Principles of Economics," *Journal of Economic Education*, Vol. 1, No. 4 (Fall 1969): 33-45.

Palmer, John, Geoffrey Carliner, and Thomas Romer, "Does High School Economics Help?," *Journal of Economic Education*, Vol. 10, No. 2 (Spring 1979): 58-61.

Ramsett, Donald E., Jerry D. Johnson, and Curtis Adams, "Some Evidence on the Value of Instructors in Teaching Economic Principles," *Journal of Economic Education*, Vol. 5, No. 4 (Fall 1973): 57-62.

Reid, Roger, "A Note on the Environment as a Factor Affecting Student Performance in Principles of Economics," *Journal of Economic Education*, Vol. 14, No. 4 (Fall 1983): 18-23.

Reynolds, Lloyd G., *Economics: A General Introduction*, Homewood, IL: Irwin, 1988.

Roby, Pamela, "Structural and Internalized Barriers to Women in Higher Education." In Alice S. Rossi and Ann Calderwood, eds., *Academic Women on the Move*. New York: Russell Sage Foundation, 1973.

Rothman, Mitchell P., and James H. Scott, "Political Opinions and the TUCE," *Journal of Economics Education*, Vol. 4, No. 2 (Spring 1973): 116-124.

Sadker, Myra, and David Sadker, "Between Teacher and Student: Overcoming Sex Bias in the Classroom," unpublished report of the Non-Sexist Teacher Education Project of the Women's Educational Equity Act Program, U.S. DHEW, Office of Education, 1979.

Samuelson, Paul, "How Economics has Changed," *Journal of Economic Education*, Vol. 18, No. 2 (Spring 1987): 107-110.

———, *Economics*, New York: McGraw-Hill, 1948.

Sandler, Bernice R., "The Classroom Climate: Still a Chilly One for Women." In Carol Lasser, ed., *Educating Men and Women Together: Coeducation in a Changing World*. Urbana, IL: University of Illinois Press, 1987.

Saunders, Phillip, "The Lasting Effects of Introductory Economics Courses," *Journal of Economic Education*, Vol. 12, No. 1 (Winter 1980): 1-14.

———, "Experimental Course Development in Introductory Economics at Indiana University," *Journal of Economic Education*, Vol. 7, No. 4 (Fall 1975), Special Issue.

Shapiro, Eileen C., Florence P. Haseltine, and Mary P. Rowe, "Moving Up: Role Models, Mentors, and the Patron System," *Sloan Management Review*, Vol. 19, No. 3. (Spring 1980): 51-58.

Siegfried, John J., "Male-Female Differences in Economic Education: A Survey," *Journal of Economic Education*, Vol. 10, No. 2 (Spring 1979): 1-11.

————, and Stephen Straud, "Sex and the Economics Student," *Review of Economics and Statistics*, Vol. 59, No. 2 (May 1977): 247-249.

Sloane, Peter E., "The Relationship of Performance to Instruction and Student Attitudes." In Arthur L. Welsh, ed., *Research Papers in Economic Education*. New York: Joint Council on Economic Education, 1972.

Solmon, Lewis C., *Male and Female Graduate Students: The Question of Equal Opportunity.* New York: Praeger, Special Studies in U.S. Economic, Social and Political Issues, 1976.

Soper, John C., "Second Generation Research in Economic Education: Problems of Specification and Interdependence," *Journal of Economic Education*, Vol. 8, No. 4 (Fall 1976): 40-48.

————, "Programmed Instruction in Large-Lecture Courses," *Journal of Economic Education*, Vol. 4, No. 2 (Spring 1973): 125-129.

————, and Richard M. Thornton, "Self-Paced Economic Instruction: A Large-Scale Disaggregated Evaluation," *Journal of Economic Education*, Vol. 7, No. 2 (Spring 1976): 81-91.

Tidball, M. Elizabeth, "Perspective on Academic Women and Affirmative Action," *Educational Record*, Vol. 54, No. 2 (Spring 1973): 130-135.

Treiman, Donald J., and Heidi I. Hartmann, eds., *Women, Work, and Wages: Equal Pay for Jobs of Equal Value*, Washington, D.C.:National Academy Press, 1981.

Tuckman, Howard P., "Teacher Effectiveness and Student Performance," *Journal of Economic Education*, Vol. 7, No. 4 (Fall 1975): 34-39.

Watts, Michael, "A Statewide Assessment of Precollege Economic Understanding and DEEP," *Journal of Economic Education*, Vol. 16, No. 3 (Summer 1985): 225-237.

Weidenaar, Dennis J., and Joe A. Dodson, Jr., "The Effectiveness of Economics Instruction in Two-Year Colleges," *Journal of Economic Education*, Vol. 4, No. 4 (Fall 1972): 5-12.

Wenthworth, Donald R., and Darrell R. Lewis, "An Evaluation of the Use of the Marketplace Game in Junior College Economics," *Journal of Economic Education*, Vol. 6, No. 2 (Spring 1975): 113-119.

PART TWO

INSTRUCTIONAL
METHODS OF
ECONOMICS

LEARNING THEORY AND INSTRUCTIONAL OBJECTIVES

Phillip Saunders[*]

An understanding of how humans learn should help us do a better job of teaching the principles of economics. Clearly established "laws" or "principles" of learning would be an invaluable aid in planning, presenting, and evaluating instruction—not only in the principles of economics course, but in other courses and other situations as well. Unfortunately, there is at present no single, generally accepted theory of learning that can be used as an infallible guide to teaching. Indeed, there is some evidence that there are different types of learning, and David Kolb (1981) argues that students have different "learning styles" and that different academic disciplines have different "learning demands." Nevertheless, an understanding of what psychologists and others have discovered to date about human learning should still be of some value in helping us do a better job of helping our students learn more about the principles of economics.

This chapter will discuss some of the findings that my review of psychological and educational literature indicates have the most relevance for teaching the principles of economics at the college level. The chapter begins with a general definition of learning that incorporates both what educators have termed the "cognitive domain" and the "affective domain." A brief review of the major "schools" of learning theory in modern psychology is followed by a discussion of four generally accepted propositions about human learning. Separate attention is then paid to the acquisition, retention, and transfer of knowledge, and the importance of focusing on clearly thought out instructional objectives is emphasized at the end of the chapter.

WHAT IS MEANT BY LEARNING?

While admitting the possibility and usefulness of many other definitions of the learning process, I offer the following: *Learning is the acquisition and retention of knowledge and habits of thought in a way that permits them to be employed in a useful way after the initial exposure has been terminated.* Learning in this sense takes place when we gain an understanding of a process, situation, fact, or thing that we did not previously possess and when we can retain this understanding in a manner that permits us to apply it to new situations. Basically, this definition contains three elements: *acquisition, retention,* and *transfer*. (We should probably also add a fourth element—*evaluation,* or some internal intellectual mechanism of checking to see if we have used our knowledge in a sensible way by judging whether or not we have made an appropriate response or behaved in a plausible manner.)

Gagne has identified and described five major categories of learning outcomes: (1) intellectual skills, (2) verbal information, (3) cognitive strategies, (4) motor skills, and (5) attitudes. And he states: "Not only do these differ in the human performances they make possible; they also differ in the conditions most favorable to their learning." (Gagne, 1985, p. 67) If it is true that there are different types of learning, it may not be possible to develop a single theory that effectively encompasses all the different varieties of learning. Further, the work of the Swiss psychologist Jean Piaget and the American educator William G. Perry, Jr., indicates that humans move through different stages of intellectual development wherein the modes of thinking are distinctly different.[1] Thus, the task of developing a single theory of human learning that can be applied to all types of learning at all stages of intellectual development is a formidable, if not an impossible, one. If we focus on student learning of the type of material typically presented in college level principles of economics courses, however, it is useful to formulate our objectives in terms of *both* what educators have termed the "cognitive domain" and the "affective domain."

The Cognitive Domain

The cognitive domain deals with intellectual outcomes such as knowledge, understanding, and thinking skills. Examples of cognitive objectives are: defines basic terms; interprets charts and graphs; recognizes logical fallacies in reasoning; predicts the outcome of an action involving economic principles. Benjamin S. Bloom and others published the *Taxonomy of Educational Objectives: Cognitive Domain* in 1956. This book describes six cognitive categories in detail and presents illustrative objectives and test items for each category. The categories in ascending order are: (1) knowledge, (2) comprehension, (3) application, (4) analysis, (5) synthesis, and (6) evaluation.

The Affective Domain

The affective domain deals with feelings and emotions such as interest, attitude, and appreciation. Examples of affective objectives are: listens attentively; completes assigned homework; participates in class discussions; shows interest in economics; appreciates the importance of economics in everyday life. David R. Krathwohl and others published the *Taxonomy of Educational Objectives: Affective Domain* in 1964. This book describes five affective categories in detail and presents illustrative objectives and test items for each category. The categories in ascending order are: (1) receiving, (2) responding, (3) valuing, (4) organization, and (5) characterization by a value or value complex.

It should be noted that the categories in each domain of these taxonomies are arranged in hierarchical order. Thus, the term "taxonomy." Each category is assumed to include the behavior at the lower levels. Thus "application" includes behavior at the "comprehension" and "knowledge" levels, and "valuing" includes behavior at both the "responding" and "receiving" levels. An excellent brief summary of the Bloom and Krathwol material is contained in Chapter 4 of Norman E. Gronlund (1970). Appendices 7-1 and 7-2 at the end of this chapter are adapted from four more comprehensive tables in Gronlund. These appendices give a brief one sentence definition of each of the categories in the cognitive and the affective taxonomies, and a few verbs specifying illustrative student behaviors are shown after each definition.

Much of the traditional learning theory research has focused on cognitive behaviors, but, as we will see, the importance of motivation in human learning implies that we must not ignore the affective domain if we want our students to acquire, retain, and use cognitive skills.

MAJOR "SCHOOLS" OF LEARNING THEORY

Psychologists, like economists, place a very high regard on "pure" as opposed to "applied" theory. Originally, therefore, they attempted to develop "principles" of learning at the highest possible levels of abstraction without much concern for classroom applications. The quest for rigorous "scientific" controls limited much early learning theory research to animals or, if humans were involved, to somewhat contrived learning exercises in laboratory situations, usually involving memorizing lists of words or nonword combinations of consonants and vowels. In the 1969 *Annual Review of Psychology*, Gagne and Rohwer (1969, p. 381) stated: "Remoteness of applicability to instruction, we note with some regret, characterizes many studies of human learning, retention and transfer, appearing in the most prestigious of psychological journals."

Since that time there have been an increasing number of attempts to apply traditional laboratory findings to more typical human learning situations, and there have been significant changes in the way psychologists and others have come to view the process of learning itself. Information-processing approaches to human learning have come to supersede and blur previous distinctions between empirically oriented, behavioral-associationist or "stimulus-response" approaches to learning and less empirical, more intuitive "cognitive-structuralist" approaches. Thus, in the 1989 *Annual Review of Psychology*, Glaser and Bassok (1989, p. 631) could state: "Instructional psychology has become a vigorous part of the mainstream of research on human cognition and development."[2]

The Stimulus-Response School

This school traditionally focused on learning as the reinforcement of associations between overt stimuli and responses, and it placed a strong emphasis on the direct observation of overt behavior. The terms "empiricists," "associationists," and "behaviorists" are sometimes used to represent the psychologists who emphasize this approach to learning. Teaching machines and programmed learning are instructional devices stemming from this school. These techniques are designed to reinforce or reward students for making the correct response (answer) to each stimulus (question). B. F. Skinner is frequently identified as the most prominent recent spokesman of the stimulus-response school. (See Skinner, 1968.)

The Cognitive-Structuralist School

This school stems from the experiments of the German psychologist Wolfgang Kohler with chimpanzees who learned to stack boxes and use short sticks to rake in long sticks so that they could obtain food that was otherwise out of their reach. This school emphasizes the introspective rearrangement of previous ideas and experience into new patterns of thought and focuses on learning as "insight" or the perception of new relationships. The terms "gestalt (the German word for configuration) theorists" and "field theorists" are sometimes used to represent the psychologists who emphasize this approach to learning. The discovery method of instruction stems from this school of learning theory, and Jerome Brunner is a prominent recent spokesman. (See Brunner, 1966.)

The Information-Processing School

While stimulus-response and cognitive-structuralist theories do not agree about what goes on in a person's mind when something is "learned," neither has a very elaborate approach to the internal processing involved when compared to more recent learning theories based on formulations from computer science, linguistics, and attempts to represent the learning process by mathematical equations. These newer "information-processing" theories propose a very elaborate set of internal processes, transformations, and structures to account for the events of human learning, and they imply that several distinct phases of processing occur during a single act of learning.[3]

A good recent example of an attempt to summarize and apply the information-processing view of learning to the problems of instruction is provided by Robert M. Gagne in the 1985 (4th) edition of his book, *The Conditions of Learning*. Figure 7-1 is reproduced from page 71 of this book. Using underlining to refer to *structures* and

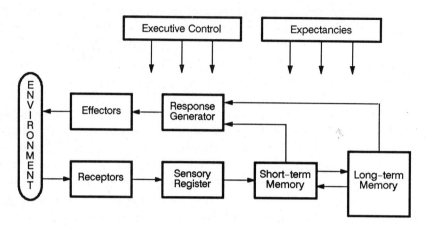

FIGURE 7-1 INFORMATION PROCESSING MODEL OF LEARNING.
Source: Figure 4.1 from *The Conditions of Learning and the Theory of Instruction*, 4th ed., by Robert M. Gagne, copyright © 1985 by Holt, Rinehart and Winston, Inc. Reprinted by permission of the publisher.

quotations to refer to "processes," my very condensed summary of Gagne's explanation of this figure is contained in the next two paragraphs.

The lower parts of Figure 7-1 indicate that information received from the environment is transformed into neural information by *receptors* and entered into the *sensory register* where a process of "selective perception" either allows it to die or, if it is attended to, be transformed into a new kind of input into the *short-term memory*. The transformed information can persist in short-term memory for only a limited period (perhaps up to 20 seconds), but this interval can be extended by a process of silent mental repetition called "rehearsal." Rehearsal may also aid the "encoding" of information for input into the *long-term memory*. Encoding is a process of meaningful organization which permits the information to be stored in long-term memory. Once stored in long-term memory, we say that information is "learned" if it can be retrieved and returned to the short-term memory or used to activate a *response generator*. Information retrieved from the long-term memory into the short-term memory can be combined with other inputs to form new encodings for long term memory or to activate a response generator. Once a response generator has been activated, some sort of performance is effected that can be observed externally and used to verify that learning has occurred.

The top parts of Figure 7-1 labeled "executive control" and "expectancies" are used to represent aspects of previous learning that are capable of affecting any or all of the phases of the information flow depicted in the lower parts of the figure. Since executive control and expectancies are the result of previous learning, they can be viewed as separate portions of long-term memory that are different from simple information storage. Control processes and expectancies are crucial parts of the learning process in determining how the attention of the learner is directed, how the information is encoded, how it is retrieved, and how it is expressed in organized responses. The terms "meta cognition" and "learning strategies" are sometimes used to refer to learners' knowledge about and control over their cognitive processes. (See Weinstein and Mayer, 1986.)

From the standpoint of learning, the most important phase of information processing is the "encoding" that meaningfully organizes the material passing from short-term memory to long-term memory. Wittrock (1974, 1978) has developed a model of learning as a generative process in which new information is related to information, concepts, and schemas already in long-term memory. Creating connections between new information and previously learned information is a key step in encoding information in a meaningful learning set rather than a rote learning set.

FOUR GENERALLY ACCEPTED PROPOSITIONS

Despite different conceptions of the basic learning process, there are some things that are generally accepted by most psychologists today with only relatively minor reservations. Fortunately, each of these generally accepted propositions has implications for helping college students learn economics. Unfortunately, not all of these implications have been empirically tested and verified in principles of economics courses to the extent one would like, and most require some generalizing beyond the actual situations in which the research was conducted.

Limited Capacity to Process Information

The limited capacity of the human mind to process information has been recognized for a long time. McKeachie (1963) has quoted the Moravian bishop and educational reformer Comenius (1592–1620) as stating:

> If we take a jar with a narrow mouth, for to this we may compare a boy's intellect, and attempt to pour a quantity of water into it violently, instead of allowing it to trickle in drop by drop what will be the result? Without doubt, the greater part of the liquid will flow over the side, and ultimately the jar will contain less than if the operation had taken place gradually. Quite as foolish is the action of those who try to teach the pupils, not as much as they can assimilate, but as much as they themselves wish. (p. 1120)

Over 300 years after Comenius made the preceding observation in his *Great Didactic*, the German-Swedish psychologist David Katz (1950) coined the term "mental dazzle" as a result of several experiments demonstrating that beyond a certain point, adding elements in an intellectual task causes confusion and inefficiency. And in 1956 George A. Miller published an important paper indicating that the number of "chunks" of independent information that an adult can keep in mind at the same time is about seven, plus or minus two. These "chunks" can vary in complexity, but the basic limitation now appears to be due to the relatively fragile nature of short-term or conscious memory compared to long-term memory. Unlike long-term memory, which has a relatively unlimited storage capacity for "encoded" or meaningful information, new items entering the short-term memory "push out" old items once the limited capacity of short-term memory has been reached. While the process of "rehearsal" mentioned above can extend the time interval that information can be stored in short-term memory, and while rehearsal may also aid in meaningfully encoding information for input into long-term memory, the number of items stored in short-term memory is not increased by rehearsal. "Overloading" short-term memory, therefore, interferes with meaningful learning and long-term memory.

The implications of the evidence on the limited capacity of the human mind to process information are clear, even if they are difficult to follow. As teachers, we must constantly resist pressure to "cover the field"—particularly in principles courses. *It is not what the instructor "covers" but what the student learns that counts.* Rather than dragging or pushing our students on a roller-skating tour through the 30-, 40-, or perhaps even 50-room mansion of our discipline, everyone might be better off if we spend more time examining the foundations on which the whole superstructure rests. We should force ourselves to settle for a few things (the most important things) done well, rather than try to "cover the waterfront" so that all, or most, is washed away by the tides that sweep through the lives of students after the final exam has been completed. Before outlining our courses or, indeed, before each class meeting, we should ask ourselves: "What will the student learn today that will make a difference in his or her life five years or more from now?" An indication of how difficult it may be to follow this advice is given by the fact that the following statement appeared in a special supplement to the *American Economic Review* in 1950! ". . . the content of the elementary course has expanded beyond all possibility of adequate comprehension and assimilation by a student in one year of three class hours a week" (p. 56). Why we haven't made any progress in reducing the content of the principles course is also suggested in the same report: ". . . the fundamental error in current practice in the teaching of the first course in economics can be summarized in one word—'indecision'" (p. 56). Hopefully, some of the discussion of instructional objectives later in this chapter will help you reduce the indecision involved in dealing with this crucial issue in your own courses.

Importance of Prior Experience or "Learning Set"

There is now a general recognition of the hierarchical arrangement of thought, and the importance of prior experience and current knowledge in establishing a student's "learning set." Whether prior learning is viewed as reinforced associations, configurations in the mind, or information stored in long-term memory, it is important that the demands we make on our students are not so unrelated to their prior experience that they are impossible to achieve.

Since most students' current knowledge and prior experiences are likely to be quite different from those of the instructor, we must be careful not to assume that the information that we give them will be interpreted and mentally filed away in the same way that it is stored in our own minds. Much that is "obvious" to the instructor may be incomprehensible or meaningless to the uninitiated student because of differences in assumptions, gaps in knowledge, and other differences in the "learning set."

The notion of "set" argues strongly for *pretesting*, so that we can get a better idea of where our students are before we attempt to take them someplace else. This is particularly true in economics where terms such as "demand" and "investment" are given precise meanings that are often at variance with what noneconomists "know" these terms mean. Ruth Beard (1972) notes: "People differ in their capacity to relinquish 'sets,' some doing so fairly readily, whereas others will distort information they receive, forcing it to fit familiar interpretation until the weight of contradictions obliges them to a change" (p. 74). Anyone who has dealt with people who "know" that the value of money is determined by its gold backing, that "investment" is buying a share of common stock, and so on will appreciate the truth of this statement. In some cases we may have to devote some time to overcoming erroneous interpretations and getting people's minds "up" to zero before we can begin getting them to accept new ways of looking at things. Whenever possible, therefore, we should use pretests to establish where our students are with respect to the learning set we want to establish. Nothing is more frustrating to a student than to be "completely in the dark." Students are unlikely to understand or retain material that is not meaningful, and new material is meaningful only if it fits in with what an individual already knows.

Carefully constructed homework problems can also be used to establish a common learning set that can help reduce much of the heterogeneity that plagues principles of economics classes by focusing student attention on a carefully structured set of questions. If students try to work the problems before coming to class, they can provide a context in which the instructor's presentation and answers to student questions can be more meaningful to more students than they would be if no such problems were used.

In addition to using pretests and carefully constructed homework problems, we should also attempt to apply the following traditional "rules" of sequence in our teaching. These rules appear in Davies (1981, p. 91), who attributes them to Herbert Spencer.

- proceed from the known to the unknown
- proceed from the simple to the complex
- proceed from the concrete to the abstract
- proceed from the particular to the general
- proceed from observation to reasoning
- proceed from a whole view to a more detailed view to a whole view

All these sequences attempt to make new material more meaningful in terms of the student's existing learning set. And, as indicated below, material encoded in a meaningful learning set is more easily transferred to new situations than is material encoded by rote.

Importance of Motivation

The learner's motivation is a crucial variable in determining how much people learn. Interest in the material to be learned and an "intent to learn" are powerful motivating factors, and the desire for self-esteem and the stimulation or satisfaction of curiosity are motivations that can also be used in the college classroom. There is also some support for the proposition that a perceived usefulness of the material or, even better, an ability to use it, stimulates student interest and intent to learn. While it is no doubt true that not all students are deeply interested in everything their teachers want them to learn, there appears to be no reason for assuming that student motives are fixed. Before we point too many fingers at uninspired students, let us first ask ourselves: "What have we done to interest them in our courses?" Beyond attempting to demonstrate the usefulness of our material to our students, we should also recognize that there is some hard evidence pointing to the value of an *enthusiastic teacher* in generating interest in a subject. Along with a host of other studies on this point, Thistlewaite (1960) has reported that National Merit scholars consider instructor enthusiasm to have been one of the most critical variables influencing their choice of a field. Mastin (1963) found that 19 of 20 classes scored higher on a multiple choice exam after an "enthusiastic" presentation than after an "indifferent" presentation of material on ancient Egypt and ancient Rome and Pompeii, and Coats and Smidchens (1966) found sizable differences in immediate recall of lecture material on classroom interaction analysis when the lecture was delivered with "dynamism" (vocal inflection, gesturing, eye contact, and animation) as compared to when the same lecture was read with good diction and sufficient volume.

With respect to *"intent to learn"* as a motivating device, an early study by Myers (1913) asked students to count the number of zeroes distributed among letters printed in color on colored paper. Later, the students were asked questions about what other letters were present and about the color of the paper and the letters. Their poor answers to these questions indicated that they had not learned much of the material to which they had been exposed but not explicitly told to learn. There have been several subsequent studies indicating the superiority of "intentional" learning, and Dressel and Mayhew (1954) have shown that even "critical thinking" can be significantly increased when it is taken as a primary objective by students. If we can generalize from such studies, carefully worded instructions, homework exercises, and exam questions can be used to encourage students to learn those aspects of our subjects we most want them to learn. The teacher who tests on the memorization of details, for example, encourages students to memorize details. But if students believe that their grades are going to be based on their ability to integrate and apply principles, they will be motivated to acquire such ability. A carefully designed course syllabus that goes beyond a simple listing of dates and chapters in a textbook and contains a clearly stated set of cognitive objectives is probably the best way to stimulate intentional learning on the part of your students—particularly if you plan to test them on skills beyond the first two levels of Bloom's *Taxonomy*. An efficient way of presenting a list of cognitive objectives that can be used for a unit in economics, or even a whole principles course, is discussed below.

With regard to students' *self-esteem*, it often helps a great deal if the instructor learns and uses their names as soon as possible. The use of students' names indicates that you take an interest in them and that they "belong" in your classroom. Self-esteem is also closely related to experiencing success and avoiding failure with respect to one's level of aspiration. The German psychologist F. Hoppe noted that a person tends to raise his or her goals after success and to lower them after failure. This process prevents one from continual failure or from too easy achievement, neither of which provides a feeling of accomplishment. An important motivating role for an instructor, therefore, is to help students set goals for themselves that are "challenging but attainable," and we should try to keep our instruction within the range of students' ability to deal with it without making it *either* too difficult or too easy. For students whose "motive to achieve success is stronger than their motive to avoid failure," Atkinson and Litwin (1960, p. 52) found that they were "most attracted to tasks of intermediate difficulty where the subjective probability of success is .50. Here the resultant positive motivation is strongest."

Similar to Atkinson and Litwin's finding that motivation may be highest in situations of moderate difficulty are D. E. Berlyne's indications that curiosity is highest in situations of moderate novelty. Berlyne (1953) contends that the interplay between the familiar and the novel is a significant factor in the development of curiosity, and he has stated:

> Our theory of curiosity implies that patterns will be most curiosity-arousing at an intermediate state of familiarity. If they are too unlike anything with which the subject is acquainted, the symbolic response tendencies aroused will be too few and too feeble to provide much conflict, while too much familiarity will have removed conflict by making the particular combination an expected one. (p. 189)

Berlyne (1954) has also emphasized the "curiosity-inducing role of questions" and has defined "epistemic curiosity" as "a drive which is aroused by a question and reduced by rehearsing its answer" (p. 256). He found that using a prequestionnaire aroused curiosity and increased the probability of college students recalling factual statements about animals. Statements recognized as answers to questions on the prequestionnaire were more likely than others to be recalled on a postquestionnaire, and "surprising" statements were more likely to be recalled as answers on the postquestionnaire than others. Frick and Coffer (1972) later repeated the Berlyne study with a better control on the test items and obtained the same results.

Somewhat related to Berlyne's results with prequestionnaires are the results of a number of studies that indicate that the insertion of questions in written prose materials facilitates learning. Rather than explaining these results in terms of curiosity, however, Rothkopf (1965, 1970) has hypothesized that inserted questions give rise to "inspective behavior" or "mathemagenic activities" which "give birth to learning." In this connection, Watts and Anderson (1971) have found that inserted questions requiring application of principles to new examples were more effective than questions simply involving recall, and they argued that:

> answering application questions facilitates later performance by encouraging students to process the content of the instruction more thoroughly, in fact to transform it, in the effort to apply it in a new situation. (p. 393)

This process of using questions to encourage students to transform information is consistent with Wittrock's model of generative learning, and in 1982 Mackenzie and White tested predictions from Wittrock's model in a geography class with impressive results.

Dominance of Visual Over Verbal Information

Bower and Hilgard (1981) report: "A large number of learning experiments have now been done indicating that imaginal or pictorial representations of information usually facilitate memory, by factors ranging from 1.5 to 3 or so" (p. 440). In trying to explain why "imagery techniques" are so effective in facilitating recall of word lists, Paivio (1969, 1971) has proposed a "two process theory of associative meaning" in which verbal information and visual information are processed or "coded" differently; and he argues that only verbal codes can be employed for abstract words whereas both visual and verbal codes can be employed for concrete words and pictures. And in answer to their question "Why are pictures, then images, and then concrete words remembered in that order, with all remembered so much better than abstract words?", Bower and Hilgard (1981) state:

> The current conjecture is what is called the "dual trace" hypothesis. . . . So a word (or word pair) that is imaged or a picture that is named has the advantage of having two, redundant copies of the memory trace laid down. The redundancy prolongs memory in comparison to abstract items, since the second, imaginal trace is likely to survive after the initial, verbal trace has decayed. That is, not only are there two traces, but the one in the imaginal system seems more resistant to forgetting.[4] (p. 440)

This clearly implies that visual aids in the classroom are much more than a "gimmick." Carefully planned use of visuals can be a valuable aid to student learning and retention. Not only do they add novelty and variation to our presentations, they also can add a concrete visual dimension to our verbal communication and permit students to process and encode information in a more meaningful learning set.

Given these generally accepted principles on the limited capacity of the human mind, the importance of prior experience or learning "set," the importance of motivation, and the dominance of visual over verbal, let us now return to the three elements of our definition of learning. There is some evidence that the things that promote acquisition also facilitate retention and, to a lesser extent, transfer. Nevertheless, there is probably an expository advantage in discussing each of these elements separately.

ACQUISITION

As indicated by some of the comments above on the importance of an "intent to learn" as a motivating device, one of the most useful things that we can do to help our students acquire new knowledge is to let them know exactly what it is that they are supposed to learn. Ausubel (1963 and 1968), in particular, has argued that providing students with "*advanced organizers*" facilitates the learning of meaningful verbal material. These "organizers" are usually brief written passages which the students are supposed to read before studying new material, and they are designed to compare and contrast the new material with what the student already knows in order to provide "ideational scaffolding" to help students integrate new material into their existing "cognitive structure." A series of experiments involving material on Buddhism, endocrinology, and interpretations of the Civil War have supported the effectiveness of advanced organizers, and Wylie Anderson's (1974) experiment with a unit on supply and demand in college introductory economics classes found:

> Organizing concepts placed immediately prior (preorganizers) to a learning unit result in significantly better retention of the concepts involved than is the case where organizing concepts are positioned following a learning unit (postorganizers). (p. 63)

The studies of the advantages of advanced organizers in classroom learning are consistent with earlier laboratory experiments that emphasized the importance of the "meaningfulness" of items in verbal word lists. Meaningfulness has traditionally been described in terms of the number of associations stimulated or the amount of "structure" that can be imposed on new material, and there is considerable evidence that initial instructions, elaborate directions, and suggested mnemonic devices can have a strong influence on rote memory tasks. The power of "mental imagery" has been discussed above. Not all mnemonic devices involve mental imagery, however, and most of us are aware of the advantages of remembering the months of the year that have a particular number of days by citing the rhyme, "Thirty days hath September, April, June and November, . . ." or recalling rules governing the placement of "i" and "e" by citing, "'i' before 'e' except after 'c,' or when sounded like 'a' as in neighbor and weigh."

Since much knowledge in economics tends to be cumulative, and since some rote learning of new terms is necessary for later retention and transfer, any mnemonic devices that we can give students at the acquisition stage should provide helpful, in part because they tend to concretize (thereby making more familiar) the abstract terms or concepts they signify. Writing out " I nelastic" and " E lastic" in this manner, for example, has proven helpful to many beginning students and beginning instructors alike.

Once material has been presented and students have tried to learn it, "*feedback*" or "*knowledge of results*" has long been regarded as a powerful aid to learning, and there is a considerable body of laboratory evidence indicating the advantage of active as opposed to passive learning and the importance of *recitation* or *verbalization* in memorizing word lists. Unsuccessful attempts to slavishly apply these findings to the construction of learning programs or "teaching machines," however, indicate that there can be too much of a good thing, and Anderson (1967) has noted: "Rather often programmed instruction research gives results at odds with the results obtained from other media, materials or techniques" (p. 137). In some programs, with low probability of error on each succeeding "frame," knowledge of results may not really convey much information; and if the responses required are not relevant to the crucial content, requiring active responses may actually disrupt thoughtful reading habits. With regard to the usefulness of feedback, McKeachie (1974) has stated:

> Knowledge of results, I would aver, *is* important for learning when the knowledge provides information and the learner knows how to correct his behavior; it doesn't make much difference if the learner already has a pretty good idea of how well he has done or doesn't know what to do differently. (p. 186)

And, with regard to the usefulness of active responses, Anderson (1967) has stated:

> Requiring an overt response from students is helpful only if the response is relevant to what is to be learned. . . . When a lesson entails technical language or foreign vocabulary, for instance, response learning becomes more important. . . . Clearly, an overt, constructed response should be required from a student if he is expected to be able to emit an unfamiliar, technical term . . . overt responding works best with difficult, unfamiliar material. (pp. 139-141)

Given the nature of most economics courses taught in the United States today, these comments indicate that we should give our students every opportunity to "respond" and "get involved" by having them complete homework problems and other assignments that are carefully graded and promptly returned with constructive comments and suggestions for improvement. There is some long-standing evidence that reward is a stronger inducement to learning than punishment. Hurlock (1925), for example, was one of the first to indicate that students show large and consistent improvement when praised for their performance, but adverse effects when reproved or ignored. So when writing comments on papers, make an effort to find some things that you can praise.

When going over homework problems and/or other examples in class, one should also be aware of the principles of "guidance." On this point Hovland (1951) has stated:

> Guidance given early apparently helps to establish the correct habits right from the start. Since, however, the learner will later have to perform the task without help, guidance must not continue too long, for the learner may become overly dependent upon outside assistance. (p. 644)

Although Hovland's observation was not based on the teaching of academic subjects in the college classroom, it suggests that after students have a broad overview and sense of perspective on the entire course, perhaps a "lecture—work example—let student work a different example" sequence may be useful in the early stages until the students have accumulated enough "tools" to work for themselves. But at a later stage of the course it is probably important to put students in problem-solving situations on their own. At this stage, we must develop patience and resist the temptation to "tell them the answer." We must let them mull it over and work it out for themselves.

Bach's Chapter 5 contains an excellent brief summary of the major findings on guidance.

RETENTION

As has been indicated previously, the things that promote acquisition also promote retention of new knowledge. Indeed, one cannot remember what one has not learned in the first place, and most tests of acquisition require the use of memory. The single most important thing in retention, therefore, is the *degree of initial learning*. Material learned by rote is not remembered as well as "meaningful" or "organized" material, and material that is used and applied is remembered much better than material that is not. In addition to an emphasis on organization, structure, and application in their initial presentations, therefore, classroom teachers can also use *repetition* and *review* to combat disuse of important ideas and concepts. In this connection, studies of verbal learning have found that *"overlearning"*—or learning beyond simple mastery—aids retention. Since getting students to the point of simple mastery is a difficult task in itself, this finding might not seem like much of a help. Yet it is probably related to the common statement among graduate students, who have just passed their qualifying exams and begun to teach at the introductory level, that only when they tried to teach their subject to others did they *really* begin to understand what it was all about themselves. Perhaps similar experiences can be provided in briefer and simpler form at the undergraduate level by having students give class reports or summaries of term papers. Such practices may help to induce overlearning in key areas carefully selected for these purposes. (See Petr's Chapter 11 on writing.)

The forgetting of material that is not used or applied has usually been explained by "decay" or "displacement." In addition, "interference theory" has also been invoked by psychologists to explain the often observed *"serial position effect"* that material presented in the middle of a sequence is not remembered as well as material presented at the beginning or at the end of a sequence. This observation can be explained as due to interference from other material in the sequence. Interference from material presented earlier is called "proactive interference," and interference from material presented later is called "retroactive interference." Material presented first in a sequence is subject only to retroactive interference. Material presented last in a sequence is subject only to proactive interference. But material presented in the middle is subject to both kinds of interference. The implication of this for classroom lectures is clear. *It is important to make your major points at the beginning and/or at the end of your presentation and not bury them in the middle.*

In addition to decay, displacement, and interference, the information-processing approach to learning has focused on still another approach to forgetting which can be called "cue dependent forgetting" to deal with situations in which the information sought for is available in the long-term memory store but is inaccessible because of inadequate retrieval cues. There is some evidence that *"priming"* can stimulate relevant recall, presumably by activating otherwise dormant retrieval cues. A study by Johnson (1965), for example, indicated the efficacy of priming in stimulating relevant recall when a group of high school seniors who had completed a unit in a physics course were given the task of solving ten problems. Half the students were given a two-minute word association pretest in which the stimulus words named concepts necessary for the solution of the subsequent problems. A significantly larger number of problem solutions were attained by the group given the prior association test than by the unprimed group.

Recalling the comments on "guidance" above, however, one should not overly rely on priming or prompting if one wants students to develop methods of recalling material on their own. Anderson, Faust, and Roderick (1968), for example, compared a heavily prompted version of an instructional program with a standard version and found that students made higher achievement scores with the latter version. So over-prompting can lead to a reduction in learning effectiveness.

TRANSFER

Transfer of learning from one situation to another has sometimes been referred to as "learning to learn." From a very early date, verbal learning experiments have indicated that the transfer of learning involves more than repetitive practice of the initial learning exercise. Indeed, without *overt stress on underlying principles*, most learning habits are apparently highly specific to the situation in which they are practiced. With regard to memory training, the experience of William James (1890) is often cited in support of this point. After memorizing the first part of a poem by Hugo, he then practiced memorizing a poem by Milton. But upon returning to memorizing the last part of Hugo's poem, James found that it was no easier, and indeed it took him longer to memorize the second 158 lines of the "Satyr" than it did the first 158 lines. He concluded that this sort of practice did not result in any general improvement in memorizing ability. Later, Woodrow (1927) reasoned that if subjects were given systematic instruction in how to memorize, the improvement would have been more marked. Accordingly, he set up a study for two experimental groups and one control group. One group devoted itself to intensive memorizing of poetry and nonword syllables. The second group spent the same amount of time but divided it between receiving instruction in good methods of memorizing and performing exercises in using these methods. The group that spent all the time in practice performed little better than the control group on subsequent memory tests, but the group given instruction in methods of efficient memory showed marked improvement.

Going beyond simple memory work, another pair of early studies indicated that in one situation in which an arithmetic teacher stressed neatness in the papers handed in by students, a gradual improvement was noted in the neatness of these papers, but no transfer was found with respect to the neatness of papers turned in by these students in other subjects. (See Bagley, 1905.) When the experiment was repeated with another group of students, however, the teacher who emphasized neatness in arithmetic also stressed the general importance of neatness in dress, business, and the home. Under these conditions, improvement was obtained in the neatness of papers not only in arithmetic but in other subjects as well. (See Ruediger, 1908.)

The main point here seems to be that *transfer is facilitated when the initial learning can be formulated in terms of general principles applicable to new learning*. It offers little support for the doctrine of "mental discipline" *per se*, for there is no evidence that courses in formal logic alone, for example, are likely to make people more logical in other areas. But if students can learn "what to look for" in solving certain kinds of problems, there is some hope that exposure to a *variety* of particular problems may lead eventually to a more general problem-solving ability. In a famous experiment involving shooting at targets underwater, Judd (1908) set up two groups. One group was first taught the principles of light refraction, the other was not. Both groups were then given practice in shooting at submerged targets. By trial and error both groups learned about equally well to adjust for refractive errors. But when the depth of the target was changed, the group previously taught about refraction learned to correct their aim for the new conditions much faster than did the other group. Katona's later experiments with geometric puzzles, card, and match tricks offer further evidence on this point (Katona, 1940), and in a recent review Bransford, Sherwood, Vye, and Rieser (1986) cite a number of studies that "provide evidence that an emphasis on executive or metacognitive processes can result in improvements in thinking and problem solving" (p. 1083). In the next chapter, Rendigs Fels discusses this problem in the specific context of the principles of economics course.

The studies of transfer of learning have implications not only for how problem-solving material is presented but also for how homework or practice problems are designed. Practice problems that emphasize computation rather than interpretation and application not only may encourage the student to relate the material to a rote learning set rather than a meaningful learning set but also may have limiting effects on the future study behavior of the student. If we want to develop in our students the capacity for meaningful (as opposed to rote) understanding and broad (as opposed to narrow) transfer, we must design our instructions and homework problems accordingly.

IMPORTANCE OF INSTRUCTIONAL OBJECTIVES

The preceding, admittedly selective review of the results of several theoretical and applied experiments in human learning indicate the importance of carefully thinking through exactly what it is we want our students to be able to do after our courses, teaching units, lectures, discussion sessions, and so on. Human learning is complex. There can be different degrees of understanding or knowledge of the same concepts. The key role of motivation in human learning also underlines the importance of the affective domain as well as the cognitive domain.

Clearly specified instructional objectives can provide helpful guidance for (1) student study efforts, (2) instructor teaching efforts, and (3) testing and evaluation efforts. Yet writing long lists of objectives for every single thing we want students to learn can often run into diminishing returns rather quickly. One way to deal with this problem is to state three or four general objectives such as "knows basic terms," "understands concepts and principles," "applies basic concepts and principles to new situations" and then follow each general objective with a *representative sample* of specific illustrative behaviors. The illustrative examples should begin with a verb that specifies observable *student* behavior, and the illustrative verbs should have the most

TABLE 7-1 OBJECTIVES FOR A COURSE (OR UNIT) IN ECONOMICS

(These objectives can be applied to various content areas depending on the length of the course/unit.)

1. Knows basic terms.
   1.1 Relates terms that have the same meaning.
   1.2 Selects the term that best fits a particular definition.
   1.3 Identifies terms used in reference to particular economic problems.
   1.4 Uses terms correctly in describing economic problems.

2. Understands economic concepts and principles.
   2.1 Identifies examples of economic concepts and principles.
   2.2 Describes economic concepts and principles in own words.
   2.3 Points out the interrelationship of economic principles.
   2.4 Explains changes in economic conditions in terms of the economic concepts and principles involved.

3. Applies economic principles to new situations.
   3.1 Identifies the economic principles needed to solve a practical problem.
   3.2 Predicts the probable outcome of an action involving economic principles.
   3.3 Describes how to solve a practical economic problem in terms of the economic principles involved.
   3.4 Distinguishes between probable and improbable economic forecasts.

4. Interprets economic data.
   4.1 Differentiates between relevant and irrelevant information.
   4.2 Differentiates between facts and inferences.
   4.3 Identifies cause-effect relations in data.
   4.4 Describes the trends in data.
   4.5 Distinguishes between warranted and unwarranted conclusions drawn from data.
   4.6 Makes proper qualifications when describing data.

Source: Reprinted with permission of Macmillan Publishing Company from *Stating Instructional Objectives for Classroom Instruction*, by Norman E. Gronlund. Copyright © 1970, 1978, 1985 by Norman E. Gronlund.

precise meaning possible—"use," "know," *really* know" are less precise than "identify," "describe," "construct," "distinguish." Gronlund (1970, p. 40) offers a good illustration of how this technique can be applied to a principles of economic course or a unit in such a course. If presented in a format similar to Table 7-1, an outline of the cognitive objectives for your whole course can be presented on a single page in your course syllabus.

Note that the statements of specific behaviors listed under each general objective in Table 7-1 describe how the student is expected to react toward the subject matter in economics, but they do not describe the specific subject matter toward which he or she is to react. (For example, the specific behaviors listed under "knows basic terms" describe what is meant by "knowing," not what terms the student should know.) Such statements make it possible to relate the same instructional objectives to different content units, and they can serve as a highly useful guide to students and to instructors in focusing their learning and teaching efforts and in preparing for exams and evaluations.

COMPLETELY STATED OBJECTIVES

The learning outcome or the *behavior* that the *student* should be able to demonstrate is the most important part of an instructional objective. Educators correctly point out, however, that a statement of what the student must do is only one component of a completely stated objective. To be complete, an instructional objective should also contain a statement of the *conditions* in which the student should be able to do it and a statement of the *criteria* that will be used to judge how well it is done. The three basic components of a completely stated objective—conditions, behavior, and criteria—are sometimes summarized in the three basic questions of *when? what?* and *how well?*

After attending the appropriate lecture, the student should be able to define the term "induced investment" with 100% accuracy.

Given 13 years of time series data on GNP, the stock of money, the Consumer's Price Index, and the unemployment rate, and with the aid of calculators being permitted, the student should be able to correctly compute the income velocity of circulation to two decimal places for four selected years in a five-minute period.

Given a hypothetical newspaper clipping with three erroneous interpretations of an economic event, the student should be able to correctly identify two of the three errors and explain fully the reason why they are wrong.

Stating complete objectives in this form, with conditions, behavior, and criteria all written out in detail for each objective is not really necessary in most instruction situations. Yet it is important to keep *conditions* and *criteria* in mind when deciding what it is we want our students to be able to do. Comparing the performance of different students or different groups on the same test, for example, is not appropriate if the conditions are not similar. Considerations such as whether or not students are allowed to consult notes and books and the amount of time allowed to work are also important in deciding what criteria to use in evaluating responses.[5]

CONCLUSIONS

The conclusions that emerge from the preceding discussion of learning theory and instructional objectives can be summarized in the following nine (7 + 2) points. If you practice these behaviors, your students should learn more in your principles course than if you do not practice these behaviors.

1 Formulate clear objectives in both the cognitive and the affective domain, and use your course syllabus and other devices to let your students know what is expected of them.

2 If you expect students to learn concepts up to the applications level, you must design presentations and exercises that go beyond recall and memory and stress transfer. You should remember the limited capacity of the human mind to process information and concentrate on a selected number of the most important concepts rather than try to "cover the waterfront."

3 Remember the importance of "learning set," and use pretests or questionnaires to make sure that you know where your students are starting from. As the course progresses, use carefully structured homework problems to focus student's "set," and don't be afraid to repeat and review frequently if major points are not being understood or cannot be applied.

4 Remember the importance of student motivation. Demonstrate enthusiasm, use clear directions to establish an "intent to learn," try to create situations of moderate difficulty and moderate novelty, and use students' names whenever possible. Also try to help students establish learning goals for themselves that are neither so low as to be unfulfilling nor so high as to be impossible of attainment.

5 Try to use variety in your presentations, and use visual aids whenever possible to activate both visual and verbal processing activities in your students.

6 Begin your presentations of new material with "advanced organizers," and try to link new material to old. Also try to begin your lectures with memorable, thought-provoking questions, and make sure that your main points are emphasized at the beginning and the end of your presentation.

7 Provide students with an opportunity to actively respond and verbalize difficult points, and provide prompt and accurate feedback on major learning exercises. In providing feedback, try to emphasize the positive, and write comments of what you can praise on papers.

8 Try to teach for transfer by emphasizing the potential usefulness of the most important general principles, and develop problems and examples that apply principles to a *wide variety* of situations.

9 In helping students with problems, use priming or cuing if necessary, but don't overprompt or provide too much guidance if you want students to develop understandings and applications on their own.

NOTES

[*]This chapter draws on Chapters 3 and 4 of the *Resource Manual for Teacher Training Programs in Economics*, edited by Phillip Saunders, Arthur L. Welsh, and W. Lee Hansen (New York: Joint Council on Economic Education, 1978).

1 Although he regarded the ages as only approximations, Piaget labeled his stages of intellectual development as: sensorimotor (birth–2 years), preoperational (2–7 years), concrete operational (7–11 years), and formal operations (11 years and older). For more information on Piaget's ideas, which have been very influential, see Ginsburg and Opper, 1969.

Although Piaget assumed that the stage of formal operational thought is reached in the early adolescent years, his work did not extend much beyond that age group. William G. Perry, Jr., later worked out a scheme that classified various stages of intellectual and ethical development in the college years. Perry's scheme outlines a process of intellectual maturation wherein college students develop from an initial stage of "basic duality" in which absolutes and authority are viewed as either totally right or totally wrong, through stages of relativism in which diversity and uncertainty are increasingly recognized and accepted, to a final stage in which students become committed to the understandings and values that determine their subsequent lifestyle. (See Perry, 1970.)

2 For a review of the evolution of the field of instructional psychology see Menges and Girard (1983).

3 Gagne (1985) notes: "The processes and structures described by learning theories are inferred from empirical studies of learning. Presumably, these processes and structures reflect the action of the human central nervous system and are compatible with what is known about the neurophysiology of the nervous system. The structures and their activities remain as postulated entities, however, since they have not yet been related to particular locations or operations of the brain" (p. 70).

4 Bower (1970) has also offered an excellent, brief discussion of dual processing systems in nontechnical terms in the latter part of his "Analysis of a Mnemonic Device."

5 An excellent brief treatment of all three aspects of a completely stated objective is Robert F. Mager (1962). Written in a format that permits you to practice and test yourself as you go along, this entire book can be completed in about one hour.

Another brief programmed approach to formulating instructional objectives is Donald L. Troyer (1977). The second part of Troyer's chapter (pp. 116-143) goes beyond writing objectives to evaluating them in terms of "worth," "fit," and "match."

REFERENCES

Anderson, B. Wylie, "A Comparison of Pre- Versus Postorganizers Upon Retention of Economic Concepts," *Journal of Economic Education*, **6**, 1974, 61-64.

Anderson, Richard C., "Education Psychology," *Annual Review of Psychology*, (Palo Alto: Annual Reviews, Inc., 1967), 129-164.

_____, G. W. Faust, and M. C. Roderick, "Overprompting in Programmed Instruction," *Journal of Education Psychology*, **59**, 1968, 88-93.

Atkinson, John W., and George H. Litwin, "Achievement Motive and Test Anxiety Conceived as Motive to Approach Success and Motive to Avoid Failure," *Journal of Abnormal and Social Psychology*, **60**, 1960, 52-63.

Ausubel, David P., *The Psychology of Meaningful Verbal Learning*, (New York: Grune & Stratton, 1963).

_____, *Educational Psychology: A Cognitive View*, (New York: Holt, Rinehart & Winston, 1968).

Bagley, William C., *The Educative Process*, (New York: Macmillan, 1905).

Beard, Ruth, *Teaching and Learning in Higher Education*, 2d ed., (Baltimore: Penguin Books, 1972).

Berlyne, D. E., "A Theory of Human Curiosity," *British Journal of Psychology*, **45**, 1954, 180-191.

_____, "An Experimental Study of Human Curiosity," *British Journal of Psychology*, **45**, 1954, 256-265.

Bower, Gordon H., "Analysis of a Mnemonic Device," *American Scientist*, **58**, 1970, 496-510.

_____, and Ernest R. Hilgard, *Theories of Learning*, 5th ed., (Englewood Cliffs: Prentice-Hall, 1981).

Bransford, John, Robert Sherwood, Nancy Vye, and John Rieser, "Teaching Thinking and Problem Solving: Research Foundations," *American Psychologist*, **41**, 1986, 1078-1089.

Brunner, Jerome S., *Toward a Theory of Instruction*, (Cambridge: Belknap Press, 1966).

Coats, William D., and U. Smidchens, "Audience Recall as a Function of Speaker Dynamism," *Journal of Educational Psychology*, **57**, 1966, 189-191.

Davies, Ivor K., *Instructional Technique*, (New York: McGraw-Hill, 1981).

Dressel, Paul L., and Lewis B. Mayhew, *General Education: Explorations in Evaluation*, (Washington: American Council on Education, 1954).

Frick, Janet W., and C. N. Cofer, "Berlyne's Demonstration of Epistemic Curiosity: An Experimental Re-Evaluation," *British Journal of Psychology*, **63**, 1972, 221-228.

Gagne, Robert M., *The Conditions of Learning and the Theory of Instruction*, 4th ed., (New York: Holt, Rinehart & Winston, 1985).

_____, and William D. Rohwer, Jr., "Instructional Psychology," *Annual Review of Psychology* (Palo Alto: Annual Reviews, Inc., 1969), 382-418.

Ginsberg, Herbert, and Sylvia Opper, *Piaget's Theory of Intellectual Development: An Introduction*, (Englewood Cliffs: Prentice-Hall, 1969).

Glaser, Robert and Miriam Bassok, "Learning Theory and the Theory of Instruction," *Annual Review of Psychology*, (Palo Alto: Annual Reviews, Inc., 1989), 631–666.

Gronlund, Norman E., *Stating Behavioral Objectives for Classroom Instruction*, (New York: The MacMillan Company, 1970).

Hovland, Carl I., "Human Learning and Retention" in S.S. Stevens (ed.), *Handbook of Experimental Psychology*, (New York: John Wiley and Sons, 1951), 613-689.

Hurlock, Elizabeth B., "An Evaluation of Certain Incentives Used in School Work," *Journal of Educational Psychology*, **16**, 1925, 145-159.

James, William, *The Principles of Psychology*, (New York: Holt, 1890).

Johnson, Paul E., "Word Relatedness and Problem Solving in High School Physics," *Journal of Educational Psychology*, **56**, 1965, 217-224.

Judd, Charles H., "The Relation of Special Training to General Intelligence," *Educational Review*, **36**, 1908, 28-42.

Katona, George, *Organizing and Memorizing*, (New York: Columbia University, 1940).

Katz, David, *Gestalt Psychology*, (New York: Ronald, 1950).

Kolb, David A., "Learning Styles and Disciplinary Difference," in Chickering, Arthur W. and Associates, *The Modern American College*, (San Francisco: Jossey-Bass, 1981), 232-255.

MacKenzie, A. W., and R. T. White, "Fieldwork in Geography and Long-Term Memory Structures." *American Education Research Journal*, **19**, 1982, 623-632.

Mager, Robert F., *Preparing Instructional Objectives*, (Belmont, CA: Fearon Publishers, 1962).

Mastin, Victor E., "Teacher Enthusiasm," *Journal of Educational Research*, **56**, 1963, 385-386.

McKeachie, Wilbert J., "Research on Teaching at the College and University Level," in N. L. Gage (ed.), *Handbook of Research on Teaching*, (Chicago: Rand-McNally, 1963), 1118-1172.

_____, "Instructional Psychology," *Annual Review of Psychology*, (Palo Alto: Annual Reviews, Inc., 1974), 161-193.

Menges, Robert J., and D. E. Girard, "Development of a Research Specialty: Instructional Psychology Portrayed in the Annual Review of Psychology," *Instructional Science*, **12**, 1983, 83-98.

Miller, George A., "The Magical Number Seven, Plus or Minus Two: Some Limits on Our Capacity for Processing Information," *Psychological Review*, **63**, 1956, 81-97.

Myers, Garry C., "A Study in Incidental Memory," *Archives of Psychology*, no. 26, February 1913.

Paivio, Allan, "Mental Imagery in Associative Learning and Memory," *Psychological Review*, **76**, 1969, 241-263.

_____, *Imagery and Verbal Processes*, (New York: Holt, Rinehart & Winston, 1971).

Perry, William G., Jr., *Forms of Intellectual and Ethical Development in the College Years: A Scheme*, (New York: Holt, Rinehart & Winston, 1970).

Rothkopf, E. Z., "Some Theoretical and Experimental Approaches to Problems in Written Instruction," in J. D. Krumboltz (ed.), *Learning and the Educational Process*, (Chicago: Rand-McNally, 1965), 193-221.

_____, "The Concept of Mathemagenic Activities," *Review of Education Research*, **40**, 1970, 325-336.

Ruediger, William C., "The Indirect Improvement of Mental Function Through Ideals," *Education Review*, **36**, 1908, 364-371.

Skinner, B. F., *The Technology of Teaching*, (New York: Appleton-Century-Crofts, 1968).

"The Teaching of Undergraduate Economics: Report of the Committee on the Undergraduate Teaching of Economics and the Training of Economists," *American Economic Review: Supplement*, vol. 40, no. 5, part 2, December 1950.

Thistlewaite, L., *College Press and Changes in Study Plans of Talented Students*, (Evanston: National Merit Scholarship Corp., 1960).

Troyer, Donald L., "Performance Objectives: Formulation and Implementation," in James Weigand (ed.) *Implementing Teacher Competencies*, Prentice-Hall 1977, 98-116.

Watts, Graeme H., and R. C. Anderson, "Effects of Three Types of Inserted Questions on Learning from Prose," *Journal of Educational Psychology*, **62**, 1971, 387-394.

Weinstein, Claire E., and Richard E. Mayer, "The Teaching of Learning Strategies," in Merlin C. Wittrock, (ed.), *Handbook of Research on Teaching*, 3d ed., (New York: MacMillan Publishing Company, 1986), 315-327.

Wittrock, Merlin C., "Learning as a Generative Process," *Educational Psychologist*, **11**, 1974, 87-95.

_____, "The Cognitive Movement in Instruction," *Educational Psychologist*, **13**, 1978, 15-30.

Woodrow, Herbert, "The Effect of the Type of Training Upon Transference," *Journal of Educational Psychology*, **18**, 1927, 159-172.

APPENDIX 7-1

BRIEF DEFINITION AND ILLUSTRATIVE VERBS FOR SPECIFYING BEHAVIORS IN EACH CATEGORY OF BLOOM'S TAXONOMY OF THE COGNITIVE DOMAIN

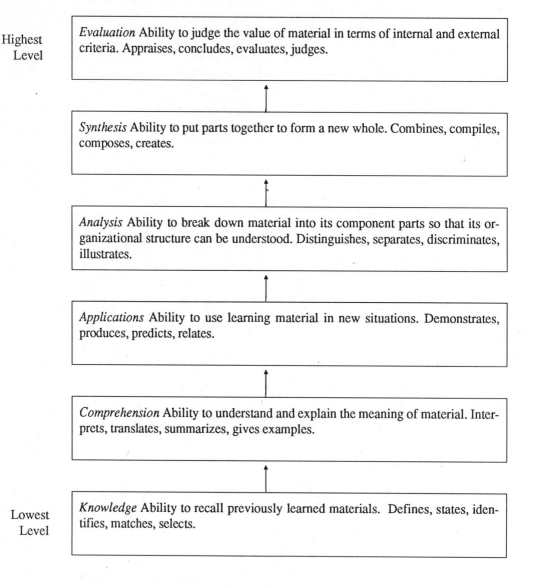

Highest Level

Evaluation Ability to judge the value of material in terms of internal and external criteria. Appraises, concludes, evaluates, judges.

Synthesis Ability to put parts together to form a new whole. Combines, compiles, composes, creates.

Analysis Ability to break down material into its component parts so that its organizational structure can be understood. Distinguishes, separates, discriminates, illustrates.

Applications Ability to use learning material in new situations. Demonstrates, produces, predicts, relates.

Comprehension Ability to understand and explain the meaning of material. Interprets, translates, summarizes, gives examples.

Lowest Level

Knowledge Ability to recall previously learned materials. Defines, states, identifies, matches, selects.

Source: Adapted with permission of Macmillan Publishing Company from *Stating Instructional Objectives for Classroom Instruction*, by Norman F. Gronlund. Copyright © 1970, 1978, 1985 by Norman F. Gronlund.

APPENDIX 7-2

BRIEF DEFINITION AND ILLUSTRATIVE VERBS FOR SPECIFYING BEHAVIORS IN EACH CATEGORY OF KRATHWOHL'S TAXONOMY OF THE AFFECTIVE DOMAIN

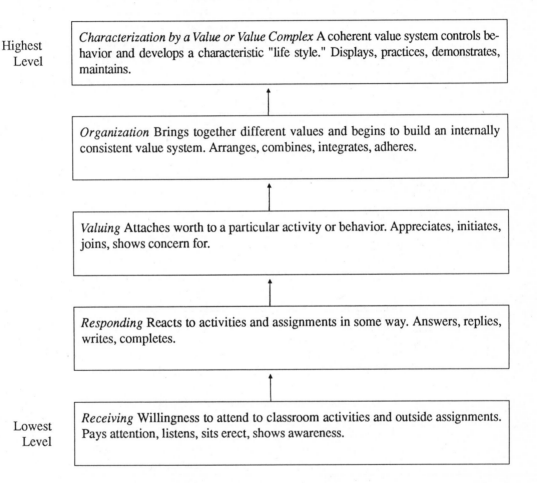

Highest
Level

Characterization by a Value or Value Complex A coherent value system controls behavior and develops a characteristic "life style." Displays, practices, demonstrates, maintains.

Organization Brings together different values and begins to build an internally consistent value system. Arranges, combines, integrates, adheres.

Valuing Attaches worth to a particular activity or behavior. Appreciates, initiates, joins, shows concern for.

Responding Reacts to activities and assignments in some way. Answers, replies, writes, completes.

Lowest
Level

Receiving Willingness to attend to classroom activities and outside assignments. Pays attention, listens, sits erect, shows awareness.

Source: Adapted with permission of Macmillan Publishing Company from *Stating Instructional Objectives for Classroom Instruction*, by Norman F. Gronlund. Copyright © 1970, 1978, 1985 by Norman F. Gronlund.

CHAPTER 8

TEACHING STUDENTS HOW TO LEARN ECONOMICS

Rendigs Fels

Those of us interested in economics education cannot afford to ignore the research by psychologists on teaching and learning. Until recently, teachers of economics paid little attention to psychology because psychologists did not have much to tell us. In the late 1960s, G. L. Bach summed up what they had to offer. In his account, motivation is the most important determinant of how much students learn. Reward is more effective than punishment, and "prompt, accurate feedback appears to be of critical importance." Bach also pointed out the value of making the material meaningful and relevant to the student and of the students doing something actively—orally or at least in their own minds.

The amount of guidance teachers need to give depends on circumstances—more at the beginning than later, more if the learning situation is complex, less for highly motivated students. Too much guidance is to be avoided; it is better to give students something to do and then provide feedback on how well they have done it. Bach concluded that "a case emerges for a mixture, and for a changing mixture, between the induction on the part of the student and guidance on the part of the instructor. . . ."

Other principles in Bach's summary included the value for retention by students of organizing the material and making it meaningful to them and the value of "overlearning" (relearning material several times). For students to become capable of transferring what they have learned to new situations, general problem solving should be stressed rather than specific techniques. Transfer is aided by having students verbalize principles.

These findings are useful as far as they go, which is why I have repeated them, but they don't go very far. Research of the last decade and a half has added significantly to them. (See Saunders' Chapter 7 and Bransford, Vye et al., and Brown et al.)

GENERAL STUDY METHODS

Students need to become self-conscious about choosing study methods appropriate to each particular discipline. We can't take it for granted that college students know how to study. Many of them don't. This is particularly true of economics, a subject that many of them have not studied before. Over the years, I have had many bright, well-motivated students who were doing poorly in economics because they were going about it the wrong way. Students are often unaware of the need to approach economics differently from, say, history. One year I asked a freshman who was having trouble how she studied economics. She answered in terms of the hours of the day and the days of the week she devoted to the subject, showing she did not understand the question. Her first need was to become self-conscious about the study methods she used, to recognize that different disciplines require different approaches, and to choose the right approach for each subject. Psychologists have developed ways to train students to do so in connection with reading and certain other subjects but not economics. One of our tasks is to develop ways to do it for our field.

Besides becoming self-conscious about study methods, students need continually to evaluate not only how much they have learned but also the learning strategies they have been using, so that in the future they will select the ones that work best.

Another lesson in the catalogue from psychology is the finding that the most general study methods are comparatively weak, that the more powerful methods are specific to particular disciplines, and that the most powerful are specific to particular tasks within a discipline. A general learning technique that we all use is self-questioning—asking ourselves questions as we read and as we listen to lectures (something you are doing now; you are asking yourself, Is Fels right? Does what he is saying make sense?). That technique is general but weak. For it to become powerful, students must learn the *kind* of questions to ask themselves when studying economics. Similarly with rehearsal, a technique we all use. Rehearsal means going over what we have just learned in the mind (or better, on paper—this is part of the value of taking notes). In studying a foreign language, it means recalling new vocabulary and trying out new words in sentences of our own devising. The challenge for economists is to convert the general but weak techniques identified by psychologists into specific, more powerful ones applicable to our field. What is applicable to our field depends on what we are trying to accomplish, a subject that needs discussion.

FEEDBACK VS. SKILL COURSES IN ECONOMICS

I once served on a review committee for the economics program of an excellent small liberal arts college. To carry out my assignment, I wanted to know to what extent economics students at this college were trained to feed back material presented in their courses and to what extent they were being trained to analyze problems for themselves. I asked for a set of final examinations and reviewed the questions. Subsequently, in a meeting with students, I asked which courses called for feedback, which courses for analysis, wrongly thinking I already knew the answer. They replied that it depended not on the course but who taught it. I demurred, naming a particular professor whose examination in macroeconomics clearly called for reproducing material in the textbook but whose econometrics exam required problem solving. The students replied that the problems on the econometrics exam were ones the professor had worked in class! With the benefit of this and other evidence, I concluded that half the faculty at this good liberal arts college wanted students to feed back what they had learned and half asked them to demonstrate skill in analysis.

There is reason to think that something like a fifty-fifty proportion characterizes economics faculties in general. The principal evidence comes from a questionnaire sent by John Siegfried[1] to graduates of forty-eight colleges two years after commencement. Indirect support is in an article by Karns and others. Before deciding what study techniques our students should use, we must choose our objective. Do we want to train them to reproduce material in the reading and lectures, or do we want to train them to use economic principles to analyze new problems? To rephrase the question, do we want feedback courses or skill courses?

To be sure, we all want to do both. Those of us who emphasize skills are well aware that students must master economic principles if they are to use them, and we want them to be able to feed them back accurately on examinations. Faculty who test mainly for feedback hope that students who learn economic theory well enough to reproduce it will know it well enough to use it. (They're wrong, of course.) Despite this qualification, the dichotomy between teachers of feedback and trainers of skill is valid, and the teaching and study techniques that are appropriate to the two kinds of courses are not entirely the same. Neither is course content. Rehearsal and schemas are crucial for both kinds of courses. Self-questioning and problem solving are equally valuable for skill courses but not for feedback courses. A feedback course, consequently, can afford to be encyclopedic, but a skill course must sacrifice coverage to mastery.

Skill courses are more appropriate than feedback courses both to the nature of economics as a discipline and to the contribution it can make to a liberal arts education. The essence of economics is analysis. Economists are above all analysts who think in a characteristic way. We are doing less than justice to our subject if we teach economic theory as a set of ideas to be learned and nothing more. Although a feedback course contributes to the goal of a liberal arts education of broadening the mental horizons of students, a skill course contributes to the greater goal of training students to think.

Teaching a skill course in economics to college freshmen is harder than teaching a feedback course. Many of the students I get come to college trained only to memorize. That approach does not work very well in economics, but it works better in a feedback course than in a skill course.

STUDENTS' SELECTION OF STUDY METHODS

The best students come to college with good study skills for subjects like mathematics and history, and they eventually learn on their own how to study economics. Many students have little skill to begin with or try in economics courses to use methods better suited to another subject. When I first taught at Vanderbilt, I gave a D to a student who, he told me in a nice way, was used to getting A's. I asked him how he had studied. He had memorized everything in the textbook, including the footnotes! This did not help him on my examination, which was analytic. I evidently had failed in my first duty. I had not made clear what he would be expected to do on the examination and how to prepare himself to do it. More serious than this isolated case is the phenomenon of junior and senior majors who after jumping to conclusions resent being asked for their assumptions or who discuss economics problems without bringing economic theory to bear.

INERT KNOWLEDGE

Inert knowledge is a common penalty for inappropriate methods of studying and teaching. The student I gave a D to had accumulated a great deal of knowledge. But it was inert. He couldn't use it. The term "inert knowledge" was used by the philosopher Alfred North Whitehead for what students know but don't use. I have had students who could state the principle that the higher the price the lower is the quantity demanded, other things remaining the same, yet when asked whether a rise in the price of gasoline will reduce the quantity bought replied no, because people have to use their cars to get to work and school. Their knowledge of the law of demand was inert. They could state it but, confronted with a problem, did not use it.

To help students acquire, understand, and use new knowledge, they need schemas. A schema is an organized body of knowledge that facilitates retrieval and use of information. When we learn something new, we mentally file it with other knowledge related to it; that is, we use schemas to facilitate future use of the new knowledge.

To illustrate, in an experiment by Gick and Holyoak, college students memorized the solution to a military problem: A fortress in the middle of a country has many roads leading into it, all of them mined. A large force of soldiers attacking it cannot travel over any one road without getting blown up, but small groups can do so safely. Since a direct attack by the entire force marching down one road is out of the question, the commanding general sends a small group on each road, timing their marches to reach the fortress simultaneously.

After students demonstrated that they had memorized the general's problem and the way he solved it, they were given a different problem involving a patient with an inoperable cancer of the stomach: the doctor can use a certain ray to destroy the cancerous tumor, but the intensity required would also destroy healthy tissue. Rays of lower intensity would destroy neither healthy tissue nor the cancer. The students were asked, "What type of procedure might be used to destroy the tumor with the rays, and at the same time avoid destroying the healthy tissue?" This problem can be solved in much the same way that the general solved the military problem. Many sources of less intense radiation could pass safely through the healthy tissue and converge on the tumor with enough intensity to destroy it.

The students had memorized the military problem and therefore had at their disposal the knowledge needed to solve the cancer problem. Only 20 percent of the students in a control group did so successfully. For the other 80 percent, the knowledge they had memorized was inert. In an experimental group advised that the military story was useful, 90 percent solved the cancer problem. If the military problem had been taught as one illustration of a class of problems and supplemented with non-military illustrations, students would have been better equipped to deal with a new problem they had not been exposed to before.

A question on the Test of Understanding in College Economics provides a similar example of inert knowledge:

> A family will be away from its house for six months. The monthly mortgage payment on the house is $300. The local utility services, to be paid by the owner, and an allowance for "wear and tear" cost $100 per month if the house is occupied; otherwise 0. If the family wishes to minimize its losses (or maximize its gains) on the house while it is away, it should rent for as much as the market will bear so long as monthly rent is above:
>
> A $ 0.
> B $100.
> C $300.
> D $400.

The question requires applying a principle from the theory of the firm to a household decision. Only 28 percent of a sample of 1,447 students from 22 schools who had just finished an introductory micro course chose the right answer (B), about what could be expected from chance.[2] It is hard to believe that the students had learned so little about sunk costs. Rather, their knowledge was inert. They did not use what they knew.

Psychologists tell us that if we want students to be able to apply a principle from one domain to another, we must teach it as a general principle, illustrating it from different domains. Economists wanting students to apply their knowledge to new problems need to teach sunk cost as a concept widely applicable and give a variety of illustrations. Better, after teaching the concept, we can ask them to generalize the idea and think of other applications.

ANCHORED INSTRUCTION

Sherwood, Kinzer, Bransford and Franks (1987) have developed a promising technique for dealing with the problem of inert knowledge. (See also Bransford, Sherwood et al.) It is called anchored instruction. They showed students the first ten minutes of *Raiders of the Lost Ark*. The students then read a series of short passages on such subjects as choosing healthy foods, using water as a measuring standard for other liquids, and making a bronze-age lamp. One group had been told merely to remember what they read. Another group read the passages with reference to the problems they might expect Indiana Jones to run into in the South American rain forest. Subsequent tests showed that the second group not only remembered more of the reading but spontaneously used a great deal more of it to deal with new problems.

Although it may not be practical to find and use anchors for economics as compellingly effective as a dramatic excerpt from an outstanding movie, the principle can be employed readily enough. Discussion of the theory of the firm can start with a problem like this one:

> Imagine that you are hired as a consultant for a company that manufactures bricks. The country is in a recession, and the brick company is losing money. Your job is to save the company from financial ruin. After conducting some research you discover that the company is capable of making twice as many bricks with very little increase in operating costs. Given this, what strategies do you suggest? (Bransford and Stein, 1984.)

Students can be asked to discuss or write a short answer in class to this problem before studying the theory of the firm and market structures. The answers will be naive but will get them to thinking about it. Then they can be alerted to keep the problem in mind as they study the theory. In this way they can be expected to bring the theory to bear on other problems to be asked later as well as this one.

It is not hard to think of other anchors to use in economics. The instructor can begin macro by describing the current rates of inflation, unemployment, and economic growth followed by the question: What do you want the President to do now? We can begin supply and demand with the drug crisis, the failure of current policies, and various proposals to deal with it.[3]

ARGUMENT RECONSTRUCTION AND EVALUATION

In *The Art of Logical Reasoning* (1980) Thomas Schwartz has developed a method of teaching informal logic that is even better suited for economics than his own field of political science. He has written an improved version (Schwartz, 1984), which I am in the process of revising for introductory economics.

In Schwartz's terminology, an argument consists of a conclusion for which reasons are given. Students are trained to reconstruct and evaluate arguments, identifying the premises (statements for which no reason is given), some of which may be implied; determining if the conclusion follows logically; and evaluating the plausibility of the premises. For example,

> Governmental regulation and taxation of a legal cocaine supply would allow the government to set prices. A higher cocaine price would reduce demand, and we see that as a primary goal. (Arnold)

This argument can be reconstructed as follows:

1 The primary goal is to reduce demand for cocaine. [express premise]

2 A higher price for cocaine would reduce the demand for it. [express premise]

3 If the government legalized cocaine, it could tax it and set a high price. [express premise]

4 Legalizing cocaine, taxing it and setting a high price would help achieve the primary goal. [intermediate step]

5 The government should legalize cocaine, tax it, and raise the price. [implied conclusion]

This argument has three premises, all of them explicit. (Sometimes premises are implied, the author thinking them so obvious that they need not be stated.) It has one intermediate step, an implication of the premises that supports the main conclusion. The excerpt quoted here does not state but clearly implies the conclusion.

Reconstruction is the first step toward evaluating the argument by asking: Does the conclusion follow logically from the premises? And, are the premises plausible? In this instance, the argument is faulty. A premise has been omitted that is not obvious, is needed for the conclusion, and is implausible, namely, that illegal sellers and buyers would stop doing business with each other.

The value of having students do exercises of this sort is to get them in the habit of thinking through the logical structure of the economics arguments they read. Skill in evaluating arguments, like any other skill, requires repeated practice. As Dale Jorgenson said, you learn calculus by differentiating hundreds of equations. Similarly for economic analysis.

It is both desirable and necessary that argument evaluation be taught as a general method of reasoning—desirable so that students will use it for other subjects and daily life, necessary because the instruction must start with extremely simple examples. Introductory economics textbooks commonly plunge the students into arguments that seem simple to economists but are too complex for beginners to reconstruct. For example, see "Idea 1" in the second edition of Baumol and Blinder's excellent textbook, p. 3. Idea 1, "The Illusion of High Interest Rates," seems simple: subtract the rate of inflation from the market rate of interest to get the real rate. But if you reconstruct Baumol and Blinder's full explanation, you find it is unsuitable—too complex—to start training students to think like economists. Throwing such arguments at them from the beginning drives them to a memorize-and-regurgitate approach to learning.

Adapting Schwartz's method to economics implies not only willingness to divert two weeks of the introductory course from content but also a commitment to follow through during an entire semester. The students must know that they will be required on tests to reconstruct economics arguments, arguments selected from the reading but not reconstructed in class. They need to be assigned problems regularly whether or not the problems are collected and corrected.

The approach also requires that the reading assignments be short. Consider the section on "Equilibrium of Supply and Demand" in Baumol and Blinder, pp. 56–58 (which follows explanations of supply and demand curves). In not quite two printed pages, it establishes that a price below equilibrium will tend to rise, that a price above equilibrium will tend to fall, and that

> In principle, in a free market the forces of supply and demand are capable of selecting an equilibrium price and an equilibrium quantity toward which, in practice, we may expect actual price and actual quantity to gravitate.

If we ask students to think through the logical structure of the five arguments in those two pages, they are more than enough for one assignment. If you don't believe it, try reconstructing the five arguments on paper and see how long it takes you.

This raises the question whether the gain in students' analytic skill is worth the loss of coverage in the introductory course. For prospective majors, the answer is yes. If they acquire early on the habit of thinking through the logical structure of what they read (and what they hear in lectures), they will learn more rapidly in intermediate courses. For those who will take only one semester of economics, coverage may be more important. The first semester of introductory economics at my school is taken primarily by students who will not become economics majors; perhaps half of them take only the one semester, a pattern that is not uncommon in American colleges. The first semester may appropriately be a survey course covering micro supply and demand, money creation, a monetarist model, a Keynesian model, and some other principles such as opportunity cost and perhaps comparative advantage, leaving no room for thorough training in logical thinking. The second semester, more heavily populated with prospective majors, can appropriately start with training in informal logic applied to reviewing supply and demand. It can then take up marginal analysis, going as far (but no further) with it as the approach sketched here permits.

LEARNING STYLES

David A. Kolb has devised a Learning Style Inventory (LSI) that throws light on the problems of learning economics (Kolb, 1976, 1984; Svinicki and Dixon). It is a questionnaire with nine sets of four adjectives, for example, receptive, relevant, analytical, and impartial. The respondent ranks the four, giving a 4 to the one that best describes his/her learning style, 3 to the next best, etc. The data from the rankings measure differences in people's learning styles, that is, the relative emphasis they put on the four modes: concrete experience, reflective observation, abstract conceptualization, and active experimentation. Different fields require different learning styles. Mismatches between the learning styles of individuals and the learning style appropriate for the fields being studied require that individuals change styles or change fields. If they don't, they get into trouble—low grades, anomie, dissatisfaction with the college.

The data from the LSI confirm the importance of abstract conceptualization for learning economics. Reflective observation is important for economics programs with a liberal arts orientation (e.g., economic history), active experimentation for programs emphasizing quantitative/theoretical and policy-formation aspects of economics.

The problem for teachers of introductory economics is to identify mismatches and help students make the appropriate adjustments. One approach would be to ask students to fill out the LSI and chart their own profiles. Those whose learning styles fit economics poorly can be advised to develop a new style for that subject while retaining the old one for courses in which it is appropriate; but if they are unable or unwilling to do so, they should be advised to study something else.

CONCLUSION

To sum up, students need to be self-conscious about the study methods they use. We cannot take it for granted that they know how to study, certainly not that they will adopt methods well suited to economics. The most general study methods are comparatively weak, more powerful methods are specific to particular disciplines, and the most powerful are specific to particular tasks within a discipline. We need to help students adapt the general methods of self-questioning and rehearsal by providing them with schemas and anchors so that their knowledge will not be inert. A particularly useful schema for economics is argument reconstruction: in learning theory, students ask themselves: What are the premises? Does the conclusion follow logically from them? Are the premises plausible? And they need to rehearse the model not solely by remembering but by following through its logical structure. But we must keep in mind the fact that students have their own learning styles. Those who come to economics with a learning style ill-adapted to economics must either learn to think like economists or shift to another field.

NOTES

*Parts of this chapter appeared previously in the *Kentucky Journal of Economics and Business*, Vol. Five, 1984-85, pp. 2-9. Thanks, with the usual disclaimer, are due to C. Elton Hinshaw, Phillip Saunders, John J. Siegfried, and William B. Walstad.

1 Responses to the question relevant here have not been published. Other results are in Siegfried and Raymond, 1984 and 1985.
2 Saunders, pp. 14, 20, and 45. This question is being deleted from the revision of the Test now in preparation.
3 See in Arnold the conclusion of Adelphi College students, based on the law of demand, that the government should legalize, tax, and sell drugs at higher prices to reduce consumption; Becker's contrasting proposal to reduce the price; and Thurow's use of elasticity to analyze the consequences of stricter enforcement of drug laws. Note the neglect of the supply side by Arnold and Thurow. Other problems that could be used as anchors can be found in Fels and Buckles.

REFERENCES

Arnold, F. Stewart, "Yes, Legalize Cocaine, and Fix Its Price," *The New York Times*, August 18, 1988, p. 26.

Bach, G. L., "Student Learning in Basic Economics: An Evaluated Experimental Course," in Keith Lumsden, editor, *New Developments in the Teaching of Economics* (Englewood Cliffs, N.J.: Prentice-Hall, Inc., 1967), pp. 77-79.

Baumol, William J., and Alan S. Blinder, *Economics: Principles and Policy*, New York: Harcourt Brace Jovanovich, 2nd ed., 1982.

Becker, Gary, "Should Drug Use Be Legalized?", *Business Week*, August 17, 1987, p. 22.

Bransford, John D., Robert D. Sherwood, Ted S. Hasselring, Charles K. Kinzer, and Susan M. Williams, "Anchored Instruction: Why We Need It and How Technology Can Help," in D. Nix and R. Spiro, eds., Hillsdale, NJ: Erlbaum, forthcoming.

———, and Barry S. Stein, *The IDEAL Problem Solver*, New York: W. H. Freeman & Co., 1984.

———, Nancy J. Vye, Lea T. Adams, and Greg A. Perfetto, "Learning Skills and Acquisition of Knowledge," in R. Glaser and A. Lesgold, eds., *Handbook of Psychology and Education*, Hillsdale, NJ: Erlbaum, forthcoming.

Brown, A. L., J. D. Bransford, R. A. Ferrara, and J. C. Campione, "Learning, Remembering and Understanding," in J. H. Flavell and E. M. Markman, editors, *Carmichael's Manual of Child Psychology*, Vol. 1 (New York: Wiley, 1983).

Fels, Rendigs, and Stephen Buckles, eds., *Casebook of Economic Problems and Policies*, 5th ed., St. Paul: West Publishing Co., 1981.

Gick, M. L., and K. J. Holyoak, "Analogical Problem Solving," *Cognitive Psychology*, 1980, pp. 306-55.

Karns, James M. L., Gene E. Burton, and Gerald D. Martin, "Learning Objectives and Testing," *Journal of Economic Education*, Summer 1983, pp. 16-21.

Kolb, David, *Learning Style Inventory: Self-Scoring Test and Interpretation Booklet*, Boston: McBer and Company, 1976.

———, *Experiential Learning*, Englewood Cliffs, NJ: Prentice Hall, 1984.

Saunders, Phillip, *Revised Test of Understanding in College Economics: Interpretative Manual*, New York: Joint Council on Economic Education, 1981.

Schwartz, Thomas, *The Act of Logical Reasoning*, New York: Random House, 1980.

Sherwood, Robert D., Charles K. Kinzer, John D. Bransford, and J. J. Franks, "Some Benefits of Creating Macro-Contexts for Science Instruction: Initial Findings," *Journal of Research in Science Teaching*, 1987:5, pp. 417-35.

Siegfried, John J., and Jennie E. Raymond, "A Profile of Senior Economics Majors in the United States," *American Economic Review*, May 1985, pp. 19-25.

———, and ———, "Economics and Faculty Attitudes on the Purpose of Undergraduate Education," *Journal of Economic Education*, Winter, 1985, pp. 71-78.

Svinicki, Marilla D., and Nancy M. Dixon, "The Kolb Model Modified for Classroom Activities," *College Teaching*, Vol. 35, No. 4, pp. 141-46.

Thurow, Lester, "U.S. Drug Policy: Colossal Ignorance," *New York Times*, May 8, 1988, p. 29.

CHAPTER 9

IMPROVING CLASSROOM DISCUSSION IN ECONOMICS COURSES

W. Lee Hansen
Michael K. Salemi[*]

"My discussion section never really had much discussion. The instructor asked a few questions but we never got into any meaty issues."

"The instructor in this course (a small upper division course) spent almost 100 percent of the time lecturing. The few times he tried to get a discussion going, it failed completely. I thought small classes were intended to permit discussion that can't occur in large principles lectures."

"Our discussions in this course have been boring and a waste of time. Neither the instructor nor the students know much about how to have good discussions."

Responses from student course evaluations

"The purpose of a college education is to teach students how to think."

"Students perceive that economics courses are hard because we expect them to show that they can think like economists not just repeat material they have memorized."

Anonymous

Most economics faculty members, when asked what they hope students will take away from their courses, mention higher order cognitive skills. They talk about the ability to evaluate an argument, to analyze some situation, to apply what is learned. Most of all, they want their students to be able to think and, in appropriate contexts, to think like economists.

Despite voicing these lofty goals, instructors rarely devote any substantial class time to honing thinking skills. In particular, they fail to recognize the effectiveness of classroom discussion both for developing these skills and in revealing whether students are actually acquiring them. Even faculty who understand the value of discussion are largely unable to capitalize on their knowledge because they do not know how to organize and lead a discussion effectively. This state of affairs reflects an obvious incongruity since it has been established that discussion is a better technique than lecturing for developing higher order cognitive skills.

The purpose of this chapter is to convince and to teach: to convince instructors that discussion (or some form of two-way talk) should be part of every teaching plan; and to teach instructors how to organize and lead fruitful discussions. Readers should keep two thoughts in mind. First, because novice and experienced instructors alike initially find it difficult to produce good discussions, both groups should find this chapter useful. Second, the technology set out in what follows really works! With careful preparation and some practice almost any instructor can lead discussions that will help students acquire and develop the thinking skills we, as economics instructors, want them to have.

THE IMPORTANCE OF USING TWO-WAY TALK IN THE CLASSROOM

The first step is to set out a hierarchy of non-lecture teaching techniques that we call two-way talk. Two-way talk is exactly what its name implies—talk between the teacher and a student or talk between students themselves. Lectures, by contrast, are one-way talk—students listen and try to understand what is said but do not formulate "talk" or responses of their own.

Several types of two-way talk can be part of a teaching plan. Instructors can initiate questions and field responses in the course of a lecture, a technique recommended by Saunders (Chapter 10) as a way of checking student understanding and of breaking long lectures into smaller chunks. Or students can initiate questions and receive answers without prompting from the instructor; while the initiative would seem to lie with the students, it is the instructor who controls the amount of time devoted to questions by being more or less receptive to them. Alternatively, instructors can have students engage in recitation or "drill" activities; though useful as a method of checking on what students know, the focus is on their providing "correct" responses to the instructor's questions. A more venturesome approach calls for students to work on a question or problem as part of a small group and then "report" the group's results or conclusions to the class as a whole. Finally, instructor and students can participate in a formal discussion of some reading assignment for the purpose of gaining a deeper understanding of what the author is saying.

This list orders two-way talk activities from initiating questions, where the instructor retains almost complete control over the flow of information, to discussion, where the instructor gives up that control. The list also orders the activities in another way—from those which provide students a minimal opportunity to acquire thinking skills to those which afford substantial opportunities to develop these skills by giving students practice in formulating answers and questions of their own.

Using two-way talk techniques thus involves important tradeoffs. More material can be covered with lectures, but discussions facilitate a deeper understanding of the material—a tradeoff between course breadth and depth. Also, in lectures the instructor can guarantee that concepts are presented clearly and accurately. In a two-way talk session, students listen to one another and must process a more extensive but lower quality stream of information. With discussion it may be more difficult for students to obtain precise concept definitions but they gain facility in applying those definitions when they use them to frame their questions and answers.

Two-way talk may leave some students confused, but, in our view, this is necessary for real learning to occur. Some students may not understand their colleagues' questions or responses. Others may be swayed by weak or even incorrect arguments. But along the way, students learn to judge the merits of an argument and to take responsibility for their own understanding. They become active learners and real learning occurs.

Why use two-way talk in the classroom? Two-way talk techniques give students practice doing in class what we say we want them to be able to do in life. These techniques require students and faculty members alike to think in class, to frame their own answers to questions, and to interpret written material using the discipline embodied in the course's content.

Discussion is a special type of two-way talk. With other two-way talk activities, students aim at providing the "correct" answer. Typically, a correct answer does exist, and the instructor will usually take pains to make that abundantly clear. Such activities are beneficial because they require students to switch from passive to active mode and to apply course concepts themselves rather than simply recognizing a correct application when it is presented. But these activities do not train students to think independently. A successful discussion, on the other hand, requires ambiguity and is designed to force each student to struggle with resolving that ambiguity. Discussion requires background reading material rich enough so that many potential interpretations and many answers exist to questions that can be asked about the material. In the course of discussion students aim at producing their own answers and interpretations and at understanding and evaluating the interpretations and opinions of their colleagues.

Good discussion is exciting. The material is interesting and relevant to the class, and students are stimulated by the realization that they alone will interpret and evaluate the material. The instructor will not provide the "right answers" at the end of class. The only answers that will be available are those which the students produce through their interaction with the material and with the comments and observations of other students during the course of the discussion. Thus, discussion offers a means for instructors to promote an appreciation for the relevance and vitality of economics while at the same time sharpening the higher order thinking skills of their students. Most of what follows is devoted to explaining the five elements which underlie effective discussion. The next five sections treat each element in turn. The last section offers some additional tips on other types of two-way talk teaching strategies.

INTEGRATING DISCUSSION INTO THE COURSE PLAN

Discussion and other two-way talk techniques are appropriate teaching strategies only when an instructor's course goals go beyond memorization of key terms and manipulation of equations. Students should understand at the outset that they are expected to develop higher level thinking skills along with an appreciation for the importance and relevance of the course material; and they should understand that discussion is an important part of the strategy for accomplishing those goals.

Students should correctly perceive that discussions "count" in the computation of grades. This does not mean the instructor should grade a student's discussion participation. In our view, grading participation is a bad idea because it is hard to do fairly and because it may make some students reticent to contribute. Instead, the instructor must make clear that widespread participation is essential in contributing to the class's understanding of the material. To lend further weight to the importance of discussion, the instructor may want to indicate that questions taken up in discussion are appropriate subject matter for examination essays.

To sum up, it is essential that students understand from the beginning that discussion is an essential part of the teaching plan of the course and that they have an obligation to participate in discussion.

SELECTION OF DISCUSSION MATERIAL

Effective discussion requires instructors to select material that is appropriate for classroom discussion. A test of appropriateness is whether an instructor can answer "yes" to the following four questions.

Does the material contain a sufficient number of ideas to warrant discussion? To test whether a particular piece is sufficiently rich and hence worth discussing, the instructor should try to write several interpretive questions concerning it. What constitutes an interpretive question is taken up later in this chapter. For now, suffice it to say that these questions should be interesting, should require the students to interpret what the author has written, and should support more than one reasonable answer.

Is the material self-contained? The selection should be able to stand on its own, so that there is no need to look up key terms or obtain supplementary information. Everyone should be able to come to the discussion equally well prepared, and the only reference necessary during the discussion is the selection itself. This does not mean, of course, that the selection cannot build on knowledge acquired from the course textbooks, lectures, and other reading selections already covered in the course.

Is the material reasonably well written? Material that is poorly written and organized will cause the discussion to get bogged down in efforts to determine what the author said. Material that is well written permits the discussion to focus on the deeper issues of interpretation. To qualify, the material need not apply economic logic faultlessly. Straightening out a confused or incorrect presentation of economic ideas is a good discussion outcome, but discussion should focus on intellectual rather than stylistic confusion.

Is the material interesting to both the instructor and the students? It is essential that the instructor find the material interesting because instructor enthusiasm for course material is an important source of motivation for students. One way an instructor can check whether students are also likely to find the material interesting is to ask whether they will think that it takes up important issues, offers new insights, or helps resolve some puzzle.

Where can the instructor find material suitable for discussion? Generally, such material will not be found in textbooks because the authors have taken pains to provide "the answer" to any and all questions the textbooks consider.

One source of material is the many books of readings published either as free-standing collections or as complements to various principles texts. These selections are usually well written and interesting, but whether they contain sufficient ideas and "ambiguity" to support discussion may not be fully clear. The test, as always, is whether the instructor can write a sufficient number of interpretive questions.

Another source of material is those business and economic periodicals oriented to the interested layperson rather than to the professional economist. *Challenge, The Public Interest, Business Week, Fortune*, and *The Economist* regularly publish articles suitable for discussion. *The Journal of Economic Education* and the *Journal of Economic Perspectives* also offer useful articles. Most regional Federal Reserve Banks publish periodic reviews which include many articles on issues of current interest; frequently these articles are suitable for discussion in upper division courses and occasionally they are suitable for discussion in a principles course.

A third source of discussion material is the financial press, particularly *The Wall Street Journal*. The *Journal* regularly includes feature articles on various aspects of the U.S. and world economies and also editorials on economic policy. Many of these pieces are rich enough to support discussion. The *Journal* annually publishes an "educational edition," a guide to reading the *Journal*, which it provides free of charge to students. One particularly good discussion article is "City of Doctors" by Marilyn Chase which appeared in the *Journal* on March 13, 1980, and which concerns the apparent surplus of doctors in the San Francisco area.

One highly useful, structured approach to discussion is that of Rendigs Fels, first described in the *American Economic Review* (May 1974) and a special issue of the *Journal of Economic Education* (Winter 1974), and later exemplified in the Fels et al., *Casebook of Economic Problems and Policies* (4th edition, 1980, West Publishing Company). Fels focuses on developing the problem-solving skills of students through two-way talk that, guided by a carefully structured approach, seeks to help students understand some economic issue or policy. One can see from Fels's approach how to select comparable material for this kind of discussion.

A final source of discussion material is the body of classic economic writings. Adam Smith's seventh chapter of *The Wealth of Nations*, "On the Natural and Market Price of Commodities," is in many respects a far more interesting and challenging treatment of prices and markets than that provided by modern textbooks. John Stuart Mill's twelfth chapter from *Principles of Political Economy*, "Of Popular Remedies for Low Wages," gives useful insights pertinent to recent debates and research on the impact of minimum wage laws. Of more recent but not current vintage, R. A. Radford's article, "The Economic Organization of a P.O.W. Camp" in *Economica* (1945) offers a fascinating description of how markets evolved within German prisoner of war camps during World War II. All three of these readings provide first-rate material for classroom discussion.

PREPARING DISCUSSION QUESTIONS

Good questions are the necessary starting point of successful discussions. But what is a good discussion question? To answer that question it is useful to classify discussion questions in two ways: by the type of answer the question seeks to elicit and by the role of the question in advancing the progress of the discussion. The two-way classification we have in mind is summarized by the matrix presented in Figure 9-1. We begin by elaborating on the matrix and then introduce the concept of a question cluster. Examples of question types, question roles, and a question cluster are given in Figure 9-2.

Question Types

Across the top of the matrix are listed the three question types: interpretive, factual, and evaluative. Question type describes the type of answer the question seeks to elicit.

FIGURE 9-1   A TWO-WAY CLASSIFICATION OF DISCUSSION QUESTIONS.

Question Types

		Interpretive	Factual	Evaluative
	Basic	yes	no	no
Question Roles	**Supporting**	yes	yes	no
	Follow–up	yes	yes	no
	Concluding	possibly	no	yes

FIGURE 9-2   CLUSTER OF QUESTIONS FOR DISCUSSION OF THE RADFORD PAPER.

Basic Question
What, according to Radford, accounts for the development of an exchange system in the POW camp?

Supporting Questions
Can the development of the system be explained by the equality or lack of equality in the distribution of supplies?

Were prisoners generally unhappy with their particular allotment of supplies and thereby motivated to develop an exchange system?

Which force does Radford think was most important in accounting for the evolution of the exchange system?

Does Radford believe that differences in preferences gave rise to exchange?

Does Radford believe that prisoners might have developed an exchange system because they were used to living in an exchange economy?

Concluding Question
What weights would you assign to the various forces Radford notes as having contributed to the development of the exchange system?

Factual Questions   A factual question asks for specific information that can be found in the reading assigned for discussion. The "facts" of the reading are the words used by the author. Sometimes these "facts" may differ from the facts as they are understood by the participants. In discussion, however, it is necessary to focus on the facts as the author presents them. In effect, factual questions all are versions of the question "What did the author say about . . .?" As mentioned before, it is important for the reading to be self-contained. In the current context, this means that the article omits no important facts and that its key facts are not controversial.

Interpretive Questions   An interpretive question asks discussion participants for an interpretation; it asks them to explore what the author meant by what s(he) said. In contrast to a factual question, an interpretive question requires the participant to use higher order cognitive skills together with the evidence, or facts, reported in the reading to arrive at an answer. Interpretive questions are the backbone of successful discussions precisely because they require students to practice using these higher order skills.

The essential characteristic of a good interpretive question is that it does not have a single right answer. If students perceive that a question has a "right answer" or that the discussion leader is looking for a particular answer, they will often switch from an active to a passive mode and wait for someone to give that answer. A good interpretive question exploits the richness of the reading in the sense that different participants, each using evidence from the reading, can provide what seem to be reasonable but yet different answers.

By asking good interpretive questions the discussion leader accomplishes two objectives. S(he) transfers responsibility for critical thinking to the students and makes the discussion challenging. The challenge comes not only in sifting through the evidence to come up with a response but also in evaluating the responses provided by other participants.

How can a discussion leader write good interpretive questions? Good interpretive questions remind participants they are to respond using evidence from the reading. To maintain this focus, it is useful to pose the question in the form "Why, according to the author, . . .?" A good interpretive question must also admit to several possible answers. To make sure that it does, the discussion leader can check the reading to ensure that the requisite ambiguity is present. If that ambiguity is not present, the question does not qualify as an interpretive question. The most successful interpretive questions are usually those whose answers are least clear to the instructor.

By way of an example, a good interpretive question about the Radford article is: "Does Radford believe that the exchange system in the P.O.W. camp operated effectively?" Some students will cite "unity of the market and the prevalence of a single price" as evidence in the affirmative. Others will point to the existence of monopoly profits. Still others will mention the ascendence of cigarettes as a numeraire. The fact that multiple answers emerge provides the challenge of the interpretive question.

Evaluative Questions   An evaluative question asks participants for a judgment. It invites them to consider the material in terms of their own experience and to determine whether they agree or disagree with the author's point of view. While an evaluative question requires the participant to relate the material to his or her own experience, participants should base their answers on the reading and discussion of the reading which has occurred. An evaluative question is not an invitation to provide unsupported opinions. It is, however, an invitation to use one's own values in answering.

A good evaluative question about the Radford article would be: "Do you believe that the ranking Allied officer in the P.O.W. camp should have allowed this exchange system to develop and operate?" One participant might answer that the system was efficient and for that reason alone was enough to make the exchange system a good idea. Another might argue that it was not fair that the lesser-skilled traders ended up with fewer goods. Still another might argue that the system gave the P.O.W.s too much individual freedom and was therefore bad for discipline. Again, the differences in responses provide an opportunity for students to understand why they answered as they did, and perhaps give them a chance to alter their view.

Question Roles

Along the side of the matrix in Figure 9-1 are listed the four roles that questions play in discussion: basic, supportive, follow-up, and concluding. Each role identifies how the discussion leader intends to use the question in the discussion.

Basic Questions A basic question is one the discussion leader uses to lead off a discussion. It is a question that can lead to an extended discussion of what the leader considers to be some of the main ideas in the reading. A basic question should concern an important issue in the reading, and it should stimulate discussion. Participants, in turn, should find a basic question interesting and should not perceive it to be rhetorical.

Supporting Questions A supporting question is one the discussion leader uses to organize discussion of the basic question. The particular organization the discussion leader plans will depend, of course, on the nature of the basic question and ultimately on the reading material itself. If the basic question addresses a complex issue in the reading, the leader might use supporting questions to break the basic question into smaller parts. If the basic question hinges on a particular concept used by the author, the leader might use a supporting question to ask participants what the author means by that concept. If some facts in the reading bear on the basic question, the leader might use supporting questions to bring those facts forward. Thus, supporting questions are used to help move the discussion toward answering the basic question.

Follow-Up Questions A follow-up question is one that probes the response to either a basic or supporting question. It is used by the leader to elicit additional responses from the participants. The following scenario illustrates how a leader might use a follow-up question. The leader has started with the basic question (Does Radford believe that the exchange system in the P.O.W. camp operated effectively?). One student responds that the system was not effective because it was not fair. At this point, the leader has several follow-up options. The student might be asked what he or she means by fair or what evidence indicates the system was not fair. Or other students might be asked whether they agree that the system was not fair.

The use of follow-up questions is the most effective strategy a leader has to ensure that responsibility for advancing and evaluating arguments in the discussion remains with the students. Because they prefer clear answers, students will often try to transfer that responsibility back to the discussion leader by asking him or her a direct question. (What is the right definition of "fair" in the context of the Radford article?) The leader can then use follow-up questions to deflect that responsibility back to the participants. (What do you think it is?)

Follow-up questions serve as a tool for the leader in directing "traffic" during a discussion. The good leader listens actively, looking for connections between the responses offered by participants. S(he) uses follow-up questions to make those connections apparent to the participants and to explore their meaning. (How does your notion of fairness differ from Susie's?) Thus, follow-up questions provide a way for the leader to get the participants to talk to one another.

Whether or not to ask a follow-up question and what kind of follow-up question to ask are decisions the leader must make spontaneously. A flow chart outlining the purpose of follow-up questioning and specific questions that the leader can use to accomplish those purposes is given in Figure 9-3.

Concluding Questions   A concluding question is used by the leader to draw a line of discussion to a close. There comes a time in the discussion when the leader perceives that participants have done as much as they can to address the issues raised by a basic question. At that point, the leader uses concluding questions to move on to another basic question or to end the entire discussion. One kind of concluding question asks participants to provide an overview of the discussion. Another asks participants directly whether the issues are sufficiently resolved. A third asks them to make

FIGURE 9-3   A FLOWCHART FOR FOLLOW-UP QUESTIONS.

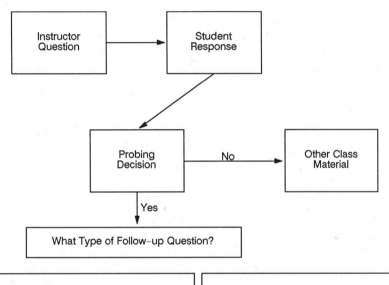

judgments about the arguments that have been raised. In all cases, the students rather than the leader wrap things up.

Question Clusters

A question cluster is a collection of questions prepared by the discussion leader to address a main idea or ideas in a reading selection. In our experience, writing question clusters is the best way, first, to decide whether a reading is suitable for discussion and, second, to prepare to lead that discussion. A good question cluster satisfies three criteria. First, it addresses an important and interesting idea in the reading. Second, it includes basic, supportive, follow-up, and concluding questions. Third, it uses the right type of question for each question role.

The principle used to choose the right question type for each question role is that participants earn the right to evaluate a reading by first interpreting it. Both interpretive and evaluative questions play important roles in a discussion. By interpreting a reading, participants develop the higher order cognitive skills that we want them to have. They develop too a deeper understanding of the reading which forms a basis for addressing the normative issues raised by it. Having an opportunity to evaluate a reading is an important source of motivation and helps bring closure or resolution to the discussion. Evaluative questions also signal to the participants that their informed opinions are important.

A good question cluster has: interpretive questions for basic questions; interpretive and, perhaps, factual questions for supportive questions; and at least one evaluative question as a concluding question. A good cluster lies along the principle diagonal of Figure 9-1. An example of a good question cluster is given in Figure 9-2.

CREATING A CONTRACT FOR EFFECTIVE DISCUSSION

Discussion can be exciting and rewarding for both the leader and the participants provided that all agree to fulfill their responsibilities. Figure 9-4 lists the responsibilities of discussion leaders and participants. It is helpful if the discussion leader distributes this and makes an explicit contract with participants to abide by "rules" of effective discussion.

For the leader, three responsibilities stand out above the rest. First, it is essential that the leader prepare question clusters in advance. It takes some work to identify those ideas in a reading that are suitable for discussion. It requires still more work to write a good interpretive question that can function as the basic question for the discussion and to write supportive questions that will break the discussion down into "bite sized" parts. Only after the leader has prepared question clusters will it be fully clear that an article is suitable for discussion.

Second, the leader must listen intently to the participants. The leader is responsible for helping the participants develop critical skills and identify the connections among

FIGURE 9-4 RESPONSIBILITIES OF DISCUSSION LEADERS AND PARTICIPANTS.

This sheet could be included as a part of the syllabus if extensive use is to be made of classroom discussion. If discussions are held only occasionally, this list could be given out when the reading assignment for the discussion is made.

Discussion Leader
1. Read the material carefully.
2. Prepare clusters of questions carefully and in advance.
3. Pose questions carefully.
4. Develop the discussion in depth.
5. Strive for answers.
6. Avoid difficult or technical terms.
7. Listen intently.
8. Involve each participant.
9. Confine yourself to asking questions.
10. Evaluate your leadership with a formal critique sheet.

Participants
1. Read the material carefully.
2. Offer evidence from the reading to support your answers.
3. Don't base your answers on outside material unless everyone has read it.
4. Listen carefully.
5. Ask for clarification of any point that you don't understand.
6. Challenge answers that you do not agree with.
7. Be willing to change your mind if someone shows you to be in error.
8. Answer the questions posed by the leader before making additional points.
9. Stick to the subject.
10. Do not interrupt when someone else is speaking. If someone else makes the point you wanted to make, don't repeat it.
11. Be as brief as possible. Do not continue to talk after you have made your point.

Note: For additional details, see W. Lee Hansen, "Improving Classroom Discussion in Economics," *Resource Manual for Teacher Training Programs in Economics* (New York: Joint Council on Economic Education, 1978), Chapter 6.

the answers they contribute. To do this, the leader must first hear what each participant is saying.

Third, the leader should confine himself or herself to asking questions. Many times in the course of a discussion the participants will "invite" the leader to provide "the right answer" or to take charge in some other way. The leader must not succumb to these temptations. Instead, the leader should ask questions that help the participants achieve their own answers.

For the participants, three responsibilities stand out above the rest. First, participants should read the material carefully before the discussion. They should read actively rather than passively, making notes of points they think are important or that they do not understand. Students who have not read the material should still be expected to participate. This may mean they will have to do a quick reading while the discussion proceeds, entering in later if they are capable of doing so.

Second, participants should strive to back up their interpretations and judgements with evidence from the reading. A well-supported view is more valuable both to the participant who contributed it and to other participants. Participants should strive always to be ready to answer the follow-up question "Why?"

Third, participants should listen carefully to what their colleagues are saying. It is as important to understand and evaluate the arguments of others as it is to frame one's own contributions. Discussion is a dialogue that requires both talking and listening.

LEADING DISCUSSIONS EFFECTIVELY

To this point, we have focused on how to prepare for a discussion. We now turn our attention to the mechanics of leading a discussion effectively. What follows is a list of tips we have found to work; the list is not exhaustive. The reader should keep in mind that there are many effective discussion leading styles and that each leader should seek to develop a style that suits their own teaching personality.

Seating Arrangements and Seating Charts

The same principle applies in the choice of a seating arrangement and the use of a seating chart: the role of the leader should be deemphasized and the role of participants enhanced. The ideal seating arrangement is a circle because it deemphasizes the importance of the leader and because it permits each participant to face the others. If a circle is impossible, a U-shaped seating arrangement with the leader at the mouth of the U is a good substitute. This means that classes which feature discussion should, whenever possible, be scheduled in rooms with movable chairs and tables.

The leader should use a seating chart. The chart facilitates calling participants by name, a practice that increases their motivation. It also assists participants in learning one another's name which, in turn, helps create a feeling of community. The chart permits the leader to keep a brief record of who has participated and what contributions they have made. This helps the leader to involve everyone and to develop connections among the contributions of different participants. (Allen, how does your idea bear on the point that Ted made earlier?)

Directing Questions to Participants

It is a controversial issue whether the leader should confine himself or herself to calling on volunteers or should be free to direct questions to participants. Our view is that directing questions is both acceptable and desirable. By directing questions the leader is able to break through the extended silence that sometimes occurs in discussions and to reinforce the responsibility of the participants to be prepared for discussion.

Direct questioning may make some students uncomfortable. A good way to remedy this problem is to give students the right to pass whenever they wish and to ensure them that they are not being graded on their contributions. When students pass the leader should come back to them later to give them a new opportunity to contribute.

Encouraging Participation

Ultimately, interesting readings and good questions will stimulate participation. But the style of the discussion leader can encourage as well. The leader should not appear to judge participants' contributions. Rather, the leader should ask follow-up questions when the meaning of a contribution is not clear. This is not to say that "anything goes." But the objectives of discussion are far better accomplished when criticism of a contribution originates with the participants rather than with the leader.

The leader should thus appear receptive and interested in what participants have to say. The leader can encourage participation by referring to insightful contributions made earlier by participants. (Susie, Joe's point seems to fit in with what you were saying earlier. Have you any reaction?) To the extent that it is comfortable to do so, the leader can also employ "warmer" body language.

Involving All Participants

One of the hardest tasks for the leader is to involve everyone in the discussion. Some participants are natural volunteers and there is a tendency for them to dominate the discussion. While the leader need not attempt to divide discussion equally among the participants, it is important that everyone who is prepared to do so contribute something. In our experience, valuable ideas often come from students who are naturally quiet.

TIPS FOR OTHER TYPES OF TWO-WAY TALK

Much of our advice about discussion organization and leading carries over to other two-way talk teaching strategies as well. Here we explain which parts of our discussion framework transfer more readily to other settings.

Using follow-up or probing questions is a technique which teachers can use in almost any setting. The purpose of these questions is always the same—to transfer the responsibility for producing a further answer back to the students.

Asking interpretive questions is also a technique that works in other settings. An interpretive question asks for a disciplined response; it requires the student to use higher order cognitive skills to arrive at an answer. Even in the midst of a lecture, it is useful to ask students to explain (to themselves if not to the class) why some particular part of the lecture makes sense. (In your own words, Joe, explain why it makes sense that price should fall in the example we have just done.)

Finally, using a seating chart, calling students by name, and directing questions to students are all practices that can be used effectively in a variety of settings. They are good ways to raise the level of student interest in classroom activities.

A CONCLUDING COMMENT

To some the approach presented here may seem overly structured and rigid. Yet this structure produces freedom—the freedom to pursue collectively and systematically the meaning of the readings we choose. The approach is based heavily on that of the Great Books Foundation. Our own experience and that of others indicate that it can and does work. Considerable effort is required to master this approach. But its benefits have lasting value by sharpening students' reading and thinking skills, deepening their understanding of economics, and contributing to the goals of a liberal education.

NOTES

*This chapter draws upon Chapter 6 of the *Resource Manual for Teacher Training Programs in Economics*, by Phillip Saunders, Arthur R. Welsh, and W. Lee Hansen (New York: Joint Council on Economic Education, 1978). That chapter, in turn, draws heavily on the training and discussion methods developed by the Great Books Foundation (Chicago, Illinois) which are reflected in the books it prepares for use by participants in its Great Books discussion groups.

CHAPTER 10

LECTURES AS AN INSTRUCTIONAL METHOD

Phillip Saunders
Arthur L. Welsh*

All instructors, at one time or another, find themselves in situations where a good lecture (one-way talk) is the most effective means of achieving their particular instructional objectives. Since good lectures are a necessary part of an effective instructor's repertoire, particularly in large-enrollment principles of economics courses, the goal of this chapter is to provide information, ideas, and suggestions that might help you, with the aid of additional effort and practice, to become a more effective lecturer. We begin by making four main points about lectures. We then discuss two common criticisms of the lecture method of instruction and what might be done to mitigate these criticisms. The heart of the chapter examines each of the four main parts of a good lecture. We conclude with a checklist that we hope will be helpful to principles of economics instructors in planning, organizing, presenting, and evaluating their lectures.

FOUR MAIN POINTS

The four main points about lectures that we want to make at the outset are:

1 There is no "one best way" to lecture.
2 Lectures are more useful for some purposes than for others.
3 A lecture does not have to last the whole class period.
4 The actual presentation is only one part of good lecturing—much more is involved than simply talking at students.

We will discuss each of these points briefly.

There Is No "One Best Way" to Lecture

The person who seeks a single "true" magic formula that will solve all of his or her problems in lecturing searches in vain. Effective lecturing is compatible with a variety of personality types and styles of presentation. People must develop the techniques that best meet their objectives, given their own personality, tastes, talents, and predilections. This is not easy, and beginning instructors must be prepared for a certain amount of hard work and disappointment as they experiment and develop a lecture style that is best for them. We can be influenced by others, and we can often get good ideas and techniques from others, but attempts to "copy" another person's lecture style often don't work unless this style is genuinely compatible with our own basic identity.

Lectures Are More Useful for Some Purposes Than Others

Bligh (1971) has argued convincingly that the lecture method's comparative advantages lie in *transmitting information* and *setting up a framework for analysis*. Lectures are often less effective than other teaching methods in promoting independent thought, developing critical thinking skills in students, and changing student attitudes. If one wants to achieve these latter objectives, one should be aware of the limitations of one-way talk (and chalk), and modify the lectures accordingly and/or supplement them with other teaching devices.

A Lecture Need Not Last the Whole Class Period

The necessity of achieving objectives for which the straight lecture is well suited, while at the same time trying to achieve objectives for which the lecture method is not well suited, often leaves instructors torn. This potential anguish diminishes considerably, however, once we recognize the simple point that more than one thing can go on during the same class period. Lectures can be combined with other modes of instruction, and a single class period can contain more than one lecture. We will have more to say about this later when we deal with one of the major objections to the straight lecture method.

The Actual Presentation Is Only One Part of Good Lecturing

The presentation of a lecture is much like the tip of an iceberg; there is more there than meets the eye. A lecture presentation must be firmly anchored on a foundation of planning, organization, and evaluation. Since all four of these tasks are important, we will return shortly to a separate discussion of planning, organization, presentation, and evaluation.

TWO CRITICISMS OF THE LECTURE METHOD

Two of the most common criticisms of the lecture method are that "books are better," and that "active participation on the part of the learner is more effective than passive listening." These criticisms are not to be taken lightly. Once recognized, however, their seriousness can be minimized. The rest of this section will discuss and partially rebut each of these criticisms. We will end up noting that the lecture, with appropriate modifications, still has an important place in college teaching. To be sure, bad lectures deserve all the criticism they get; but a good lecture, used under the right conditions, is a tremendously efficient vehicle for transmitting information and setting up a framework for analysis.

Books Are Better

Boswell reported that Samuel Johnson criticized lectures as far back as 1766 on the general grounds that "I can not see that lectures do as much good as reading the books from which the lectures are taken." Johnson also noted: "If your attention fails, and you miss a point of the lecture, it is lost; you cannot go back as you do upon a book."

Ignoring the facts that lectures and books can be complementary goods as well as substitute goods, that many students do not and will not read the assignments in the text until they have been to class to "find out what's important," and that even in today's atmosphere of publish or perish there is still much that is not readily accessible to large numbers of students in printed form, there are three other points to be made in rebuttal to this criticism.

First, listening to a lecture can be a very different experience from reading a transcript of the same material. Hawkins, Davies, and Majer (1973, p. 23) have noted that "The content may be the same, but the process is different." "Social facilitation" may occur during a lecture when students can see others simultaneously concerning themselves with the same ideas, and each member of the class may be stimulated by the awareness that other students are responding to the lecturer at the same moment.

Second, a lecture can be more flexible than a written presentation. A good lecturer can organize his or her presentation to allow for the "attention failures" noted by Johnson (we call them "micro sleeps" now), and in college classrooms the opportunity to ask clarifying questions and review unclear points should be much greater than in the type of public lecture to which Johnson may have been referring. Also, no book ever got any instant feedback from a reader; all but the most obtuse lecturers can get clues from their students about how well things are or are not going over, however, and they can modify their presentation accordingly.

Third, and most important, the one thing that a lecture can do much better than a book is to provide a *live model of a person thinking*. An enthusiastic lecturer setting up a problem and thinking it through can provide a memorable experience for students that is hard to duplicate in any other way. Facial expressions, body language, and changes in pace and inflection all give clues to aid comprehension and understanding that are not available from a printed page.

Active Participation Is Better Than Passive Listening

The reasons most people object to passive listening as opposed to active participation are usually based on learning theory and experiments that emphasize the importance of verbalization, reinforcement, and feedback to the student. It is true that most conventional lectures do not provide a great deal of opportunity for student verbalization, reinforcement, or feedback. But once this weakness is recognized it can be dealt with by encouraging students to question you, by asking your students questions, by combining lecture demonstrations with problem solving assignments given as homework, and/or by breaking up the lecture at certain key points. We should also note here that simply because a student's body is sitting still during a lecture does not necessarily mean that his or her mind is passive. Indeed, the student's mind is often highly active—many times with the wrong activity—during the lecture. The trick is to get the student's mental activity working in the right direction.

In the last chapter of his 1972 book, *The Summer Game*, Roger Angell uses the fascinating term "The Interior Stadium" and refers to the "interior game—baseball in the mind."[1] Later David Bergman used the term "internal dialogue" to explain why students in his lecture courses commented that he brought the class out in discussion even though there were no formal class discussions. He hypothesized that they had the "illusion of a discussion" and stated:

> Somewhere between the lecture and their notebooks a dialogue had quietly taken place. This internal dialogue is often as stimulating as, and more open than, any classroom discussion. Moreover, the internal dialogue always focuses on just those issues that interest us. . . . It always concerns itself with what bothers us most. (Bergman, 1983, p. 49)

In lecturing we want to try to make sure that it is our game, and not some other, that is being played in the student's interior stadium. We can use rhetorical questions and other techniques to initiate an internal dialogue in the student's mind. In this way active participation, learning from listening, and even reinforcement can occur during a lecture if the student tries to anticipate and implicitly predict the outcome of the speaker's discourse or argument. The student is reinforced if the speaker's next idea confirms the prediction.

Returning to our third main point—that a lecture need not last a whole class period, or that one class period can be broken into different parts—it is often a good idea to stop lecturing and solicit some form of response from students.[2] A general "Are there any questions?" is not likely to be as effective as asking some particular question of your own in a nonthreatening manner. Rather than singling out a particular student, you might put a question on the board or the overhead projector and have the whole class meditate on the answer for a minute or so before discussing it in detail. Or you might give your students a problem and let them break into small "buzz" groups to discuss it for 2 to 5 minutes before reporting their answers and/or their confusion about what the problem or question means. If it is feasible, the small group technique has the advantage of promoting social interaction among classmates and giving vent to any latent needs for self-expression. Students are more likely to ask questions of each other in such situations than they are to ask the instructor. Fear of asking "dumb" or "obvious" questions is also lessened when students find out they are not the only ones who don't have a clear notion of what is going on. And when questions from the group are discussed in front of the whole class, it is possible to cloak some individual problems in the guise that "some members of the group aren't clear on . . ." or "one or two of us wonder why. . . ."

The first time such a "break" to discuss a new question or problem is used, it is important to put the class at ease with a statement to the effect that "This is a tough point, and I want to make sure you understand it before going on to the next one. I'm going to put a question on the screen (board) so you can see if you really grasp the idea. Don't get nervous; this is not a pop quiz or anything like that. Just study the question for a few minutes, and think out an answer. Then we will discuss any ambiguity in the question or any problem you might have in arriving at the answer."

If a lecture-demonstration is coupled with going over homework problems, it's important that the instructor does *not* do all the work, show off his or her superior knowledge, and make the answers appear to be self-evident. If the answers are self-evident, why go to the bother of assigning homework problems? If the answers are not self-evident, let the students know that you appreciate the effort they have expended. Give them some guidance at first and then gradually allow them to take over and present their own solutions. Studies have shown that in teaching students to solve problems, knowledge of how to go about them is more important than knowledge of the principle involved (Bligh, p. 136). A live demonstration of setting up a problem and working it through can be useful for students at first, and it is probably important for the instructor to point out the answer or the conclusion if it appears that many students have not arrived at it by themselves. But there is a lot of evidence that the discovery of a conclusion by oneself can have considerable motivational value for a student, and Beard (1970, p. 38) reports that "teachers who solve all the problems, displaying their own superior skills, tend to depress interest in all but their most able students."

THE MAIN PARTS OF A GOOD LECTURE

Let us now turn to the four main parts of a good lecture: planning, organization, presentation, and evaluation. We will discuss each of these parts separately.

Lecture Planning

Lecture planning should start with a consideration of your students' "learning set" (see Chapter 7). In principles of economics courses the background and prior experiences of most students are likely to be quite different from those of the instructor. This is often particularly difficult for young, beginning economics instructors to appreciate. The fact that they have recently been students themselves often misleads them. The problem is that most new instructors have recently been successful, strongly motivated students, with a deep interest in the subject. This is not likely to be typical of the students entering a large (usually "required") principles of economics class. Some planning effort must be directed to motivating students, and you should plan to open each lecture with some indication to students of why the topic is of importance to them. You should also try to work out specific examples that will be meaningful to them.

Even experienced instructors sometimes fall into the trap of trying to jam too much material into a single lecture. An important step in lecture planning for new instructors, therefore, is deciding what material to leave out. Instructors who have just won professional status and are full of their subject must *strongly* resist the temptation to try to cover too much material and to go into too great detail. As emphasized in Chapter 7, the human mind has a limited capacity to process information, and adding too many elements to an intellectual task causes confusion and inefficiency. Wilbert J. McKeachie, a psychologist who has devoted his professional career to analyzing learning and teaching, has emphasized this problem and offered a suggestion to deal with it. McKeachie (1980, pp. 32-33) states:

> Probably one of the greatest barriers to effective lecturing is the feeling that one must cover the material at all costs. While it may seem irrational to cover material when students are not learning from it, one should not underestimate the compulsion one feels to get through one's lecture notes. A remedy for this compulsion is to put into the lecture notes reminders to oneself to check the students' understanding—both by looking for nonverbal cues of bewilderment or of lack of attention and by raising specific questions that will test the students' understanding.

Instructors vary considerably in the type of notes they prepare in planning a lecture. Ruth S. Day discusses several different formats ranging from verbatim transcripts to pictorial and tree diagram formats, and she notes: "The process of devising the notes may become more important than its product" (Day, 1980, p. 111). In general, you should not plan to cover more than three to five major points in a 50-minute lecture, and you should carefully work out elaborating examples and the transitions from one major point to another. Too little detail is to be preferred to too much, and the concrete is to be preferred to the abstract. Instead of talking about equilibrium prices in general, for example, it helps to start by focusing on a particular price that has some meaning for the student, such as tuition, beer, or movies. Initial examples dealing with diagrams should have specific numbers attached, and it is wise to work them out in advance on an overhead transparency, rather than relying on blackboard work where it is difficult to get things drawn exactly to scale. Overlays are useful in ways that conventional blackboard diagrams are not. They are especially useful for building up complex diagrams piece by piece. Moreover, they have the added advantage that they can be reversed or "peeled" back for clarification. A transparency is also available for later reference, whereas limited space often forces lecturers to erase the board.

If you plan to make frequent use of diagrams in your presentations, it is a good idea to work out one or two homework problems that require the students themselves to draw and interpret simple diagrams. This way you can be sure that they are aware of what variables are on what axes, and it helps them get a "feel" for the data through their fingers as they connect the points on a demand curve, for example. Once students have worked out an example involving a specific set of prices, it is easier to move to a more general form where exact numbers need not be specified and we can simply refer to diagrams where "P_1 is greater than P_2," "Q_1 is less than Q_2," and so on.

Since it usually involves a considerable amount of effort, forcing yourself to work out specific numerical examples and homework problems in the planning stage is one good way to insure that you keep your learning objectives limited and avoid the common error of trying to cover too much material. If you can't, or don't, take time to work out examples and problems, how can you expect the typical student to get deeply involved in what you're trying to teach?

Another important point to consider in planning your lectures is that your students' learning set will probably change as the semester progresses. As they become more familiar with the techniques and procedures of economics, and as they become more familiar with your lecturing style, they should be able to process larger and more complex "chunks" of information later in the course than at the beginning. The amount of detail and elaboration you plan to devote to a topic or a concept, therefore, should be related to where it will appear in the course sequence. Topics and concepts which require knowledge of prerequisite concepts and understanding should be covered toward the end of the course rather than at the beginning. But in cases where there is some flexibility in the sequence of topics, consideration must be given to what topics have preceded the lecture you are planning. A well-planned lecture at one point in the course might not be a well-planned lecture at another. A lecture on derived demand in factor markets, for example, would have to be planned differently if it preceded your lectures on noncompetitive product market structures than if it did not.

Lecture Organization

Everything we know about learning emphasizes the importance of organization or "structure." Some structure or framework for analysis is necessary to make a subject comprehensible, and unless ideas and facts can be placed in a structured pattern in the student's mind, they are easily forgotten. A knowledge of how things are related is also the easiest way to facilitate the transfer of ideas to new situations. What may seem like a well-organized set of ideas to the lecturer may not appear to be nearly as clear or so well organized to the listener, who typically has far less familiarity with and sophistication in the subject matter, and who may not know where the material fits in with other ideas, how it will be used, or why it is important. The lecturer must help students forge these links. Therefore, it is important to state the organization at the beginning of the lecture, to outline or itemize the main points to be covered, and to summarize and pull things together at the end.

1 *State the organization at the beginning.* The classic dictum "First tell 'em what you're going to tell 'em. Then tell 'em. And, finally, tell 'em what you've told 'em" has much to be said for it. Many beginning lecturers feel there may be too much repetition using this format. But experience indicates that repetition, which may seem "redundant" to the speaker, is actually "reinforcing" to the listener.

Several different organizational patterns are possible for various lectures in economics, and each has its uses for particular purposes. If one wants to cover a lot of ground dealing with an overall framework or a series of definitions, a *classification hierarchy* may be the most appropriate organization. The notions of total cost, fixed cost, variable cost, and marginal cost, for example, might best be structured in this way. For other purposes, a *problem centered* organization may be most appropriate. In introducing the notion of price elasticity of demand, for example, one might pose the question: Why is it that raising the price of some products (gasoline or alcohol) seems to bring in more revenue while raising the price of other products (a specific brand of gasoline) may bring in less revenue?[3] The organizational principle of *comparison and contrast* might be the most appropriate one for dealing with an issue such as the national debt where problems of false analogies abound. Other organizational patterns to consider are concept to application and familiar to unfamiliar.

Regardless of which organizational principle is being used in any particular lecture, it is important that the students know what it is, so they know what to listen for and so they can set up some of the implicit anticipations and predictions mentioned above. (Letting students lay out the bases in their interior stadium is a great aid in helping them to deal with Abbott and Costello's immortal question "Who's on first?") The introduction to the lecture should also indicate to students why it is important that they understand the material to be covered.

2 *Itemize the main points.* Itemizing the main points of a lecture on the blackboard, the overhead, or a mimeographed handout has several advantages for both lecturer and student. The items provide "memory pegs" on which details and examples can be hung, and they help to make it clear when the lecturer is moving from one point to another. If points are itemized, the student who daydreams or has a "micro sleep" finds it easier to realize that he or she has missed something, and can ask a fellow student or the lecturer to fill him or her in later. Itemizing also aids memory when we can say "there are three points on this topic" or "there are two items in this category and three in the other." In itemizing, it helps to keep lists relatively short. If you have more than four or five points, try to break the list into parts or subgroups.

3 *Summarize at the end.* In summarizing the lecture, it may be more helpful to pose significant questions than to simply repeat statements of fact. McKeachie (1986, p. 222) notes that experiments by D. E. Berlyne "found that asking students questions, rather than presenting statements of fact, not only improved learning but also increased interest in learning more about the topic." And Hawkins, Davies, and Majer (1973, p. 26) state that questions "remind students of material they should have gained and what implications they should consider. Questions help the student structure what he has learned on the topic, in that particular lecture and cumulatively." And they continue "At the end, it is also useful to review concepts, noting how they relate to each other and to previous ones."

Lecture Presentation

The beginning is by far the most important part of the lecture presentation.[4] At the beginning of each lecture the day's topic(s) should be tied in with familiar material, perhaps by reviewing the main points of the preceding lecture or by citing some current event that relates to the day's lecture. As indicated above, you should indicate why the topic(s) is (are) important for the students to understand and try to motivate them to want to pay attention. Beyond the other points already discussed above under "organization," much of what remains to be said about good lecture presentations appears to be simple common sense; lectures should be delivered in a clear and confident voice that does not go too fast and varies in emphasis and intonation; they should be aptly illustrated with a variety of stimuli and specific examples, accompanied by abundant eye contact with the listeners; time should be allowed for students to absorb difficult points and take notes; and so on. Yet it is often saddening to sit in a college lecture room and witness the extent to which such obvious maxims of common sense are ignored, disregarded, or simply overlooked.

Seven specific things that lecturers should keep in mind in thinking about their presentations are: enthusiasm is important; nonverbal behavior, or body language, is important; silence, as well as voice inflection, can be golden; some apparently mundane considerations can be crucial; a sense of humor, a stock of catchy examples, and/or a few special "tricks" can be valuable aids; variety in *stimuli* is the spice of living through a lecture; it helps to develop a more-or-less standard *procedure* in dealing with major points in your presentation.

Let us elaborate briefly on each of these items before turning to evaluating lecture presentations.

1 *Enthusiasm is important.* There is a lot of evidence that the lecturer's own enthusiasm is an important variable in arousing student interest and motivation, and experimental studies show significantly higher exam performance by students who have been exposed to enthusiastic as opposed to passive lecturers. If lecturers do not convey some sense of intellectual excitement in the topics they are presenting, it is very difficult to arouse student interest or attention.

2 *Nonverbal behavior is important.* If you don't think that body language, such as facial expressions, posture, and gestures, is an important communicator, compare a transcript or a radio tape with a TV tape of the same presentation.

Much of an instructor's enthusiasm or lack of enthusiasm is communicated nonverbally rather than with the actual words spoken.[5] If you *really* want to encourage students to ask questions, greet questions with a smile and an approving nod, and preface your answer with a "good question" or "I'm glad you asked that." If you appear irritated or appear to resent an interruption of your beautiful spiel, it doesn't make much difference what you say; students will get the "cue" not to ask questions.

3 *Silence can be golden.* Closely related to nonverbal behavior and voice inflection is the use of silence. A pregnant pause can be useful, and in encouraging student response to questions be sure to allow sufficient time for them to digest, meditate, and react. What may seem like a long time to you standing in front of the room may not really seem very long to students. Develop patience in resisting the temptation to "plug" silent "gaps." How do you do this? Recall the person who stopped a man on New York's Lower East Side and asked, "How do you get to Carnegie Hall?" The reply was, "Practice, practice, practice."[6]

4 *Some mundane things can be crucial.* If your classroom is hot and stuffy, if the "black" board is a "gray" board thick with fine white chalk dust, if the window blinds are not drawn to shield the board from glare, if a light bulb is missing, if you don't have chalk, if your handouts aren't typed on time, or if your reserve readings are not available in the library when the students need them, then it is foolish to ignore these problems and blunder about on the grounds that such mundane details are beneath your professional dignity. Modesty compels us to recognize that on some days opening a window, getting a wet paper towel, drawing a blind, arranging to have a bulb or a broken chair replaced, or moving the class outside may be our most significant contribution to student understanding. Your concentration may make you oblivious to your surroundings, but not many students have the powers of concentration or the desire to overcome bad physical conditions. Cultivate janitors, secretaries, and librarians if you want to be sure that you have enough chalk, your handouts are ready on time, and your reserve readings are available. Bobby Burns noted that "The best laid schemes o' mice an' men gang aft a-gely." Don't get tripped up by mundane details. Allow lead time and PLAN AHEAD.

5 *Humor, catchy examples, and special tricks.* Robert M. Kaplan and Gregory C. Pascoe (1977) conducted a study with 508 university students that found that humorous examples were recalled better than nonhumorous ones, and most lecturers have one or two favorite "tricks," ploys, especially dramatic examples, or jokes that they like to employ. If some way could be devised to pool and access this accumulated "wisdom" of the thousands of principles instructors, we would probably all be better off—although what works for one person might not work for another.

Prolonged silence, flipping an overhead projector on and off, or letting a permanently mounted screen roll up with a bang have their value as attention getters at certain key points if they are not overworked. Developing one or two ploys of continuing "in-humor" can be useful in establishing rapport with large classes. Try to keep them limited in number and reserved for key points. One that we have used, for example, deals with a repeated harping (at our expense) on the point that the price where "the amount bought equals the amount sold" is not the same thing as an equilibrium, or a market clearing, price. This is akin to the instructor who is worried about the audibility of his voice and asks all students who cannot hear him to please raise their hands. Or the instructor who takes attendance by asking all students who are not present to please stand up. These ploys usually go over with most of our students, but we don't know if other instructors could use them effectively or not.

Another device we use when we think that students are not getting the material but are afraid to ask questions is to set up a dialogue with ourselves in which we play the part of both the instructor and the prudent student ("prude") or the casual observer ("cas") who just happens to wander in and start asking questions. The simulated dialogue can also be used to dramatize other points, such as the independence of the Fed if one wants to play the part of both Harry Truman and Marriner Eccles or George Bush and Alan Greenspan. You don't have to be a professional actor to pull this one off, but a certain amount of ham (or corn) helps.

In working out numerical examples in class, we sometimes make simple errors in addition, subtraction, or multiplication, and then use these occasions to dramatize our human frailties and let students know that we appreciate some of the agonies they have gone through by exclaiming "Hell, that's only the 12th mistake I've made so far today" or an exaggerated "Heavens, that's the first mistake I've ever made in my whole life" accompanied by an elaborate show of anguish accompanied with a wink.

"Salty" language is a dangerous weapon, but a confident instructor can sometimes pull it off without offending—particularly if he or she invents new words such as "bass ackwards." A confident instructor is also not afraid to admit to mistakes or that he or she doesn't know the answer to a question, and humor is far more effective when it is at the instructor's, not the student's, expense. In talking about the importance of the items selected for measurement in dealing with price indexes, for example, we sometimes dramatize the notion of a "market basket" of goods by drawing a ludicrous picture of a market basket on the board. Our artistic "talent" then becomes a source of amusement as well as a focus for understanding. Evoking mental images of Alfred Marshall basking on a roof top in Palermo or the "bad guys" tying a cowboy to two horses headed in the opposite directions can be useful in arousing student interest in the price elasticity of demand, and so on.

A stock of "tricks" and vivid examples can be a real aid in lecturing. They best serve as devices to stimulate interest and attention; and like fertilizer, they can be useful in encouraging growth—in this case, student understanding of economics.

6 *Variety of stimuli.* In addition to voice inflection and avoiding the common error of letting sentences trail off at the end, presentations can be varied by using a combination of overhead projector, blackboard work, and mimeographed handouts. In listing main points or key definitions, the blackboard or the overhead is sometimes preferable, since students may pay more attention to things they have copied themselves. (An overhead promotes more eye contact and student feedback than the blackboard, and as mentioned above, flipping the on/off switch gets attention.) But, if a series of related points is to be covered in a cumulative sequence over several periods, a mimeographed outline, with space for a student's marginal notes, may be preferable. Mimeographed outlines can provide the students with an opportunity to concentrate on the big ideas unhindered by the necessity of taking detailed notes. They are also very useful to students who miss classes, but students should be encouraged to keep them and bring them to class.

If the blackboard or overhead is used, be sure the print is large and legible to all, and try not to stand in front of what is written or projected. Hawkins, Davies, and Majer (1973, p. 26) have also suggested some helpful techniques for blackboard work:

a Write down complete statements (or words) not just symbols. Students tend to copy down just what you write and later wonder what you meant. Your notes should help recollection, not hinder it.

b Start at the top of one panel, move down and then go up to the next. Do not skip around, and do not erase a panel until all available ones are used.

c If you are right-handed, why not start with the right-handed panel (as seen by the class), and when this is full, move to the left. This insures that you will not stand in front of what you have written.

7 *Standard procedure in making major points*. It may help your students under-stand your lectures and take better notes if you use a standard procedure in making major points. Such a procedure might be to first make a concise statement of the point and write it on the board or an overhead transparency; then restate the point in more detail with illustrations and examples that relate this point to others that students already understand; then solicit some student response that will indicate if they understand the point before offering a final, brief recapitulation and restatement. (See Bligh, 1971, pp. 79-88.)

Evaluating Lectures

In the most fundamental sense, your lectures are a success if the students learn what you want them to learn. If your appropriately established objectives are met, other forms of evaluation are secondary. Yet most lecturers don't have to wait until the test results are in to see how their presentations are going over—just watch the students! Do they come on time or straggle in? Do they sit upright and appear to be interested in what's going on, or are they slouched over and extending their "micro sleeps" into "macro sleeps"? Is there sparkle or haze in their eyes? Are they taking notes on the right things? Do they ask the right questions? If you are getting preliminary warning signs from these observations, there are better reactions than sulking and nursing your bruised ego in silence, or boiling up with indignant rage. Even if you are not getting preliminary warning signs, you may want to pass out an anonymous question-naire occasionally as a visible sign to students that you're trying to do a good job and are interested in improving. The questionnaire need not be elaborate, but it might in-clude some questions on the classroom environment (such as light, noise, tempera-ture) and the student's usual condition during your class (fatigue, hunger) as well as comments on the audibility of your voice, amount of material covered, speed of delivery, and clarity of board work or overhead transparencies.[7] Whatever question-naire you use, don't wait too long to use it. If students are asked to take question-naires seriously, they want their comments to benefit them *before* the course is over. They, legitimately, are more concerned with their own experiences than the experi-ences of students who follow them.

In addition to obtaining student feedback, you might want to ask a trusted friend to sit in on some of your lectures and make suggestions for improvement. This type of feedback usually works best if it is focused on a limited number of specific points. Without some form of checklist focusing on classroom atmosphere and lecturing techniques, conversations with colleagues often become excessively dominated by discussions of content rather than lecturing skills. Appendix 10-1 shows a "Class-room Observer Checklist" that we have found useful to help avoid this problem. Rather than trying to cover all the points on this checklist, it often helps to have the observer concentrate on only the four or five points you are most interested in.

Although comments from your students and friends can be helpful, the best critic of all may very well be yourself. Remember another of Bobbie Burns' gems:

O wad some power the giftie gie us
To see ourselves as ithers see us!
It wad frae mony a blunder free us
And folish notion.

The advent of videotape now makes it possible "To see ourselves as ithers see us." It takes courage, but it can be done in private, and reviewing videotapes of one or two of your lectures offers a powerful tool for self-study and self-evaluation. Many of us have unconscious annoying or distracting personal mannerisms that even our best friends, let alone semidependent students, are reluctant to tell us about. Often, they have to be seen to be believed—and corrected. Chapter 17 covers videotaping in more detail.

CONCLUSIONS

Good lecturing, far from being an artistic talent with which people are born, is a skill which can be developed and improved with thoughtful consideration and practice.

If we may be permitted one final example from the world of baseball, consider the case of George Shuba, an outfielder from the Brooklyn Dodgers in the early 1950s, who Roger Kahn (1972, p. 224) notes was called "The Shotgun" because of his ability to spray line drives to all fields "with a swing so compact and so fluid that it appeared as natural as a smile." In compiling his wonderful book *The Boys of Summer*, Kahn visited Shuba at his home some years after his retirement from baseball and had occasion to comment on his "natural" swing. Shuba, then in his basement, reached up to a beam in the ceiling and lowered a rope with a clump of knots that hung waist high. Then he showed Kahn a bat which had been drilled and filled with lead, and went to a file and pulled out a whole ream of charts marked with X's. Kahn notes:

"In the winters," he said, "for fifteen years after loading potatoes or anything else, even when I was in the majors, I'd swing at the clump six hundred times. Every night, after sixty I'd make an X. Ten X's and I had my six hundred swings. Then I could go to bed. You call that natural? I swung a 44 ounce bat 600 times a night, 4,200 times a week, 47,200 swings every winter. Wrists. The fast ball's by you. You gotta wrist it out. Forty-seven thousand two hundred times."

Fortunately, it doesn't take this much practice to become a "natural" lecturer.

NOTES

*This chapter draws on Chapter 5 of the *Resource Manual for Teacher Training Programs in Economics*, edited by Phillip Saunders, Arthur L. Welsh, and W. Lee Hansen, (New York: Joint Council on Economic Education, 1978).

1   Angell (1972, pp. 308-310) notes: "At first, it is a game of recollections, recapturing, and visions. Figures and occasions return, enormous sounds rise and swell, and the interior stadium fills with light. . . . Any fan, as I say, can play this private game, extending it to extraordinary varieties and possibilities in his mind. Ruth bats against Sandy Koufax . . . Hubbell pitches to Ted Williams. . . . By thinking about baseball like this—by playing it

over, keeping it warm in a cold season—we begin to make discoveries. With luck, we may even penetrate some of its mysteries."

2 Peter Frederick (1986) suggests several ways in which the degree of student-faculty interaction can be increased in lecture situations.

3 One of our favorite ploys on the topic of the price elasticity of demand is to project a picture of farmers dumping milk from a truck or Brazilian coffee fields burning and ask, "why would they do this?" When students say, "to drive up the price," we ask, "But won't they have less to sell at the higher price?" "What good is a high price if you don't have anything to sell?" Thus, we are off and running.

4 McKeachie (1980, p. 29) notes: "Studies of the attention of students during lectures find that, typically, attention increases from the beginning of the lecture to ten minutes into the lecture and decreases after that point. One evidence of this was that after the lecture students recalled 70 percent of the material covered in the first ten minutes, and only 20 percent of the material covered in the last 10 minutes."

   If attention starts to wane after ten minutes, pause and ask questions or, as indicated above, "break" the lecture with some activity so that when you start again it seems like the first ten minutes of a new lecture.

5 Ivor Davies (1981, p. 152) has noted: "Albert Mehrabian has estimated that only about 7 percent of the emotional impact of a person's message comes from words. Vocal elements contribute something like 38 percent of the message. Facial expressions, on the other hand, contribute 55 percent. Thus, nonverbal communication is an important part of instructional technique."

6 Patricia Andrews (1989, p. 4) has noted: "Research has shown that if an instructor asks a question and then counts to 10 (slowly and silently) he is likely to elicit some student response. One study showed that the number of student responses increased by 80% when instructors used this technique."

7 A questionnaire form developed to evaluate lectures at London University is reproduced in Beard (1970, p. 110-111). One thing we like about the London form is that it solicits the students' perceptions of some of the "mundane" factors such as light, visibility, and temperature mentioned above, and it also obtains information on the students' own condition in terms of fatigue and hunger. Not all the problems in maintaining interest or attention are the instructor's fault, and if it turns out that a large number of students are always tired or hungry at the time your class meets, you want to be aware of this problem and try to deal with it, perhaps by allowing students to bring snacks or by trying to schedule your class at a different hour in the next semester.

REFERENCES

Andrews, Patricia H., "Improving Lecturing Skills: Some Insights from Speech Communications," *Teaching and Learning At Indiana University*, February, 1989.

Angell, Roger, *The Summer Game.* New York: Poplar Library, 1972.

Beard, Ruth, *Teaching and Learning in Higher Education.* Baltimore: Penguin Books, 1970.

Bergman, David, "In Defense of Lecturing," *Association of Departments of English (ADE) Bulletin*, Winter, 1983, *76*, pp. 49-51.

Bligh, Donald A., *What's the Use of Lecturers.* London: University Teaching Methods Unit, 1971.

Frederick, Peter J., "The Lively Lecture—8 Variations," *College Teaching*, 1986, *34*, (2), pp. 43-50.

Davies, Ivor K., *Instructional Technique.* New York: McGraw-Hill, 1981.

Day, Ruth S., "Teaching from Notes: Some Cognitive Consequences," in McKeachie, W.J., (ed.) *Learning, Cognition, and College Teaching: New Directions for Teaching and Learning.* No. 2, San Francisco: Jossey-Bass, 1980, pp. 95-112.

Hawkins, Susan, Ivor Davies, and Kenneth Majer, *Getting Started.* Bloomington, Indiana: Mimeographed guide for beginning Instructors at Indiana University, 1973.

Kahn, Roger, *The Boys of Summer.* New York: Harper and Row, 1972.

Kaplan, Robert M., and Gregory C. Pascoe, "Humorous Lectures and Humorous Examples: Some Effects Upon Comprehension and Retention," *Journal of Educational Psychology,* 1977, *69*, 6, 1-65.

McKeachie, Wilbert J., "Improving Lectures by Understanding Students' Information Processing," in W. J. McKeachie (ed.) *Learning, Cognition, and College Teaching: New Directions for Teaching and Learning,* 2. San Francisco: Jossey-Bass, 1980, 95-112.

————, *Teaching Tips: A Guidebook for the Beginning College Teacher,* Eighth Edition. Lexington, Massachusetts: D.C. Heath, 1986.

APPENDIX 10-1

CLASSROOM OBSERVER CHECKLIST

Make written comments under any item that is particularly strong or particularly weak, and try to identify the one strongest and the one weakest aspect of the lecture presentation.

Overall Classroom Atmosphere

_____ 1 Instructor appears enthusiastic.

_____ 2 Students appear alert and attentive.

Organization

_____ 3 Initial outline of content clearly stated.

_____ 4 Initial statement of why this content is important for students to understand.

_____ 5 Main points organized in logical sequence.

_____ 6 Use of examples and elaboration to emphasize and clarify main points.

_____ 7 Clarity of transition between main points.

_____ 8 Effectiveness of summaries of main points.

Presentation

_____ 9 Speaks audibly and understandably.

_____ 10 Makes effective use of voice inflection.

_____ 11 Maintains eye contact with students.

_____ 12 Makes effective use of blackboard or overhead projector.

_____ **13** Makes effective use of nonverbal behavior.

_____ **14** Allows adequate time for students to think and organize material presented.

_____ **15** Provides adequate time for student questions and responses.

_____ **16** Responds to students' questions in a helpful manner.

_____ **17** Has no distracting mannerisms.

CHAPTER 11

STUDENT WRITING AS A GUIDE TO STUDENT THINKING

Jerry L. Petr

Maybe...it's time to redefine the 'three R's'—they should be reading, 'riting and reasoning. Together they add up to learning. It's by writing about a subject we're trying to learn that we reason our way to what it means.

Zinsser, 1988, p. 22

INTRODUCTION

This chapter is grounded on the knowledge that there is a close relationship between writing and thinking. Clear writing reflects clear thinking. Because one of our goals in teaching economics is precisely student "clear thinking" about our subject, this chapter addresses the use of writing to attain that goal.

Resting on that foundation, this chapter is built upon several related corollary ideas. First, writing in a college classroom, although most frequently seen as an evaluation tool in the form of essay tests, term papers and the like, should be recast as a learning-facilitator. A major theme of the vigorous contemporary "writing across the curriculum" movement is that the first purpose of student writing is to *create* learning, rather than to evaluate it. Viewing writing as a productive learning tool, rather than primarily as a grading aid, permits a refreshing reconsideration of types and timing of useful writing activities.[1]

Second, the concept of writing to learn clearly emphasizes enhanced cognitive functions as a writing outcome, placing higher priority on an instructor's contribution to a student's thinking than on that instructor's more technical editorial skills. To most economics professors this is a liberating notion as it allows them to focus on understanding and expression rather than on spelling and grammar. And it is certainly a more efficient notion as it maximizes time spent on areas in which we have a comparative advantage.

Third, as we consider writing in its more traditional role as an instrument of "evaluation," we should be quick to ask "evaluation of what?" It is, or should be, much more than evaluation of student knowledge of subject matter, although that is a valid and valuable objective. But writing can be even more effectively used for evaluation of the mental processes by which the student generates and manipulates economic ideas. Used in that way, it becomes a diagnostic tool in the hands of a skilled professor, who can then try to direct those processes more toward coherence with what we call "the economic way of thinking."

A fourth premise that undergirds this chapter is the potential for writing to serve the function of student "self-evaluation" of economic understanding. William Zinsser (1988) asserts "We write to find out what we know. . . ." If that is true, and I share Zinsser's conviction on that point, writing is a direct and immediate way for the serious student to assess his/her progress in our discipline. In many cases, "I don't know what to write," really means "I don't know what I think." As a student recognizes that fact, opportunities for learning to take place may be created. Too often we educators slip into the habit of mind which views determination of grades as the primary function of evaluation. It is not. The primary function of evaluation is assessment of student learning. And who better to be immersed in that assessment process than the student him/herself?

Such assessment activities likewise add a facet to our understanding of the "revision" process in writing. If we insist that what is being revised is student understanding of the concepts of our discipline, revision is a much more enriching process for student and teacher than if revision is only a mechanism for editorial corrections. "Writing to learn" is not the same thing as "writing to publish." The first wants the process of cognitive growth; the second wants the polish of product perfection.

A fifth virtue of classroom writing is its requirement that students actively participate in the learning process. Educators may not agree on the many particulars of pedagogical tactics, but few can be found who would deny the superiority of "active" over "passive" learning modes. ("Passive learning" may even be an oxymoron, like "lucid economist.") To write is to engage one's mental talents with the task at hand. Such active engagement leads to the construction of knowledge—to learning.

Finally, while the previous points have been focussed on the merits of "writing to learn," the corollary activity, "learning to write" is a beneficial by-product. While economic knowledge is a wonderful thing, particularly to its purveyors, it is considerably devalued if not accompanied by the ability to communicate. Because effective writing depends upon having something to write about, by providing a subject matter and a motivation for writing we, as economic educators, may have better opportunity to contribute to student writing skills than the professors of English composition.

This chapter, then, is designed to present some ideas (and to stimulate others) about using a variety of forms of writing to initiate, facilitate and evaluate student learning in economics. We will consider briefly the most common classroom writing form, the essay exam, but we will also discuss other opportunities for students to explore their ideas by presenting and examining them on paper. Economic writing may include notetaking, journals, in-class commentaries, news analyses, essays, research papers, data interpretations, lecture summaries, poetry, and more. It can be beneficial whether graded or not, or even whether seen by the professor or not. Students of economics can write to query, to clarify, to explore, to understand, and to learn. In the process, not only their economics but their writing will benefit.

WRITING TO LEARN

Fundamentally, any teaching strategy or method rests upon an epistemology, explicit or implicit. Our assumptions, beliefs and understandings about learning and the learning process must, at least subconsciously, shape our classroom activities.

I like Zinsser's description of learning, quoted at the beginning of this chapter, because it is consistent with my epistemological ideas. It emphasizes learning as an action, a process, and not as the accumulation of information. To learn is to build.

What is built is an always changeable notion of the way the world works. How it is built is through repeated, progressively more thorough engagement by the learner with that world, its events, its ideas, its people, its diversity, its challenges. Knowledge is not built, I think, through absorption, adhesion, or osmosis. Writing is one method of accomplishing the requisite interaction of student with world.[2]

And—as our English department colleagues have been trying to tell us for years—because "writing is a form of thinking," (Zinsser, 1988, p. viii) to write economics requires the ability to "think economics." Good writing is, to some extent, discipline-specific, relying on a unique blend of vocabulary, concept, method, precedent and history, typifying that discipline and reflecting its thought-patterns (its metaphors, if you will). That may be especially true in economics, where, for decades, our textbook writers have emphasized precisely that "economics is a way of thinking." For that reason, a generalized freshman course in "English composition" does not automatically create competent writers of economics; conversely, developing competent writers of economics in our classrooms will lead to more competent economics being done there.

Asking our students visibly to reason their way into our discipline via written exercises obviously allows us one means of evaluating how well they're doing. But the "doing" we are able to focus on here is the reasoning process itself, the footprints of the mind at work, rather than the final product of learning, the answer, which is conventionally the subject of our evaluation.

Surely every educator has painfully sharp experiences of the adage "there's many a slip 'twixt cup and lip" as s/he recalls the mystifying and discouraging differences between the pearls of wisdom placed before the student on one day and the shards of shattered glass the student offers back on the test short days later. Where have they (or we, depending on your generosity) failed?

Evaluating student writing allows us to answer precisely that question. By tracking that errant mind through the thickets of misunderstood concepts, misapplied jargon and faulty relationships, we can locate the misapprehension and retrieve the misdirected thought. The evidence, provided by student writing, of how and why my carefully prepared instruction comes unravelled as it passes through their thought processes is my single greatest asset as I seek to improve student learning. The "aha" experience occurs regularly as I trail the student intellect into the quagmire and follow the footprints to the edge of the quicksand. Prior to the next learning adventure, I can place a warning sign or guidepost at each such trouble spot.

Writing, therefore, is a both a means to learning and a diagnostic tool for assessment of strengths and weaknesses in the teaching-learning process. To accomplish each of those ends, writing tasks can be varied in form and in audience. In one form or other, then, writing is a valuable component in any economics course.

TYPES OF CLASSROOM WRITING

Many different educational objectives can be achieved through diverse types of writing assignments. Several of these will be discussed in the paragraphs that follow. Let's work from the more imaginative to the more traditional, starting with interesting processes of student-faculty written dialogue and then moving through a variety of less or more familiar writing assignments.

Economic Issues Notebooks

One of the most successful writing exercises I've used works on several levels of writing and thinking—and, as a by-product, produces a wealth of raw material for yet additional writing activity. The project involves student preparation of an annotated economic issues notebook or journal. Throughout the academic term the student is required to maintain a notebook of news clippings relevant to a topic the student has selected at the beginning of the term. In a macro-principles course, topics have included inflation, unemployment, budget deficit, trade deficit, and more.

One level and form of student writing generated by this project results from the requirement that each clipping be "annotated" with the comments of the student. Annotations are not to be summaries of the clippings, but rather are to be the students' intellectual interaction with the news and opinions they contain. Annotations can express bewilderment, reinforcement, extensions, comparisons with other news items or with class or textbook interpretations, or may raise questions for further discussion. In each case they require some active student mental involvement with economic ideas, and in all cases they again provide, for the instructor, a window on the student mind.

Thus, as I thumb through student notebooks, I see students concentrating on the impact of extended unemployment benefits on the well-being of distressed families and can ask them also to consider the macroeconomic consequences on aggregate demand. Or relating to another student who uses her notebook to report politicians' claims of inability to deal with the budget deficit, I can ask her to go one additional step with the question, "Why?"

The accumulated annotations need not, and probably should not, be "graded." Better used, they initiate dialogues between students and instructor. When using the issues notebook as part of my class, I accept the responsibility of maintaining my part of the dialogue by responding in writing, briefly, to annotations made by each student. I try to alleviate the bewilderment, acknowledge the reinforcement, evaluate the extensions, react to the comparisons, and answer the questions. In other words, each student and I have a unique written "conversation" about the economic material at hand.

It is important that the clippings accumulate at a rate sufficient to maintain the student's involvement and interest, and that the notebook be reviewed by the instructor frequently enough to sustain an effective dialogue. I have found that requiring the student to obtain at least three clippings per week, and requiring myself to collect and respond to each student's notebook once every three or four weeks, works well. (And "work" it is.) It obviously is important *not* to collect and hold student notebooks for lengthy periods of time; I therefore stagger the collection and review activity so that I nearly always have a few notebooks for a day or two, but never have the entire set weighting down my desk and my conscience.

As the notebook grows during the course, it becomes the informal raw material from which a more structured and organized writing product can grow. Therefore a natural conclusion to the project is student preparation of a summary paper on the selected topic which gathers and presents the student learning, as reflected in the notebook, in a concise document. Not only does the student use the annotated notebook as raw material for this final paper, but the student is also able to see and recognize the pattern of growth of his/her understanding as the term has evolved. What had been rather concrete lamentation about the impact of job loss on family well-being has become more analytical awareness of economy-wide repercussions of unemployment, or unemployment compensation. Unreflective hand-wringing at the horror of deficit spending becomes modestly reflective consideration of trade-offs involved in deficit reduction. The activity generates a tangible written product, but, more importantly, it enhances the student's sense of intellectual growth and accomplishment.

The most surprising, and rewarding, aspect of this annotated notebook project is the approval with which it is greeted by students. I introduced this activity into my classroom believing that it had great potential for contributing to learning, and greater potential for generating student hostility. I was right on the first count and wrong on the second. It requires more student work, it places increased demands on student time, but apparently the sense of learning which it provides outweighs those costs and leads to overwhelming student support. Can we reach the rash conclusion that students do desire to learn and will accept the associated costs? What we often view as student laziness or hostility may be sensible resistance to costs which are unaccompanied by learning. The notebook project seems to give them a sense of *quid pro quo*.

Obviously, as we discuss student preparation of a significant paper as a possible outcome of the annotated notebook project, we have entered the realm of paper-writing as a component of "writing to learn."

Student Papers

Like most of us who use student writing as a component of our pedagogical tool-kit, for many years I created writing assignments that mirrored the writing assignments I was asked to do in my own student days. "Term papers," 20 pages or so in length, requiring library "research" for completion, were the typical expectation. The growth of a significant mail-order industry which provides such papers to our students indicates I was not alone in those term paper assignments. It also is a clue to the utility of those assignments in reaching our educational objectives. The small percent of students who retrieve their term papers, if alternative ways to obtain grades are available, is further indication of the low value such papers, and our responses to them, have for the students.

Regrettably, I continued to make those assignments despite my introspective acknowledgement that they did little for me as a student and despite my awareness that they seemed to produce little for my students beyond one or two sleepless nights as the "due date" drew near. In general, the students hated writing them and I hated reading them—our hatreds perhaps mutually originating in our shared tacit understanding of the futility of the task—the costs unaccompanied by learning.

However, if we transfer our focus from the desired "product"—a term paper with its accumulation of relevant information and analysis—to a preferred "process" of student engagement with and reflection upon the substance of our discipline, alternative writing assignments appear more attractive. In my classes, a series of essays that require frequent student confrontation with their own economic understanding and analytical ability have replaced the term paper.

These essays repeatedly ask the student to review, reorganize and reassess important ideas and concepts in order to enhance analytical ability rather than research skills. Such an essay might, for example, request an application of the "comparative advantage" concept to discussion of a trade bill before Congress. Or a different essay assignment might ask for student evaluation of the impact of a defense "build-down" on U.S. macroeconomic well-being. In an upper-level comparative systems course, my students are frequently asked to use substantial data sets to evaluate "The United States as a Representative Mixed Economy" or to assess the "convergence theory" of capitalist and socialist homogenization.

My aim, in substituting these essay assignments for term papers, is to foster writing, and thinking, which is more frequent, more immediate, more closely related to classroom activity, and more productive in generating classroom interaction. It is also closer to real-world encounters with economics for those relying primarily on a Principles course. It has been a successful substitution on all counts.

Problem Sets and Data Interpretation

I include discussion of problem sets and data interpretation in this chapter because such tasks may present interesting puzzles about which students can write. They can be yet one more source of intellectual footprints thereby giving them value beyond their obvious contribution to quantitative economic analysis or mastery of model manipulation.

Traditional problem sets clearly have value as checks on student mastery of economic models and utilization of concepts with quantitative dimensions. Problem solving requires active student interaction with our subject matter, an additional benefit. And, of course, students can be asked to write about the significance of the problem, or its solution, or the method by which its solution is to be sought, which may promote or tap the most useful learning of all. From my perspective, doing is better than not doing, where learning is at stake, so I advocate using problem assignments. Worded more elegantly, as my colleague Campbell McConnell reminds me, is proverbial language which notes: "I hear and I forget; I see and I remember; I do and I understand."

Traditional problem sets, however, such as those which appear in study guides or end-of-chapter assignments, useful though they may be for the purposes mentioned above, are perceived by student and teacher alike as artificial and "make-believe." Experienced educators recognize that students have no trouble separating the game of academic "let's pretend" from the real world of their interests and activities in ways which effectively erase the classroom material from their consciousness.

Therefore, I am more intrigued by the implications and possibilities involved in a somewhat different use of data and data manipulation for the purposes of learning economics and evaluating that learning. Suppose we assume, as I have for two decades, that a major purpose of an introductory economics class is to foster "economic literacy." Suppose further that we define "economic literacy" to mean comprehension of day-to-day journalistic presentation of business and economic information. What happens if we ask our students to "explain" a chart, graph, table or diagram from the front page of a daily newspaper, a copy of a corporate report, or the latest edition of the *Economic Report of the President*?

I can answer that question confidently, because I have performed the exercise over and over again. The answer, over and over again, is that many students exhibit a discouraging amount of functional illiteracy in data interpretation. The charts and tables in texts are ignored, the data displays and graphs in periodicals are slipped over because our students don't know what to make of them. As instructors, we overlook that illiteracy because the prose in the text tells the student what the table shows (provides an interpretation). But ask the student to provide the explanation for a data display for which the accompanying interpretation is lacking, and the results are stunning. Many (most?) students cannot draw useful inferences by correctly integrating title, headings, data, footnotes and structure of the display into a meaningful statement.

Ignorance revealed is opportunity presented. If learning takes place through interaction of student with environment, we can place students in circumstances where data interpretation is necessary for success. Asking students to write about data taken from current and significant source materials is one avenue toward achieving an interpretive literacy which, I'm afraid, most of us have simply, and wrongly, taken for granted.

My response has been to include data interpretation as a significant aspect of at least one-half of the assigned course activities. In a typical course, one out of three semester essay assignments will have a data focus. "Using selected tables (which I specify) from the 'Government Finance' section of Appendix B of the *Economic Report of the President*, write an essay comparing the taxing and spending activity of the federal government with the taxing and spending activity of state and local governments." Two out of three exams will contain tables from the text, or other relevant sources, which illustrate key points of our study. In those cases, I am normally satisfied if the student can correctly explain the contents of the table. (A simplified version of a balance of payments following a unit on international economics is sufficient challenge for most students. What a boost for economic literacy if they can successfully read such a document!)

My attempt to involve students with "real" rather than "make-believe" economics echoes suggestions made by Lee Hansen. He argues, persuasively, that students need to read more "real" economics and less "textbook" economics because it is "real" books that "reveal economists doing what economists do" (Hansen, 1988, p. 272). Likewise, I want students to wrestle with "real" problems that are daily newspaper headlines, rather than "pretend" problems that have no significance beyond the door of the classroom.

Data interpretation is one aspect of our educational task in which we can reinforce the notion that learning can be a collective activity. To ask small groups of students to solve data arrays cooperatively is to encourage students to learn from one another and actively to build on knowledge already existing in the classroom. Group endeavors and group reports (written) achieve many of the learning objectives we share while allowing student interaction and exploration to take the place of some of the unidirectional communication that normally fills our classrooms. And, as one of my English department colleagues observes, it also dignifies and encourages the most regular form of informal learning in which we participate.

A somewhat more sophisticated use of data interpretation as a learning activity is to request students to affirm or refute an argument or position through the use of a table, or chart or graph which is provided for them. (Almost any supposedly empirically based political assertion will serve very well.) Such a request may require students to consider aspects of the information or interpretation which are more subtle or complex than they might voluntarily explore by presenting their own analysis. You may be amazed to discover, as I was, that students are often willing to affirm almost any marginally plausible inference supplied for a data array.

Students have, in rather large numbers, been willing to use comparison of 1980 data with 1970 data to illustrate the impact of the Reagan administration on the role of government in the U.S. When asked to make international comparisons of countries' expenditures on health care, they are typically willing to ignore definitional distinctions between public or government spending and total (public plus private) spending from one economy to another. "Millions" and "billions" become interchangeable. Per capita and aggregate data are indiscriminately compared. Critical distinctions are not overabundant in our students' intellectual tool kit. They may become more abundant if they are more frequently needed.

Student writing about data is some of the most productive raw material which educators can obtain. By observing the visible grappling, on paper, of the student mind with quantitative information, we, as teachers, can learn amazing amounts about student assumptions, powers of observation, ability to relate concepts, fundamental grounding in basic mathematical principles and more. Armed with such knowledge, we are much better prepared to aim our educational fire at the most appropriate targets. I believe you'll find that we've been overshooting.

Cartoon Analysis

Although political/economic cartooning (editorial page variety) seems related to data arrays only to the extent that both are visual representations of information or ideas, I think there is a more fundamental tie which merits a brief discussion of cartoon analysis in this portion of this chapter. Drawing appropriate inferences from data, and discerning figurative insight from a fanciful cartoon, both require high-level cognitive skills. For me, the two tasks are closely related because asking students to perform them and to write about that performance has revealed closely related problems and has provided similar insights into student learning difficulties in our discipline. I also group the activities together because interpreting charts, graphs, and tables and interpreting political/economic cartoon messages are both skills requisite to the economic literacy we seek as an educational objective.

Asking students to interpret economically targeted editorial cartoons, like asking them to interpret media-presented data displays, often reveals shockingly concrete (mis)understandings of subtly witty allusions intended by the cartoonists. One reviewer of an early draft of this chapter observes that both cartoon and display interpretation "assumes symbol literacy in the special dialects of economics." The fact that political cartooning is frequently metaphorical or representational seems lost on many students who struggle to understand at the literal or concrete level, or who don't possess the requisite "symbol literacy." On the one hand, I've come to feel sorry for the cartoonists' profession whose work so regularly goes unappreciated; on the other hand, I see these revealed misunderstandings as fertile raw material with which we should be able to craft helpful learning experiences. The "bottom line" is that it is difficult to understand or appreciate any of these by-ways of the student mind unless one asks students to map them for us via their written reactions to a variety of intellectual stimuli.

Essay Exams

For the most part, the writing activities discussed to this point are primarily learning activities and only secondarily evaluation activities. They do, as we have emphasized, facilitate self-evaluation by the student; and they most emphatically are of diagnostic help to the instructor.

But when we look at writing activities in which the emphasis most clearly shifts over to the evaluative function, our eyes must finally fall upon the essay exam. The essay question or the essay exam is unquestionably the most common use of writing for evaluation purposes. Since the construction and grading of essay examinations is discussed in detail in Chapter 16 below, I will simply emphasize the point that exams serve pedagogical as well as evaluative purposes. Our exams should not simply assess content mastery. They should also attempt to promote learning by encouraging reflection, integration, synthesis, and by creating yet one more building block in the edifice of the course.

Essay questions are best used to assess and develop more sophisticated cognitive skills (application, synthesis, evaluation) rather than simple recall or association. An essay question that asks students to evaluate the consequences of alternative fiscal policy proposals of Democratic and Republican politicians is more likely to promote learning and reveal understanding than an essay question that asks students to define and explain Federal Reserve monetary policy tools. Likewise, an essay question which requires student analytical thinking certainly provides more interesting intellectual tracks for the instructor to follow than one which only reveals memory. And it is the existence of those intellectual tracks which provides the most significant benefit of essay questions over multiple-choice questions.

Essay exams, paper writing, problem solving, notebook preparation provide varied opportunities for student writing. These types of writing activities include those most often used in economics courses. But they do not exhaust the list of productive writing exercises which can promote learning economics.[3]

Other Writing Activities

Most of the discussion to this point involves out-of-class writing (with the exception of essay exams). But other in-class writing exercises provide much less stressful learning experiences. Such activities need not be long and they need not be graded.

It can be useful, for example, to ask students to write for one another—the instructor need not always be the audience—as they work through the understanding and implications of an economic concept. Each student can be asked to devote five minutes of class time to writing a paragraph explaining or applying a specific economic concept under discussion. Then, allowing small groups (four or five students) to distill from their collected paragraphs a single preferred explanation can lead to highly constructive learning activity. While each group's final product may not have the polish and subtlety of a professor's well-honed lecture notes on the same topic, the student work has the advantage of direct involvement and internalization. May we not assume that more learning takes place as student "A" and student "C" compare their interpretative paragraphs than when their colleague, student "B," transfers the professor's lecture into sketchy notes?

Another form of in-class writing that I believe has particular pedagogical merit is student preparation of "summaries." These can either be summaries of reading assignments the students are to have completed, or, more revealingly, summaries of a class session which is drawing to a close. For the instructor receiving immediate reaction to a lecture-discussion session in the form of student capsulation of their perception of what it was all about, summaries can be wonderfully helpful indicators of teaching effectiveness. Why wait until the periodic hour exams to find out how woefully misinterpreted your instruction has been? Finding out the same thing earlier and regularly allows more immediate and effective corrective steps to be taken. And then have the students summarize the corrective steps.

Of course when the summarization focuses on what has taken place in the immediately preceding class time, it will rely upon the most common form of in-class writing, student notetaking. Education research has consistently shown notetaking to be a positive component of the education experience (Carrier, 1983) but, among economic educators, it is surely one of the most neglected variables of effective learning. If it is true that students can "write to learn," presumably we can usefully pay some attention to the writing they do daily, in their notes.

Deliberate involvement of the instructor with student notes and notetaking skills can pay dividends for both teacher and learner. Notetaking incorporates some degree of active student involvement with our subject matter. If, with help, students can regularly move beyond simply using notetaking as a "recording" activity and instead use it as a "processing" activity, it becomes increasingly valuable. Such "processing" could involve *relating* a lecture idea to prior class or text material, *questioning* the meaning or applicability of a lecture concept, or *suggesting* a follow-up line of investigation, for example.

But even when notetaking serves only the recording purpose, it can be an opportunity for strengthening specific student skills. One of the inadequately developed student skills is the ability to discern the "big idea," to tap the "key concept," to separate major points from minor filler. An instructor who occasionally examines student notebooks, or thumbs through textbooks which have been "highlighted" by students, will quickly encounter this inadequacy. Deliberately planning brief activities which improve those notetaking skills may pay significant learning dividends.

Simply interrupting a normal lecture session after the first twenty minutes to discuss what a "good" set of notes on those twenty minutes should contain would make a significant contribution to most students. Asking them to share and discuss their notes with each other will allow them to learn from their peers. Brief class discussion of why specific elements are included and others are excluded will generate notetaking patterns which can be replicated. And providing an instructor-prepared set of notes on that twenty-minute segment (fairly representing the amount and sophistication of notes which could have been taken by an astute student) will show a student what developing such a skill can add to his/her educational benefits.

Of course the various forms of writing activities discussed in these pages often can be combined in educationally useful ways. As is indicated above, a paper requiring analysis of a significant body of economic data is frequently included in the series of short paper assignments I ask of students in any class. Essay examination questions can incorporate thought-provoking elements from other class writing assignments. (For example, after asking students to write a short paper on the trade-offs involved in various deficit-reduction plans, I would consider following up with an exam question which required students to offer macroeconomic policy advice to an incoming President.) The primary objective is to provide opportunities for students to grapple with the subject matter in ways which cause them to expand their understanding and to provide, to their instructors, evidence of how well that is happening.

The creation of writing assignments which involve students intellectually, generate learning opportunities, and provide insight on student progress is limited only by faculty imagination. And, in some cases, perhaps it's true that "the more imaginative, the better."

Consider a playful, and effective, writing assignment used by a faculty colleague of mine who, probably not coincidentally, is a wonderful writer.[4] A biologist who is also committed to the concept of writing to learn, he requires each of his many students to submit 40 lines of original poetry about a biological organism of their choice. This becomes writing the students want to do, that requires them to learn something about the organism, that sends them to appropriate source material, and that stimulates their expressive imagination. What more could we as educators want?

Writing poetry as a method of learning economics? Try it. Or better yet, develop your own equally creative collection of assignments which target the same objectives. Writing is an immensely flexible activity which can assist us in seemingly limitless ways.

CONCLUSION

Writing facilitates learning, and vice versa.

More specifically, this chapter has argued that active student involvement in the processing of ideas is an essential element of learning, in economics as in any other academic area. Further, a written record of that idea-processing is crucial to instructor assessment of what is happening in the students' minds as a result of classroom instruction. Such assessment should go beyond *what* the student thinks is correct to *why* the student comes to that conclusion. A variety of carefully considered writing forms and assignments can contribute to the teaching process, the learning process and the assessment process, thereby better grounding the entire educational endeavor.

As the economics educator considers the use of writing in his/her teaching activities, the following appear to be salient points for consideration and reflection.

1 Learning occurs as student minds interact with our subject matter and thereby construct meaning and understanding. Listening is not learning. Writing is one possible method of generating the desired student intellectual engagement.

2 Writing allows each of us to find out what we know. The plaintive student lament, "I knew the answer, but I just couldn't write it down," is false. If we know it, we can write it; if we can write it, we know it. Even more amazingly, we are often surprised, after writing it down, that we know as much as we do. All this is true of students, as of ourselves.

3 More important, I think, than showing us what students know, writing shows us why they think they know it. Student writing reveals student thought-processing and provides a "snapshot" of that process. Such a snapshot allows processes to be compared, and defended, and amended. It is immeasurably more helpful to a classroom instructor to know *why* students are misunderstanding our discipline rather than simply once again to find out that they are.

4 Although writing as an evaluation tool is a common educational notion, we too often ignore the self-assessment dimension of the writing process. It is not only the instructor who benefits from the diagnostic insights offered by student writing. The student him/herself often arrives at even more helpful insights and understandings via the process of organizing and explicating latent notions.

5 Multiple and creative types of writing can each contribute variously to a learning environment. Annotated issues notebooks, economic journals, in-class writing, concept paragraphs, summaries of class activities, poetry writing are but a few of the possible written forms which can contribute to learning. Many of these forms of writing can serve their purpose without being read and evaluated by the instructor.

6 Assignment of frequent, short, analytical essays which require reflection on the applications and implications of class material are typically more effective learning-generators than are the commonly assigned "research" or term papers. They are so primarily as a result of the regularized student interaction with subject matter which they require. Such repeated interchange allows (perhaps requires) the growth and refinement of ideas and the continually closer approximation of ihe language and thought, the dialect, of our discipline. Term papers, with their "one shot" constraint, offer no such growth dimension.

7 An overlooked area of student economic illiteracy is inability to interpret and analyze data presentations with precision and accuracy. Such illiteracy can be reduced by using writing assignments which require and develop those interpretive skills. Again, the student writing reveals the problem areas and allows instructional assistance to be applied efficiently.

8 If developed carefully, essay examinations can be one effective aid in the assessment of student understanding. To help with that process, essay questions should probe high-level cognitive skills and should require careful explication of thought.

9 Writing to learn in the college classroom fosters instructor awareness of student individuality and enhances student ownership of the educational process. Being reminded of student individuality improves our educational function as we respond more directly to the diverse needs and problems reflected in our students. Student ownership of learning removes the teacher or the text from the center of the educational process and puts the student there instead. The student whose individual educational needs are being addressed, and who accepts his/her role as active agent in the academic environment, is much more likely to attain academic success.

10 Writing activities, although often individual, can also be used to stimulate group interaction which leads to formation of shared understandings, focus discussion, generate stronger arguments, encourage revision, and lead to new and sharper reexaminations of material and concepts.

11 Finally, writing to learn also contributes to learning to write. Good writing is mostly about the cogent presentation of ideas. The processes and activities discussed in this chapter produce that cogency about economics, which enhances the students' ability to communicate in our subject matter. Once the substance is present, the editorial aspects of spelling, grammar, and other technical details can be addressed as needed. But that's another chapter.

All in all, then, "writing to learn" can be a significant part of a successful economics classroom. "Writing across the curriculum" is an important pedagogical emphasis, as vital to our segment of the curriculum as it is to any other. Economic educators who increase their awareness of developments in this currently energized educational area should find that enhanced student interaction with material, and improved instructor diagnostic ability combine to increase instructional effectiveness and student satisfaction dramatically.

NOTES

1 Chapter 16 below focuses on the topics of constructing and grading essay exams.
2 These points are also made with power and clarity in Knoblauch and Brannon (1983).
3 Crowe and Youga (1986) offer a good discussion of a number of writing alternatives.
4 I refer to John Janovy, author of many and varied works including the highly acclaimed naturalist essays in *Keith County Journal*, New York: St. Martin's Press, 1978.

REFERENCES

Carrier, Carol A., "Notetaking Research: Implications for the Classroom," *Journal of Instructional Development*, 1983, *6*, 19-25.

Crowe, Douglas, and Janet Youga, "Using Writing as a Tool for Learning Economics," *The Journal of Economic Education*, Summer 1986, *17*, 218-222.

Hansen, W. Lee, "'Real' Books and Textbooks," *The Journal of Economic Education*, Summer, 1988, *19*, 271-274.

Janovy, John, *Keith County Journal*, New York: St. Martin's Press, 1978.

Knoblauch, C. H., and Lil Brannon, "Writing as Learning Through the Curriculum," *College English*, Sept. 1983, *45*, 465-474.

Zinsser, William, *Writing to Learn*, New York: Harper & Row, 1988.

CHAPTER 12

THE PRINCIPLES OF ECONOMICS TEXTBOOK: HISTORY AND CONTENT

William B. Walstad
Michael Watts

The principles of economics textbook is a major, and in many cases, the only source of information for students taking their introductory courses in the discipline. Today, a wide range of ancillary materials for the textbooks reinforces its influence over the character of the course. Test banks are used to create exams and extensive instructor's manuals provide classroom ideas for presenting the text content. Study guides take students through out-of-class reviews of the course material. Computer programs demonstrate and animate graphical analysis, review basic concepts and sometimes simulate "the real world." Despite this pervasive influence, few new instructors know much about the history of principles textbooks, the market forces that shape current textbooks or, in a comparative sense, the specific content of many different textbooks. This chapter offers insights into each of these areas.

The tradition of textbook writing is a long one in the economics profession, perhaps beginning with *The Wealth of Nations*. This history is briefly described in the first section of the chapter. The next two sections describe the structure of the textbook market and several specific complaints frequently aimed at the current textbooks. The final two sections of the chapter examine the content of seven leading textbooks. This content analysis shows how the text material is allocated across major concept clusters—fundamental, microeconomic, macroeconomic, and international—and subcategories under each cluster. The chapter ends with a description of a "consensus" text, which provides a kind of benchmark for reviewing both the content and pedagogical features of other leading principles textbooks.

A SHORT HISTORY OF PRINCIPLES TEXTBOOKS

As Paul Samuelson notes in his foreword to this volume, there is a long tradition of textbook writing in the economics profession that has attracted the interest and efforts of many different kinds of economists. Among the principles books currently in print, we find some authors at leading research institutions, some at urban commuter campuses, and others at small liberal arts colleges. Some are Nobel laureates or prominent candidates for this award; most are not.

This research versus teaching orientation has existed among textbook authors since shortly after the publication of *The Wealth of Nations*, which was certainly more than a basic textbook but did serve that role too for many decades, and through several editions. Malthus, Ricardo, and especially Mill and Marshall wrote principles books that are still in print today, and are seen by many contemporary economists as the leading texts of the 19th and early 20th centuries. But in fact these books, written by the intellectual giants among the classical and neoclassical economists, were often not the leading textbooks of the previous century, at least in terms of their market share. Many of the best sellers were written by less familiar figures. For example, Jane Marcet's *Conversations on Political Economy* (first published in 1816) ran through many editions, and Harriet Martineau's monthly issues of *Illustrations of Political Economy* (published from 1832-34) sometimes sold 10,000 copies per issue, and counted the Czar of Russia and Princess Victoria on its list of dedicated readers (Shackleton, 1988).

Marshall expressed a strongly negative opinion of Marcet's and Martineau's work, but Ricardo and Mill were more favorably impressed and supportive of these "popularizing" efforts for the new discipline. Around the same time, works by Robert Owen and William Cobbett dealing with political economy and a wide range of other topics were popular with workers and tradesmen, including those organized by the fledgling trade unions. Because of this partisan support, and the authors' generally populist and often idiosyncratic approaches to this material, these works have usually been treated as somewhat suspect by academic economists.

From 1870-1914, Millicent Fawcett's *Political Economy for Beginners* ran through nine editions, and in this same period of time the early American and Austrian textbooks began to appear. But Marshall's *Principles* held strong and prevailed into the 1920s, particularly in terms of prestige within the discipline and in maintaining the neoclassical approach as economic orthodoxy despite challenges from the German historical school and institutionalists like Veblen and John R. Commons. Then things became more unsettled, especially in the United States.

From 1920-1930, college enrollments in the U.S. approximately doubled. Between the 1910-11 and the 1925-26 academic years, credit hours of economics offered in American institutions of higher education increased about 500%. That meant that by the mid-1920s there were not enough qualified instructors to staff these courses in traditional (i.e., small) class formats. This also appears to be the time when a large number of the most prominent economists in the country first moved out of the principles classrooms to specialize in coursework designed for economics majors, and eventually in courses for graduate students.[1]

Fairchild, Furniss, and Buck adapted Irving Fisher's textbook to take the "best seller" position in the U.S. market during this period of flux. Their book remained dominant until Paul Samuelson refocused the textbook market, and our introductory courses, with the publication of his *Economics* in 1948. Samuelson's book is now seen as the first of the "modern" textbooks. In one sense his text continued the direct line from the classical and neoclassical schools, since he added Keynesian macro-economics to basically neoclassical microeconomics—and recall that Keynes himself was strongly influenced by his one-time teacher, Alfred Marshall.[2] This brings us to a discussion of the present generation of principles texts and a look at the current textbook market.

THE CURRENT TEXTBOOK MARKET: MONOPOLISTIC COMPETITION OR OLIGOPOLY?

In the fall of 1987 a conference on principles textbooks was sponsored by Purdue University. The proceedings were published in the Spring 1988 issue of the *Journal of Economic Education*. Kenneth Boulding, Carolyn Shaw Bell, Michael Boskin, and Joseph Stiglitz offered their views of today's principles texts, and responses to each paper were given by a group of textbook authors including Campbell McConnell, Ryan Amacher, Karl Case, Edwin Dolan, Werner Sichel, and Bradley Schiller. Numerous criticisms of the current crop of textbooks were offered, leading Robin Bartlett and Dennis Weidenaar to state in an introduction to the proceedings volume that "the principles of economics textbook has become the book that economics professors love to hate—or at least berate" (p. 109).

Such criticisms are nothing new, but in retrospect two of the critiques were novel in offering a market structure perspective to explain the general pattern of development, organization, and limitations among the present generation of textbooks. There was also considerable focus on one particular book—Paul Samuelson's seminal text of 1948 and its subsequent editions.

The Samuelson text was repeatedly described as "revolutionary" and "innovative." It may not have been the first to attempt to introduce Keynesian macroeconomic theory at the principles level, but it was the first successful book to offer this new dimension. As McConnell remarked: "In some ways, this pedagogical revolution was as remarkable as the Keynesian intellectual revolution itself" (p. 150). There was also much discussion at the conference about the need for a "new Samuelson" to appear and launch a new generation of textbooks; but that debate was much less cohesive and definite than the discussion on what the "old Samuelson" had done for, and to, the current textbook market.[3]

Samuelson's text soon captured a large market share, and was a dominant sales leader in the industry for a number of years. Over time, other books appeared with similar formats, but offering different features which were received as improvements in the marketplace, at least for some groups of students. The "improvements" included easier reading levels and other differences in writing style, increased use of purely pedagogical aids, and some variation in content. As the industry became even more competitive, more new textbooks offered slightly different products to pursue different "niches" in the market. But in retrospect it is clear that during this century no other textbook has fit the role of innovative leader on anything like the order of magnitude achieved by Samuelson's book.[4]

Stiglitz raised the question of how to best characterize the current textbook market, and then classified it as monopolistically competitive. Certainly there is a high degree of differentiation and nonprice competition in the market. We now have one and two semester textbooks, books for high- and low-ability students, books with differing emphases on economic theory and ideology, some books with extensive ancillary packages and others with minimal packages, etc. The competition has also produced a wide range of pedagogical aids, such as two- and four-color printing, the use of cartoons, "boxed features," and learning objectives, all designed to make the product more attractive and useful for students and instructors. Among ancillary materials, study guides, instructor's manuals, test banks, computer tutorial and simulation programs, books of readings on current issues, and even anthologies of teaching tips offer students and instructors additional help. When these new content or pedagogical features prove attractive to text adopters, they are quickly incorporated into future editions of many old and new textbooks.

The perception of the principles textbook market as monopolistically competitive is also compatible with several well-known and widespread complaints about the textbooks. Stiglitz notes that there may be "too many similar products at the center of the market and too few products at the fringes" (p. 172). He predicts a pattern of "subtle" innovations, and quick imitation of successful improvements and gimmicks by the competition. While some books will cater to special needs and serve special markets, they still cannot represent a radical departure from the "standard" text. Most publishers and textbook authors believe that only a small degree of innovation is acceptable if a book is to have a chance in the main part of the market.

Stiglitz also argues that effective barriers to entry into the market tend to limit the degree of innovation. The standard books tend to be of high quality in terms of appearance and content presentation and the many supplements that are now expected to be available from major textbook publishers. Whether or not all of these features are effective pedagogically—and we have no major research on that question for the economics discipline—the extensive support packages clearly represent both product differentiation and barriers to entry.

Stiglitz ends his paper by suggesting that the textbook market substantially shapes the principles course, and *vice versa*. He writes that:

> market forces may actually serve to inhibit important innovations and to promote a high degree of standardization of the curriculum: courses have been designed around the current set of textbooks. Any fundamental innovation would require a fundamental alteration in the courses (pp. 173-74).

Most professors are not likely to bear the cost of changing their courses given the prospect of limited and uncertain benefits, including minimal financial incentives for doing this work. So little impetus for change in the textbooks comes from that direction. Thus, the textbook market may be in an inefficient Nash equilibrium, which may explain much of the dissatisfaction with principles textbooks and courses.

One alternative to Stiglitz's monopolistic competition model is oligopoly, a view expressed at the textbook conference by Werner Sichel. He observed that although there are many principles textbooks there are few textbook publishers, and claimed that the top ten firms probably account for 90 percent of textbook sales. Sichel also feels that in this concentrated industry the practice of price leadership prevails, with dominant firms' price increases soon followed by other firms in the industry. On a day-to-day basis, the firms compete on the basis of the textbook (and ancillary) products, not prices.

Sichel argues that a new textbook "clone" has less chance of capturing significant market share in an oligopoly than in a monopolistically competitive market, because of the barriers to entry by established textbooks and their publishers. Truly innovative books, if successful, may capture a significant market share and reap the great rewards, but only after a high degree of risk is faced by the textbook author and large investments are made by the publisher. The advantage of being established also gives incumbent authors and publishers ample time (editions) to adopt any new features which appeal to buyers, even when those features come from competing textbooks (including new entrants). Sichel claims that the monopolistically competitive model suggests that the allowable time lag for imitation would be shorter. For these reasons, he believes that oligopoly is a better way to describe the textbook market. This position is also consistent with complaints about the widespread homogeneity among texts, and a lack of radically new approaches.

SPECIFIC CRITICISM OF TEXTBOOKS

Regardless of which of these general models of the textbook market seems most convincing and comprehensive, both claim to explain why there will be a prevailing standard for features, format, and content in the principles textbooks. Innovations in the existing textbooks will tend to be minor, and imitation of the successful minor innovations will occur quickly. Still, there may be lags before there is widespread adoption of these changes as the industry standard. This general background provides some perspective for examining specific criticisms of the principles texts.

The Need for More International Economics

One widespread criticism of current textbooks at the 1987 conference was the limited attention then being given to international economics, both in terms of the quantity of the coverage provided and the degree to which it was integrated throughout the texts. Carolyn Shaw Bell went so far as to claim that:

> The notion of a world economy, of aggregate analysis applied to open economies of nations interdependent in staggeringly various ways, should be the new paradigm for the introductory textbook. As a unifying theme, it can go far in integrating micro and macro analysis as well as the market for goods and the markets for financial instruments. Aside from being truthful, the vision of a world economy can also rejuvenate the introductory course and its textbook (p. 133).

Many books do relegate their international material to two or three chapters at the end of the book. And while the authors/publishers are now stressing their increased coverage of international issues—responding to the popular complaints and such things as AACSB guidelines calling for a more internationalized business curriculum—past practices are certainly not due to a conspiracy of textbook writers or their lack of appreciation of the significance of the world economy. Rather, several pedagogical and practical issues are at stake. McConnell observes that:

> In general, a meaningful discussion of international economics and finance presumes that the student already has a fair grasp of micro and macro theory. I am fairly confident that this is the basic reason that international trade and finance constitute the closing chapters of most textbooks; it is not because of the failure of textbook authors to appreciate the increasing importance of the topic (p. 149).

International issues seem likely to become a more prominent feature in the principles texts and courses. But we can't know with certainty if, or to what degree, the stress on international economics will prove to be just part of the "fad and fashion" pattern of focusing on the most current issues in a text revision year. Passing fancies clearly do occur: witness the attention devoted to energy, radical economics, pollution, and other topics that were more pressing concerns for students and instructors in the 1970s. And today, no other topics are receiving more attention than international trade deficits and other facets of world trade and finance, with the possible exception of federal budget deficits which also have international consequences.

Micro or Macro First?

For many years principles instructors have debated whether microeconomics should be presented before macroeconomics. The original (i.e., Samuelson) position was that macro should be taught first because it more powerfully develops or exploits a student's initial interest in the subject. After all, macroeconomics covers the "big" issues of unemployment, inflation, and economic growth that are found in daily media reports and affect all of us to some degree. When taught well, a first course in macroeconomics helps sustain student interest even when they go on to learn microeconomics.

But the micro-first proponents have been gaining ground in recent years for several reasons. Most important, perhaps, is that such courses provide the necessary micro foundations for macro theory, and avoid the need to repeat material on supply, demand, elasticity, etc. Michael Boskin wondered "how anyone can be serious about teaching macro to students who have not had micro, and simultaneously avoid repeating much of what is taught in the micro half of the course?" (p. 157). In a survey for a new principles book co-authored with Ray Fair, Karl Case found that about 85 percent of the respondents said that micro should be presented first for exactly these reasons (1987, p. 165). A recent study (Fizel and Johnson, 1986) found empirical evidence that students who took a micro-first principles sequence learned significantly more than other students, as measured on a nationally normed, objective test. And following the lead of Gary Becker, microeconomists have demonstrated that economic principles can be applied to a wider range of topics than might have been imagined in 1948, with results even principles students find interesting.

Most texts have yet to change to a micro-then-macro format, but the explanation for that, according to Dolan, is found by viewing textbook writers as royalty maximizers. He believes that the textbook format will change when a large percentage of economics departments change to a micro-first *course* sequence. The advent of micro/macro "splits" has made such changes both easier to make and less important for textbook writers, publishers, and adopters, but not less important for departments deciding which course to teach first. With splits, few books are summarily eliminated from adoption decisions on the basis of whether micro or macro comes first, even if both halves of the same textbook are to be used.

Textbook Bulk

The average size of the leading texts has grown from about 600 pages to over 900 pages in the past 30 years. Boskin commented that the "encyclopedia-like structure of most principles textbooks tends almost *de facto* to underemphasize basic economics concepts such as scarcity, opportunity cost, and marginality" (p. 161). Bell complains that "today's bulging textbooks are overcrowded by modern macroeconomic models, none of which has achieved general agreement" (p. 135). And Stiglitz argues that it is a major problem to sort through the "fads and fashions" in current texts, wanting books which more clearly stress the "central messages" of the discipline (p. 175).

This particular criticism prompted a spirited defense by the textbook authors attending the Purdue conference. Dolan thinks that the reason that textbook writers don't spend more time on basic economic concepts is because professors who teach the principles course tend not to spend much time on them, and are not demanding that more attention be placed on basic concepts in the textbook (p. 169). McConnell believes that it is not competing macro theories that have increased the size of the principles text, but rather the addition of chapters on urban economics, radical economics, energy and other "miscellaneous" chapters that textbook writers have included over the years to accommodate the wishes of their adopting customers. Case worries that by focusing on the central messages and the basic concepts we may increase the gap between what is covered in the principles course and what we do as professional economists (p. 167). He also notes that the American Economic Association sponsored a conference as early as 1952, which resulted in a suggestion that there was, even then, too much material for the principles course to handle.

No one, neither textbook users nor authors, seems particularly happy about the size of the textbook. But again, the size problem is probably the result of market forces rather than a conspiracy among publishers. Amacher explains that:

> Textbooks are rarely excluded from consideration just because they have material that some instructors do not want; rather, they are excluded because some pet topics are excluded. Authors and editors therefore find themselves in a position where it is better to include than to exclude (p. 155).

Thus, product competition leads to more material being included in the text than can reasonably be covered in the course. And there is a pedagogical defense of the encyclopedic approach, consistent with the idea of letting instructors tailor the books to better fit their own classes. That defense is most directly stated in the preface to the current edition of the Samuelson/Nordhaus text:

> The book has been through a searching review for superfluous elements: every paragraph, every figure, and every table has been scrutinized to ensure that it is both necessary and clearly expressed. Many a sentence and appendix has fallen before the merciless scissors. While we have ruthlessly trimmed unnecessary details or outmoded theories, nothing essential has been sacrificed.
>
> . . . Above all, we want this book to be authoritative, comprehensive, and clear. . . . A *comprehensive* survey of modern economics needs 950 pages. Reports of teachers advised us that no major topic has been omitted. . . . There is freedom to choose (p.x, emphasis in the original).

Miscellaneous Criticisms

Many other criticisms emerged at the Purdue conference, including: (1) the need for more real world data in the textbooks; (2) a perception of reduced reliance on graphical analysis in the books in recent years; (3) limited explanations of basic economic measures and statistics; and (4) publication lags in the production of textbooks. Principles instructors can probably find many more candidates for the list, especially when the textbooks are examined from a narrow content or ideological perspective.[5]

More generally, Stiglitz concluded that there is a simultaneity problem at the heart of our criticisms of the principles books and courses:

> The textbooks we use no doubt influence our courses, but the type of course we teach influences the type of textbook that we demand from the market. The courses we teach are also influenced by the nature of academic economics in the United States and in the curriculum decisions we've made at our colleges and universities for teaching that course.

This simultaneity problem led Stiglitz to ask: "To what extent are the deficiencies that some see in the textbooks really deficiencies that we see in ourselves" (p. 177). Or as Walt Kelly might have said, it's Pogo *deja vu*.

Evaluating Texts

Over the years there have been numerous attempts to use new pedagogical approaches in the principles course, such as television, computers, and programmed learning. As these innovations were introduced, there were usually a number of research studies that investigated the effectiveness of the new approaches (Siegfried and Fels, 1979). Few showed significant, let alone cost-effective, improvements in student learning. So the textbook-lecture approach remains as the dominant type of pedagogy, perhaps in a more secure position than ever. Yet solid research on the use of textbooks in the principles course is almost nonexistent.[6] We know very little about how they are or might be used, or if some texts can serve students (or certain types of students) better than others.

The need to evaluate textbooks was suggested several times at the Purdue conference. Bell noted that "physicians know more about the effectiveness of new drugs than economists know about the usefulness of new textbooks. . . . Nor do we have the equivalent of the Food and Drug Administration standing watch over publishers' claims" (p. 135). Even textbook writers endorsed the call for more research on the books, as with McConnell's comment that "we somehow need to do a more objective job of evaluating textbooks" (p. 151). Shiller complained that "textbooks are now evaluated and adopted on the basis of sporadic, ad hoc consideration of specific topics, special features, or extremely limited comparison shopping"; and called for the Joint Council on Economic Education to support "comparative evaluations of principles textbooks" (p. 184).

Key reasons why textbook evaluations have not been undertaken on a systematic basis are that the costs to do so are high, and the benefits uncertain, limited, and subject to free-rider problems. Results suggesting a negative effect from the use of a particular textbook are likely to initiate strident rebuttals, while the product differentiation discussed earlier makes it more difficult to compare books, and the periodic but nonstandard revision dates across books limit the useful "shelf-life" of both individual and comparative reviews. Finally, many evaluation systems might well favor established textbooks. These books have already met the market test, whereas innovative new entrants are particularly susceptible to first-edition "bugs" which make them more vulnerable in direct comparisons. Of course, many economists would claim that the market test/evaluation is the only one worth passing in these lucrative fields. Despite these problems, we decided to conduct a limited content analysis on a small sample of books. Those results are presented in the following section.

A CONTENT ANALYSIS OF SOME LEADING TEXTBOOKS

Table 12-1, below, reports various measures of content coverage and pedagogical features in current editions of seven leading textbooks: Baumol and Blinder (1988); Byrns and Stone (1987); Gwartney and Stroup (1987); Heilbroner and Galbraith (1987); Lipsey, Steiner and Purvis (1987); McConnell (1987); and Samuelson and Nordhaus (1989). These particular books were selected for a variety of reasons. The books by McConnell and Byrns and Stone were included because they are popular entries in a "middle of the road" position, both in terms of level of their analytical rigor and any "liberal/conservative" sentiment. Samuelson and Nordhaus is here by virtue of the "first-innovator role" discussed above and because, with Lipsey, Steiner and Purvis, it caters more to the "upper" end of the market in terms of rigor in content coverage and presentation. Baumol and Blinder is perhaps a bit upper-level in orientation, but primarily a major competitor in the middle part of the market featuring prominent authors known for their "liberal/Keynesian" tendencies. Gwartney and Stroup was one of the first books to stress public choice theory and a conservative viewpoint at the principles level, while Heilbroner and Galbraith check in much further "left" on the political/policy spectrum and at the lower end of the analytical rigor scale. All of the books are in at least a third edition, and sold by major publishing houses.

A series of broad content categories with an extensive list of subtopics under each of these general headings was prepared from a page-by-page review of one of the texts (Lipsey/Steiner/ Purvis), and expanded as necessary in completing later reviews. A similar list of basic pedagogical features (e.g., numbers of graphs and tables) was also prepared (see the Appendix for the full list). Then a written list of "counting rules" was established, with the basic rule being that a concept was considered to be treated on a page if at least three complete sentences of text or a table or graph were devoted to its explication.[7] All concepts and features treated on a page of text were then recorded on a "pages occurring" list, which was later converted into our classification table as presented below.

One other review feature was adopted to facilitate cross-book comparisons. Because the texts vary in terms of page size, and some books use a one-column format while most use two columns of text per page, we established a "Samuelson/Nordhaus-equivalent" (S/N-E) page standard. In each book, we literally counted words on three pages of "pure" text (i.e., pages with no graphs, major section breaks with large typefaces, long quotations with small or indented typesetting, or extensive "white space" areas). From these values, we determined the percentage of words per page in each of the books relative to the 1989 edition of Samuelson and Nordhaus, and used that index to convert the "raw" page counts shown in the table to the values shown in the S/N-E column.[8] This is our best comparative measure of the total amount of coverage on a given topic in each of the books, subject to the limitations of our basic

TABLE 12-1 TEXTBOOK PAGE CONTENT ALLOCATED BY CATEGORIES

Broad Categories	(1) #	(1) %	(1) S/N-E	(2) #	(2) %	(2) S/N-E	(3) #	(3) %	(3) S/N-E	(4) #	(4) %	(4) S/N-E
Fundamental Concepts	52	5.5	42	40	5.0	44	56	5.1	49	72	9.8	53
Micro Theory	290	30.7	237	285	35.8	310	292	33.9	253	194	26.3	143
Micro Topics	151	16.0	123	127	16.0	138	143	16.6	124	116	15.7	85
Macro Theory	292	30.9	238	266	33.4	289	248	28.8	215	176	23.9	130
Macro Topics	145	15.4	118	86	10.8	94	49	5.7	42	74	10.0	55
International Theory	45	4.8	37	35	4.4	38	25	2.9	22	25	3.4	18
International Topics	41	4.3	34	25	3.1	30	35	4.1	30	27	3.7	20
Comparative Systems	49	5.2	40	28	3.5	30	48	5.6	42	32	4.3	24
Pedagogical Features	263	27.9	215	241	30.2	262	288	33.4	250	241	32.7	178
Biographies	10	1.1	8	19	2.4	21	16	1.9	14	11	1.5	8
"Blank" Pages	15	1.6	12	7	.9	8	27	3.1	23	29	3.9	21
Total Pages Occurring	1353		1104	1159		1261	1227		1063	997		734
Actual # of Pages	944		770	796		866	862		747	737		543

Note: The texts are: (1) Baumol/Binder (1988); (2) Byrns/Stone (1987); (3) Gwartney/Stroup (1987); (4) Heilbroner/Galbraith (1987); (5) Lipsey/Steiner/Purvis (1987); (6) McConnell (1987); and, (7) Samuelson/Nordhaus (1989). Columns under (8) are the average percentages and average S/N-E across the seven books.

counting system noted earlier. With that background in mind, we can now turn to Table 12-1.

The "Consensus" Text

There is more homogeneity among the books in considering the broad subject headings among the review categories than among the individual topics that are classified under those different headings. The fundamental concepts group is covered on 5 to 7 percent of the pages in all but two of the books: Heilbroner and Galbraith check in with nearly 10 percent of their pages including this material; Lipsey, Steiner and Purvis move very quickly on to more advanced topics, with less than 4 percent of their pages treating these basic concepts. The micro theory sections comprise 31-36 percent of five of the books, but only 29 percent of McConnell and 26 percent of Heilbroner and Galbraith. Micro topics and institutions get 15-16 percent page coverage in six of the books, with McConnell running slightly higher at 20 percent. Macro theory and basic models get 29-31 percent page coverage in four books, with Byrns and Stone a bit higher at 33 percent, Lipsey, Steiner and Purvis and Heilbroner and Galbraith lower at 24 percent. Five of the books allocate 10-15 percent page coverage to the material we have classified as macro topics and institutions, but Gwartney and Stroup shows some deemphasis of these topics with less than 6 percent coverage, and McConnell shows slightly more emphasis at 17 percent. International theory topics are less extensively covered than any of the groups mentioned thus far, with only 3-6 percent of the pages in any of the books. International topics and institutions adds another 3-6 percent, and comparative systems yet

TABLE 12-1 (CONTINUED)

Broad Categories	(5) #	(5) %	(5) S/N-E	(6) #	(6) %	(6) S/N-E	(7) #	(7) %	(7) S/N-E	(8) %	(8) S/N-E
Fundamental Concepts	34	3.6	34	65	7.1	69	58	5.7	58	6.0	50
Micro Theory	294	31.2	295	263	28.8	280	333	32.9	333	31.4	264
Micro Topics	147	15.6	147	181	19.8	193	162	16.0	162	16.5	139
Macro Theory	229	24.3	230	280	30.6	300	297	29.3	297	28.7	243
Macro Topics	142	15.1	142	155	17.0	165	146	14.4	146	12.6	109
International Theory	40	4.2	40	28	3.1	30	35	3.5	35	3.8	31
International Topics	54	5.7	54	45	4.9	48	54	5.3	54	4.4	39
Comparative Systems	36	3.8	36	51	5.6	53	39	3.9	39	4.5	38
Pedagogical Features	376	39.9	377	350	38.3	373	321	31.7	321	33.4	282
Biographies	0	0.0	0	2	.2	2	0	0.0	0	1.0	8
"Blank" Pages	17	1.8	17	12	1.3	13	21	2.1	21	2.1	16
Total Pages Occurring	1369		1372	1432		1527	1466		1466		1218
Actual # of Pages	942		944	914		974	1013		1013		887

another 3-6 percent; but no one book's total of these three international topic areas exceeds the 14 percent level. Whether that represents too much or too little coverage of international issues is, still, a matter of some debate; but far more text space is allocated to other topics in these texts.

The pedagogical features other than graphs, tables and charts (which are counted under the various topic areas they are used to illustrate or discuss) appear on roughly 28-40 percent of the pages in the books. Glossaries, indexes, end-of-chapter discussion questions, graphing reviews/primers and "boxed features" are literally standard features in these texts. Chapter summaries and lists of key concepts are nearly so, with each of these features appearing in six of the seven books. The variations in coverage in this section are usually tied to the inclusion of learning objectives (in Gwartney/Stroup and Heilbroner/Galbraith); sections on math notes or extensions (treated briefly in Baumol/Blinder, extensively in Lipsey/Steiner/Purvis, and not at all in the other books); a "data reference section" (provided only in Gwartney/Stroup—apart from cover-liner pages in several of the books); and to differences in length in the standard features.

The average coverage for each broad category, in terms of the percentage and S/N-E measures, is shown in the last two columns of Table 12-1. While no current textbook exactly meets this consensus specification, it is worth noting that, particularly on core concepts and content allocation over the broad concept headings, none of the seven books reviewed here is very far from it, either. Some observers will no doubt view this as reflecting a high degree of consensus in the discipline, others as an indicator of effective barriers to entry into the textbook market, and perhaps a few as an outright conspiracy (implicit or explicit) among publishers and authors. Whatever the reason, the broad category data indicates that the broad division of content coverage in the textbooks is fairly standard, and that there is a "consensus" textbook in this regard.

Comparisons within Categories

Within the major content blocks, the differences across books are more pronounced, both in terms of identifying what material has not been universally accepted as important by the authors, and in identifying how authors target particular market levels, segments or "niches" by expanding, contracting, or even deleting coverage on certain topics.[9]

Fundamental Concepts The least amount of difference in topic treatment within categories is found in this division. Most of the observed differences simply reflect the decision on how much total coverage to include on these topics. But even here some of the books treat methodological issues much more extensively—occasionally as a separate topic—than others (Lipsey/Steiner/Purvis, Heilbroner/Galbraith, McConnell and Samuelson/Nordhaus are the most thorough; Gwartney/Stroup and Byrns/Stone the least). Three books keep their discussion of production possibilities frontiers to three or four pages (Gwartney/Stroup, Heilbroner/Galbraith, and Lipsey/Steiner/Purvis), Samuelson and Nordhaus have six, and the others devote eight to ten pages to it.

Gwartney and Stroup devote more space to the gains from voluntary exchange than the other books.

Micro Theory Some similarities in coverage are as important as any differences in the micro theory category. For example, basic supply and demand models get between two and four percent page coverage in all of the books. Coverage of price controls, elasticity, cost curves, and the four basic market structures is similarly close across all authors. But key differences are also observed. The most striking difference involves indifference curves and isoquant models, where at least one text in the group entirely avoids any kind of coverage (Heilbroner/Galbraith say nothing about either topic; McConnell treats indifference curves but not isoquants or isocosts; the rest of the books cover both sets of material). The books that do provide this coverage spend as little as five to six pages on indifference curves (Byrns/Stone and McConnell), sometimes eight pages (Baumol/Blinder, Gwartney/Stroup and Samuelson/Nordhaus), but never more than thirteen (Lipsey/Steiner/Purvis). All books that cover isoquants and isocosts do so in four to seven pages. That pattern raises the obvious question: Do four to seven pages of text on these topics give students enough support to learn this advanced material? Or, as we have discussed earlier, is this a clear example of market forces at work to assuage the instructors/adopters who plan to teach these topics at considerably greater length than the textual coverage implies, without offending those who plan to skip the material and who may believe that their colleagues should skip it too, with little textual encouragement to do more? Certainly not all principles classes should be trying to teach these concepts, but with perhaps only one exception it is not clear that what is included in these texts is adequate for those schools or classes where covering this material may be justified.

Micro Topics and Institutions Looking at what is unanimously covered from this section of micro topics, we found that everyone discusses types of firms and corporate securities, mergers and antitrust policy, government regulation, minimum wage laws, unions, public finance topics, poverty, and income redistribution policies. There are certainly inter-book differences in the extent of coverage on this list of topics—indeed, some of the books have full chapters on one or more of these issues. To take one specific example, unions get 10-23 pages in six of the books, but only 5 pages in Heilbroner and Galbraith.

Coverage differences in this section are, predictably, more a matter of tastes, product differentiation or market segmentation than an issue of global concern, except in the role this plays in promoting encyclopedic texts. The number of topics that are treated in one to three pages in this and other sections does show that such an approach affects all of these books to some degree, but that observation constitutes only a little more fuel for the long-standing debate about the practice. How the books vary in their coverage is more interesting to see: three books deal with the Berle-Means-(John Kenneth)Galbraith issue of the separation of ownership and control in large corporations (Byrns/Stone, Heilbroner/Galbraith and, at much greater length, Lipsey/Steiner/Purvis); the other books don't. Brief treatments of the effects of tax rates on the supply of labor are now in all of the books except Byrns and Stone; and comparable worth appears, though sometimes only as a "boxed insert," in all but two books (Gwartney/Stroup and Heilbroner/Galbraith). Energy/OPEC sections or even chapters appear in most of the books, but not all (Heilbroner/Galbraith). Environmental sections (excluding simple pollution examples from the externalities passages) occur in all but two of the texts (Gwartney/Stroup and Lipsey/Steiner/Purvis). Agricultural issues draw special coverage in all of the books except Byrns and Stone, who with Heilbroner and Galbraith are also the only authors to pass on the issue of rent controls.

Macroeconomics In both the macro theory and topics sections, where professional disagreement is so well publicized in both the policy and research arenas, we found a surprising degree of consensus among the textbook authors. Measures like GNP, CPI, and national income accounts make it into all of the books at closely comparable coverage levels. Aggregate expenditure analysis, as derived from Keynes and Samuelson's first edition, is still featured prominently, but especially so in three books (Heilbroner/Galbraith, Baumol/Blinder and Samuelson/Nordhaus). The "alternative" approach of aggregate supply and aggregate demand curve analysis has, in these books, become a complementary tool instead, receiving 3-6 percent page coverage in all of the books except Heilbroner and Galbraith, where it is covered more briefly. Other major topics from the macro theory section, in terms of most extensive page coverage, are monetary and fiscal policy, comparisons and contrasts of the competing "schools" of macroeconomic thought, and Phillips curves (short run and long run).

There is similar agreement on several topics covered more briefly as well, including business cycles, the process of money creation, money supply and demand schedules, and rational expectations. Areas that all of the books cover, but with pronounced differences in emphasis, include the equation of exchange (a one-page entry in Lipsey/Steiner/Purvis, but five to eight pages in Baumol/Blinder, Byrns/Stone, Heilbroner/Galbraith and McConnell), interest rates (which Gwartney/Stroup, Lipsey/Steiner/Purvis, and Samuelson/Nordhaus treat at greatest length), and the natural rate of unemployment (which Byrns/Stone, Gwartney/Stroup, Lipsey/Steiner/Purvis and Samuelson/Nordhaus cover most fully).

As for macro topics and institutions, everyone devotes considerable space to the misery-index linked problems of inflation (though Gwartney/Stroup are by far the briefest) and unemployment (where all books are in the 2 or 3 percent coverage range). Economic growth/productivity issues are treated extensively in three books (Baumol/Blinder, McConnell and Samuelson/Nordhaus), moderately in three (Byrns/Stone, Heilbroner/Galbraith, and Lipsey/Steiner/Purvis), and quite briefly in one (Gwartney/Stroup). Also, Lipsey, Steiner and Purvis, McConnell, and Samuelson and Nordhaus all deal with the institutional arrangements of money, banking and central banking on more than 20 pages.

International Categories In international theory, everyone has 1 or 2 percent coverage on comparative advantage and the gains from international trade, and like amounts on exchange rate determination and price controls. Balance of payments accounts take about 0.5-1 percent of page coverage in all of the books, and only the terms of trade issue appears briefly in most of the books, but not at all in two (Baumol/Blinder and Gwartney/Stroup).

In the international topics and institutions category, tariffs and quotas are unanimously covered at the 1-2 percent level. Development and LDC issues get as much or slightly more coverage in all of the books, though, which we found a little surprising. The rest of the categories are treated briefly or, in the books noted below, not at all: recent history and current events with exchange rate markets, the gold standard and the Bretton Woods agreement (Heilbroner/Galbraith); U.S. trade deficit issues (Gwartney/Stroup); the LDC debt crisis (Gwartney/Stroup and Heilbroner/Galbraith); and purchasing power parity (Byrns/Stone, Heilbroner/Galbraith and McConnell).

In the comparative systems section, we found everyone using the Heilbroner market/command-economy distinction in about equal coverage levels, but only Byrns and Stone, Heilbroner and Galbraith, McConnell, and Samuelson and Nordhaus use the third descriptor, traditional economies. All of the books except Heilbroner and Galbraith include at least one country-specific comparison and some discussion of Marxian economics. Byrns and Stone and Samuelson and Nordhaus stand out by having much less on country-specific comparisons, and Baumol and Blinder by including much more than anyone else (fourteen pages, a full chapter) on Marxian economics.

CONCLUSION

The selection of a textbook is a major instructional decision, which influences what the student learns in the classroom and beyond. That decision is more complicated today than in past eras, because of the far greater number of textbooks on the market.

But that variety and the critical nature of the text adoption decision is somewhat illusory, given the high degree of standardization in the textbooks. At least over the broad content categories and pedagogical features of texts, there appears to be a high degree of consensus about what material should be included and how it should be presented. In fact, most differences in textbooks for the principles course come at the smallest of margins: some books include a page or two on a subject not covered in other books, or devote a few more pages to a topic than other books.

Alternative reasons for this pattern were discussed earlier in this chapter. Apart from the possible existence of a professional consensus on core concepts, that is not admitted in the deeply felt and widely expressed criticism of these textbooks, the main explanation focuses on the market structure of the industry producing the books and packages of ancillary materials. Monopolistic competition or oligopoly, with both product differentiation and extensive nonprice competition, is probably the best way to characterize the market. Although the basic content and format of the leading principles textbooks are fairly standard, most product differentiation in the books comes from the slight variations produced by topic emphasis or omission. Most of the other nonprice competition occurs in the range of ancillary products offered for a textbook, and other components of the marketing effort including the size of a company's sales force. The structure of this market may well contribute to the many criticisms instructors have voiced concerning principles texts.

NOTES

1 This paragraph is based on Leamer (1950).
2 On this, see the memoir of Marshall in Keynes' *Essays on Biography*.
3 One of the rare "outlier/innovator" texts of the 1980s was written by Edmund Phelps (1985). This book was reviewed by Michael Weinstein (1987), who commented: "Phelps ain't Samuelson. Or Bronfenbrenner, Baumol, Lipsey or anyone else. *Political Economy* is a scintillating excursion into modern economic thinking" (p. 179). But Weinstein argues that the time is not ripe for a new Samuelson-like revolution among the textbooks, because no revolutionary in the discipline, like Keynes, has succeeded in achieving the same kind of consensus that Samuelson announced at the principles level, with a great sense of market timing and considerable writing/teaching skills, in 1948.
4 The exception to this view is offered by Ryan Amacher. He agrees that "Samuelson is an ancestor in that he 'invented' a more efficient way of organizing the material and in this sense he defined the format" (p. 152). But he also thinks that a group of more free-market oriented texts owe their ideological and genealogical heritage to Alchian and Allen's *University Economics*.
5 For an example of a free-market critique of some textbooks, see Taylor (1982). Feiner and Morgan (1987) find flaws with textbooks on the basis of coverage of women's issues (Ferber discusses these points in her chapter in this volume). Kent (forthcoming) criticizes textbooks for neglecting the entrepreneurial perspective.
6 See Meinkoth (1971) and Watts and Lynch (1989) for two of the few quantitative studies of the effects textbooks can have on student performance.
7 This counting system obviously results in many pages being counted in more than one concept category, and in some overstatement of how much coverage is allocated to some topics (compare total pages occurring to absolute number of pages in Table 12-1); however, the concepts developed earlier in the text that are used to develop another concept are not counted as occurring again (e.g., supply and demand is not counted again when the supply and demand for money are introduced).
8 The index numbers used for the S/N-E conversion were: Baumol and Blinder (.816); Byrns and Stone (1.088); Gwartney and Stroup (.867); Heilbroner and Galbraith (.737); Lipsey, Steiner and Purvis (1.002); McConnell (1.066); and Samuelson and Nordhaus (1.000).
9 The table data on topic coverage within categories is extensive, covering some 140 topics. For brevity, that table is not reproduced here and only a summary of the major highlights is provided. All of the specific topics are listed in Appendix 12-1.

REFERENCES

Baumol, William J., and Alan S. Blinder, *Economics: Principles and Policy*, San Diego, California: Harcourt Brace Jovanovich, 1988.

Byrns, Ralph T., and Gerald W. Stone, *Economics*, Glenview, Illinois: Scott, Foresman, 1987.

Fairchild, Fred R., Edgar S. Furniss, and Norman S. Buck, *Elementary Economics*, New York: Macmillan, 1926 and subsequent editions. Two volumes.

Feiner, Susan F., and Barbara A. Morgan, "Women and Minorities in Introductory Economics Textbooks: 1974 to 1984," *Journal of Economic Education*, Fall 1987, *18*, 376-392.

Fizel, John L., and Jerry D. Johnson, "The Effect of Macro/Micro Course Sequencing on Learning and Attitudes in Principles of Economics," *Journal of Economic Education*, Spring 1986, *17*, 87-98.

Gwartney, James D., and Richard L. Stroup, *Economics: Private and Public Choice*, San Diego, California: Harcourt Brace Jovanovich, 1987.

Heilbroner, Robert L., and James K. Galbraith, *The Economic Problem*, Englewood Cliffs, New Jersey: Prentice Hall, 1987.

Kent, Calvin, "The Treatment of Entrepreneurship in Collegiate Principles of Economics Texts," *Journal of Economic Education*, Spring 1989, *20*, 153-164.

Leamer, Lawrence E., "A Brief History of Economics in General Education," *American Economic Review*, December 1950, *40*, 18-33.

Lipsey, Richard G., Peter O. Steiner, and Douglas D. Purvis, *Economics*, New York: Harper & Row, 1987.

McConnell, Campbell R., *Economics: Principles, Problems, and Policies*, New York: McGraw-Hill, 1987.

Meinkoth, Marian R., "Textbooks and the Teaching of Economic Principles," *Journal of Economic Education*, Spring 1971, *2*, 127-130.

Phelps, Edmund, *Political Economy: An Introductory Text*, New York: W. W. Norton, 1985.

Samuelson, Paul A., and William D. Nordhaus, *Economics*, New York: McGraw-Hill, 1989.

Shackleton, J. R., "Why Don't Women Feature in the History of Economics?" *Economics*, Autumn 1988, *24*, 123-126.

Taylor, James B., *American Economics Texts: A Free Market Critique*, Reston, Virginia: Young America's Foundation, 1982.

Watts, Michael, and Gerald J. Lynch, "The Principles Courses Revisited," *American Economic Review*, May 1989, *79*, 236-241.

Weinstein, Michael M., "Review of Political Economy: An Introductory Text, by Edmund S. Phelps," *The Journal of Economic Perspectives*, Fall 1987, *1*, 179-182.

APPENDIX 12-1

LISTING OF PAGE-COUNT CATEGORIES

Fundamental Concepts

Definitions of Economics

Scarcity and Choice

Opportunity Cost

Productive Resources/Factors of Production

Basic Economic Questions

Specialization and the Division of Labor

Gains From Voluntary (Inter-Personal and Intra-National) Exchange

Production Possibilities Frontiers

Circular Flow

Methodology

Positive vs. Normative Concepts

Micro Theory

Supply, Demand and Price
Price Controls (Floors; Ceilings)
Elasticity Measures
Utility Theory
Consumer Surplus
Producer Surplus
Indifference Curves/Budget
    Constraints
Production Schedules (SR and LR)
Isoquants/Isocosts
Economic vs. Accounting Costs
Cost Curves/Schedules (SR and LR)
Normal and Economic Profits
Industry/Market Structures
    (General Discussion)
Perfect Competition
Monopoly
Monopolistic Competition
Concentration Ratios
Oligopoly
Game Theory
Contestable Markets
Kinked Demand
Price Discrimination
Principal-Agent Issues (Generic)

Competitive Labor/Resource Markets
Human Capital
Monopoly Hiring in Labor Markets
Monopsony
Economic Rents
Capital (and Loanable Funds) Markets
Discounting/Net Present Value/
    Capitalization
Technological Change/R&D Efforts
Measures of Economic and Market
    Efficiency (Including Comparisons
    of Industry Structures)
Moral Hazard
Risk and Uncertainty
Futures Markets
Information
Property Rights
Public Goods
Externalities
Cost-Benefit Analysis
Public Choice/Government Failure
Transactions Costs
Input-Output Analysis/Tables
General Equilibrium Analysis

Micro Topics and Institutions

Types of Firms and Corporate
    Securities
Separation of Ownership and
    Control (Non-Profit-Maximizing
    Objectives)
Antitrust Policy
Merger Activity
Regulation (Includes Natural
    Monopoly Regulation)
Unions
Taxes and the Supply of Labor
Minimum Wage Laws
Tax Incidence
Discrimination (in Labor Markets)
Comparable Worth

Energy/OPEC
Environment (see also Externalities)
Public Finance (Goals of Government,
    Basic Types of Taxes and Spending
    Programs)
Agriculture
Advertising
Rent Controls
Urban Economics/Problems
Income Distribution and Effects of
    Government Redistribution Programs
Poverty
Health Care/Medical Economics
Dual Labor Markets

Macro Theory

GNP

CPI and Implicit Price Deflator

National Output and National
Income Accounting

GNP Gap

Aggregate Expenditures (Desired
and Actual—Including C, I,
G, X-M Schedules and Rationales
of Spending/Savings/Tax
Multipliers)

Aggregate Demand

Aggregate Supply

Business Cycles

Money Creation by Commercial Banks

Fiscal Policy

Equation of Exchange

Monetary Policy and Tools

Supply and Demand for Money

Interest Rates

Rational Expectations

IS/LM Analysis

Competing Schools of Thought
(Classical; Keynes; Monetarism;
Supply Side; Rational Expectations, etc.)

Index Numbers (General)

Phillips Curves

Natural Rate of Unemployment

Incomes Policies

Okun's Law

Macro Topics and Institutions

Inflation/Deflation

Unemployment and Employment

Money, Banking and Central Banking
—Descriptive/Institutional/
Definitional/Functions

Financial Securities and Securities
Markets

National (Federal) Debt (Distinct
From or In Addition to Deficits,
Which Are Counted in Expenditures
and/or Fiscal Policy Sections)

Economic Growth and LR Determinants
of Productivity

Industrial Policy

Limits to/Costs of Economic Growth

Indexing

The Share Economy

The Underground Economy

The Laffer Curve

Reaganomics

International Theory

Comparative Advantage and Gains
From (International) Trade

Exchange Rates (Flexible and Fixed)

Balance of Payment Accounts

Terms of Trade

International Topics and Institutions

Tarriffs and Quotas; Free Trade
vs. Protectionism

Current and Recent Events in
Foreign Exchange Systems

The Gold Standard and Bretton Woods

Trade Deficit Issues

The LDC Debt Crisis

Economic Development (International
Orientation—e.g., LDCs)

Purchasing Power Parity

Comparative Systems

General Discussion:
  Market Economies
  Command Economies
  Traditional Economies

"Case Studies"
Marxian Economics

Biographies

CHAPTER 13

MICROCOMPUTER SOFTWARE FOR PRINCIPLES OF ECONOMICS COURSES

DeVon L. Yoho
William B. Walstad

INTRODUCTION

Many instructors think that microcomputer software heralds a new era for the principles of economics course, and that economics appears to be well-suited for the microcomputer revolution given its graphing and quantitative emphasis. Before this conclusion can be accepted, however, the idea needs to be put in a historical perspective because the computer (now the microcomputer) is just the latest in a series of educational "innovations" expected to improve instruction in economic principles.

In the 1960s, television was going to revolutionize economics instruction in the classroom (Coleman, 1963). It did not have a profound effect on principles instruction simply because it is very difficult to use capital in an effective and cost-efficient way to replace labor in teaching. Television became a complement to rather than a substitute for teaching labor. This innovation simply became one of the many supplementary aides for principles teaching.

The most recent example of a new television series and textbook for the principles course is *Economics USA* (Mansfield and Behravesh, 1986). These programs show students some of the historical background to macro- or microeconomic theory and acquaint students with the economic decisions policy-makers face. When used on a selective basis, the programs offer variety and they supplement the lectures and the textbook materials. This use of different instructional methods probably improves instruction because one of the major conclusions from research in economic education at the college level was that: "Different students learn economics in different ways.

161

The best teaching strategy provides alternative learning methods directed toward the different needs of different students" (Siegfried and Fels, 1979, p. 953). No doubt good television programs give instructors some alternatives to the traditional methods.

In the 1970s, computer instruction on the mainframe took center stage as the new educational innovation for the principles course. Extensive research was conducted on computer-assisted instruction in economics, but the positive results were limited (Soper, 1974; Siegfried and Fels, pp. 940-42).[1] Computer-assisted instruction was found to generate no more (and no less) economics understanding than more conventional methods. The problem was the cost: these methods cost the instructor more time to set up; they cost the students more time to use; and they cost institutions more equipment and maintenance expense. Comparing the few cognitive benefits relative to the cost, computer-assisted instruction was not going to sweep the principles of economics curriculum. It did not cause revolutionary changes in economics courses, except for the few "dedicated" faculty whose "psychic" benefits from this innovation outweighed their costs.

What about the prospects for the microcomputer? Computer-assisted instruction in economics will certainly be better than the mainframe use of the computer according to Lovell (1987). Microcomputer hardware offers more flexibility for the instructor to use software in class and for the student to use it outside of class. Students also learn a skill in a class that uses a personal computer that can be more easily transported with them once they leave the campus. The extensive microcomputer education at the precollege and college level means that more students are familiar with microcomputers and may be more willing to accept microcomputer-assisted instruction. These reasons and others make Lovell optimistic about effective microcomputer-assisted learning compared to the mainframe experience.

But how much use microcomputers will get in the principles course is still unknown. A few instructors who like personal computers and the software programs will find effective uses in the classroom. It is doubtful that microcomputer use will ever become widespread. The principles course is just too "packed" at present to include microcomputer programs as anything more than a supplement to lectures and the texts, unless the instructor is dedicated to microcomputer use and finds innovative ways to use the programs as a basic part of instruction. As Sumansky (1986, p. 482) notes: Instructors see the programs as "appendages to a curriculum or a course in economics—optional but not integral, interesting but not important." Microcomputer programs are more likely to be used with intermediate or advanced courses than the principles course because there is more latitude to make them an integral part of the course (Yohe, Schenk, and Walstad, 1987; Millerd and Robertson, 1987).

TYPES OF SOFTWARE AVAILABLE

Microcomputer use will depend on the type and quality of the software that is available for classroom use. There are two basic types: tutorials and simulations/games. Each has its advantages and disadvantages for classroom use. There are also other possibilities for software use in the form of computer-managed instruction and testing.

Publishers of textbooks have concentrated their development of software on drill and practice exercises, tutorials, and problem sets that are designed to complement the textbook used by the instructor. The main justification for tutorial software lies in the complexity of the material. As most instructors know from years of teaching the principles course, economics is difficult for students to master. A tutorial provides a way of reinforcing the text and classroom presentations without spending additional instructor or class time. It can be an efficient alternative to instructor time for students who need help.

Tutorials are not without problems. They may cover the content, but certainly not in the most imaginative way. Students need to be sufficiently motivated and interested to learn economic content from the video screen. Tutorials are unlikely to change the character of the text-dominated courses that have resisted change for 30 years.

While the primary contribution of the text publishers to the principles course has been tutorials and problem sets, the primary contribution of economics instructors and private developers has been simulations/games (Post, 1985; Walstad, Hallows, and Ross, 1986). Instructors may prefer them because they have more potential for getting students involved in the subject matter. Simulations allow students to make decisions and examine their effects on the modeled phenomena, so that they become active rather than passive learners. Games use competition to excite students and give them an incentive to cover the material. A simulation/game combines the best features of each to get students to look at complex situations. A simulation/game will not guarantee student interest, but, if well constructed, it can generate excitement and serve as an effective instructional activity.

The penetration of microcomputer simulation/gaming into the principles course is still limited. Most simulations/games do not explicitly present an economic concept and may cover several interrelated concepts. The instructor has greater teaching responsibilities and must use scarce class time to make certain that students understand the concepts underlying the simulation/game. The programs also vary in quality and may be difficult or expensive to obtain from private developers or commercial vendors compared to captive text software. Thus, the use of simulation/gaming in the principles course, already overcrowded with other materials, requires more determination by the instructor and the students than that of a tutorial or the traditional textbook-lecture method. Only computer-oriented instructors are likely to accept the challenge.

A promising line for software development would be to use the research results from computer-managed instruction on the mainframe. An example of the computer-managed program for the mainframe was the TIPS package developed by Allen Kelley (1972). With TIPS, students took weekly quizzes and received immediate feedback on performance. The mainframe computer then gave students grades on quizzes and reported to the instructor how well each student and the class was doing. This method gave effective feedback to both students and the instructors. The original research showed that it did produce positive cognitive benefits for students. There may be an opportunity for an instructor or a company to develop a microcomputer-managed instructional system that would be both beneficial for students and maybe even cost-effective.

A more subtle and perhaps widespread influence of computer software on the principles course may come from the testing software provided free of charge by text publishers. The major text publishers produce microcomputer test banks and an operating program to create tests. For example, McConnell's *Economics* (1987) contains two microcomputer test banks, one with about 2,900 and the other with about 2,300 multiple choice and true-false questions. These test banks can be used to create tests on IBM PCs or compatibles, or on Apple II-family computers with Brownstone's EXAM software.

Testing software is less captive than tutorials software in that once the instructor has a copy of the exam program and the test bank(s), he or she can in time develop a personal test bank that matches the characteristics of the course the instructor wants to teach. Most exam programs allow the instructor to take existing questions and use them as is, edit them, or delete them as well as to write original questions and store them in the personal test bank. Questions from test banks prepared by other publishers that the instructor would like to include in a personal test bank can be entered as new questions or, depending on the software, the other publisher's test bank can be entered as a new file. These capabilities are powerful, for they allow principles instructors to tailor tests to the type of course they like to teach and thereby overcome the severe restrictions of printed test banks.

Despite the variety of software available, most principles instructors will use the "captive software" of tutorials and problem sets produced by book publishers for the text used in the course. Most of this software will be used as a supplement rather than as an integral part of the course. Instructors will demonstrate the microcomputer tutorials in class and let the student do the exercises on their own time in the microcomputer lab. This development may be beneficial because it can give students more choice and provide variety for different learning styles. Because this captive software is the most likely type to be used in the principles course, the remainder of this chapter provides a detailed description of the software available in 1988.

PRINCIPLES OF ECONOMICS SOFTWARE

Fourteen software packages available from eight textbook publishers are examined.[2] The software are provided as companions to publishers' textbooks like instructor's manuals, study guides, and test banks. Therefore they are readily available to instructors and students. Software from other sellers has a more limited availability. If it is available from a commercial vendor, it is usually very expensive for instructors and students; however, most of this software is not available commercially and is difficult to acquire. It is characterized by a higher variability in content and technical quality than is the software available from textbook publishers.

General descriptions and comments about the packages based on ease of use, documentation, availability, content, potential for learning economics, and selection follow.

Description

The available software varies greatly in type, ease of use, content, and quality of graphics. All of the software except those available from Dryden Press, Scott, Foresman & Co., and McGraw-Hill's DRI software include test questions with some form of feedback. Thus, as a group, the software is essentially computer-managed instruction. However, this generalization is inadequate because many packages include interactive tutorials. Three packages, **COMPUTER-AIDED INSTRUCTION, GRAPHECON II** and **PRINCIPLES SIMULATIONS,** aid the instructor by storing students' records on quizzes and examinations. Such records are usually a salient feature of CMI software but not of the reviewed software.

Two publishers, McGraw-Hill and Scott, Foresman & Co., provide problem sets. McGraw-Hill's DRI software requires the use of a spreadsheet. The program is written especially for **Lotus 1-2-3** but can be used with other spreadsheets. Students calculate statistics on a set of data using the tools of the spreadsheet and are asked to interpret their findings, but this is not an interactive program. Students can access content hints, text references, and graphs. Both packages require instructors to provide students with feedback on the correctness of their computations and the quality of their interpretations of the data.

Another McGraw-Hill package uses *Framework*[3] and asks students to use its word processor, spreadsheet, database, and graphing features to answer a selected group of questions in the *Study Guide* for the Samuelson-Nordhaus textbook. Students are not provided on-screen hints on how to proceed with the software to answer the study guide questions.

TARGET, available from Scott, Foresman & Co., contains many problems that students might be asked to calculate in a class in economic principles.[4] Students may select any item in the data set and can access it either as a problem or as an example. In the example mode, the answer is provided. This software does not use real databases and the problems are usually quite simple.

The problems posed in McGraw-Hill's DRI software use real data and tend to be more complex. However, students rarely need to calculate anything more complicated than a percent or a percentage change. The spreadsheet program does the calculations and any repetitions. This is an efficient use of the microcomputer.

Students using **TARGET** have access to the computational capacity of the computer. **ECO TALK** also allows use of the computer when calculations are required to answer questions. **TARGET** accepts the result of the calculation without additional student key strokes. **ECO TALK** does not. Students must remember the answer and input it after the calculator window with the answer is cleared from the screen. The inclusion of a window in which students could access a calculator function would improve nearly all of the remaining programs.

All of the programs, except **MICROSTUDY,** use graphs, but not all of them with the same finesse. Horizontal intercepts from equilibrium points extend beyond the equilibrium point in **GRAPHECON II.** Several programs expect students to answer questions using inadequately marked graphs. As a result students must guess. One program, **ECONOMIC PRINCIPLES**, attempts to deal with the problem by accepting any answer within a predetermined range.

Ease of Use

User-friendly microcomputer software requires limited use of the keyboard, is menu driven, monitors student inputs, provides easy access to feedback, and has an efficient help system. Some of the reviewed programs are easier to use than others. **CAPER** is unforgiving of any typos and students must often input complete words rather than a single letter or number to execute functions. Most programs require students to input one character or a number rather than complete words. In addition, most programs use menus, the most user friendly of all access systems.

Since McGraw-Hill's two DRI software packages use spreadsheets, they are unique. Spreadsheets are very easy to use once a few very basic procedures are learned. **Lotus 1-2-3** has a very effective help system. The DRI software for the Samuelson-Nordhaus text contains a tutorial on the spreadsheet and the software which is well written and very helpful. Both of McGraw-Hill's DRI packages include a written tutorial. However, both written tutorials contain errors—a most unfortunate problem for the novice user. Many students unfamiliar with computers and/or spreadsheets will require significant start-up costs, which may spill over into class time and/or office hours.

ECO TALK and **INTERACTIVE ECONOMICS GRAPHIC TUTORIAL** both use a single output screen. Students input answers and receive feedback on different sections of the same screen. This is an efficient use of the computer since the information students need to answer questions remains on the screen as feedback is provided. The text portion of the **ECO TALK** screen is conveniently placed on the left side. The text in the window of the **INTERACTIVE ECONOMICS GRAPHIC TUTORIAL** scrolls.

Documentation

Instructional microcomputer software must include instruction on how to boot the disk. Users might also expect to find suggestions on how to use the software in a course in economic principles. All the reviewed software except for **PRINCIPLES SIMULATIONS** met this minimum and a few provided additional information and teaching suggestions. **CAPER**'s Student's Manual contains a detailed description of the contents of the software. The documentation for McGraw-Hill's DRI software includes a listing of questions and preformatted data that students can use with the spreadsheet to answer the questions. In addition, users are provided empirical models for "what if" exercises. While usually not extensive, the documentations are adequate.

Availability

Software needs to be readily available for review and purchase by faculty. Most of the reviewed software packages are available for examination prior to textbook adoption. The software programs are available at no cost to faculty adopting the textbooks. The costs of student disks are noted in the accompanying reviews of the software. A few publishers grant permission to make copies for students' use at the educational institution or temporarily at home.

Content

The content of instructional microcomputer software must provide adequate coverage of basic concepts. In addition, the concept presentation must be accurate. Most of the packages were comprehensive in their coverage of principles of economics. This is not surprising since they were designed to complement comprehensive textbooks. Content errors emerged in very few cases. These errors are detailed in the individual reviews.

Potential for Learning Economics

The research findings are mixed on the question of whether CAI increases student achievement for all classifications of students (see footnote 1). It may be that students with the greatest difficulty with economics might benefit the most from the tutorials and drills typical of CAI. By using many of the available software packages, except for **MICROSTUDY**, students having problems with graphs might benefit considerably, although there is no solid research to support this conclusion.

The existing packages are essentially electronic workbooks. As such, most instructors are likely to use the software as a supplement to their regular economics course. Such use would not require significant adjustments to principles of economics courses. For some students the nominal changes would have significant achievement benefits. Dalgaard et al. (p. 313) suggest that, "Students can be taught with computer in less time than with conventional methods for some content and tasks, even when there is no difference in achievement." Although the software could be improved, their use is suggested by the general CAI research literature.[5] Student use of microcomputer software in principles of economics courses is likely to increase student comprehension while requiring less time on tasks. The potential for gain seems to warrant their trial use.

Selection

There exist substantial differences between the available software. Instructors who prefer to use exercises should consider McGraw-Hill's DRI software. **TARGET** is available for those instructors who prefer exercises but wish to avoid spreadsheets. McGraw-Hill's *Framework* package may best suit instructors who want students to extensively use the computer as a productivity tool.

On the other hand, for instructors who prefer interactive tutorials and mini-simulations, then **ECO TALK** would be the software of choice. But note that except for **CAPER**'s and **COMPUTER-AIDED INSTRUCTION**'s text page references and some differences in the depth and breath of economics content coverage, the software packages in this category are nearly perfect substitutes. Therefore, you can select the best of the preferred type.[6]

CONCLUSION

No matter what type of software is used in the principles of economics course, there is a need for empirical research. Previous studies on the effectiveness of computers used mainframe programs and techniques. The conclusions from those studies may not be applicable to microcomputer uses in the classroom. Whether students learn more or their attitudes improve from using microcomputer programs on economic principles remains a matter of speculation. At present there is not a significant body of research in economic education on which to base claims.

Most of the available software for the principles of economics course are drill, tutorials, and testing packages—the lowest level of computer use. Producers of software may have advanced about as far as they can without additional research. To the extent software developers must "rely on personal classroom experience and professional intuition to design instructional activities on the computer" rather than research findings, economic education software is less likely to require "intensive intellectual participation on the part of the student, guide students through optimal sequences of discrete pieces of economic knowledge accumulating to a desired learning objective, diagnose and treat errors in reasoning, and build on the unique characteristics of individual students" (Sumansky, 1985, p. 82). None of the programs reviewed came close to meeting these desirable features. A detailed description of the fourteen programs follows.

CAPER (Computer Assisted Program for Economic Review)

Authors: Calvin A. Hoerneman, David C. Howard, Karen Wilson, and D. John Cole

Publisher: Harcourt Brace Jovanovich, College Department, 1250 Sixth Street, San Diego, CA 92101 Telephone: 619/231-6616

Materials: Two disks and a fifteen-page student manual.

Cost: None to adopters of *Economics: Principles and Policy* by William J. Baumol and Alan S. Blinder. Students: $16.00 net bookstore.

Machine: IBM PC with 128K, monochrome or color display (may work with IBM Compatibles if GWBASIC or a similar Basic is available)

Type: Drill and Practice, Interactive Tutorials

Documentation. Student Manual contains a detailed description of the contents of the software and easy to follow operating instructions.

Features. Four interactive tutorials are included: graph, multiplier, elasticity, and marginal analysis. Following correct responses to multiple choice questions, students may choose to go on or to get an explanation. This procedure permits guessing, while allowing students an opportunity to explore why the guess was correct. An incorrect response brings a hint and another try. Failure on the second try brings an explanation and text references. Diagnostic messages direct students to content areas for further study. In some instances, they were too general to be really helpful.

Ease of Use. No prior computer experience is required to effectively use **CAPER**. On-screen instructions for the test are succinct and clear. Students must input complete words rather than a character or a number. The input must be typed without error before the program continues. Poor typists will require additional time to use this software.

Content. The software contains eleven multiple choice tests. Each test consists of an average of fourteen questions drawn from the textbook's forty-one chapters. The discussion of elasticity implies that P and Qd are not inversely related if the good or service in question is a necessity. "If something is a necessity, you will purchase it no matter what happens to the price (within reason)."

Comments. The software uses a friendly, bantering tone as feedback. It accepts the student's name to personalize the dialogue. Student records are not maintained.

COMPUTER-AIDED INSTRUCTION

Author: Stephen E. Lile

Publisher: C. V. Mosby Company, 11830 Westline Industrial Drive, St. Louis, MO 63146 Telephone: 314/872-8370

Materials: Seven disks.

Cost: None to faculty who adopt *Economics* by Lila Truett and Dale Truett. Students: None, permission is given to make copies for students' use.

Machine: IBM PC and IBM PC Compatible with 256k of RAM, two floppy disk drives, and an IBM or compatible color graphics card.

Type: Drill and Practice

Documentation. None provided. The software required start-up inputs that were not provided. A disk to access students' scores is included but without explanations on how to access it.

Features. Students have access to two microeconomics and three macroeconomics lessons. Each lesson consists of approximately thirty questions, most of which are multiple choice. Expected learning outcomes are shared with students. After two or three incorrect responses students are automatically told the correct response. Page references to the Truett and Truett textbook are provided when a student's answer is incorrect. In addition, explanations are frequently provided for correct answers. Student scores are maintained and are accessible by the instructor. Students are frequently provided feedback on the number right on the first try during the lesson and at the end of the lesson. The student's name appears in feedback statements.

Ease of Use. The software is easy to use. Student input is limited to a few keystrokes. Input prompts and other instructions occur at the top of the screen. This may require some user adjustments since it is unconventional. Many space bar inputs are required to advance the software.

Content. Limited coverage of principles of economics content.

Comments. Graphs clear from the screen before questions are asked. To reference prior graphs students must enter the word "info" and then return to the screen with the question. This procedure is time consuming and inefficient. Students also have access to a "back" command. It is helpful but also inefficient. The graphs contain incomplete reference lines and are generally of poor quality. The Demand and Supply lesson contained two very poorly written questions. In one, students are shown a graph with one supply and two demand curves and are asked the question, "The equilibrium price is?"

COMPUTER SIMULATIONS IN ECONOMICS

Author: Rae Jean Goodman

Publisher: McGraw-Hill Publishing Company, College Division, Manchester Road, Manchester, MO 63011 Telephone: 314/227-1600

Materials: Two disks.

Cost: None to faculty who adopt *The Economy Today* by Bradley R. Schiller. Students: $21.00 net bookstore.

Machine: IBM PC and compatibles with graphics.

Type: Simulation.

Documentation. A ten page user's manual that includes start-up instructions, a description of the microeconomics and macroeconomics modules, and a correlation of the modules to the Schiller textbook.

Features. Students have access to six simulations. In the three microeconomics simulations students assume roles as a business decision maker or as the chairman of the Council of Economic Advisors. The three macroeconomics simulations also place students in decision making roles.

Ease of Use. The software is menu driven and thus easy to use. Student input is limited to a few key strokes. The information students need to answer questions is cleared from the screen before questions are asked. This practice encourages guessing and is frustrating to users who need to review graphs and data before answering questions.

Content. Most of the major concepts presented in a principles of economics course are presented in the software. Students are asked to use what they know. They are not presented with on-screen review of content.

Comments. The graphs are not continuous functions and therefore are very difficult to read. In addition, students must answer questions about graphs that are inadequately marked. After several wrong attempts, students will become frustrated and resort to guessing. The program attempts to deal with this by accepting any answers within a predetermined range. Students can answer incorrectly simply because the graphs are so inadequate.

ECONGRAPH II

Authors: Charles Link, Jeffrey Miller, and John Bergman

Publisher: CBS College Publishing, The Dryden Press, P.O. Box 36, LaValette, NJ 08735 Telephone: 312/323-0205

Materials: Two disks and three-page pamphlet.

Cost: None to faculty who adopt *Economics* by Edwin G. Dolan. Students: $12.00 net bookstore (or $13.75, price of textbook plus $5.00 net bookstore).

Machine: IBM PC with 128K, DOS 2.0, graphics card, and double-sided disk drive and most IBM compatibles

Type: Interactive Tutorial; Mini-Simulations

Documentation. A very brief pamphlet describes the software and how to use it.

Features. Key concepts are identified and objectives are listed for students. Students proceed by selecting an objective they want to work on. Excellent and thorough feedback is provided to incorrect responses. Correct responses are also followed by feedback.

Ease of Use. In ECONGRAPH II almost all questions are answered by entering a single letter or a number. To accomplish this, special coding and cursor movements are required. Initially students may find the procedure confusing. Once the procedure is understood, it is very easy to use.

Content. ECONGRAPH II is comprised of nine interactive lessons designed to improve student understanding of principles of economics, particularly in topic areas where the use of graphics enhances comprehension. The nine lessons cover material from eleven of the textbook's thirty-seven chapters.

Comments. "Return" without input is not accepted. Student must provide input before the program will continue. Students are warned to use the software only after reading relevant chapters in the text. The graphics are very good.

ECO TALK

Authors: Michael Claudon and Kipley Olson

Publisher: Harcourt Brace Jovanovich, College Department, 1250 Sixth Street, San Diego, CA 92101 Telephone: 619/231-6616

Materials: One disk and a fifty-three page user's manual.

Cost: None to adopters of *Economics: Principles and Policy* by William J. Baumol and Alan S. Blinder, *Economics: Private and Public Choice* by James D. Gwartney and Richard L. Stroup, and *Cost and Choice* by J. R. Clark and Michael Veseth. Students: $14.00 net bookstore.

Machine: IBM PC, XT, or AT, and compatible equipment with 256k RAM, a color monitor, and MS DOS 2.0 or higher. The software will run without a graphics card but the card is highly recommended.

Type: Drill and Practice; Simulations

Documentation. The User's Manual contains a detailed description of the contents of the software and easy to follow operating instructions.

Features. Students are provided with three distinct learning modes to use with ten micro models and ten macro models. Using the practice mode students can explore the diagrams and determine how the graphs, numbers, and equations relate to one another. Students can check their knowledge in the quiz mode. After two unsuccessful attempts **ECO TALK** provides both the answer and how it is arrived at. The policy mode presents students with a macro policy target and requires students to manipulate government spending, taxes, and/or the money supply to accomplish the policy target. In the Micro Business simulation the student seeks to minimize production costs, maximize company growth, and maximize profits as the chief executive officer of a firm. As the newly elected President students in the simulation Economy must minimize the gap between full employment and Net National Product and simultaneously keep inflation, unemployment rates, the interest rate, and economic growth close to targeted levels.

Ease of Use. No prior computer experience is required to effectively use **ECO TALK**. Users have ready access to help screens and to a calculator. The calculator is a valuable feature not often found in economics software. It worked well but could be improved by allowing the calculation to be input as the answer to the question without additional key strokes.

Content. Students can work with the usual micro and macro concepts including cardinal and ordinal utility theory, supply and demand, markets, cost and production theory, aggregate supply and demand, and national income determination with or without government and different assumptions about taxes and investment. The content coverage, while not comprehensive, is excellent especially in terms of student use of graphic models.

Comments. ECO TALK is excellent economics software. The screen format is efficient. Students always have on display the numbers and graphs needed to answer questions. In addition they can access help and a calculator. Student performance for the quiz and simulation modes is available to the teacher.

FRAMEWORK

Author: Thomas F. Goldman

Publisher: McGraw-Hill Publishing Company, College Division, Manchester Road, Manchester, MO 63011 Telephone: 314/227-1600

Materials: Two disks, two keyboard templates and a 74-page student instructions manual.

Cost: None to adopters of *Economics* by Paul A. Samuelson and William D. Nordhaus. Students: $21.95.

Machine: IBM PC and IBM compatible computer with 256K, two disk drives or a hard disk drive.

Type: Problems

Documentation. An extensive student instruction manual is provided. It supports student learning of **FRAMEWORK**, an integrated computer program involving several applications—word processing, spreadsheet, database, and graphing.

Features. Students are provided an extensive print and computer tutorial introduction to a special limited version of **FRAMEWORK**. Once students have a working knowledge of **FRAMEWORK**, they may use **FRAMEWORK** to answer 105 questions representing twenty-five of the textbook's forty chapters. The questions are from a *Study Guide to accompany Samuelson & Nordhaus Economics* by Gary W. Yohe.

Ease of Use. To use the software effectively, students with limited computer literacy will need extensive practice with **FRAMEWORK** before they will be able to work any of the suggested problems. If students already know one software application package, they may be very reluctant to learn another.

Content. The economics content is determined by the content of the study guide.

Comments. Using this package would require considerable commitment by instructors to helping students learn **FRAMEWORK**. There are no on-screen hints on how to proceed with the software for a given question. Evaluation of student work is not assisted by the software.

THE GRAPHICS TUTOR

Authors: William D. Gunther and Thomas M. Gunther

Publisher: McGraw-Hill Publishing Company, College Division, Manchester Road, Manchester, MO 63011 Telephone: 314/227-1600

Materials: Two disks.

Cost: None to faculty who adopt *The Economy Today* by Bradley R. Schiller. Students: $22.00.

Machine: IBM PC and compatibles with graphics.

Type: Drill and Practice

Documentation. A twelve page user's manual that includes start-up instructions, a description of the microeconomics and macroeconomics modules, and a correlation of the modules to the Schiller textbook.

Features. Students can review the major microeconomic and macroeconomic concepts. Student quiz records are maintained.

Ease of Use. The software is menu driven and thus easy to use. Required student input is not indicated on the screen. Since the text portion of the screen is only three lines, many keystrokes are required to advance the software. Students answer fill-in-the-blank questions by typing in a complete word. Poor typists may become frustrated and use return without input to advance the program.

Content. Most of the major concepts presented in a principles of economics course are presented in the software.

Comments. Graphs are inadequately marked thus encouraging student guessing. Incorrect answers are followed by very brief hints. The software waits for the student to input the correct response or return. Return is accepted as a correct answer. In the command mode students can access help, key terms, and test grades.

GRAPHECON II (An Interactive Introduction to Economics)

Authors: Lee D. Olvey & James R. Golden
Publisher: Addison-Wesley Publishing Company, Inc., Reading, MA 01867 Telephone: 617/944-3700
Materials: Five disks and 20 page instructor's manual.
Cost: None to adopters of *Economics* by Allen R. Thompson. Students: $30.50.
Machine: IBM PC or compatible with 256K memory, CGA-compatible graphics card, and color monitor.
Type: Interactive tutorial and applications
Documentation. The Instructor's Manual is well written and very easy to use. It includes a chapter on instructor options and suggestions on how to use the software in a principles course. A user's manual comes with the disks. The instructions on the Introduction Disk contain all of the information students need to operate **GRAPHECON II.**
Features. Extensive use is made of graphs. Graphs are used to explain and illustrate end-of-chapter questions. Graphs are also used with the text material. Interaction is required as students read the text materials. Correct entries are rewarded with $ signs and incorrect answers receive brief explanations. Succinct explanations are also given for right answers. An "Introduction to Graphs" tutorial is provided as part of the Introduction Disk. A final examination of forty-two questions is available for each of the four disks. Student records are maintained on quiz and final examination scores.
Ease of Use. GRAPHECON II is very easy to use. Student input is restricted to a single key, space bar, and, infrequently, one or two words.
Content. The software includes extensive content coverage, equivalent to that of most college textbooks. There are four volumes: introduction, microeconomics, macroeconomics and international trade. Each volume has seven tutorials and two applications. During each tutorial students are asked questions. A short quiz follows each tutorial. The emphasis is on graphics analysis.
Comments. The graphics are very good. However, in some instances the horizontal intercepts with equilibrium points extend to the right beyond equilibrium points. When curves are shifted, old curves are erased from the screen.

INTERACTIVE ECONOMICS GRAPHIC TUTORIAL

Authors: H. Scott Bierman and Todd A. Proebsting
Publisher: McGraw-Hill Publishing Company, College Division, Manchester Road, Manchester, MO 63011 Telephone: 314/227-1600
Materials: Two disks and a 12-page user's manual.
Cost: None to faculty who adopt *Economics* by Campbell R. McConnell. Students: $16.96.
Machine: IBM PC and IBM PC Compatible with 128K of RAM, one floppy disk drive, an IBM or compatible color graphics adapter, and a single color or RGB monitor.
Type: Tutorial

Documentation. The Instruction Manual includes a thorough description of how to run the software and a list of the forty-five macroeconomic and thirty-five microeconomic content topics covered by the software.

Features. By using the software students can practice graphing techniques used in a wide variety of economic applications. A diagram and a series of questions are provided for each of eighty content topics. Using a single output screen, students input answers to questions based on typical principles of economics graphs. Return without input is treated as a wrong answer. Wrong answers are corrected with an explanation on screen. Students do not actually move curves but input the direction of changes by a single key stroke response to the options "shift to the right" or "shift to the left." In several incidences, students are asked to calculate answers. The calculating capacity of the computer is not available for them to use. A few advance exercises are marked with an asterisk. Score-keeping is not used.

Ease of Use. The software is easy to use. Students are only required to input a letter or several numbers. Students can easily and independently operate the program with very limited orientation. The graphics displays are crisp, clear, and quickly redrawn.

Content. Comprehensive coverage of principles of economics content is usually presented in graphic format. Movement of functions are referenced as shifts left and right rather than the preferred increase and decrease. The terminology excess supply and excess demand is used instead of the preferred surplus and shortage.

Comments. The text screen window is too small and located inconveniently. Users might find text placed on the left side of the screen easier to read. The text in the window scrolls.

McConnell DRI/DATA DISKETTE

Author: Elizabeth Allison

Publisher: McGraw-Hill Publishing Company, College Division, Manchester Road, Manchester, MO 63011 Telephone: 314/227-1600

Materials: One disk and a 174-page instructor's manual. The System Disk of Lotus 1-2-3 or another spreadsheet must be provided by the user.

Cost: None to faculty who adopt *Economics* by Campbell R. McConnell. Students: $45.95 (includes copy of textbook and software).

Machine: IBM PC and IBM Compatibles, other requirements determined by the spreadsheet selected.

Type: Problem sets; Exercises

Documentation. The Instructor's Manual includes a listing of questions and preformatted data that allow students to answer these questions using the computational power of the spreadsheet. Worksheets and suggested answers are included. The database is organized by economic concept. It can be used to provide a variety of additional questions and exercises. The appendix includes empirical models for "What if" exercises and instructions on how to use Dataware with Lotus 1-2-3 and other spreadsheets. Documentation for using the database is on the disk. Also included on the disk are instructions for using Lotus 1-2-3.

Features. This software is a work-alike to that accompanying Samuelson/Nordhaus.

Ease of Use. Spreadsheets are very easy to use once very basic procedures are understood. Many students unfamiliar with computers and/or spreadsheets will no doubt encounter significant start-up costs.

Content. Students can work forty-nine problems representative of the content of thirty-four of the textbook's forty-four chapters.

Comments. The preformatted graphs should help students visualize problem data. Relevant passages from the text can be accessed by the student with a single keystroke.

MACROECONOMICS AND MICROECONOMICS: AN INTERACTIVE DEMONSTRATION

Author: Darryl Strickler

Publisher: South-Western Publishing Company, 5101 Madison Road, Cincinnati, OH 45227
Telephone: 513/271-8811

Materials: Two disks and one-page instruction sheet.

Cost: None to faculty who adopt *Principles of Economics* by Ryan C. Amacher and Holley H. Ulbrich. Students: None, permission is given to make copies for students' use at the educational institution or temporarily at home.

Machine: Apple IIe, Apple IIc, IBM PCjr, IBM PC, and Tandy 1000. The Tandy 1000 must have 256K. The other microcomputers must have 128K. A color monitor is required to run this software on the IBM PC or IBM PCjr.

Type: Interactive Tutorials

Documentation. The instruction sheet provides a very brief description on how to run the software.

Features. The software is menu driven. Students may choose from four microeconomic topics, three macroeconomic topics, and international trade. Each content area is cross referenced to a chapter(s) in the textbook. Students are encouraged to read the textbook chapters before proceeding with the computer programs. Learning objectives are provided for each content area. High quality graphs are used extensively. Students are not provided explanations for incorrect responses to questions.

Ease of Use. The software is very easy to use because it is menu driven. Students with no prior experience with computers will be able to use this program without difficulty.

Content. Students can access eight tutorials written for fourteen of the textbook's thirty-seven chapters. Content coverage, although not comprehensive, is adequate.

Comments. This is a nuts and bolts tutorial. Only the very basics for each content area are presented. The use of applications/examples is minimal. The graphics are excellent. Price is listed as a determinant of demand and supply, thus confusing the distinction between demand and quantity demanded; supply and quantity supplied. When elasticity of demand is calculated, the negative sign is dropped without explanation. The software worked flawlessly on a Compaq computer not equipped with a color monitor.

MICROGRAPH AND MACROGRAPH

Author: Darryl Strickler and Steven Paul Peterson

Publisher: South-Western Publishing Company, 5101 Madison Road, Cincinnati, OH 45227
Telephone: 513/271-8811

Materials: Two disks.

Cost: None to faculty who adopt *Economics: A Contemporary Introduction* by William A. McEachern. Students: None, permission is given to make copies for students' use at the educational institution or temporarily at home.

Machine: IBM PC, and Tandy 1000. A color/composite graphics monitor is required.

Type: Interactive Tutorials

Documentation. None.

Features. The software is menu driven. Students may choose from five microeconomic topics and four macroeconomic topics. Expected learning outcomes are provided students after they have completed each topic. High quality graphs are used extensively. Students are not provided explanations for incorrect responses to questions.

Ease of Use. The software is very easy to use because it is menu driven. Students with no prior experience with computers will be able to use this program without difficulty. Too many keystrokes are required to advance the program. Only infrequently are students asked to input an answer to a question. Users are not returned to DOS when they exit the software.

Content. The content coverage is not comprehensive but it is adequate. The micro modules present supply and demand, short run and long run perfect competition, and monopoly. Consumption and investment, aggregate expenditures and aggregate demand, aggregate supply, and fiscal policy are the topics included in the macro module.

Comments. The graphics are excellent. The software would not produce high quality graphics on a Zenith IBM compatible equipped with a color/composite graphics monitor.

MICROSTUDY

Author: Delta Software

Publisher: Houghton Mifflin Company, 1900 South Batavia Avenue, Geneva, IL 60134 Telephone: 312/232-2550

Materials: Four disks and instructions on how to boot the disk.

Cost: None to faculty who adopt *Economics* by Martin Bronfenbrenner, Werner Sichel, & Wayland Gardner. Students: None, permission is given to make copies for student use.

Machine: IBM PC and IBM PC Compatible with 192K of RAM, two floppy disk drives. The Apple II version requires 64K and an 80-column card.

Type: Quiz/Drill

Documentation. A four page on-screen documentation that can be printed.

Features. The software is menu driven. Users select from chapter titles and options permitting the study of learning objectives, content overview, key terms, and true-false and multiple choice questions. Questions are scrambled so no two learning sessions are identical. The software is not copy protected. Student performance on the T/F and MC questions is recorded and reported to the student. It is not available to the instructor.

Ease of Use. The software is easy to use. Required student responses are limited to a few key strokes. Help screens are available during any module. A series of three or four screens provide students with a description of the software.

Content. The content coverage is comprehensive, including the economic concepts commonly taught in principles of economics courses. Students have access to study aids for the thirty-nine chapters of the textbook.

Comments. The student using the software is passive and does little more than punch keys occasionally. The computer is used as an electronic page turner. The software does not use graphics. Several problems were encountered during the review. Feedback on a T/F question was for another T/F question. The software aborts to the system if no disk is present in drive B. In one instance, it was necessary to abort to the system to exit the definition window. A toll free telephone number is available to users with questions about or problems with the software.

Samuelson DRI/DATADISKETTE

Author: Elizabeth Allison

Publisher: McGraw-Hill Publishing Company, College Division, Manchester Road, Manchester, MO 63011 Telephone: 314/227-1600

Materials: One disk and a 272-page instructor's manual. The System Disk of Lotus 1-2-3 must be provided by the user.

Cost: None to faculty who adopt *Economics* by Paul A. Samuelson and William D. Nordhaus. Students: $42.95 (includes copy of textbook and software).

Machine: IBM PC and IBM Compatibles

Type: Problem sets

Documentation. The Instructor's Manual includes a listing of questions and preformatted data that allow students to answer these questions using the computational power of the spreadsheet. Worksheets and suggested answers are included. The database is organized by economic concepts. It can be used to provide a variety of additional questions and exercises. The appendix includes empirical models for "What if" exercises and instructions on how to use Dataware with Lotus 1-2-3.

Features. DRI/DATADISKETTE provides on-screen assistance to help students learn the basics of the spreadsheet. Students can also access the extensive help screens of the spreadsheet. The on-screen help specific to the problems includes content hints, text references, and graphs. Prepared graphics on the data are available for student use.

Ease of Use. Spreadsheets are very easy to use once very basic procedures are understood. Many students unfamiliar with computers and/or spreadsheets will require significant start-up costs.

Content. One to three problems are available for twenty-eight of the textbook's forty chapters.

Comments. The on-screen tutorial for the spreadsheet was very helpful. The printed version contained errors which could result in unfortunate outcomes for novice users. The suggested answer for question 1, Chapter 2 contained a reference error.

TARGET 2.0

Author: Jeffrey Parker

Publisher: Scott, Foresman Higher Education/Professional Division, 1900 East Lake Avenue, Glenview, IL 60025 Telephone: 312/729-3000

Materials: Four disks and a two-page instruction sheet.

Cost: None to faculty who adopt *Economics* by Roy Ruffin and Paul Gregory. Students: $13.00 net bookstore.

Machine: IBM PC and compatibles with graphics card and 256K RAM

Type: Drill and Practice; Problems

Documentation. The instruction sheet provides a very brief description on how to run the software.

Features. TARGET is organized as a series of menus. The initial menu is a list of economics topics referred to as modules. Students select a topic module, e.g., "Money & Price." Each module is organized by lesson, e.g., "Classical Quantity Theory," and each lesson includes a set of activities, e.g., "Computing Velocity of Circulation." After two wrong answers, **TARGET** shows the student how to get the right answer. When needed, students receive comprehensive feedback on the problem. No student records are maintained. When mathematical calculations are required students have access to the computer's computation capabilities.

Ease of use. The software is menu driven so it is very easy to use. Student input is usually only a number.

Content. Content coverage is adequate and representative of the content presented in the textbook.

Comments. Students requesting "Introduction & Definitions" are presented with too much text on one screen. It is very difficult to read. The program accepts "return" without student input. **TARGET** makes excellent use of graphs. The calculator function failed to operate correctly in the pre-release version of the software that was reviewed.

NOTES

1   The Siegfried and Fels findings are in marked contrast to those of Dalgaard et al., 1984, pp. 311-315. Schenk and Silva, 1984, p. 240, offer several explanations for the scarcity of positive results for the use of CAI in economics compared to the more extensive positive results for other subjects. They suggest "that the computer materials [in economics], not the method, are poorly developed." In addition they suggest "that even when the computer programs are of good quality, they have been improperly used."

2   The textbooks are: Ryan C. Amacher and Holley H. Ulbrich, *Principles of Economics*; Willliam J. Baumol and Alan S. Blinder, *Economics: Principles and Policy*; Martin Bronfenbrenner, Werner Sichel, & Wayland Gardner, *Economics*; J. R. Clark and Michael Veseth, *Cost and Choice*; Edwin G. Dolan, *Economics*; James D. Gwartney and Richard L. Stroup, *Economics: Private and Public Choice*; Campbell R. McConnell, *Economics*; William A. McEachern, *Economics: A Contemporary Introduction*; Roy J. Ruffin and Paul R. Gregory, *Principles of Economics*; Paul A. Samuelson and William D. Nordhaus, *Economics*; Bradley R. Schiller, *The Economy Today*; Allen R. Thompson, *Economics*; Lila Truett and Dale Truett, *Economics*.

3   This is a special limited version of Ashton-Tate's *Framework*.

4   A pre-release version was reviewed.

5   Some suggestions for improvement are included in this review; others must await the results of the research called for by John Sumansky (1985).

6   See Mark Walbert (1989) for another discussion and evaluation of computer software for principles of economics courses.

REFERENCES

Amacher, Ryan C., and Holley H. Ulbrich, *Principles of Economics*, Cincinnati: South-Western Publishing Co., 1986.

Baumol, William J., and Alan S. Blinder, *Economics: Principles and Policy*, San Diego, CA: Harcourt Brace Jovanovich, Publishers, 1988.

Bronfenbrenner, Martin, Werner Sichel, and Wayland Gardner, *Economics*, Burlington, MA: Houghton Mifflin Company, 1987.

Clark, J. R., and Michael Veseth, *Cost and Choice*, San Diego, CA: Harcourt Brace Jovanovich, 1987.

Coleman, John R., "Economic Literacy: What Role for Television," *American Economic Review*, 53:2 (May 1963), 645-652.

Dalgaard, Bruce R., Darrell R. Lewis, and Carol M. Boyer, "Cost and Effectiveness Considerations in the Use of Computer-Assisted Instruction in Economics," *Journal of Economics Education*, 15:4 (Fall 1984), 309-323.

Dolan, Edwin G., and David E. Lindsey, *Economics*, New York: The Dryden Press, 1985.

Gwartney, James D., and Richard L. Stroup, *Economics: Private and Public Choice*, San Diego, CA: Harcourt Brace Jovanovich, 1987.

Kelly, Allen C., "TIPS and Technical Change in Classroom Instruction," *American Economic Review*, 62:2 (May 1972), 422-428.

Lovell, Michael C., "CAI on PCs - Some Economic Applications," *Journal of Economic Education*, 18:3 (Summer 1987), 319-329.

Mansfield, Edwin, and Nariman Behravesh, *Economics USA*, New York: W. W. Norton, 1986.

McConnell, Campbell R., *Economics*, New York: McGraw-Hill Book Company, 1987.

McEachern, William A., *Economics: A Contemporary Introduction*, Cincinnati, OH: South-Western Publishing Company, 1988.

Millerd, Frank W., and Alastair R. Robertson, "Computer Simulations as an Integral Part of Intermediate Macroeconomics," *Journal of Economic Education*, 18:3 (Summer 1987), 269-286.

Post, Gerald V., "Microcomputers in Teaching Economics," *Journal of Economic Education*, 16:4 (Fall 1985), 309-312.

Ruffin, Roy J., and Paul R. Gregory, *Principles of Economics*, Glenview, IL: Scott, Foresman and Company, 1986.

Samuelson, Paul A., and William D. Nordhaus, *Economics*, New York: McGraw-Hill Book Company, 1985.

Schenk, Robert, and John E. Silvia, "Why Has CAI Not Been More Successful in Economic Education: A Note," *Journal of Economic Education*, 15:3 (Summer 1984), 239-242.

Schiller, Bradley R., *The Economy Today*, New York: Random House, 1986.

Siegfried, John R., and Rendigs Fels, "Research on Teaching College Economics: A Survey," *Journal of Economic Literature*, 17:3 (September 1979), 923-969.

Soper, John C., "Computer Assisted Instruction in Economics: A Survey," *Journal of Economic Education*, 6:4 (Fall 1974), 4-28.

Sumansky, John, "College Economics and the Computer Revolution," *Social Science Microcomputer Review*, 4:4 (Winter 1986), 480-486.

_____, "Computer Applications in Pre-College Economics," *The American Economic Review*, 75:2 (May 1985), 80-84.

Thompson, Allen R., *Economics*, Reading, MA: Addison-Wesley Publishing Company, 1988.

Truett, Lila, and Dale Truett, *Economics*, St. Louis, MO: C. V. Mosby Company, 1987.

Walbert, Mark S., "Grading Software Programs Accompanying Selected Principles Texts," *Economic Inquiry*, 27:1 (January 1989), 169-178.

Walstad, William B., Karen S. Hallows, and David Ross, *An Annotated Catalog of Microcomputer Software in Economics*, New York: Joint Council on Economic Education, 1986.

Yohe, William P., Robert E. Schenk, and William B. Walstad, "Instructional Microcomputing in Economics," *Social Science Microcomputer Review*, 5:4 (Winter 1987), 476-484.

CHAPTER 14

THE USE OF MATHEMATICS AND STATISTICS IN THE TEACHING OF ECONOMICS

William E. Becker[*]

In the late 1960s D. V. T. Bear advanced the notion that the teaching of introductory economics required a mathematical treatment. For the principles of macroeconomics he stated that "with a little extra care—primarily quick review of how to solve one linear equation in two or more variables for one of those variables in terms of the others—the mathematics of macroeconomics should not constitute an obstacle to mastery of the material . . . the algebra is so straightforward that, as an expository device, it puts the corresponding geometry to shame!" (1967, p. 155). For microeconomics, he stated that differential calculus is essential to the treatment of utility and profit maximization. He advocated the teaching of static as well as dynamic models, with special attention given to cobweb models of price adjustment. "Of course," he added, "explicit mathematical treatment of the simple cobweb does require the student to learn how to solve a linear, first-order difference equation." He asserted that this was not too advanced for the average student (1970, p. 180).

Although some may have tried to follow Bear's advice, few succeeded, as evidenced by the content of principles texts of today. Books that have attempted to incorporate differential calculus in the main body of the text have failed or been revised, with calculus relegated to footnotes and appendices. Principles texts do not engage the student in the solving of difference equations; calculations of "multipliers" in multisector macroeconomic models have been downplayed.

The lack of extensive mathematical treatments in principles texts today may reflect a resource misallocation arising from consumer sovereignty in education, as alleged by Bear twenty years ago. That is, a Gresham's law of textbooks may have caused the mathematical treatment to be driven from the market, as students and their professors select the cute, easy, verbal texts over the good, hard, mathematical ones. I doubt that this is the case, however. A mathematical method for the teaching of economics has not become dominant because mathematical symbolism as used in economics is not conducive to learning economics.

Efficiency in learning requires communication in the language most familiar to both the student and the teacher. In the United States that language is English. Mathematics is a shorthand form of communication between parties who already know what is being said. In the teaching of economics, even when it may be appropriate to use the shorthand of mathematics (because students have fulfilled an algebra, calculus or statistics requisite, for example), student learning is impaired because the mathematical shorthand used in economics is inconsistent with the symbolism used in other courses.

This chapter advances a rule for including mathematical and statistical concepts and symbolism in the teaching of economics. A few quantitative concepts that are essential for an understanding of the principles of economics are identified and discussed. Examples of abuses of mathematics in the teaching of economics and suggestions for ways to correct these problems are presented.

THE USE OF MATHEMATICS IN THE LEARNING OF ECONOMICS

I doubt that anyone will argue with the premise that the study of economics requires some knowledge of mathematics and statistics. Few would disagree with the idea that the mathematical skills of differential and integral calculus, difference equations, and the like may be appropriate requirements to pass certain qualifying exams for a Ph.D. in economics. I assert, however, that requiring such skills of graduate students does not imply that they are necessary for an understanding of economics. That the American Economic Association has found it necessary to introduce two journals to convey and review ideas in a nontechnical manner suggests that its elected executive committee recognized that most of the AEA membership prefer to learn without the excess baggage of specialized mathematics. As asserted by McCloskey (1985, p. 188),

> Economics depends much more on the mastery of speaking and writing than on the mastery of engineering mathematics and biological statistics usually touted as the master skills of the trade. Most of the economist's skills are verbal.[1]

How can an instructor of economics justify the use of a mathematical treatment to teach freshmen and sophomores when colleagues are relying on *The Journal of Economic Perspectives* and *The Journal of Economic Literature* to stay current in areas in which they may not specialize? *The Wall Street Journal*, *Business Week*, and other well-known periodicals of economic news do not use mathematics for exposition; yet instructors of economics read them faithfully. To expect that students who enter or complete an introductory course will have quantitative skills beyond those required to read these publications is hypocritical and inefficient.

In theorizing about how people learn economics we need to look at what economists do rather than what they say they do. The majority of economists appear to be buying and reading less mathematical writing even though many are attempting to produce more.[2] As teachers we might be wise to respond to the majority of our students and rely on only those mathematical concepts that are absolutely needed for an understanding of the principles of economics. To identify those concepts look at the periodicals economists regularly read. If the concept is not used in those periodicals, think twice about including it in your teaching.

In what follows I identify a few mathematical and statistical concepts that have become part of the language of economics, as reflected in current periodicals. I discuss how the use of mathematical shorthand may have impaired the learning of even these concepts. I also make suggestions on how to improve our use of mathematics in the teaching of economics.

ALGEBRA AND FUNCTION NOTATION

The idea that one event or variable affects the outcome of another is necessary for an understanding of economics. The concept of causality is not difficult to grasp, as seen in the writings of numerous journalists. Students become confused, however, when functional notation is introduced as a shorthand for the relationship between two variables. This confusion has nothing to do with the idea of a relationship between variables. Rather, it is the consequence of the notation used.

From algebra classes students are acquainted with writing the relationship between two variables as

$$y = f(x)$$

where y is the (dependent) variable, which is plotted on the vertical axis of a two dimension diagram, and x is the (independent) variable, plotted on the horizontal axis. They have been taught that this relationship implies that for every value of x (in the domain) there is one and only one value of y (in the range). They most likely have done many exercises aimed at reinforcing the idea that only relations that assign to each element in the domain a single element in the range are functions (e.g., M. P. Dolciani, R. G. Brown, and W. L. Cole, 1986, p. 404).

In macroeconomics, we confuse the student by introducing consumption c as a function of income y. Consumption is typically ill-defined as either planned, expected, or observed consumption, and is written in functional notation as

$$c = f(y)$$

In a two dimensional graph, income y is measured along the horizontal axis (the domain), while in algebra this letter represented the vertical axis (the range). Even within macroeconomics textbooks the confusion over the axes on which the domain and range reside is magnified by having a chapter on graphs, where the vertical axis is labeled y (range) and the horizontal is labeled x (domain), while in the chapter on consumption the independent variable income is on the horizontal axis while the dependent variable consumption is on the vertical. To make matters worse, the hypothetical consumption-income relationship typically is drawn through a scatterplot that has more than one value of consumption associated with a given level of income. (One person making $2,500 dollars per month is observed spending $2,300, while another person with identical income is observed spending $2,450.)

In microeconomics, students must be confused when the direction of functional mapping (causality) appears to be reversed. We write the demand relationship as

$$q_d = f(p)$$

but we place the price p on the vertical axis (the range) and the quantity q on the horizontal axis (the domain).

Making algebraic relationships explicit will not necessarily help the student. It may just add to the confusion. For example, we typically write the consumption function as the straight line

$$c = a + by$$

where the letter b represents the slope of the consumption line. Algebra books, however, define a straight line in "slope-intercept form" to be

$$y = mx + b$$

where the letter b is the y-intercept (e.g., Dolciani et al., p. 397). When an instructor of economics defines the marginal propensity to consume to be the letter b, is it the concept of a marginal propensity to consume or the notation that causes difficulty in learning?[3]

Students are not perplexed by the idea of a function. Working with a straight line relationship between two variables is not overwhelming. It is the economist's shorthand notation that is confusing. To the student this notation may appear to contradict that which he or she learned in algebra classes. While D. V. T. Bear's "average student" may have little problem making the transition from an algebra class to an economics class, remember that the distribution of intelligences is right skewed. Most of our students are below the average. For these students it is not reinforcing to learn that b is the intercept of a line in algebra but is the slope of a line in economics. Seeing functions graphed one way in algebra and another way in economics is not conducive to learning either algebra or economics.

The fact that algebraic and economic functional notation differs is not a sufficient reason for its exclusion from the economics principles classroom. The use of functional notation is so widespread in economics that a student must be familiar with it. Instructors, however, must be cognizant of the manner in which students are taught about functions in algebra classes. At a minimum, instructors should call attention to the differences in notation. Ideally, economists would adjust to the notation of algebra.

BASIC MEASUREMENT AND QUANTITATIVE SKILLS

To understand economics students must be familiar with some measurement concepts such as ratios and index numbers. They must be able to make calculations with these concepts.

In teaching undergraduates I am no longer shocked to find students who cannot convert ratios into decimals, percentages, and equivalent fractional forms. As a matter of routine I now show every step in the formation of a ratio and alternative representations as a decimal and percentage. Students are expected to have these skills by the time they reach high school. By the time they reach college it seems that a large number of students have conveniently forgotten arithmetic.

I find that remedial work with arithmetic and algebra is essential. For reinforcement to be effective, however, instructors of economics cannot be sloppy with notation. As an example of sloppiness, consider the form of a consumption function that I have seen in workbooks

$$c = 2 + 8/9y$$

where c and y are measured in hundreds of dollars. The fraction 8/9 is defined to be the marginal propensity to consume; a rise in income from \$900 to \$1,800 is said to result in expected consumption rising from \$1,000 to \$1,800. But how many students calculate a fall in consumption from \$209.88 to \$204.94, when income rises from \$900 to \$1,800? Those students are correct; the term "8/9y" states that 8 is divided by the product of 9 and y. If 8/9 is the marginal propensity to consume, then the consumption function must be written as

$$c = 2 + (8/9)y$$

A working knowledge of ratios, decimals, and percentages is essential to understanding elasticities, discounting, relative prices, index numbers, and other measurement concepts that are specific to economics. Of these measurement concepts I believe that index numbers are the least appreciated by college students, even though they are among the most frequently cited statistics in economics. This may be because our emphasis in teaching has been on the calculation of index numbers as opposed to their use. To work with the consumer price index, gross national product deflator, or any other index one does not need to know the intricacies of their construction. What is important to know, at least for reading articles in the popular press, is that a movement from 240 to 264 is a 24 base point change and a ten percent rise in whatever the index represents.

CONCEPTS FROM PROBABILITY AND STATISTICS

Students need to be able to use information on averages and expected values. With articles appearing in *Business Week* on rational expectations, and discussions of the efficient wage hypothesis on the front page of *The Wall Street Journal*, the concept of an expected value cannot be ignored. While some might argue that the introduction of the concept of an expected value, and a distribution around that value, is in conflict with the call for less mathematics in the teaching of the principles of economics, these concepts are part of the vocabulary of economics and public policy debate, as seen in the popular press. They are concepts that are used in everyday discussions of decision making. They also are not difficult to understand if the complexities of probability are circumvented. Their use can aid in the teaching of other economic concepts (such as the consumption function).

By the end of the first term every college freshman knows how to calculate his or her grade point average, or is in the process of flunking out. An extension of the concept of an average to an expected value as an average calculated over an extremely (infinitely) large number of courses (trials) follows easily. This discussion can show that because the magnitude of future measurements is unknown, there is no unique way to formulate expectations about the future.

Complex equations are not needed for a discussion of an expected value. Students have no problem grasping the idea that chance factors make the actual outcome of any future event uncertain. A shorthand notation to differentiate the expected value of a variable from any other occurrence of the variables may be helpful; this notation need not go beyond $E(\ )$. Students, however, do not need to learn about density functions or see an integral sign. They only need to be able to visualize a distribution around an expected value.

The idea that there is a distribution of course grades around the grade average for a specific term is understood by students. Similarly, the notion of a distribution of values around the expected value of consumption for a specific level of income can be understood. A consumption function, in which there is only one value of expected consumption associated with an income level while there are many values that can be observed by chance, is made consistent with high school algebra books by reference to the distribution of consumption about an expected level.

For those instructors who wish to make consumption functions explicit, any value of consumption can be written as

$$c = \beta_0 + \beta_1 x + \varepsilon$$

and the expected value of consumption then can be written as

$$E(c|x) = \beta_0 + \beta_1 x$$

where ε is the chance factor, $E(c|x)$ is expected consumption at income level x, and the βs are, respectively, the intercept and the slope. One might think that it would be easier for the student if this consumption function were written as

$$E(c) = \beta_0 + \beta_1 x$$

but such notation is contrary to what they will be or have been exposed to in an introductory econometrics or statistics course. The expected value of consumption notation $E(c)$ is the mean calculated for the entire distribution of consumption regardless of the value of income.

In presenting this mathematical structure for the consumption function I am not arguing that it should be presented in principles classes. I am sympathetic to the notion that the consumption-income relationship (as well as other relationships in economics) can be taught without ever writing down an equation. I am arguing that this mathe-

FIGURE 14-1 CONSUMPTION FUNCTION

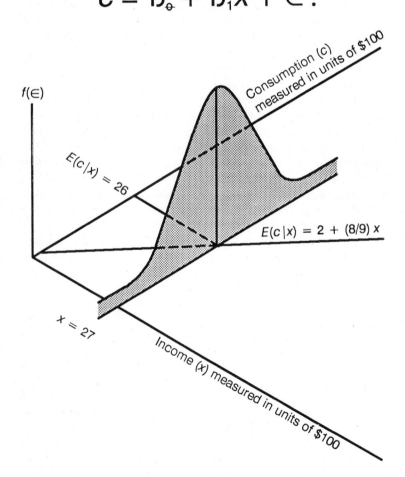

$$C = \beta_0 + \beta_1 X + \epsilon.$$

matical notation is preferred to the consumption function notation that is employed currently in principles texts.   The use of the βs is not in conflict with the notation used in high school algebra classes and it is consistent with the regression notation used in statistics and econometrics courses.   Similarly, the use of x to represent income does not conflict with the use of x in algebra books.   The difference between expected consumption and realized consumption, at given income levels, is explicit in the notation.

Consumption and its expected value can be graphed in a three-dimensional diagram such as that in Figure 14-1. In Figure 14-1 note that all lines are labeled and points of interest are marked. For instance, at an income level of $2,700 per month, where $x = 27$, expected consumption is $2,600, $E(c|x = 27) = 26$. The bell-shaped curve (density function) centered at this expected consumption level shows the dispersion or distribution around a consumption level of a $2,600 that is possible when income is $2,700. Students can see how more than one value of consumption can be associated with a given level of income when the random disturbance ε is introduced. (The use of $100 units is deliberate. As discussed below students must be able to make unit of measurement conversions to understand tables published in business and economics periodicals. Similarly, an ability to read three dimensional diagrams is a requirement for reading these periodicals.)

The concept of a distribution also is essential to an understanding of risk and uncertainty. Modern day microeconomics requires some consideration of the role of uncertainty in decision making. As a starting point I do not advocate the introduction of formulas for the variance, standard deviation, or any other weighted measures of dispersion. The absolute difference between the highest (or the lowest) value in a data set and the expected value can be defined to be a measure of risk. For example, if the expected return on an investment A is 9 percent and the lowest return ever recorded is 3 percent, then a measure of the downside risk for investment A is 6 percent. If another investment B has an expected return of 10 percent, with downside risk of 8 percent, then which investment is preferred depends on the decision maker's attitude toward risk.[4]

MAGNITUDES

To work with economic concepts students need some idea of what is "big," "small," and a "reasonable" value; as Ann Landers (March 25, 1988) put it, "Figuring in the trillions is confusing to most folks." The difference in the number of individuals unemployed for a six versus a seven percent rate of unemployment is not apparent to students. Without seeing the values they could not be expected to associate a one percentage point change with approximately one million more people unemployed. Similarly, the consequence of compounding at a five versus six percent rate of interest cannot be appreciated until the calculations are made.

At a minimum students should be made aware of the tables in the back of the *Economic Report of the President*, as transmitted to the Congress in February of each year. They should learn how to order their own copy from the Superintendent of Documents, U.S. Government Printing Office. Comparing current interest rates, unemployment rates, and other economic measures that appear in newspapers with the historical values in the *Economic Report of the President* will give students a sense of magnitudes. Without this historical perspective there is no way for them to know whether current values are out of line with past occurrences.

CONCLUDING COMMENTS

As with theories of learning, messiness in economics occurs when models are applied to observable phenomena. This does not mean that theoretical relationships should not be considered in the principles course or when considered that they should not be applied to actual situations. It does suggest that emphasis on mathematical detail could mask disagreement among competing schools, impair discussion, and retard the learning of economics. My former teacher, Martin Bronfenbrenner, made this point when a classmate of mine asked what to study for the Ph.D. qualifying exams. Bronfenbrenner responded that Samuelson's principles text should be known from cover to cover. This response was disturbing since at that time (early 1970s) I was trying to learn from the mathematics in Samuelson's foundations; Samuelson's principles text relied on English.

I have come to learn that Bronfenbrenner's advice is grounded in the history of economic thought. In trying to decide how much mathematics to include in our teaching of economics, we may be wise to remember what Marshall wrote to Bowley:

> But I know I had a growing feeling in the later years of my work at the subject that a good mathematical theorem dealing with economic hypotheses was very unlikely to be good economics; and I went more and more on the rules— (1) Use mathematics as a shorthand language; rather than as an engine of inquiry. (2) Keep to them till you have done. (3) Translate into English. (4) Then illustrate by examples that are important in real life. (5) Burn the mathematics. (6) If you can't succeed in 4, burn 3.[5]

Any economist can think of measurement concepts and quantitative skills that he or she feels are essential to an understanding of economics. The question to be asked is at what point do we draw the line and say that additional concepts from arithmetic, algebra, geometry, statistics or other areas of mathematics are not needed for a basic understanding of economics? To use Marshall's words, what mathematics do we burn and not show the students? What quantitative skills are important in real life?

I have argued that answers to those questions can be found in the current periodicals economists read. If articles in *The Wall Street Journal, Business Week, Forbes, Barrons,* and the like do not require readers to have specialized mathematical knowledge and skill, then students in an introductory economics course should not be expected to know or to learn such things.

Many of the articles in current periodicals that deal with economic issues and policy rely on a knowledge of percentages, indices, expected values, and distributions. Some articles require a knowledge of elasticities, standard deviations, functions, and even the marginal propensity to consume. An ability to read charts and tables is taken for granted. Clearly these are quantitative concepts and skills students of economics principles should know on completion of their study. But differential or integral calculus and more specialized quantitative skills have no place in an introductory class; such knowledge is not required to read the publications from which economists learn.

NOTES

[*]Bruce Dalgaard, Colleen Davidson, Catherine Melfi, and William Walstad provided constructive criticism on earlier drafts of this chapter.

1 For a debate on this point see the comment by High (1987) and the reply by McCloskey (1987). Grubel and Boland (1986) show the growth in mathematical economics.
2 This is a testable proposition that has troubling theoretical implications for the reward structure within academic institutions. For instance, if economists (and other academics as well) are willing to pay to have their work published, while the journals have trouble maintaining nonlibrary subscriptions, doesn't this imply that the product of the academic economist is that of a hobbyist? If this is the case, why do departments and university deans count articles in those journals as making someone worthy of promotion?
3 This question has received no attention in empirical work; yet, it gives rise to hypotheses that can be tested in the traditional paper and pencil, pre-post exam, control-experimental classroom design.
4 There is no need for an instructor to introduce the variance or standard deviation as a measure of risk. In an introductory statistics course, the variance is defined as the average squared deviation of observations around their average value. In accordance with this definition, the variance can serve as a measure of risk. Because the variance is measured in squared units, the standard deviation (positive square root of the variance) typically is used as a measure of riskiness. The standard deviation is in the original units of measurement. To appreciate the definition of the variance and the calculation of a standard deviation, students will have to calculate a finite population variance from the formula

$$\sigma^2 = \Sigma (f_i/N)(x_i - \mu)^2$$

and in probability form from the formula

$$\sigma^2 = \Sigma P(x)(x - \mu)^2$$

These procedures are best left to statistics courses.
5 From Marshall's February 27, 1906, letter to Bowley as it appeared in Pigou (1956, p. 427). I am indebted to my colleague Scott Gordon for bringing this volume to my attention.

REFERENCES

D. V. T. Bear. "The Use of Mathematics in the Teaching of the Principles Course," *New Developments in the Teaching of Economics*, Keith Lumsden (ed.). Englewood Cliffs: Prentice-Hall, Inc., 1967.

————. "More on the Use of Mathematics in the Teaching of the Principles Course," *Recent Research in Economics Education*. Englewood Cliffs: Prentice-Hall, Inc. 1970.

M. P. Dolciani, R. G. Brown, and W. L. Cole. *Algebra Structure and Methods*. Boston: Houghton Mifflin Company, 1986.

Herbert Grubel and Lawrence Boland, "On the Efficient Use of Mathematics in Economics: Some Theory, Facts and Results of an Opinion Survey," *Kyklos*, 39(3), 1986, 419-442.

Jack High. "The Costs of Economical Writing," *Economic Inquiry*, 25(3), 1987, 543-547.

Ann Landers. "Figuring in the trillions is confusing to most folks," Los Angeles Times Syndicate and Creators Syndicate (March 25, 1988).

Donald McCloskey. "Economical Writing," *Economic Inquiry*, 23(2), 1985, 187-221.

———. "Reply To Jack High," *Economic Inquiry*, 25(3), 1987, 547-548.

A. C. Pigou (ed.). *Memorials of Alfred Marshall*. New York: Kelley & Millman, Inc., 1956.

THREE

EVALUATION OF INSTRUCTION

CHAPTER 15

MULTIPLE CHOICE TESTS FOR PRINCIPLES OF ECONOMICS COURSES

William B. Walstad

The evaluation of students is one of the most taxing responsibilities for instructors in principles of economics courses. To make that task easier, multiple choice tests are often administered in those courses. Ease of use, however, provides no guarantee of the quality of the test. Test constructors must have solid understanding of this fixed-response method if they are to assess student knowledge of the content covered in a course with any degree of accuracy.

This chapter, therefore, is designed to help economics instructors make better multiple choice tests for classroom use. The first section of the chapter discusses the positive features of multiple choice tests because many economics instructors are not aware that this method is often superior to the essay method for evaluating students. The second section outlines procedures for constructing mid-term or final exams, and presents guidelines and examples of how questions should be prepared for multiple choice tests. The final section explains how statistical analysis of the test data can be used to identify weaknesses in questions and to improve the quality of future tests.

THE CASE FOR MULTIPLE CHOICE TESTING

Multiple choice tests have distinct advantages over the other major alternative, the essay test, or its short-answer derivative. The most compelling advantage arises from the constraints facing teachers. When class sizes are large, as they often are in principles sections, it is very time-consuming to grade essays and more difficult to give quick feedback to students. Spending hours reading essays means less time available for other duties—preparing lectures, seeing students, serving on committees, and conducting research. The grading time for multiple choice tests is negligible.

Some instructors think that the economy in scoring offered by multiple choice tests cheapens the education of students. Personal preference aside, there is no evidence to suggest that multiple choice tests are less effective ways to measure student achievement in economics. In fact, multiple choice tests provide more objective assessments of economic understanding because there is no bias in scoring. Bias in essay scoring comes from such factors as knowing the name of the student, the mood of the instructor, the order in which essays of the class are read, how many times the essays are read, and the importance given to matters of composition. None of these sources of bias enter the scoring of multiple choice tests. Fixed-format questions are also highly structured with one correct answer, and contain none of the vagueness that affects the grading of essays.

Another benefit comes from the ability to sample more of the content domain. A look at the content of major principles textbooks (see Chapter 12) shows that there are a multitude of topics covered in any text. Essay tests with three questions, or short-answer tests with five to seven questions, may assess only a limited portion of the content domain of the textbook chapters or the lectures for which the tests are designed. Multiple choice tests, in contrast, usually contain 30-40 questions and allow the instructors more flexibility to evaluate students on a much wider range of content. The instructor can also measure the depth of understanding by placing a series of questions about a topic on the exam.

The advantages of less bias and wider sampling of the content domain mean that multiple choice tests are more reliable indicators of student performance than essay tests. With essays, there is a much stronger element of chance influencing the test score because students may be unlucky if the instructor asks one of three essay questions on a topic that the student did not study; it is less likely that one-third of the multiple choice questions will be on material that the student did not study. The measurement error introduced from the subjective nature of grading compounds the problem. A recent study of college tests of English composition (Breland et al., 1987) illustrates the difference: the reliability of single essays read once ranged from .36-.46, and only rose to the range of .53-.62 after being read three times; the reliability of the multiple choice tests were in the range of .84-.92.[1]

It is sometimes argued that multiple choice questions are less desirable because they work only on recall, whereas essays tap higher-order thinking in students and allow students to express themselves. This argument really depends on the quality of each test. Multiple choice questions can be written at different cognitive levels. For example, the *Test of Understanding of College Economics* (TUCE) (Saunders, forthcoming) is a standardized achievement test that has multiple choice questions written at three cognitive levels: (1) recognition and understanding; (2) explicit application; and (3) implicit application.[2] The first level focuses on the identification of concepts and terms and mainly taps student recall or identification skills. An example of a recognition or understanding question is:

Which of the following is counted as "investment" in national income accounting?

*A building a new factory.
B buying an existing house.
C purchasing corporate stocks and bonds.
D depositing money in a commercial bank.

Questions at the higher cognitive levels, however, require students to use economic concepts either when the concepts are directly mentioned or when they are implied in the question. An example of an implicit application question from the TUCE is:

In an economy where there is unrestricted competition in all markets, coal is the primary source of heat for most households. Suppose a supply of natural gas which can provide heat at a much lower cost is discovered. What is the most likely effect of the natural gas discovery on the price of coal and the quantity of coal produced?

	Price	Quantity
*A	decrease	decrease
B	decrease	increase
C	increase	decrease
D	increase	no change

This question is not necessarily more difficult than being able to identify an example of investment, but it does require that the student apply supply and demand analysis to determine the correct answer.

Essay tests may not always demonstrate that students show complex understanding. Asking students to "explain why we have a Federal Reserve System" may not reveal higher-level thinking because the students will most likely "regurgitate" the five reasons you gave in your lecture or that were listed in the textbook. Essays, moreover, can be so vague and unstructured that there might be several possibilities for student response. An essay question such as "criticize minimum wage laws" may produce several responses that are valid from an economic perspective but that do not necessarily require the student to use the supply and demand analysis that the instructor wanted students to use in explaining the problems with an increase in the minimum wage. Several well-written items in choice format could handle either the Federal Reserve topic or the minimum wage topic at several cognitive levels with more precision and in less time for the student to answer and the instructor to grade.[3]

The other consideration is the purpose of the assessment. If the purpose is to find out what students know and whether they can apply basic concepts to new situations, then multiple choice tests can handle the task quite well and even better than essays. If the purpose is to find out how well students write, then essays might have an advantage, but the time limitation for responding to essay tests certainly makes them suspect as an accurate gauge of student writing. There are also better ways to assess student writing—term papers, short papers, in-class exercises. These writing assignments make the essay test a poor substitute (see Chapter 11 on student writing).

If these arguments still raise doubts about the worth of multiple choice tests in your mind, you might conduct the following experiment in your class. Give students a test with multiple choice questions for half the period and essay questions (or short-answer) for the other half. Score each half of the test and then correlate the scores. What you are likely to find is that students who do well on the multiple choice questions are likely to do well on the essay questions, and vice versa.[4]

CONSTRUCTING CLASSROOM TESTS

There are two elements to constructing a classroom test. The first element is the creation of a test plan or log for covering the content. The second element entails preparing questions for the exam. Each element is discussed in the sections that follow, but special attention is devoted to guidelines for preparing test items.

The Test Log

What do you need to do first to make a good quality test for classroom use? The initial step is basically an iterative process that results in the development of a table outlining the content covered by the items on the test. You can begin by identifying the economic concepts for the test and then finding or writing questions that will be used to assess that content; or, you can start by selecting or writing questions, and then describe what economic content the questions cover. In the end there should be a content descriptor for each item on the test. An example of a test log for a mid-term exam in a microeconomic principles course is shown in Table 15-1.

With this test log, you now know how many questions are being used to cover the material in five chapters assigned for the test and some of the characteristics of the test questions. A quick scan of this 35-item test tells you the percentage of questions that will be allocated to each chapter. For example, the largest percentage (26) of questions is devoted to the material in the chapter on pure monopoly. The listing shows you if you missed any central concepts and should add questions, or if you should delete questions that duplicate material covered by other questions. The test log also gives you a sheet to use in review sessions to give students hints about what to study.

Other information about the characteristics of the test can be obtained from the test log. You can count how many questions use tables (5) or graphs (7), and how those stimuli are distributed across the test. The source of the question is also reported in the table, with a column indicating the test bank or department file number (#). A plus (+) after the number denotes that the questions have been revised and asterisks (**) in the column mean that the question is new. This item information gives you a detailed record for this exam or for constructing future exams.

Finally, you might want to classify items for the test log according to a taxonomy of the cognitive level. This classification work will give you a good indication about how much of the test requires higher-level thinking. With this data, you can produce a content and cognitive level matrix for the test showing the relative distribution of questions in two areas.

TABLE 15-1   TEST ITEM LOG

Chapter 26: Costs of Production (17.1% of questions)
1. #4   when diminishing marginal returns begin
2. #57   (graph) which graph is correct?
3. #66   diseconomies of scale—why they occur
4. #67+   (table) total variable cost calculation
5. #52   average fixed cost as output increases
6. #26   marginal product and marginal cost relationship

Chapter 27: Pure Competition (20.0%)
7. #23   (table) profit maximization and normal profit
8. #32   total revenue-total cost—the shutdown condition
9. #49+   reason for increasing cost industry
10. #73   increase in demand in increasing cost industry
11. **   (table) on average total cost, average variable cost
12. #68   marginal revenue = marginal cost problem
13. #87   (graph) on short-run and long-run equilibrium

Chapter 28: Pure Monopoly (25.7%)
14. #1   demand curve for pure monopolist
15. #6   (table) demand schedule and total revenue
16. #7   marginal conditions for profit maximization problem
17. #9   marginal revenue and price elasticity
18. #19   (graph) setting price and output by monopolist
19. #22+ (table) cost data and profit maximization calculation
20. #24   when monopolist will close down from losses
21. #33   optimal social price for monopoly
22. #35+ economic incentives for price discrimination

Chapter 29: Monopolistic Competition (17.1%)
23. #3   comparison to pure competition
24. #29   wastes of monopolistic competition
25. #7+   (graph) long run equilibrium
26. #24   (graph) costs of advertising
27. **   demand curve for monopoly
28. #42   allocation of resources

Chapter 30: Oligopoly (20%)
29. #20   joint profit maximization for cartels
30. #25+ price leadership
31. #32   comparisons of structures when price > mc
32. #33   (graph) monopolistic competition in long run
33. **   concentration ratios
34. **   kinked demand curves
35. #39+ cost-plus pricing

Test Banks and Software

The availability of test banks for principles of economics texts means that the time to produce tests that match the content in the textbook has been considerably reduced. It used to be the rule that essay tests take less time to prepare but more time to grade, while multiple choice tests take more time to prepare and less time to grade. Some instructors think that now all you have to do to create a test is to make a list of the item numbers from the test bank and then let the departmental secretary produce the test.

That procedure is the wrong one to follow because it assumes that all the questions in the test bank are good. Anyone who has looked at test banks knows the quality of items varies widely.

Fortunately, complimentary test software for textbooks gives you much greater control over test construction.   The software lets you print selected questions from the test banks that come with principles textbooks.[5] You also have the option to create new questions or to revise the existing questions. This means that the instructor, and not the test bank writer, is responsible for the quality of the questions on course exams: if the test bank questions meet your approval, fine; if not, the questions can be modified to correct perceived deficiencies. New questions can also be written that require higher-order thinking or that cover special applications that were only presented in the lectures.[6]

Preparing Items

Selecting a multiple choice question from a test bank, revising a question, or writing a new question are tasks that require careful scrutiny of the two parts of a multiple choice question. The first part of the question is called the *stem* and it sets up the problem for the student to consider. The second part presents the *alternatives* to the student. The set of alternatives consists of a correct answer and incorrect alternatives which are also called *distractors*. The following points highlight desirable features that should be exhibited by the stem or the alternatives before the question is included on the test. Table 15-2 provides a summary listing of these guidelines.

A Central Idea   The stem in a good test question should present one central idea and not several concepts or terms. A stem that simply states: "Trade barriers:" is vague and confusing for the students because there are a variety of "trade barriers"— tariffs, import quotas, voluntary export restraints, nontariff barriers. A better stem

TABLE 15-2   GUIDELINES FOR WRITING, REVISING OR SELECTING MULTIPLE CHOICE QUESTIONS

1   The stem should present one central problem or concept and relevant qualifying phases.
2   The stem should include all words that would otherwise appear in each alternative.
3   The stem and alternatives should be written as clearly and simply as possible with words whose meaning are clear to students.
4   Alternatives should be homogenous in form, have a consistent grammatical structure, and be in logical order.
5   Alternatives should not provide irrelevant clues to the correct answer because of response length, repetition of phrases, or grammar.
6   Alternatives should not use "all of the above," "none of the above," or a type of "some of the above" as possible responses.
7   The stem should not be negatively stated with words such as "not," "least," "incorrect," or "except."
8   Each item should be independent, so that answering one item does not help in answering another item.
9   The item should have only one correct or best answer, but all distractors should be plausible.

would be one that asks: "Which statement about tariffs is true?" and then lists the alternatives. The question clearly focuses on one concept—tariffs.

Clarity and Brevity   The question should be written as clearly and simply and be as brief as possible. Extra words, unnecessary jargon, and confusing language make a question harder, even if students know the concepts. There is no need for the item to become a test of reading skills when it is designed to test understanding of introductory college economics.

Consider how this tariff question might be improved:

Which one of the following statements about tariffs is true?

   A Tariffs decrease employment in domestic industries, whose products they protect.
*B Tariffs benefit some groups at the expense of the national standard of living.
   C Tariffs increase the market for our exports by reducing our imports.
   D Tariffs encourage the growth of our most efficient industries.

When this question was administered to a large group of students who had taken economics, only 29 percent could correctly answer it. When the alternatives were rewritten as follows to make them simpler and more direct, 58 percent of a similar group of students provided a correct answer:

Which one of the following statements about tariffs is true?

   A Tariffs increase the market for exports.
   B Tariffs decrease employment in protected industries.
*C Tariffs benefit some groups at the expense of others.
   D Tariffs encourage the growth of the most efficient industries.

Use the Stem   Another rule to make items easier to read can be illustrated with the above question. The stem could be simplified further by stating: "Which statement about tariffs is true? Tariffs:". The rule here is that the stem should include all words that otherwise would appear in each alternative, thereby reducing the reading load for students.

Form and Grammar   Alternatives should be consistent in form and grammatical structure, and be listed in logical order. In the revision of the alternatives for the tariff question, the switching of original option C to make it revised option A, and placing original option A as revised option B was done to pair the verbs *increase* and *decrease* as the first two options. The two unrelated verbs (benefit and encourage) are paired as the final two options. This change gave the alternatives more balance.

No Clues   Irrelevant clues to the correct answer provided by response length, repetition of phrases, or grammar should be avoided in items. Notice that the above item is typed so that the alternative with the shortest length comes first, and then longer alternatives follow in ascending order. The alternatives could also be typed in order of descending length. By typing alternatives in ascending or descending order, you do not give any clues to the student about the right answer. When possible, the position of the correct alternatives should be randomized, so that the answers do not fall into a logical pattern that can be decoded by students. In other words, on a four-option test, each option should be the correct answer about 25 percent of the time.

All, None, or Some Options   Another mistake made is the use of alternatives which say "All of the above," "None of the above," or "Some of the above" (e.g., "both A and C"). These alternatives violate the rule that responses should be independent and mutually exclusive. These options also force the student to make sure that the alternative selected is absolutely correct, rather than having the student select the most correct response. Consider the question:

The location of the product supply curve depends on:

A   production technology.
B   costs of required resources.
C   the number of sellers in the market.
*D   All of the above.

For option D to be chosen, the other options must be thoroughly correct. Although ambiguity does not appear to be a problem with this question, selecting the D option places extra burden on students to make sure that A, B, and C are absolutely correct rather than asking students to select the most correct answer. What is more important, however, is that you do not get independent and mutually exclusive assessment of alternatives. Once students know that two options are correct (A and B), then students can assume that D is the correct answer, without having to judge the option C. Students are also given a conflicting message when choosing A, B, or C: they would be penalized for selecting a correct response *because* there are other correct responses.

For a "None of the above" example, consider the following question drawn from a principles test bank:

A perfectly competitive firm might first consider exiting from an industry when:

*A   price is less than average variable cost.
B   price is greater than average variable cost.
C   the price is set so that accounting profit is being made, but economic profit is zero.
D   None of the above.

The correct answer is supposed to be A. When "None of the above" is included, students have to decide if A is absolutely correct. Some students could correctly think that the firm may shut down in the short-run when price is less than average variable cost, but that does not necessarily mean that the firm begins thinking about exiting the industry at that point. Under those circumstances, option D could be correct.

Problems also are present when a combination of alternatives are used. In the above question, "None of the above" could be replaced by an option that read "A and C, but not B." This combination violates the independence and mutual exclusivity of alternatives; if the students know that C is incorrect, there is no need to consider the combination ("A and C, but not B").

Avoid Negatives   Negative items should be avoided, if possible. These items are easily identified because they include such words in the stem as *not*, *least*, *except*, and *incorrect*. There are many negatively stated items in test banks because it is often easier to ask students to identify something that is not characteristic or incorrect rather than writing a question that asks them to identify something that is characteristic or correct.

The reason for the caution is that negative wording requires a change in mental set and tends to be more confusing for students. Students are also more likely to misread the item because it is easy to skip over terms like "not" or "least," especially when they are *NOT* highlighted with italics, capitals, or underlining. These items should be written in the positive direction to test if students know that something is correct rather than incorrect. An awkward item from one principles test bank that begins, "Which of the following is not what an economist would call a productive resource," could be revised to, "Which of the following is considered a productive resource by economists."

Item Independence   Sometimes test banks have a series of questions based on a table or a graph. Care should be exercised in the selection of more than one question related to a table or graph because items should provide an independent assessment of student understanding. When the answer to the second question depends on the answer to the first question, you increase the potential for a double penalty to students who answer the first question wrong and for a double credit for the students who answer the first question right. For example:

The next *two* questions refer to the following consolidated balance sheet for the commercial banking system. Assume the required reserve ratio is 30 percent. All figures are in billions of dollars.

Assets	*Liabilities and Net Worth*
Reserves $200	Demand deposits $600
Loans 600	Capital stock 700
Property 500	

1 There are excess reserves in this commercial bank system of:

   A $10 billion.
  *B $20 billion.
   C $30 billion.
   D $180 billion.

2 The commercial banking system can expand the supply of money by a maximum of approximately:

   A $23.5 billion.
   B $36.5 billion.
   C $51.9 billion.
  *D $66.6 billion.

To answer question 2 you have to be able to answer question 1. Rather than putting students in a double jeopardy situation, select one question (preferably item 2 because it assesses an understanding of excess reserves, the calculation of the multiplier, and deposit expansion). Most questions that follow a table or graph in test banks are not independent. It is best to select one question to use based on the stimulus.

One Correct Answer   Finally, multiple choice items are written so that there is only one correct alternative or one best answer. The other alternatives are to be plausible, but incorrect. You need to double check each item to make sure that there is only one correct answer because distractors are sometimes too plausible. It is more embarrassing for you to have students detect a problem with a question or discover a wrong answer in class while they are taking your test than it is for you to find the problem in the privacy of your office. Most errors of this type can be avoided by taking the exam first, as if you are a student taking it.

Despite these precautions, there are still occasions when students find more than one correct answer. For instance, consider this test bank item:

As price increases along a linear demand curve, the price elasticity of:

  A   supply increases.
 *B   demand increases.
  C   demand decreases.
  D   demand does not change.

Response B is keyed as correct based on material in the textbook. A clever student, however, might have selected D and would be correct if an assumption was made that the linear demand curve was vertical. Since you are not told what the shape of the demand curve is in the stem, students who marked D must be given credit and their grades changed. If the question is to be used in the future, the stem needs to have the qualifying phrase "that is downward sloping" inserted after "curve" to insure that there is one correct answer.

At other times, an instructor has to explain why an answer to a question is correct from an economics perspective, even if students challenge the answer on ideological grounds or some other basis. Consider the following question from a national economics test that was published in many newspapers:

To promote economic growth, a developing country must:

 *A   increase investment.
  B   increase consumption.
  C   use the market system.
  D   use central economic planning.

An editorial in the *Wall Street Journal* criticized the experts for selecting A as the correct answer and commented that if the majority of students picked C "rather than the hoary Keynesian answer, we won't worry too much." The question, however, assesses understanding of the crucial role of investment for economic growth; it is not assessing students' economic philosophy or asking students what they think the best economic system is for achieving growth. The reason A is correct is that for economists investment is the production and accumulation of capital that can be used to produce other goods and services. With investment, nations are able to produce more goods and this additional production is the basis for economic growth (a relationship recognized by both Adam Smith and Keynes). The other options are neither necessary nor sufficient conditions for creating economic growth.[7]

Although few instructors face public debate over the test questions they write, the classroom can become the courtroom when tests are returned. Some students, especially the more able, want to know why the answer they selected is not correct or the option you selected is correct. You must be prepared to defend your answers and give a good rationale for your chosen option; otherwise you must give students credit for their responses. If you don't clearly respond to students' objections, then they think that you are being "unfair," and this perception can affect their evaluation of your instruction. You should also remember that the situation need not be adversarial. The test discussion period can be used to reinforce points made during instruction: "Remember when I described the cost curves for a pure monopoly in class, well this multiple choice question . . ."

Another technique for minimizing adversarial relations in multiple choice question reviews is to have a standing offer to students that they can submit a short written explanation of why they think a particular option is correct, and that you will read the explanation as the answer to a short essay question. This technique permits bright students who make plausible assumptions not considered by the instructor to get credit, and it also prevents giving credit to other students who do not have a good reason for selecting an alternative, or who simply say "I thought that way too" after a good student gives a good oral argument in class. This technique works best if the written explanations have to be submitted after an answer key is posted but before there is a verbal discussion in class. Experience with this technique indicates that few students actually use it, but most feel better about having the option of doing so. Many of the written explanations received also permit questions to be improved.

TEST ANALYSIS

Information is vital to effective classroom instruction. One benefit of multiple choice testing is the opportunity to analyze the test data. From the statistical analysis, you can study overall class results to determine grades, assess individual performance to spot areas of weakness, and use item data to evaluate how well individual questions worked with students. Most colleges and universities have an office where you can turn in the exams and have them scored within twenty-four hours. The test analysis comes back with more data than you probably need, but it can all be helpful in judging the overall test and individual items. Selected test data is shown in Table 15-3 for the test that was described in Table 15-1.

TABLE 15-3   SELECTED TEST DATA

A.   Overall Test Data

Number of Subjects =	40	Number of Questions =	35
High Score =	35	Low Score =	18
Test Mean =	27.13	Test Median =	28.17
Standard deviation =	4.43	Variance =	19.66
Coefficient alpha =	0.76		

B.   Frequency Data for One Item

	Options				
	A	**B**	**C**	**D**	**Total**
1. Number	6	2	29	3	40
2. Percent	15.0	5.0	72.5	7.5	100
3. Group Data					
High	0	0	18	1	19	94.7%
Middle	3	1	6	1	11	54.5%
Low	3	1	5	1	10	50.0%
Option Means	23.7	22.5	28.2	27.0	– – –	– – –

C.   Item Statistics

1. Difficulty = 0.73
2. Correlation (r_{pbis}) = 0.38
3. Discrimination (high-low) = 0.45

Overall Statistics

Most instructors are familiar with basic statistics such as the mean, standard deviation, and range, so there is no need to discuss those in detail here. You can see from the overall data in Table 15-3 that for the 40 students taking the test the scores ranged from 18 to the maximum possible score of 35. The class average was 27.13, which means that the average percent correct on the test items was 77 percent. The large majority of students appeared to show good knowledge of the test content, which was expected because this class contained a larger proportion of high ability students than normal. When the test grades were assigned, 55 percent received an A or a B grade.

The meaning and interpretation of the coefficient *alpha* may not be familiar and merits further attention. Alpha measures the internal consistency reliability of a test. Internal consistency indicates whether the items in the test are assessing a common characteristic, which in this case would be student ability to understand the costs of production and the four market structures. One way to conceptualize the meaning of internal consistency is to think of splitting the test in half and correlating student scores on both halves. The alpha coefficient provides an estimate of the average of all possible split-half correlations. The formula for alpha is:

$$\alpha = \frac{n}{n-1}\ [1 - (\Sigma V_i/V_t)]$$

where, n is the number of items on the test, V_t is the variance of the total test; and ΣV_i is the sum of the variance of individual items.

Alpha can range from zero to one. When scores on individual items are uncorrelated, alpha is zero, and when there is perfect correlation, alpha is 1.00. Between the extremes, the more highly items correlate with each other, the higher the coefficient will be. There is no absolute standard for judging reliability, but the higher the coefficient, the better. The alpha for most standardized achievement tests in economics is in the range of .80-.90. Classroom tests in economics will more likely be in the range of .60-.85. For this test, the alpha of .76 suggests that it is a very reliable measure of student knowledge over the chapters covered.[8]

Item Difficulty

Before you return the exam to students it is best to check the item statistics on each multiple choice question to see how the item performed with your sample of students. Item difficulty is the ratio of the number of students who answered the item correctly to the total number of students who took the item. In item data shown in Table 15-3, of the 40 students who took the item, 29 marked the correct answer, so item difficulty is .73. This ratio is sometimes referred to as a p-value, or it can be expressed as a percentage.

There are no hard rules for determining whether an item was "too hard" or "too easy" for students. That decision will depend on such factors as the purposes of the test, the characteristics of the students in the class, or the circumstances of the testing. For nationally normed tests of achievement such as the TUCE, the p-values tend to range from about .30 to .70, with an average difficulty of about .50. If everyone guessed, the p-value would be expected to be .25, on average, so values below .25 are considered too hard. Values above .75, conversely, are thought to be relatively easy.

The .50 average p-value and .30-.70 range are probably too exacting for classroom tests because the students would get only half the test questions right. Unless you plan to curve the test, this .50 level will result in many low grades. Item difficulty on classroom tests is more likely to range from .50-.90. Those instructors who design classroom tests as an achievement measure will be on the lower end of the range, while those instructors who design mastery tests will probably be on the higher end. The general point is that a sound test consists of items with a range of difficulty at the level at which you think the students should be performing.

What may be more enlightening is the frequency data for each option. You should question any item where the percent marking a distractor is greater than the percent marking the correct answer. If that is the case, check the key to see that you correctly marked it. If you did not make an error, then try to determine why students selected that option. The study of the incorrect responses of students should give you some insight into why they are confused about a question and help prepare you for the class discussion when you return the examination.

You can also use the response data to improve items for future use: item difficulty can be changed by making distractors more or less plausible. In Table 15-3, data on option B indicates it is weak because only 5 percent of the sample selected it; option D is a stronger distractor because 15 percent of the sample selected it. Keep a file on test questions you would like to use again with the difficulty and option frequency data so you can make improvements in questions.

Item Discrimination

The other major piece of information to be extracted from item analysis is the discrimination of the item. A discrimination index provides an estimate of how well an item does in separating students with more economic understanding from those students with less understanding. There are two types of discrimination measures that are usually reported: point biserial and high minus low.

Point Biserial The point biserial correlation coefficient measures the correlation between the students' total test scores (a continuous variable) and their scores on a single test item (a dichotomous variable). The formula is:

$$r_{\text{pbis}} = \frac{X\,\overline{R} - X\,\overline{W}}{S_T} \quad [p/(1-p)]^{1/2}$$

where: $X\,\overline{R}$ is the mean test score for the students getting this item correct, $X\,\overline{W}$ is the mean test score for the students getting the item incorrect, S_T is the test standard deviation, p is the proportion getting the item right, and $(1-p)$ is the proportion getting the item wrong.

With this item the r_{pbis} was .38. What does this number mean? An ordinary Pearson product-moment correlation would have a range of +1.00 to –1.00. The r_{pbis} is a special type of Pearson correlation and its range is somewhat restricted. The general rule is that items with a negative correlation are probably defective, or the key is incorrect, because this would indicate that students who got this item right had lower mean scores than students who got the item wrong.

On national achievement tests, the point biserial correlation sought is at least .20, but on classroom tests, the correlation will probably range from .10 – .50. If you have data from past administrations, items with higher correlations are usually preferred in making up a test, but you should be aware that the correlation formula that indicates higher correlations are more often found with items of average difficulty. Items with low correlations are candidates for inspection and revision because of possible problems with ambiguity or other defects.

High-Low Discrimination A simpler, but less accurate, way to measure discrimination is to break the sample into three groups as shown in Table 15-3. The "high" and "low" headings for the box represent the students scoring in the upper and lower 25-30 percent of the class on the overall test. This method is only approximate because it is difficult to make precise percent cutoffs, especially with smaller samples. For this item, 48 percent of the sample is in the "high" group and 25 percent of the sample is in the "low" group.

This discrimination index is determined by subtracting the proportion correct of the group with a high score on this test from the proportion correct of the group with a low score on the test. For this item, there was a proportional difference of .45 (.947 − .500). Again, there is the problem of interpreting the meaning of this "high-low" number. The index can theoretically range from +1.00 to -1.00, but a negative number is a clear indication of a poor item. A good discriminator will be .40 or greater, although any positive discrimination level indicates that the item is helping to differentiate students. As the index number moves toward zero there is more reason to suspect the discrimination power of the item.

Sample Size and Group Character

Caution must be exercised in the analysis of items from class tests. Decisions about questions based on small class sizes should be very tentative. Large sample sizes are sometimes recommended before you can be confident of the item results. The difficulty and discrimination characteristics of items can also vary from one group to another. It would not be unusual to find that with one group of students a question was hard (.50) and very discriminating (.45), while with another group the question was easier (.70) and less discriminating (.20). These factors, however, should not dissuade you from having the test scored because the item data can be very useful in identifying flawed questions, how questions "worked" with students, or in revising questions for future use. Just keep in mind that the results will depend, in part, on the sample size and student characteristics.

CONCLUSION

Multiple choice tests are probably the predominant method of assessment in principles of economics courses. The reason has to do with the many advantages of this method, including the ease of scoring, the ability to sample the content domain, and greater test reliability. No matter what the advantages, however, the soundness of the tests and the questions still depend on the quality of input from the instructor. Economics teachers need to know how to write good multiple choice questions and how to prepare a well-constructed test. They also need to know what to look for in the follow-up analysis of the test data. This chapter has outlined basic points of multiple choice test construction so that economics instructors can prepare mid-term or final exams that accurately measure student knowledge of principles of economics.

NOTES

1   Reliability is measured on a scale from .00 to 1.00, with higher numbers indicating a more consistent measure (see test analysis section). For a further discussion of the reliability and validity of standardized achievement tests in economics, see Walstad (1987).

2   There are many other taxonomies of the cognitive domain. The most widely used was outlined by Benjamin Bloom and others (1956) and has six levels: (1) knowledge; (2) comprehension; (3) application; (4) analysis; (5) synthesis; (6) evaluation.

3   Multiple choice tests in economics, however, have been criticized because of gender bias. See Chapter 6 or Chapter 20 in this volume for a discussion.

4   A landmark study by Godshalk et al. (1966), replicated by Breland et al. (1987), showed high correlations between scores on multiple choice and essay tests of English composition and concluded that multiple choice tests provided valid indices of students' ability to write.

5   In large classes, you may want to produce several forms of an exam to restrict opportunity for cheating. Test software lets you scramble the order of questions. Recent research by Spector and Gohmann (forthcoming) indicates there is no difference in performance between students who take a scrambled test or students who are tested with questions in the order in which the material was covered in the class or the text.

6   You should beware of the cognitive level of test bank questions. Karns, Burton, and Martin (1983) found in six principles of economics textbooks that the large majority of the questions (70-90 percent) were written at the knowledge and comprehension level of Bloom's taxonomy (see footnote 2).

7   For the complete editorial, see "Quizzical Quiz" (*Wall Street Journal*, December 30, 1988, p. A6). For responses, see letters to the editor by William Walstad (January 12, 1989), John C. Soper (February 3, 1989) and Wallace Peterson (February 10, 1989).

8   Be careful when interpreting alpha, or when comparing alphas across tests. It should be remembered from studying the formula that alpha can be increased by increasing the number of test questions or by administering it to a more heterogeneous group. The opposite changes tend to produce decreases in alpha. There are other tests and formulas for reliability in addition to the alpha or "split-half" test, but they will not be discussed here.

REFERENCES

Bloom, B. S., M. D. Englehart, E. J. Furst, W. H. Hill, and D. R. Krathwohl, *Taxonomy of Educational Objectives Handbook I: Cognitive Domain*, New York: David McKay, 1956.

Breland, Hunter, Roberta Camp, Robert J. Jones, Margaret M. Morris, and Donald Rock, *Assessing Writing Skill*, New York: College Entrance Examination Board, 1987.

Ebel, Robert, *Essentials of Educational Measurement*, Englewood Cliffs: Prentice Hall, 1979.

Godshalk, Fred I., Frances Swineford, and William E. Coffman, *The Measurement of Writing Ability*, New York: College Entrance Examination Board, 1966.

Karns, James M. L., Gene E. Burton, and Gerald D. Martin, "Learning Objectives and Testing: An Analysis of Six Principles of Economics Textbooks, Using Bloom's Taxonomy," *Journal of Economic Education*, Summer 1983, 14, 16-20.

Nunnally, Jum C., *Educational Measurement and Evaluation*, New York: McGraw-Hill, 1972.

Saunders, Phillip, *Test of Understanding in College Economics (3rd. ed.): Interpretive Manual*, New York: Joint Council on Economic Education, forthcoming.

Spector, Lee and Stephen F. Gohmann, "Test Scrambling and Student Performance," *Journal of Economic Education*, Summer 1989, 20, 235–238.

Walstad, William B., "Measurement Instruments," in William E. Becker and William B. Walstad, eds., *Econometric Modeling in Economic Education Research*, Boston: Kluwer-Nijhoff, 1987, 73-98.

CHAPTER 16

ESSAY QUESTIONS AND TESTS

Arthur L. Welsh
Phillip Saunders[*]

Although objective-type tests such as multiple choice and true-false examinations have become increasingly popular in large-enrollment principles of economics courses, essay questions and tests still remain an important part of teaching economists' testing repertoire. Indeed, for many economists the essay test is the only appropriate type of examination, notwithstanding the fact that it has been subjected to over a half century of criticism by testing experts. The purpose of this chapter is not to completely resolve the differences economists might have in choosing between objective tests and essay tests, nor, certainly, is it to intrude into the debate among experts in the field of testing and measurement. Rather, the somewhat more modest goals of this chapter are to review the strengths and weaknesses of essay examinations and explore situations in which essay tests can be used to advantage. The chapter then discusses some general guidelines to use in preparing essay questions and tests, and it concludes with some suggestions for grading student answers. Careful preparation and grading can overcome some of the weaknesses of essay examinations and can help instructors take advantage of more of their strengths—not only in testing student knowledge but also in influencing student study habits.

STRENGTHS OF ESSAY TESTS

The greatest strength of the essay exam is that if carefully constructed, it permits us to *assess and develop higher level cognitive skills* such as synthesis and evaluation in ways that are not possible in multiple choice examinations. While multiple choice questions can be written which require the use of sophisticated cognitive skills to arrive at correct answers, we can never be certain that individual students actually use these skills, since there are no intellectual "tracks" or "footprints" left by either the skilled or the unskilled student.

A student answer on a multiple choice question tells us *what* the student thinks the answer is. The answer on an essay question tells us *why* the student thinks that is the answer. In many cases, of course, the *why* can be very significant. Jerry Petr, for example, has supplied us with a set of two student responses to the following question: "Assume that a monopolistic publisher has agreed to pay an author 15 percent of the total revenue from the sales of a text. Will the author and the publisher both want to charge the same price for the text?" This question, following a unit on profit maximization under monopoly, is supposed to get the student to differentiate between profit maximization and revenue maximization and, if written in multiple choice or true-false format, would require an answer of "no" in some form or other.

Consider, however, two possible student responses to this question in essay form. Student A says, essentially: "No; because the author gets 15 cents on every dollar of price, ($1.50 on a $10 book—$3.00 on a $20 book) s/he will want to charge a higher price than the publisher thinks would be good for sales." Student B says: "Yes; even though the author would be better off in the short run by urging the publisher to produce until marginal revenue is driven to zero, thereby maximizing total revenue, the intelligent author knows that long run existence of his/her publisher would be better served by maximizing profit at a lower volume, and lower revenue, where marginal revenue equals marginal cost." In this example, the students' intellectual "tracks" are obviously more revealing of underlying economic sophistication than the simple affirmative or negative answer to the question.

In addition to what they can reveal about students' knowledge and thought processes, essay questions can also *encourage the development of writing skills*. If one thinks that training in expression, organization of content, and techniques of outlining and summarization are important, one will probably want to use at least some essay questions on examinations. It has been our experience that students who know in advance that they will be required to write out answers study differently than those who know that they will be required only to select answers. No matter how many times we tell our students that our multiple choice questions will require interpretation and application and not just memory we have found that it is only when we tell them that they will also have to write out answers and explain things that they really begin to look for relations between concepts and try to integrate their understanding of various points. And, of course, there is the obvious point: writing is writing is writing. If we want students to develop writing skills, we must give them opportunities to write (see Chapter 11).

A third strength claimed for essay tests is that they are superior to objective tests in *eliciting students' opinions and attitudes*. Economists who make a strong distinction between positive and normative economics may not be too interested in opinions and attitudes for grading purposes. For purposes of relating their instruction to their students' "learning set" (see Chapter 7), however, information about student attitudes and opinions can be helpful. Since there are other ways of eliciting information about student attitudes and opinions besides essay tests, however, we doubt that many principles of economics instructors use essay examinations for this purpose.

A fourth strength of the essay test is one, perhaps, that we don't always fully acknowledge to ourselves. It is simply the fact that *good essay exams are more easily prepared than good multiple choice exams*. This does not always imply that a good essay question is easier to write than a good multiple choice question. It simply means that an essay test with four good questions takes less time to prepare than an objective test with 25 to 30 good multiple choice questions. It has been suggested by experts in testing and measurement that this feature of the essay test is what keeps it popular.

WEAKNESSES OF ESSAY TESTS

Despite the fact that essay tests are the best instruments for measuring certain objectives, one of the most common weaknesses in actual practice is that instructors often *fail to exploit their potential advantage*. Instead of challenging students to analyze and evaluate, our questions are sometimes trite and ambiguous in form. A good essay question requires at least as much specificity and thought from its creator as from its respondents.

A second weakness, and one that is hard to overcome, is that essay questions are *time consuming to score*. Unlike multiple choice or true-false questions, they cannot be assigned to a computer to score. With large classes and/or frequent testing, the opportunity costs to an instructor can be considerable.

Two other weaknesses of essay examinations are limited content sampling and inconsistent scoring.

Limited content sampling simply means that 4 essay questions are not likely to probe student understanding of as many concepts as 40 multiple-choice questions. A partial antidote for this problem is to draft a larger number of more sharply focused essay questions. And, of course, "limited content sampling" diminishes as a problem if we admit that any reasonably sized segment of our course material may contain only a few major concepts suitable for essay probing, along with a lot of other material more amenable to objective testing.

The problem of *inconsistent scoring* of essay answers is the problem of human fallibility. Our evaluation of written work is "subjective" and can vary from one reading to another and from one evaluator to another. We are sometimes influenced by the legibility of handwriting, cleverness or awkwardness of phrasing, grammar, punctuation, and other factors which may be extraneous to a student's economic understanding. There are ways by which the careful instructor can minimize the problem of imprecise scoring, however, and they will be discussed below.

WHEN TO USE ESSAY TESTS

Putting together and administering examinations is an important part of a teacher's responsibilities. It is primarily through the use of examinations that we inform our students about what we think is really important and obtain feedback on how well or poorly they are achieving. If examinations are to provide accurate information for the instructor and be fair to students, the format should be selected with great care. Unfortunately, such care is sometimes lacking in principles courses. All of us, of course, do some thinking about test format before we put our exams together; but, too often, our thinking is not as precise as it might be. Generally, we have an idea of the broad content areas we are testing for. However, we tend to be less aware of the type of student knowledge we are attempting to measure. It is because of this that we sometimes misuse the essay test and fail to exploit its advantages.

If our essay questions begin with words like "who," "what," and "where," we are misusing the essay format. Such questions usually do not get us beyond simple memorization and can be tested for more efficiently and effectively by objective tests. If our essay questions test the student's ability to select ideas, organize these ideas, and present them in his or her own words, however, then we are exploiting the superior advantage of the essay test over other formats.

Keep in mind that the key consideration in selecting a test format (essay versus objective) is a precise knowledge of what it is you want to measure. Now, let us turn to some practical things to consider when preparing essay questions and tests.

STEPS TO IMPROVE ESSAY QUESTIONS AND TESTS

Devote More Time to Planning the Test

We generally have an idea of the broad content areas for which we are testing. In improving our test planning, however, we should go beyond "broad content areas." A useful first step is to specify in some detail the content we wish to cover and then to prepare the examination to meet these specifications, allowing sufficient lead time to permit careful editing and last minute revisions.

A simple matrix, sometimes called a *table of specifications* is often helpful in planning the test. In the left-hand column of the matrix we list the content areas we wish to test, i.e., elements of national income accounting, the GNP deflator, real vs. nominal, real GNP per capita, etc. In the horizontal categories we describe the intellectual or cognitive levels for each content item. For example, we may only want our students to be able to recognize the differences among GNP, NNP, NI, PI and DI—fairly low levels of cognitive understanding. On the other hand, we move up the cognitive ladder if we want to measure how well students can relate the idea of a price index to a real-life situation in macroeconomics. The idea here is to get students to apply the concepts they learned to perhaps a novel situation. This, of course, requires a more sophisticated thinking process than mere memorization of terms.

There are several things that a simple matrix can do for us: (1) by stating the content categories we are forced to specify the content we wish to examine, (2) the cognitive categories show us at a glance the type of student behavior to be tested (and whether the essay test is the appropriate format!), and (3) since presumably all content areas are not equally important, we get a clue on how essay questions should be structured to focus on the more important content areas.

Devote More Time to Constructing Questions

We have already mentioned that one of the strengths of the essay test is that they are easier to prepare than objective tests. But, remember, we were talking about preparing *good* essay tests as opposed to good objective tests. Good essay questions—the features of which we will describe below—are not easy to write. If essay questions are intended to elicit the behaviors we reserve for these types of tests, then sufficient time and care should be given to their preparation.

In discussing when to use the essay test we also noted that essay questions which begin with words like "who," "what," and "where" constitute a misuse of the essay format. The reason questions like these persist is that they take virtually no time to write. Consider the following:

1 Who are the members of OPEC and what are their current aims?
2 What are the conditions for perfect competition?
3 Where are most of the world's current supplies of oil located?

One can think of scores of questions like these in a short period of time, but they are of limited educational value. What we should be seeking instead are essay questions which call for contrasts and comparisons, causes and effects, statements of relationships, analyses and synthesis, and the like. Moreover, we should try to motivate our students by posing challenging and interesting introductions to our questions. For example:

Currently the Fed seems preoccupied with the problem of inflation. However, some critics of Fed policy believe that Fed actions are too timid to tame inflation while others believe that the Fed is overreacting to inflation fears and risks bringing about an early recession.

If you were chairman of the Fed, how would you respond to your critics? Restrict your answer to an analysis of the current economic situation and the likely effect of the Fed's policies on short-term employment and prices.

or:

You were required to read the following books:

An Inquiry Into the Nature and the Causes of the Wealth of Nations—Smith
The Theory of the Leisure Class—Veblen
Value and Capital—Hicks
The New Industrial State—Galbraith

Which of these books gives the most complete account of the workings of the market economy? Briefly summarize what you found in that book. How do the findings of the other books differ from those in the book you selected?

and:

The following two headlines might have appeared in newspapers somewhere:

"J.M. Keynes, Socialist Economist, Dies at the Age of 63"
"J.M. Keynes, Savior of Capitalism, Dies at the Age of 63"

Select either headline and defend it by giving your understanding of Keynes's main arguments expressed in the *General Theory*.

Keep in mind that the foregoing questions are illustrative only; they are simply meant to indicate that essay questions should not be, nor need be, trite. But searching questions require time to think about and compose.[1]

Provide Adequate Instructions for the Students

Even though some students may not know the answer to a question, every student should know what question is being asked. Oftentimes we need instructions calling the student's attention to what we expect in the way of content coverage and detail. Don't be afraid to use detailed instructions in order to keep students on track. Failure to do this can result in some students attacking the problem the way you intended, while others, for legitimate reasons, do not. The upshot of this situation is that there is no fair way to compare students' answers.

Consider the following questions:

1 You are the President. What economic policies would you pursue?

2 You are advising the President of the U.S. What economic policies would you recommend be currently pursued with respect to employment, the price level, and the rate of real economic growth? Restrict your analysis to the instruments of fiscal and monetary policy and how conscious changes in these policy instruments might affect these goals.

Neither of these questions is technically perfect, but clearly the second is more explicit than the first. The first question gives the student great latitude for discourse; the only limitation being that it be restricted to "economic policies." The second question, while longer, directs the student but also allows latitude to demonstrate synthesis and evaluative skills.

Another pair of questions is:

1 Discuss the publically financed income maintenance system in the United States.

2 Discuss the publically financed income maintenance system in the United States. In your discussion, identify the two main elements in the system. Give a specific example of a program in each element, and compare and contrast each element with respect to basic underlying rationale, source of financing, eligibility for benefits, and relative size.

Which question would you prefer to answer if you were a student? Which one would you prefer to grade if you were an instructor?

Several Short-Answer Essay Questions May Be Preferable to a Few Long-Answer Questions

An examination covering the first third or half semester is typically no more than 50 minutes in length. In such a limited period of time only a fraction of the content you might wish to test for can be included. It becomes important, then, to specify carefully the content you are testing for and to design your exam accordingly.

Three or four long- or extended-answer essay questions are probably the most that can be used in a typical exam situation. Unless these questions are very well thought out and tightly phrased, the risk of unreliability due to limited content sampling becomes very real. While content unreliability can result in any type of examination of any length, it is *more likely* to occur in tests with few questions—especially the long-answer essay test.

To get around the problem of content unreliability—and thus minimize the risk of drawing unwarranted inferences about students' abilities—it is sometimes wise to use 10 to 15 short-answer essay questions in place of three or four extended-answer essay questions. By spacing the questions on the examination form you can indicate the desired length of each answer. One type of short-answer essay question combines the essay with the multiple choice exam. You can do this by asking students to write several sentences explaining the process by which they selected one option on a multiple choice question and explaining why each of the other options they rejected were "incorrect." This type of exercise is not only useful in gaining insights into students' analytical processes but is also a good method for determining whether the multiple choice question has weaknesses you might have overlooked.

Examples of two such questions that we have used are:

With the same overall level of aggregate demand, which combination of fiscal and monetary policy might do the most to increase the rate of economic growth? *Why*? (Circle the alternative and explain below.)

A "Easy" fiscal policy and "easy" monetary policy.
B "Tight" fiscal policy and "easy" monetary policy.
C "Easy" fiscal policy and "tight" monetary policy.
D "Tight" fiscal policy and "tight" monetary policy.

The following table gives the number of tons of apples and bananas that can be produced in Country X and Country Y by employing the same amount of productive resources.

	Apples	Bananas
Country X	10	5
Country Y	8	2

Under these conditions, *Country X* would find it advantageous to: (Circle one alternative and explain below.)

A export apples and import bananas.
B export bananas and import apples.
C export both apples and bananas and import nothing.
D import both apples and bananas and export nothing.

Another form of "mini-essay" that can sometimes be used to improve content sampling and also help improve future multiple choice questions is the "true-or-false-and-why" question. If the bulk of the grading is based on the "why" part of the answer rather than on the "true or false" part, considerable insight can be gained into students' thinking, and a fairly large number of questions can be used. Some student answers to this type of question can also be edited and made into options for future multiple choice questions.

One of the most difficult problems in constructing multiple choice questions is to come up with plausible wrong answers, or "distractors." While it's difficult for instructors, who know the right answer, to think of plausible wrong answers, students can often provide us with more than we might want to consider. Seeing what students write on "true-or-false-*and-why*" questions can provide you with a good source of short, plausible wrong answers in constructing good multiple choice questions.

Another form of short-answer essay question that permits a wide range of content sampling and also permits an evaluation of different levels of learning is a set of terms for which students "define and explain the significance." As this form of question is used by Professor Jerry Petr at the University of Nebraska, students are required to write two sentences about each term on the list. The first sentence is to be used to "define" the term; this is often a matter of recall or mastery. But the second sentence is to "explain the significance" of that term in the context of the course. The ability to place a concept in context requires higher level cognitive skills, skills which are not reflected in a response which says "'Externalities' are significant because we study them in Principles of Economics." A number of such terms ("elasticity," "concentration ratio," "crowding out," "currency devaluation" are all examples) can be incorporated into an examination without making unreasonable time demands on the student.

Keep in mind that the short-answer essay can improve content reliability, but it does not guarantee that result. Many short-answer questions, for example, which cover a narrow range of the subject matter may not adequately sample the universe of understanding you wish to measure. Thus, it is vitally important that serious prior thought be given to content planning *before* you actually write your exam questions.

Make Sure Sufficient Time Is Allowed for Student Response

There are three main considerations to keep in mind when allotting time to answer a question. The first concerns the breadth of response you intend. If long, written responses are your intention, you should use few questions or extend the testing period. Since the latter is usually not possible, the number of items must be reduced. But remember that this may cause you a content sampling problem.

A second consideration concerns the depth of response, or complexity. If an in-depth treatment of a particular topic is required, then the extended essay is most appropriate and sufficient time to complete the task is required. It is the in-depth question which often provokes student complaints—and they are not all groundless. We tend, at times, to overestimate our students' abilities and maturity levels, and believe that they can accomplish complex tasks in a short period of time. This is a mistake we should try to avoid. A good way to do this is to actually write out an answer yourself. After you see how long it takes you, add a time allowance of 10 to 15 percent for students who will come to the question less prepared to formulate an answer than you are, and use this as a guide. (Your written answer can later serve as a basis of a carefully worked out scoring key. See below.)

Lastly, we should clearly indicate the number of points assigned to each question on an exam. Some concepts and principles are more important than others, and we rightly attach more weight to questions requiring use of the more important ones. Our students should know at the outset of the test which questions have the greater value so they can budget their time accordingly.

The Use of Optional Essay Questions Should Be Avoided

Permitting students to answer any three of five questions on an essay test, or two of three, or whatever combination, is common practice. Perhaps the reason for this is that the instructor may feel vaguely uncomfortable with the content sampling and wishes to broaden it with optional questions. But whatever the reason, it is a practice to avoid, with minor exceptions. Keep in mind that the purpose of a test is to assess student performance in responding to a representative sampling of the course content. An examination in which individual students can select different questions is no common examination at all. Since the questions presumably deal with different content matter, any attempt to apply the same grading scale to dissimilar tests is unfair to students and, therefore, generally unwise.

As noted above, there are possible exceptions to this rule. At some institutions a "common" examination is given to multiple sections taught by several instructors. While all instructors are required to teach a "common core," latitude may be given to the various instructors to emphasize additional material according to their wishes. In such a situation, optional questions in conjunction with a common core exam may be appropriate to accommodate class variations. Another closely related exception is the case where students are doing independent learning under the tutelage of different instructors and a common exam is given to all. Again, optional questions may be appropriate to capture variations in content emphasis and approach.

GRADING ESSAY QUESTIONS

Prepare an Answer and a Scoring Key

The importance of writing out the answer and making a key for marking exams should be obvious; the key should indicate the elements desired in an acceptable answer and the credit points assigned to each element, thus reducing the chances of unreliability in scoring. Let's assume, for example, that we have presented the following statement to students and asked them to indicate whether they agree or disagree, to identify the main issue(s) involved, and to show by way of examples their supporting argument.

> **Question:** "Clean air, clean water, green grass, and redwoods are all good things, but so are electricity, newspapers, houses, and bread, and I don't see any reason to believe that the market wouldn't give us the right combination of them all."

> **Model Answer:** *Disagree.* The problem of third-party costs and third-party benefits (externalities) makes it unlikely that a free market based only on private costs and benefits would provide optimum combinations of all goods. Goods with third-party costs (negative externalities) would tend to be overproduced, and goods with third-party benefits (positive externalities) would tend to be underproduced.

If burning coal to produce electricity fouls up the air, for example, an unrestricted free market would not count the cost of air pollution and this cost would not be covered by the price paid by the consumers of electricity. Part of the cost of electricity is thus shoved off on "third parties," and since the price charged consumers is lower than it would be if it covered all costs, this would tend to cause overconsumption and overproduction by the parties directly involved.

Likewise goods that have third-party benefits such as neat, trim lawns are likely to be underproduced in a free market. Since the person who improves the appearance of his lawn can't effectively charge all of the passersby who derive aesthetic enjoyment or charge his neighbors who benefit from the general neighborhood improvement, he is likely to devote less time to improving his lawn than would be the case if he could charge for the third-party benefits of his private lawn improvements.

If we're satisfied with our written answer we can now assign credit points to the elements in the answer we feel are most important. For this question an instructor might assign 15 points, weighted as follows: 3 points for disagree; 3 points each for noting third-party costs and third-party benefits (or negative and positive externalities); and 3 points each for examples showing third-party costs and third-party benefits and their consequences.

Why this particular assignment of points? It is largely *subjective*: what the instructor thinks is important based on what he or she has emphasized in class. If you were to prepare an answer for this question and assign credit points, in all likelihood your results would differ somewhat from this example. Because of this, it becomes especially important that all instructors agree on a suitable answer and a scoring key on common departmental examinations.

A well-thought-out scoring key not only facilitates more objective scoring but can also help instructors achieve a greater degree of discrimination among students' responses. For example, some instructors are loathe to give a student zero credit on an essay question unless the question is left blank. In the absence of substance some instructors can find redeeming merit in anything the students put down on paper and give them 2 or 3 credit points. On the other end of the grading scale, these same instructors may embrace the notion that students are inherently incapable of a "perfect" answer and assign as a best score one that is 2 or 3 points below the maximum allotted.

The difficulty with adding points at the lower end of the scale and shaving them at the upper is that one automatically restricts the range of scores. A 10-point question with a 0 to 10 theoretical range becomes for all practical purposes a 2 to 8 range or even a 3 to 7 range. By restricting the range, scores tend to cluster and the question loses much of its discriminating power; that is, it does not reveal significantly different performance levels among good and poor students.

Of course, the range of scores may be narrow because the question is too difficult or too easy. This will happen sometimes but can be overcome with experience. However, restricting the range of scores because one does not have an adequate scoring key is avoidable.

Don't Make the Scoring Key Too Rigid

Before grading examination questions it is a good practice to glance through some of the students' responses. Sometimes students come up with valid points you may not have thought about, or you might have worded your question in such a way as to lead students toward an unintended—but valid—answer.

Suppose, for example, you asked students to "describe the process of inflation and identify the groups in society which suffer from price inflation." You then write out your answer to the question and assign credit points. After glancing through some of the students' responses you notice that some students are answering on the basis that the price inflation was anticipated by all groups in society, while other students assumed that the price inflation was unanticipated. You had "unanticipated" in mind. Are your answer and key valid? Probably not, since your question is ambiguous on this point.

The ideal solution is to construct questions which leave no room for unintentional ambiguity. Regardless of how hard one might try, however, mistakes do happen. In such situations recognize the error as yours and not the student's, and prepare an alternate key.

Also, in some situations, you may want an essay question that permits or encourages different responses depending on what assumptions are made. You may even want to test for students' ability to recognize and respond to this point. In these cases an answer key should be constructed to reflect this situation (see below).

If you want to use your examinations as learning devices as well as grading devices, it is a good practice to distribute your preliminary, tentative answer key to the students as soon as they hand in their answers, before you have had a chance to read them. Our experience is that these answers are read with an intensity that is rare in other, more conventional study situations. Regardless of what students have written on their own exams, they concentrate on a set of good answers to what are, hopefully, the most important questions in the course while the questions are fresh in their minds. This is a rare opportunity to focus student learning; having a carefully prepared, but reasonably flexible, answer key enables you to take advantage of it.[2]

An example of a flexible answer to a "true-false-*and-why*" question that we have used for learning as well as grading purposes is the following.

Question: "A change in the stock of money will lead to a proportional change in the price level." (Source: The "Classical" Quantity Theory of Money)

Model Answer: True, or False, or Uncertain depending on the assumptions made about V and Q in the classical equation $M \times V = P \times Q$. The statement would be true *if* the velocity of circulation (V) and real output (Q) *both* remain constant. It would be false or at least uncertain if V or Q changed. Realistically, V is not always constant, and real output also varies, so there is more empirical evidence for a false or an uncertain answer than a true answer. But, for grading purposes, a person who says that the statement is true if one assumes a constant V and Q will get full credit if these assumptions are clearly specified.

Grade Each Question for All Students Before Moving to the Next Question

Grading one student's entire exam before moving to the next exam can result in unconscious scoring bias. If, for example, the first few responses on a student's exam are excellent, there is sometimes a tendency to award more credit on the next question than is perhaps warranted by the answer. The reverse situation holds also. Thus, grade each question *seriatim.*

Don't Look at the Student's Name Before Grading the Exam

Knowing the identity of the student whose exam you are grading can be a source of unconscious scoring bias. Instructors often gain quick impressions of who their better and poorer students are. In grading exams there is sometimes a tendency to legitimize prior impressions by reading more into the answers of "better" students than is actually there. The opposite holds true for "poorer" students. One can minimize the potential for bias by not looking at the name on the examination until all questions are marked, or by having students put only identification numbers on their answers.

SUMMARY

The essay-type test can be an effective and useful device in principles of economics courses, despite strong criticisms. Essays are excellent devices for assessing student thought processes and their ability to write effectively. Well-written essay questions can probe higher level cognitive skills and require students to synthesize and evaluate ideas. Moreover, unlike objective questions, essay questions require students to supply an answer rather than select one. Essays are also a superior method of eliciting student opinions and attitudes, although most instructors do not do this extensively in principles courses. Finally, good essay tests generally take less time to prepare than good objective tests, chiefly because fewer questions are involved in a typical essay examination.

Criticisms of the essay format center around four general points: (1) they are often used inappropriately, (2) they are time consuming to score, (3) they are more susceptible to content unreliability than objective tests, and (4) they are vulnerable to human scoring error.

A common problem concerning examinations in general is that too little planning takes place prior to writing them. We should know beforehand the precise content we wish to cover on our exams and the cognitive processes we wish to measure. Once we have determined this, we can apply some general guidelines in preparing our exam. A list of these guidelines would include the following: (1) devote more time to constructing questions, (2) provide adequate instructions for students, (3) use several short-answer questions rather than a few extended-answer questions, (4) allow sufficient time for student response, and (5) avoid the use of optional essay questions.

When grading essay questions keep the following in mind: (1) prepare an answer to each question and a scoring key, (2) don't make the scoring key too rigid and be prepared to alter it if it becomes necessary to do so, (3) grade each question for all students before moving to the next question, and (4) don't look at the student's name before grading the exam.

NOTES

*We are indebted to Jerry Petr for some of the ideas and examples used in this chapter.

1   One of our favorites, originally inspired by Michael Sattinger, is:

Read the following three passages and answer the questions below.

Exodus, Chapter 30, verses 12-15. "Each who is numbered in the census shall give this: half a shekel according to the shekel of the sanctuary (the shekel is twenty gerahs), half a shekel as an offering to the Lord. Every one who is numbered in the census, from twenty years old and upwards, shall give the Lord's offering. The rich shall not give more, and the poor shall not give less, than the half shekel, when you give the Lord's offering to make atonement for yourselves."

Leviticus, Chapter 27, verses 30 and 33. "All the tithe of the land, whether of the seed of the land or of the fruit of the trees, is the Lord's; it is holy to the Lord. And all the tithe of herds and flocks, every tenth animal of all that pass under the herdsman's staff, shall be holy to the Lord."

Deuteronomy, Chapter 16, verse 17. ". . . every man shall give as he is able, according to the blessing of the Lord your God which he has given you."

Questions:

A   In terms of *"vertical equity,"* how does the Lord's tax system seem to be changing as one moves from the second to the third to the fifth books of the Old Testament? (i.e., What kind of a tax is indicated in the passage from Exodus? What kind of tax is a tithe? What principle of taxation is implied in the passage from Deuteronomy?)

B   If you were chief angel in charge of economics, which of these three kinds of taxation would you favor? Why? (Explain fully the reasons you favor one kind of taxation over another. Make clear the difference between any analytical concepts and any value judgments you use in your explanation.)

2   It has also been our experience that this practice reduces student complaints about grading. Students looking at the model answer almost always implicitly grade themselves harder than we do. Thus, they often have a sense of relief when they get back answers with partial credit. Without a prior look at a model answer, students with only partial credit are often prompted to ask "why were points taken off?" Once they have seen a model answer that usually contains things that might have been included that they didn't think of, however, they are less inclined to ask this question.

ADDITIONAL READING

If you wish to read further, you might try the following:

Mehrens, William A., and Irvin J. Lehman, *Measurement and Evaluation in Education and Psychology*, third edition, New York, N.Y.: Holt, Rinehart & Winston, 1984.

Test Construction: Development and Interpretation of Achievement Tests, Columbus, Ohio: Charles E. Merrill Books, Inc., 1961, pp. 93-107.

CHAPTER 17

USING VIDEOTAPE FOR TEACHER DEVELOPMENT AND SELF-EVALUATION

Michael K. Salemi[*]

Videotape is a nearly ideal medium for providing feedback to teachers. It is useful both in the training and development of new teachers and for self-evaluation by experienced teachers.

There are three reasons why videotape is a superior medium for development and self-evaluation. Chief among these is that videotape can provide a literal record of what went on in the classroom. It permits the teacher to sit down in the classroom and see what the students see. No other medium permits the teacher to see what actually occurred and decide what worked well and what did not.

Videotape also provides a permanent record of a class session. An instructor can watch the tape more than once and can rewind it to review a part of the class. This permits the teacher to "interact" with the tape. S(he) can watch, then think about what s(he) has seen, and then watch again.

Finally, videotape is convenient and inexpensive by today's standards. Colleges and universities of all sizes have recording facilities capable of producing tapes that can be watched on the standard home videotape player. Today's portable equipment is lightweight, convenient and produces clear images from available light. This means that the teacher's regular classroom may be used for taping.

Videotape is a powerful tool, one that must be used with care. Most teachers, novices especially, are frightened at the prospect of seeing themselves on videotape. They are inclined to be embarrassed and self-conscious about their appearance and the sound of their voice. The powerful impact of videotape makes it a two-edged sword. On one hand, it is usually easy to get teachers to take their videotaped sessions seriously. On the other, it requires careful planning and management to make the videotape experience constructive.

This chapter suggests how to use videotape successfully in a teacher development program. The first section sets out the ways in which videotape can be used in such a program. The second and third sections discuss more specifically how to use videotape to provide constructive feedback to both new and experienced teachers. The fourth section provides specific examples drawn from the teacher training program run by the Department of Economics at the University of North Carolina. The last section suggests how videotape can be used for self-evaluation.

USING VIDEOTAPE IN TEACHER DEVELOPMENT PROGRAMS

There are several ways in which videotape can be used as part of a training program for new teachers or a development program for experienced teachers.

First, videotape can be used as it would be in the typical classroom—to bring information to the participants. Programs for new teachers do more to improve teaching performance when the participants find it easy to connect the principles of good teaching offered in the program with actual classroom situations where they can be employed. Videotape is an effective way to make this important connection. A session on teaching styles can be enhanced by a videotape providing examples of both a formal, professorial style and an informal, conversational style. A session on questioning techniques has greater impact when participants can view a tape of a teacher using follow-up questions to probe the students' understanding and to prompt them to dig deeper for answers. A session on lecturing skills can illustrate those skills by showing several ways of presenting, say, the "revenue test" for the elasticity of demand.

The use of "trigger tapes" as a discussion-starting strategy is a second important use of videotape in teacher training programs. Trigger tapes are collections of short episodes. Each episode is an enactment of a potentially troublesome teaching situation. One type of trigger tape sets up the situation but does not show its resolution. Instead the narrator asks questions intended to begin discussion among the participants about the nature of the problem and strategies for correcting or resolving it. A second type illustrates poor teaching practices and asks participants to discuss ways of improving the performance.

Consider some examples. Novice teachers are rarely prepared for the first time a student, under stress, breaks down in their office. While they may have received good advice for dealing with such a situation, they are unlikely to recall it when faced with reality. By using a trigger tape depiction of such a breakdown, new teachers can experience the emotion of the situation and practice responding to the distraught student. Good teachers know that it is important to listen carefully when students ask questions. A trigger tape segment showing an instructor answering the "wrong question" can drive this point home and stimulate useful discussion about how to listen carefully.

Trigger tapes can focus on content as well as on teaching skills. One of the hardest concepts to explain to beginning economics students is the application of demand and supply analysis to the foreign currency market. A trigger tape might show a weak presentation where an instructor confuses the forces which underlie each schedule. Participants might then discuss strategies for presenting the material clearly and correctly.

The Joint Council on Economic Education has two trigger tapes that have proved quite useful in teacher training programs. The first was produced by the psychology department at the University of Michigan. It contains a segment showing a beginning instructor making a bad impression on the first day of class. Watching the segment can lead to a fruitful discussion on how to get ready for that first day. The second tape was produced by the economics department at the University of North Carolina at Chapel Hill. It depicts a number of "critical moments" which teaching assistants face when teaching recitation sections of an economics principles course. It helps new TAs think through issues such as the level at which to pitch recitations, how to stimulate student participation, and the types of questions students are likely to ask. It is also possible for a department to produce its own trigger tapes which address specific needs.

The third way that videotape can be used in teacher training and development programs is as part of the microteaching process. Microteaching is a small group training procedure that uses videotape to provide feedback to a trainee who is attempting to master a specific teaching skill, such as the use of probing questions or advance organizers. The typical microteaching exercise has three steps. In the first step, the supervisor demonstrates or models the skill. In the second, the trainee practices the skill. The practice session is videotaped. In the third step, the supervisor replays the tape for the trainee and the group and leads a discussion in which suggestions are given by the group members to the trainee.

For example, microteaching can be used to teach participants how to ask follow-up or probing questions in class. In the first step, the person leading the training session defines follow-up questions, explains why they are used, and then shows how to use them. (See Chapter 9 for an explanation of follow-up questions.) In the second step, participants practice asking follow-up questions. Each begins the practice session by explaining some concept and quickly asks the group a question. When other participants respond, the practicer follows up with another question designed to stimulate further student participation. In the third step, the videotape is replayed and the group members offer suggestions possibly pointing out probes that worked well and places where probing opportunities were missed.

Microteaching is more effective than many other methods for teaching new techniques such as questioning skills. Often teachers are reluctant to try these techniques in the classroom simply because they have had no opportunity to practice them and are reluctant to try them out in a "game situation." Microteaching provides not only intensive practice but also nearly instantaneous feedback. The trainee is able to practice the technique until s(he) does it well and feels comfortable with it.

The fourth use of videotape in teacher training and development programs is the one to which the rest of this chapter is devoted—the use of videotape to obtain feedback on the effectiveness of one's teaching.

TYPES OF VIDEOTAPE CRITIQUING PROGRAMS

A two-way classification will describe most videotape feedback programs. The first factor which differentiates programs is the type of teaching performance which is taped and critiqued. Short, simulated lectures and actual class sessions are the most common types. The second factor is the type of videotape procedure used to review the tape and critique the participant. Some programs use formal, objective procedures to review the tape. Most use a relatively informal, subjective approach. Some programs count on participants to critique themselves. Others provide critiquing sessions.

Intensive programs confine videotape critiquing to short, simulated lectures prepared in advance by the participants. For example, each participant in the Joint Council on Economic Education workshops offered between 1979 and 1983 prepared the first five minutes of an economics principles lecture and was videotaped while presenting this material to fellow participants. Critiquing and, in some cases, retaping occurred during the workshop.[1]

Extensive programs such as those offered over the course of a semester by the departments of economics at Indiana University and at the University of North Carolina at Chapel Hill critique participants on the basis of one or more tapes of actual classroom performances. The UNC program is described in detail in section four.

Programs differ also as to the formality of their videotape reviews and instructor critiques. At one extreme are programs that simply provide participants with videotape of their class and permit them to view it privately. No review and no formal critiquing occurs. At the other extreme is the program that was used by the University of Minnesota in the 1970s.[2] There, a specialist undertook an elaborate, numerical review of each videotape to document how an instructor used class time. The critiquer introduced that objective data as part of the instructor's critique.

There are trade-offs involved in choosing any model for videotape critiquing. Intensive programs can use consultants to critique instructors and free the department from the cost of developing in-house critiquing expertise. Participants are simply taped at the beginning of the program and critiqued before the program is concluded. These critiques are useful. They provide an instructor with some basic feedback on voice level and quality, the use of the blackboard, and on body language. However, because they are based on simulated lectures, such critiques cannot provide feedback on other aspects of teaching such as the instructor's mastery of content or the way that the instructor handles student questions.

A related trade-off faced by intensive programs involves the choice of consultants. Critiquing specialists who are educational specialists may provide the most knowledgeable feedback on teaching skills. But critiquers who are economists are clearly better able to provide feedback on the content itself and alternative ways of presenting it.

There are also trade-offs involved in choosing how formal a critiquing program will be. Providing instructors with tapes of their class sessions is inexpensive, but there is no guarantee that they can use the tapes to improve their teaching. Reviewing tapes with the Minnesota procedure provides objective data on each instructor's performance, but at a cost of two to three hours of analysis per class. At UNC, we have found that it is not important to provide instructors with a detailed statistical analysis of how they used their class time. It is important, however, to conduct a critique.[3] Our "semiformal" approach is described later.

MAXIMS FOR A SUCCESSFUL VIDEOTAPE CRITIQUING PROGRAM

A successful videotape critiquing program ultimately improves instruction. It helps instructors change by providing them both with useful information on their teaching and with a framework within which they can evaluate that information. In my view, a successful program must obey several rules. The way the rules are implemented may depend on the type of critiquing program but the rules themselves will not vary.

First and foremost, the program must, as far as possible, provide a nonthreatening experience for the participants. If the critiquing experience is threatening, the participant will be more concerned with self-defense and less concerned with improvement. One might think that the shock value of seeing oneself perform miserably would produce great resolve to improve. "I had no idea I was that bad! I have to do something about this. And fast!" But resolve will not necessarily lead to constructive change, especially when it is coupled with panic. There are several things that the critiquer can do to minimize the threat associated with a first videotape critique. First, the critiquer should state "up front" that the critique is designed to be a rewarding experience. To assuage some fear, the critiquer might show participants a taped demonstration critique of an experienced faculty member. Second, all the arrangements for the taping and critique should be made in consultation with the critiquee. As far as possible, the critiquee should choose the class session for the critique. Third, the critiquer should make a point of emphasizing those teaching practices that worked well for the critiquee. It is as important to reinforce effective teaching practices as it is to change ineffective ones. Fourth, the critiquer should limit the critique to the two or three areas for improvement that appear to be most important. The critiquee should come out of the critiquing session with the clear impression that the proposed agenda for change is manageable.

The second rule of a successful videotape critiquing program is that the videotapes and the results of the critique should be confidential. The principle here is that teacher development and teacher evaluation are, to an extent, incompatible objectives. Videotape critique will be a more effective tool for improving instruction when the critiquee trusts the critiquer and does not feel compelled to defend the teaching practices recorded on the videotape. It is far easier to create an atmosphere of trust when the critiquee knows that he will not be evaluated on the basis of the tape or the critique.

The third rule of a successful videotape critiquing program is that steps are taken to help instructors watch their tapes in a disciplined way. It is not enough for instructors to gain a general impression of their style and effectiveness. The desired outcome is improved instruction so that instructors should watch the tapes in a way that helps them decide what to change.

A useful device for introducing discipline is to have instructors write down before the taping, on a form like that in Figure 17-1, the objectives and teaching plan for the class session. (See Chapter 7 for an introduction to instructional objectives.) After the class, but before viewing the tape, the instructor should also complete a self-evaluation, like that given in Figure 17-2. While watching the tape the instructor should be invited to identify those teaching techniques that worked best. S(he) should also be asked to identify a few places in the tape that indicate a need for improvement and to suggest some alternatives. Finally, the instructor should reevaluate how well the class objectives were met and decide where improvements are most needed.

FIGURE 17-1

PREVIDEOTAPING SURVEY.

1   You are asked to complete this survey for the class which is being taped. When is this class session?

Section 304, Econ 10, September 13, 2:00 pm

2   What are the objectives for the class? What should the students know or be able to do by the end of the class?

The objective for this class is to engage students in a discussion of scarcity, choice,

and opportunity cost, the most important concepts introduced in chapter three. The

students should learn from the class the definitions of those concepts and how to

apply them in a discussion of the allocation of water to the competing uses of irriga-

tion and production of textiles. They should be able to draw a production pos-

sibilities frontier and explain how it shifts when less rainfall occurs or when water

quality improves.

3   What is your teaching plan for the class? What materials, if any, will you use?

I will begin class by defining scarcity and explaining that a scarcity of inputs implies

a tradeoff between outputs. I will give as an example the scarcity of student time

and draw myself a ppf where study time is on one axis and recreation time is on

the other. I will then ask the students how to draw the ppf for the example given

above and lead them through its construction. I will then ask the students how the

ppf will shift in a number of cases.

FIGURE 17-2   POSTVIDEOTAPING SURVEY.

Please fill out this survey after your taping and before your critique.

1   Did your students meet their objectives? How do you know?

I think so. My example went over nicely and a number of students asked questions

and participated in a discussion of it. But they had some trouble understanding

how to shift the ppf.

2   How well did your teaching plan work? Did you stay with the plan? If not, why? Which aspects of the plan worked best? Less well?

My lecture on the ppf went well. But I was surprised by the number of questions

that the students asked about my simple example. Also, no one volunteered when

I asked how to draw the ppf for the water quality example. I explained how but ran

out of time before I could give them much practice on shifting the ppf.

Please fill out the checklist on the following page and use it as a guide when answering the next three questions.

3   What were the two greatest strengths of your performance? Explain.

I think I did a good job of maintaining eye contact with the students. By maintaining

eye contact, I was able to address my answers to the whole class and not just to

the person asking the question. I also made good use of gestures. I also think my

ppf examples were good illustrations of the concept.

4   What were two weaknesses of your performance? Explain.

I think I repeated myself too often when I introduced scarcity and went off on a tan-

gent about the invisible hand. Also, I think I might have asked better questions

about the water example. I looked at the blackboard after class and found that my

writing and drawing was a little sloppy.

5   How will you overcome the weaknesses mentioned above? Explain.

I will plan a little more carefully so that I don't go off on tangents. I will write out my

questions for students in advance. And I will plan to write more carefully.

FIGURE 17-2 (CONTINUED)

Checklist

	Very pleased	O.K.	Would like to improve
1 Delivery			
a I spoke clearly		x	
b I used good vocal inflection and was not monotone.		x	
2 Enthusiasm			
a I appeared interested in the lesson.	x		
b Students appeared interested.			x
3 Poise and self-confidence			
a I appeared confident and natural.		x	
b I was free of distracting mannerisms.		x	
c I kept eye contact with students.	x		
4 Lecture skills			
a My explanations were coherent.		x	
b I made good use of examples.			x
c I used the blackboard well.			x
d I showed mastery of the subject.		x	
e My notation was clear and precise.		x	
f The pace of the class was appropriate.			x
5 Discussion skills			
a I made good use of questions.		x	
b I fielded questions well.			x
c I used follow up questions well.			x
d I listened carefully to answers.		x	
6 Planning			
a My lesson was well organized.	x		
b I emphasized important ideas.	x		

Since improved instruction is the most important objective of videotape critiquing, a final rule for such a program is the use of a contract for change. Instructors should be asked from the beginning to agree that they will implement in their classes the improvements that they identify as most important in their videotape critiques. In some cases they might agree to seek help with specific problems from teaching specialists on their campus. The contract might be a formal one but will more likely amount to an informal agreement between the critiquer and the critiquee. If the instructor is taped again at a later date, the second critique should begin with a review of the original contract for change.

The key here is that the *instructor* should make all the important decisions. The instructor should decide what worked and what didn't. The instructor should decide whether the class objectives were met. The instructor should decide where improvement is most needed. And the instructor should make an explicit commitment to change in the indicated ways. In this way, the videotape critiquing program helps the instructor begin a process of self-evaluation and improvement that can continue after the videotape critique is concluded.

There is the question of what to do with an instructor who does not take the critiquing process seriously and ignores needed change. A second critique can help in this case by pointing out to the instructor that the same problems exist. This is about as far as a development-oriented program can go. An instructor who will not cooperate may be a problem better dealt with by the school's separate evaluation program.

VIDEOTAPE CRITIQUING MODELS

It is now time to set out some specific models of videotape critiquing programs beginning with the model currently in use at the University of North Carolina at Chapel Hill.

In the Department of Economics at UNC, videotape critiquing is one part of the department's annual teacher training program (TTP). The TTP consists of a series of lectures, discussions, and practicums, a set of written assignments, and videotape critiquing. The TTP sessions are organized and conducted by a regular faculty member as part of his/her departmental committee chores. The videotaping and critiquing is done by a senior graduate student chosen and trained by the faculty member. Although mandatory for all new teaching assistants and faculty, the program is very popular so that attendance is regular and participation spirited. The lectures, discussions, and practicums occur at the beginning of the participant's first teaching assignment. Videotaping occurs midway through that first semester.

The first teaching assignment for most of our graduate students is to be a teaching assistant for an economics principles course. There are typically four TAs assigned to each major professor. The TAs are responsible for conducting weekly recitations to groups of about twenty-five students each. After serving two or more semesters as a principles TA, graduate students are assigned to teach their own course in summer school and to be an assistant for an advanced course or a TA coordinator for principles.

The first step in the UNC critiquing process is scheduling the class session to be taped. The TAs are consulted to determine an appropriate week and the recitation section in which they prefer to be taped. Classes where exams are given or reviewed or which immediately precede a holiday are not appropriate for taping. Because we frequently use group critiques, all the TAs for a principles course are taped in the same week so that they all have the same objectives for their recitation sections.

Prior to the taping, each TA completes a survey (Figure 17-1) in which the TA states the objectives and teaching plan for the recitation. We use the survey to reinforce the idea that teachers should begin planning by asking what students should be able to accomplish as a result of the lesson. We also use it to emphasize that self-development requires, as a first step, that the teacher set some objectives.

Next comes the taping of the class. We urge the TAs to tell their classes a week in advance that they will be videotaped and to explain why. The students tend to be more relaxed and more responsive when they understand the purpose of the taping. They are also pleased to learn that the department has a program designed to improve instruction. We use standard "consumer" equipment: a one-half inch videocassette deck, a camera, and a TV monitor. By using the TV monitor rather than the tiny camera monitor, the operator is better able to watch the class and stay alert to what is going on.

We have modified the standard equipment in only one way. We override the built-in microphone and use instead the mixed input from two microphones. We position one microphone near the rear of the class to capture the instructor's voice. We position a second near the front of the room to record students' questions, responses, and comments. Because it is very important to the critiquing process to have a clear recording of student questions and answers, we experimented with microphone positions and mixer settings until we achieved the needed clarity.

The camera operator for our program is the same experienced graduate student assistant who critiques the videotape. This is not essential and a large program might prefer either to hire an undergraduate assistant as operator or to ask for help from the campus media center. In our case, it is simpler to consolidate tasks and the same senior TA tapes, critiques, reads and comments on participants' written exercises, and assists with the TTP seminars.

It is highly desirable that the taping occur in the TA's regular classroom. The technical quality of the tape is clearly less than that obtainable in a media lab. But the tape is *much more* useful because it gives a *much more* accurate picture of the TA's in-class behavior and the interaction between the TA and the students. The equipment we use is so compact and quiet that most instructors report that after a few minutes they largely forget that it is there.

While taping, the camera operator should obey a number of simple rules. Above all, the operator should be as unobtrusive as possible. S(he) should set up the equipment and check the sound level well before the beginning of class. There is a trade-off involved in deciding where in the classroom to position the camera. To be able to record the facial expressions of students who are asking and answering questions, the ideal position for the camera is on one side about half way toward the back of the room. Because this positioning tends to distract some students, we have chosen to tape from the rear of the classroom. In a large lecture hall, it is necessary to position the camera nearer the front of the room.

During the taping, the operator should be careful not to disturb the class. S(he) should either use earphones or operate without a sound monitor and should remain stationary. Most of the time s(he) should focus the camera on whoever is speaking, taking particular care to obtain a clear record of student questions and answers. The operator should also tape the instructor's physical reaction to student questions and answers since that "body language" may affect students' willingness to participate. The operator should use the zoom lens to vary the shot from a head-and-shoulders closeup to a shot that takes in a width of about ten feet. S(he) should get a clear shot of several seconds' duration on whatever is written on the blackboard. From time to time the operator should pan the class so that the instructor will later be able to reflect on the attention level and reaction of the students.

After the taping, both the instructor and the critiquer prepare for the critique. The instructor fills out a self-evaluation survey (Figure 17-2). This self-evaluation is an important part of the process for two reasons. First, critiques are more effective when instructors have first evaluated their own performance because they learn during the critique whether their self-assessment is realistic. Second, videotape critiques have a more permanent impact if they teach instructors how to critique themselves.

The critiquer prepares for the critique by reading the teaching plan and the self-evaluation and then watching the tape. A novice may need to watch the tape twice— first to get a general impression of the session and then to plan the critique. An experienced critiquer will generally watch the tape only once unless the session presents some special problems.

In addition to gaining an overall impression of the session, the critiquer should come away armed with three kinds of specific information. First, s(he) should be prepared to point to two or three parts of the performance that were particularly good. One of these should be chosen to begin the critique even if it means showing some of the tape out of sequence. In this way, the critique begins on a positive note and the instructor will be more likely to deal constructively with problems that the tape may reveal.

Second, the critiquer should identify sections of the tape that bear directly on the objectives that the instructor set out for the class. These are sections that the critiquer plans to discuss with the instructor. It is helpful for the critiquer to take notes so that s(he) can later recall how to use these segments. S(he) should also note the "counter number" associated with each segment in order to cue the tape.

An example should help to clarify the sort of segment that might be used in a critique. Suppose an instructor has stated that the objective for a class is that students practice using demand and supply analysis by solving comparative statics exercises. Early in the class the instructor sets the first practice problem. One or two students unsuccessfully attempt to work it. Thereafter, the students no longer volunteer. After a brief pause, the instructor solves that problem, reviews the rules for shifting demand and supply schedules, and goes on to solve some other practice problems.

The critiquer should plan to focus on the tape segment that shows the instructor giving up the questioning strategy and beginning to lecture. S(he) should plan to ask why the instructor abandoned the questioning strategy. S(he) should also ask the instructor to think of some ways to make the questioning strategy work even though students have stopped volunteering. If possible, the critiquer should show the instructor another segment of the tape where things went better—one, perhaps, where the instructor managed to restate the original problem in a simpler way and stimulate additional participation. The critiquer's ideal plan points out important contradictions between the instructor's objectives and the taped performance but leaves decision making to the instructor. If the instructor is not persuaded, the critiquer should plan to drop the issue rather than to place the instructor on the defensive.

Finally, the critiquer should decide on one or two areas where the instructor might improve. For example, s(he) might decide that the instructor should listen to student questions more carefully and should ask more follow-up questions. S(he) should present suggestions for improvement that flow naturally from the tape segments on which the critique has been focused and, ultimately, from the objectives set by the instructor for the class. If possible, the critiquer should relate these suggestions to the instructor's self-evaluation.

Above all, the critiquer should recognize that the decision to change is the instructor's. At most, the critiquer can facilitate change. The critiquer must be prepared to adjust to the attitude of the instructor. If the instructor seems resistant or defensive, the critiquer should be prepared to make fewer suggestions for change. If the instructor is receptive, the critiquer should be prepared to do more.

The last step of the critiquing process is the critique itself. We employ two types of critiques in our program: private critiques and group critiques. If the taped class went badly or if the instructor does not like the idea of a group critique, the critiquer will conduct the critique one on one.

Typically, the critiquer begins with a brief review covering the instructor's objectives for the class and self-evaluation. S(he) explains the ground rules of the critique, how the tape player works, and that the critique is confidential. Next, the critiquer plays the tape, pausing the tape to ask questions or make a point. Often instructors will be interested in stopping the tape to ask questions or make points of their own. The critique continues in this way until the tape is concluded or until the critiquer believes that it is time to conclude. The critiquer always offers the instructor the opportunity to borrow the tape or watch it again on the department's equipment.

Often we conduct group critiques for two or three TAs whose taped classes were on the same subject matter. In a group critique, ground rules are very important. The most critical rule designates the level of involvement of the critiquees. Allowing other critiquees to offer criticism carries a very high risk of compromising the positive attitude of the session. It is preferable to require that only the critiquer and the person whose tape is being played may talk; the others watch. At the completion of all tapes, some time can be set aside for group discussion and additional comments.

The advantage of the group critique is that TAs see how one another tackled the common teaching assignment. They often make helpful suggestions to one another and exchange ideas. The disadvantage is that less of any one tape can be shown so that it is more difficult to focus on any one individual and to work on developing a commitment to change. For this reason, group critiques are probably a better strategy for more experienced TAs.

A second model for videotape critiquing closely resembles microteaching and was used for some years by the department of economics at Harvard. In this model, videotape critiquing is used as part of an intensive training program for new TAs. TAs are instructed to prepare a short lecture suitable for presentation in the principles course. They are then taped while delivering that lecture to the training group. A critiquer replays the tape immediately and makes suggestions to the TA. TAs modify their teaching plans and are retaped the following day giving the same lecture.

There are several benefits to the microteaching approach. First, TAs receive rapid feedback on their lecture technique which permits them to make needed adjustments and assess the success of those adjustments. This feedback appears to work well since the second-day tapes usually show significant improvement. Second, the program is easy to implement. One need only arrange to use videotape equipment for two or three days each year. Third, the program is particularly valuable for teaching a specific skill. For example, if a TA's blackboard writing was poorly organized in the first taping, the critiquer can point this out and suggest specific improvements. At the second taping, the critiquer will see whether the TA understood how to correct the problem and then can provide additional instruction as needed.

There are likewise some disadvantages to the microteaching approach. Above all, it does not provide feedback on an instructor's actual in-class performance. It cannot realistically simulate, for example, how instructors adjust their presentation when students signal that they do not understand. Nor can it show how well instructors field spontaneous questions. Because it does not provide sustained reinforcement, instructors may revert to their previous practices once the program is ended. Overall, it would seem sensible to think of the microteaching model as a complement to, rather than a substitute for, in-class videotaping. (Klinzing and Klinzing-Eurich also reach this conclusion.) One benefit of using both types of video feedback is that experience with microteaching at the beginning of a TTP should lower the TA's anxiety about the full scale taping and critiquing to come later.

USING VIDEOTAPE FOR SELF-EVALUATION

This section is addressed to those readers who do not have access to video tape critiquing services or who prefer not to involve someone else in the critiquing process. Fortunately, much of what has been said in the previous sections is relevant to the use of videotape for self-evaluation.

A Five Step Approach to Videotape Self-Evaluation

1 Request your media center, teaching resources center, or anyone owning a "camcorder" and tripod to tape one of your classes. Show them the suggestions for taping given above.

2 Fill out the preclass questionnaire (Figure 17-1).

3 After the class is over and before you watch the tape, fill out the self-evaluation (Figure 17-2). You are now ready to watch the tape.

4 Watch the tape with an eye toward making a list of the three parts of your performance that worked best. Write these down and ask yourself why they worked. At the end of the tape, write down two (and only two) parts of your performance that you believe could be improved.

5 Reread the pre- and postclass forms and remind yourself why you liked the parts you liked and why it is important to change the parts you didn't like. Write down a manageable plan for change.

It is a good idea to keep the videotape and watch it again at a later date, possibly in preparation for repeating the self-evaluation process. In this way you can monitor whether your plan for change has been effective and adjust it if necessary.

NOTES

*I would like to thank Steve Cobb of North Texas State University, Matt Klena and Ed Neal of UNC, Phil Saunders of Indiana University, and my friend Joan Worth for making many useful comments on an earlier draft of this chapter. Ed Neal contributed the services of the Center for Teaching and Learning at UNC to conduct a literature search. Steve Cobb was the videotape critiquer for our department between 1984 and 1986. Matt Klena now holds that post.

1 See Hansen, W. Lee, P. Saunders, and A. L. Welsh, "Teacher Training Programs in College Economics: Their Development, Current Status, and Future Prospects," *Journal of Economic Education*, Spring 1980, 11, 1-9.

2 See William E. Becker et al., "Development and Evaluation of Teaching Skills through the use of Videotape," Chapter 11 of Saunders, Phillip, A. L. Welsh, and W. L. Hansen, (eds.) *Resource Manual for Teacher Training Programs in Economics*, Joint Council on Economic Education, New York, 1978.

3 Juliette Venitsky in a paper prepared for the 1982 Annual California Great Teachers Seminar entitled "Using videotape for self-improvement," argues that effective use of videotape requires positive feedback, the provision of immediate and private feedback, and the provision of multiple opportunites to be taped and critiqued. There is other literature documenting that videotape critiquing improves teaching. See Ellett, Lowell E. and E. P. Smith, "Improving performance of classroom teachers through videotaping and self-evaluation," *AV Communication Review*, 23, 1975, 277-288. See also Klinzing, Hans G. and G. Klinzing-Eurich, "The effects of self-confrontation via TV and of additional training components: group discussion, discrimination training, and practice in a scaled-down situation on the indirectness of teacher trainees," paper presented to the annual meeting of the American Educational Research Association (New Orleans, La., April 23-27, 1984).

CHAPTER 18

STUDENT EVALUATIONS OF INSTRUCTION: DECIPHER THE MESSAGE

James W. Marlin, Jr.

Faculty members have always been responsible for teaching, research, and service. As competition for tenured jobs has become more intense, evaluating performance of these duties has become more important. A major problem in this evaluation process is how performance should be measured. Of the three areas, teaching performance is perhaps the most difficult to measure. The purpose of this chapter is to examine one of the major aspects of teacher assessment, the student evaluation of instruction. To provide some background for this discussion, the first section of the chapter examines the problem of determining what should be measured. The next two sections deal with the two major purposes for conducting student evaluations: for improving teaching and for making personnel decisions. The final section of the chapter provides some practical advice on using student evaluations in a positive manner, particularly emphasizing what should be done if you find yourself with a poor evaluation. Sample evaluation forms and a sample summary table are provided in three appendices.

WHAT THE STUDENT EVALUATION IS AIMED AT MEASURING

Teaching performance is difficult to measure for several reasons. In the first place, there is no complete agreement on the purpose of a college education. At first blush it would seem obvious that student learning should be the sole criterion by which teaching performance should be gauged and, therefore, evaluation of how much students have learned should be all that is necessary. While learning information is vital, there are many people within the university community who believe that education is more than the acquisition of facts and figures. Many economics professors, for example, feel that not only factual information is important, but the ability to think, analyze, and make decisions in an economic environment may be more important than the factual information learned. It is particularly difficult to determine if students have acquired these attributes.

Other aspects of education that defy measurement are also present. Much of what is learned in college is learned outside the classroom. Maturation, acculturation, and the acquisition of values also occur during a student's college career. In many cases the professor contributes to the student's education by serving as the role model through which students achieve these ends. Finally, many economics professors believe that a college education revolves around learning to love learning and particularly to get excited about economics. All these aspects of a professor's "teaching" are almost impossible to measure, yet they may be as important a contribution to the student's overall education as is the assimilation of material that appears on final examinations.

To make the situation more confusing, there is no clear agreement among faculty and administrators on the role of the professor. Much of the opinion on that role is, of course, based on the professor's view of the purpose of the educational process. If the professor sees the goal of education to be the simple acquisition of knowledge and skills such as the ability to manipulate supply and demand curves, then the role of the professor is rather straightforward—the role is to provide that information. You will find professors who agree with this view whose classes tend to be dominated by a straight lecture accompanied by specific reading assignments. In their classes, a lecture might be delivered on the complexities of market structures and an exposition, using curves and mathematics, to show how oligopolies maximize profits. Other professors, who believe that decision making and honing of thinking skills are important, tend to teach through discussion and problem solving exercises. Such a professor might present students with a situation potentially faced by decision makers in the automobile industry and then ask them to determine what they would do to solve the problem presented by the situation. Professors who see their role as a mentor and guide tend to have rather free-wheeling, open-ended class sessions. Their classes might again start with a situation, but then go on to examine how the situation might be faced in different markets, evaluate the welfare implications of the situation, or discuss the moral aspects of oligopoly. What happens in the classroom depends, to a large extent, on the professor's view of the educational process and the teacher's role in it. None of these techniques is the *only* way to teach, yet all these views should be accommodated by an effective evaluation scheme.

Methods for evaluating teaching performance include student evaluations of instruction, self-evaluation by the professor, classroom visits by administrators or peers, examination of materials prepared for the classroom such as syllabi and tests, complaints by students, and (unfortunately) gossip in the faculty coffee lounge on who is "still using that dumb Keynesian cross." It has even been argued that good research and good teaching go hand in hand; therefore, a long list of publications is evidence of good teaching and evaluation of teaching is unnecessary.[1] The epitome of an outstanding scholar who was not a "good" teacher is Thorstein Veblen. Few doubt his contribution to economics, yet stories of his dislike of, disrespect for, and avoidance of students are legion. He mumbled, was boring, had office "minutes" at impossible times—he wasn't a very good teacher!

Despite these difficulties and disagreements, most faculty members and administrators agree that evaluation of teaching is both desirable and necessary. They further agree that *student* evaluations do provide useful information (Centra, 1980). In addition to providing assistance in making personnel decisions, the student evaluation of instruction can provide valuable input to the professor regarding his or her own teaching performance.

USING STUDENT EVALUATIONS FOR THE IMPROVEMENT OF INSTRUCTION

Any assessment of student evaluations should differentiate between evaluation for diagnostic feedback to the instructor and evaluation to provide information for making personnel decisions. Both purposes are important, but since the information to be gleaned from the process will be used for different purposes, different types of questions and a different number of questions should be asked. If improvement of teaching is the goal, the questions can be more subjective in nature, and the number of questions used can be larger.

At times, student evaluations can tell you things about your teaching performance that you can get in no other way. For example, only the student can tell you if your brilliant exposition on comparative advantage makes any sense to a nineteen-year-old whose only experience is one in which a premium is placed on the ability to memorize by rote. Learning is an active process—the student must be actively involved for learning to take place. The teacher's job is to help the learner *do* the learning. Therefore, the student's *perception* of your part in the process is unique and cannot be simulated by a peer or supervisor. For most students, what you are presenting is totally new. Money has always been that green stuff in your wallet—not figures on a computer printout at First National Bank. Only a neophyte can appreciate whether or not you are getting your points across to a neophyte.

New faculty members, enthused with all they have learned in their graduate school experience, have a tendency to try to teach everything they learned in their Ph.D. program in one principles of economics course. After four years or more of graduate economics courses, the new professor is completely comfortable with thinking in terms of a curve or an equation on a blackboard representing a real world phenomenon. On the other hand, most beginning economics students are completely mystified by the abstraction of a demand curve. It is a mark on the blackboard only. Without some input from the student to say "slow down—I don't even understand what a graph *means*," new faculty are often surprised when students completely "bomb" the first test. Student input on an evaluation can provide the necessary feedback to allow faculty to know whether or not they are communicating.

Students are also the only ones who can really say whether or not they understand the encyclopedic, 950-page principles of economics textbook you choose. The economic theories may be explained just the way you think they should be, but if they are not clear to the student, your text may be of little help in the learning process. Students can point this out during an evaluation. Your organization may be perfectly reasonable to you, but if students aren't able to perceive the logic of it, they will get lost. Student evaluations will point this out to you. These are but a few examples of what students can do to help you teach well. However, you must give them the opportunity to tell you, and you should not wait until the end of the semester to do it.

Student evaluations can be both verbal and written. Periodic oral evaluations are particularly helpful for improving either the course content or your own teaching performance. When conducting oral evaluations, attempt to keep the atmosphere informal. Stress the need for two-way communication to make the learning experience the best it can be. If you can convince students that their opinions *are* important and that you will *do* something, they will be very open and helpful in their suggestions.[2] The real advantage of the oral evaluation is the two-way communication that is possible. You will be able to follow up and determine exactly what the students are recommending rather than guess at some awkwardly worded student suggestion that is clear to the student but ambiguous to you. For instance, a student might write "you go too fast." In the oral discussion you can find out whether she means simply that "you talk too fast" or whether she is saying "I am having difficulty with the concept of elasticity and you didn't explain it several different ways so that I could understand it."

There are two major disadvantages to oral evaluations. The first is that in large classes, the method is difficult to administer.[3] The second is that students may be reticent about providing feedback, particularly if they feel that you might "get even" on the next test. Whether or not this "drawback" exists depends on the level of trust and rapport you have been able to establish with your students.

Perhaps the most helpful method for obtaining student feedback on a course is a combination of written and oral evaluations. Plan to give a written evaluation and then go over it orally the next class period after you have had a chance to review the comments. In this way you can get the benefits of both methods.

If improvement of instruction is the purpose, then the timing of the evaluation should also be different than if the purpose is for making personnel decisions. If the purpose is to improve instruction, particularly in the current course, then it stands to reason that the evaluation should be given early in the course. This way corrections can be made in "mid stream." You can, for instance, "slow down" the remaining classes in the semester (however the students may have *meant* that comment). Beginning teachers may also wish to conduct more than one diagnostic evaluation in a term. For example, in your principles class, you might wish to take part of a class period after you have completed the coverage of supply and demand to determine whether your techniques have aided or confused the students.

It may be appropriate to conduct an evaluation at the end of the term also if the purpose is to learn student opinion about course content and order of presentation. Many intermediate macro students may not "catch on" to the complex model you have explained until all the parts are fit together near the end of the semester. A premature student evaluation might give a wrong picture of whether students have followed the organization or not.

Since only the individual teacher is involved with an evaluation to improve his or her particular instructional presentations, standardized forms designed for making personnel evaluations are probably not the best choice. As the instructor, only you can design the form to meet your needs. If written evaluations are used, they can be open-ended. However, a blank sheet of paper as an evaluation form will probably not elicit much helpful information. You know what is important for you to accomplish in the class. Questions on the form should be fairly specific, such as, "Were graphic explanations clear to you? If not, why not?" They should also be aimed at finding out how well you accomplished your goals and what you could do differently to help the student to accomplish them better. Students *will* write but they may need a nudge.

Whether or not your college or department has a formalized student evaluation process, evaluation of individual performance as described above is highly recommended, particularly for new instructors. Some of the best ideas about teaching come from students, but if you do not ask them, they will probably not volunteer. However, don't be surprised if your first set of diagnostic evaluations reveals that you are not yet God's gift to the teaching profession. Students can be brutally frank. They also may say one thing and mean another. Don't get too uptight. Remember your own frustrations as a student.

Student evaluations of instruction *do* improve instruction in the students' eyes. Marsh (1984) found that "instructors who received midterm feedback were subsequently rated about one-third of a standard deviation higher than nonfeedback instructors on the total rating" and particularly in the items "Instructor Skill, Attitude Toward Subject, and Feedback to Students." Marsh also found that when feedback was coupled with consultation between the teacher and another more experienced teacher, there were substantially larger differences. As Marsh puts it, "feedback from students' evaluations, particularly when augmented by consultation, can lead to improvement in teaching effectiveness" (Marsh, 1984, p. 746).

WHAT IS "GOOD" TEACHING?

Although there are certainly differences of opinion as to what constitutes "good teaching," research has shown that for teachers and students alike, there does seem to be (for at least a majority) some consensus. The question then arises, "What are students identifying as 'good teaching' when they fill out the forms?" Kenneth Feldman (1988) reviewed a number of studies which attempted to find out what students and faculty think are the most important factors in good teaching. In these studies, students and faculty, prior to the time of the student evaluation, were asked to rank order a number of factors which might indicate good teaching. Student and faculty rankings on the top five items chosen by students were as follows:

Factor	Student Ranking	Faculty Ranking
teacher's concern for student progress	1	3
teacher's preparation and organization	2	4
teacher's knowledge of the subject	3	1
teacher's stimulation of students' interest	4	12
teacher's enthusiasm (for subject or teaching)	5	2

The faculty's fifth choice was "teacher's clarity and understandableness." With a rank of 12, faculty apparently did not think stimulation of student interest all that important.

What students *said* they considered most important and what they *actually rated* as most important at the time of the actual evaluation were somewhat different. Feldman found that students actually ranked in order of importance:[4]

1 teacher's stimulation of student interest (the item ranked 12th by faculty)
2 teacher's clarity and understandableness (fifth in the teacher's list but not in the top five for students)
3 students' perception of the outcome or impact of instruction
4 teacher's preparation and organization
5 teacher's concern for student progress

What this research tells us is that students are really indicating two basic things. To the learner, "good teaching" means that the teacher is able to make the student *want* to learn the material, and that the material is presented in such a way that it is *easy to learn*. Stated another way, the role of the teacher is to *motivate* and *organize*. The major difference in opinion between teachers and students seems to be on the importance of what the teacher *knows* and selects for the student to learn. Since presumably the student does not know what is important it is probably inappropriate for the student to evaluate this aspect of "good teaching," and, indeed, students have indicated the right list of priorities on what they can evaluate.

USING STUDENT EVALUATIONS TO ASSIST IN PERSONNEL DECISIONS

From sophisticated research to faculty coffee lounge conversation, most attention is given to student evaluations as a tool for personnel decisions. Since jobs and pay are involved, this is only natural. Most of the vast number of articles written on student evaluations deal with topics bearing on personnel decisions.

The Evaluation Instrument

Many student evaluation instruments tend to be used for several purposes. Although logic might dictate that there should be a different student evaluation instrument for each purpose being attempted, this is not generally the case. Few departments or faculty members take the time to go through the self-diagnostic procedures outlined in the previous section, or create forms specifically for this purpose. The reality of the matter is that for most departments or colleges, a standard form is developed which is used for *all* purposes from analysis of teaching methods for improving instruction to determining promotion or tenure. Many evaluation forms have an "objective" section and a "comments" section.

Researchers studying student evaluations describe teaching as a multidimensional activity. Activities include preparation, presentation, evaluation, interaction with students, and so forth. Teacher behavior may be inconsistent over different areas of the educational process (e.g., a well-organized professor may have little rapport with students, or the enthusiastic lecturer may be highly disorganized). With different purposes and different behaviors to be measured, it would seem logical that any rating instrument would be multidimensional; but this is not always the case. There are thousands of evaluation forms currently in use in economics departments ranging from departmentally designed instruments to those mandated by the college or university. All too often these forms are not designed by experts and only a few dimensions of teaching are measured, but there are also several excellent forms which do attempt to measure the multidimensionality of the performance being evaluated. Marsh's (1984) Student Evaluations of Educational Quality (SEEQ) form has nine basic areas: learning/value, enthusiasm, organization, group interaction, individual rapport, breadth of coverage, exams/grades, assignments, and workload. The version of a SEEQ questionnaire used to evaluate economics instructors and courses at the University of Southern California (Aigner and Thum, 1986) is included as Appendix 18-1.

This questionnaire has 35 questions distributed over the nine basic areas (including 2 "overall" questions: one dealing with the course, and one dealing with the instructor) and 6 additional questions dealing with characteristics of the student completing the questionnaire. While this form allows instructors and administrators to get a complete picture of students' perception of a faculty member's teaching performance, the large number of questions makes compact summarization difficult. The layout of questionnaires with over 40 questions also makes it difficult for students to add written comments on individual items, and some students may be tempted to "lock in" on a single standard response for most questions rather than reading each question carefully.

Questionnaires of over 40 items may best be used for diagnostic rather than personnel decision purposes.[5] It is very difficult to present a compact summary of a large number of questions for each course an individual instructor teaches over the five- or six-year period usually preceding a tenure decision. In such cases administrators and faculty committees often look at only the mean rating on the single overall summary question as the "teaching" input to personnel decisions. At the very least, if some form of summary "number" is necessary, a weighted average of the scores on various dimensions should be used. The weighing should be based on a logical assessment of the importance attached to the various behaviors described (e.g., an overall high rating for a highly enthusiastic presentation of bad information should not be allowed to have much positive affect on a personnel decision).

If teaching evaluation numbers are going to be used in personnel decisions that affect your fate, you might devise or encourage others to use a fairly brief form that covers several dimensions of teaching performance and yet can be easily summarized. Ideally the summary should show the number and percent of students responding to the questionnaire, and it should show a distribution of the responses on each question in addition to a simple mean number.

An example of a brief questionnaire that evaluates several dimensions of teaching performance and still permits a reasonably compact summary is shown in Appendix 18-2. This questionnaire is laid out in a way that encourages students to read each question carefully and discourages them from simply making an overall standard response such as "agree" or "very descriptive" to different questions. This questionnaire, with instructions and space for written student comments on each question, fits on the front and back of a single 8 1/2 x 11 inch sheet of paper. If used with a separate machine readable answer sheet, the responses can be easily tabulated and summarized.

Appendix 18-3 shows a tabular summary of responses to each question on the 10-item questionnaire shown in Appendix 18-2. This format permits a relatively easy examination of the distribution of responses in addition to the mean rating on each question. Separate columns can be used for each course an instructor teaches in a given semester or for each semester an instructor teaches the same course. A time series of rating summaries for each course taught can show patterns of improvement (if they exist) better than a format that shows more than one course each semester.

In selecting the 10 questions to be put on a questionnaire such as the one shown in Appendix 18-2 and summarized in Appendix 18-3 consideration needs to be given to what dimensions seem most important in individual situations. Dimensions that might be important in smaller upper division courses (such as "group interaction") might not be as important in large introductory courses. It might also be a good idea to change the referent in the phrases "compared to other ___ courses" and "compared to other ___ instructors" to reflect different situations. The referent might be by course level—"sophomore level," "senior level"—or by orientation—"lecture oriented," "discussion oriented," "mathematically oriented." Separate summary tables by course level or course orientation may reveal comparative advantages that should be considered in evaluating an individual instructor's teaching performance and in making future teaching assignments.

Factors Which Affect the Student's Evaluation

The student evaluation should measure what it is supposed to measure, presumably teaching behavior. There have been a number of attempts to determine if teaching behavior is actually measured by the student evaluation. These studies center on two possible measures of teaching performance—student learning and evaluations of the teacher by persons other than the student.

The most commonly used research method to determine if teacher effectiveness is measured by the student evaluation is to compare that evaluation with the amount that students actually learned. Attempts have been made to correlate student test performance with teacher evaluations holding all other things constant. While there are some real difficulties in conducting such research, existing studies indicate that there is such a correlation.[6]

Another way to determine the validity of students' evaluations is to measure them against evaluations by the teachers themselves, other faculty members, alumni, or administrators. When student ratings have been compared to teacher's self-ratings, the results have been positively correlated. Even in cases where the instructor was asked to rate his or her own performance in two different courses, students' ratings paralleled the instructors' self-ratings. Likewise, ratings by administrators, colleagues, and alumni have been shown to correlate highly with student ratings.[7] These findings tend to give credence to the contention that student ratings do indeed measure teacher performance.

As important as whether the student evaluation measures teacher performance is what *else* it is measuring. If the evaluation is measuring other factors, it is incumbent on the administrator to consider these factors in assessing the degree to which the student evaluation is indeed a measure of teaching performance. It is also helpful to the faculty member to know these other factors exist.

There are many possible external factors which might affect student ratings. However, some which we might expect to affect the rating process have been found to have little or no effect on student evaluations.[8] The sex of the instructor seems to have little to do with the students' evaluation, as does the age of the instructor. No particular instructor personality characteristics seem to produce either high or low student ratings. Most interestingly, there seems to be little connection between research productivity and the students' evaluation of instruction. Student characteristics such as age, sex, grade level, previous GPA, or personality seem to have little effect on the evaluation. Class size, the time of day of the class or the time during the term when the evaluation was made likewise seem to have little effect.

The most common external variables cited[9] in studies that may affect student evaluations are:

• *Faculty rank*—Regular faculty tend to be rated higher than graduate assistants or adjunct faculty. Assistants and full professors tend to be rated higher than associates (Aigner and Thum, 1986).

• *Expressiveness*—This variable relates to the so called "Dr. Fox" effect which is based on an experiment in which a professional actor who had no knowledge of the subject was given a script to follow and then received higher ratings than knowledgeable professors. So far the studies in this category have been so methodologically flawed that any evidence of bias is almost surely incorrect.[10]

• *Student motivation*—Students are likely to rate instructors higher in classes where students are more motivated (such as elective classes or classes chosen within a major).

• *Expected grades*—The research has shown that there tends to be a positive but very low correlation between expected grades and student evaluations. Several reasons are cited to explain this effect—grading leniency (teachers attempting to buy a good evaluation), the fact that students who learn more *should* rate their teachers higher, and the observation that certain characteristics lead to both higher grades *and* higher evaluations (such as higher motivation). Much of the literature in this category has been shown to be methodologically flawed.[11]

• *Course level*—Graduate classes tend to rate more highly than undergraduate, and seniors rate higher than freshmen.

• *Difficulty of the class*—Some studies have shown a *positive* relationship between course difficulty and evaluations; that is, the harder the course, the higher the evaluation. This in spite of the fact that faculty tend to think the bias goes the other way.

- *How the evaluation is conducted*—If the instructor is present during the evaluation process, if students know that the rating is for purposes of personnel decisions, or if the ratings are signed, the evaluations tend to be higher.[12]

Despite these other factors, student evaluations do present evidence which is useful in personnel decisions. Note, however, that this is not a ringing endorsement of student evaluations as the *only* source of information on instructor performance which should be used for making personnel decisions. They are *useful*, but not complete.

Almost all department chairs *do* use information from the evaluation forms. In a recent survey of department chairs from all departments at two large universities, all but one indicated that they looked at either summary data or student comments from evaluations when making personnel decisions. Over 90 percent of the chairs indicated that they always looked at summary data, and over 80 percent said they always read most of the student comments. Seventy-five percent of them agreed with the statement "In this department, student evaluations of instruction have a significant impact on promotion and tenure decisions," while over 80 percent agreed that "student evaluations of instruction are a good indicator of teaching performance" (Marlin, 1987, p. 712). *Your student evaluations will be used in making personnel decisions.* Chairs will use student evaluations, but most of them will also analyze as much other information as there is available in making their decisions.

WHAT TO DO IF YOU GET A BAD EVALUATION

The odds are that your first evaluations will not be as good as you would like—after all, there is something to be said for experience. No matter how good you are, you will, at one time or another, receive results of an evaluation that will not please you. *Nobody* enjoys being told that a semester's work is bad. How you respond to these evaluations is up to you.

It is human, when receiving a poor evaluation, to respond in one of three different ways. The easiest response is to say that you had a bad class of students. The second most common excuse is that the students were rating something other than your instruction. The most difficult is to admit the possibility that your performance may not have been on a par with Socrates, and that improvements are possible. This is not to say that every class is a "good" class—they aren't. Nor is it to say that other factors than your performance could have affected the rating—they could. Both of these factors may have had an influence on the rating. My point, however, is that the *first* thing that you should consider is that your performance might not have been what you wished. From there you should try to determine, if indeed it was a problem in your teaching, what it was specifically that made the evaluations poor.

Recommendation 1: Look for what the students mean, not what they say. It is sometimes difficult to discern what it is the students are complaining about. Many times students may be upset about one thing yet write another. Such statements as "Fire him, he's the worst teacher I ever had" are not particularly helpful in improving your teaching. They do, however, indicate that the student is upset about something!

Look for specific items. Often students might say that the lectures were boring, when what they are indicating is that they were not able to understand or they got lost and were therefore bored. Such statements are a hint that you might work more on organizing the material more logically and even provide additional written aids to students to help them understand your organization. Too many beginning instructors follow the organization of the textbook too closely. Make sure your class organization makes sense to *you*.

Recommendation 2: Let students know that economics is "different." One problem that new economics professors encounter is a reflection of students' previous training and the fact that economics is *different*. Most students beginning their initial course in economics are faced with their first taste of the abstract. It is possible to be a high school valedictorian by memorizing and regurgitating facts and figures on an exam booklet. Economics requires more of the student. The student must be able to think—to analyze and combine information to reach a conclusion. Be prepared for the fact that *most students will have great difficulties doing this*. Unless you help them to understand this difference, you are likely to get evaluations on which you are rated low on clarity of presentation. You will be criticized for "too many graphs" and "no relationship to the real world." You may find that you are accused of tests that are "too hard" and cover material "that was not covered in class."

Recommendation 3: Tell students what you expect from them. Take time at the beginning of a principles of economics class to cover the whys and wherefores of using graphs and mathematical concepts. (You can be pretty well assured that no one else will have given them this little talk before!) Tell students up front that you give "trick exams." Then go on to explain that the "trick" is that they will be given tests on material they have never seen before—they will have to *apply* the principles they have learned.

Much of the secret to getting good evaluations in economics courses (which students will have heard through the grapevine are "hard") is to practice good teaching to start with. Tell them what you expect. Take the time to teach them the methods you plan to use.

Recommendation 4: Use examples. Show how economics principles are used in the real world. (If you doubt the value of good examples, pick up a student's notebook and see what is included from your lecture. You will probably find that *all* of your examples are included.)

Recommendation 5: Cover "tools" thoroughly. Allow adequate time at the beginning of the semester or quarter to *assure* that a majority of the students understand how to use economic tools, even if it means that you leave something else out later in the course.

Recommendation 6: Put grades in perspective. Students tend to be obsessed with grades. If they think they are being treated unfairly, particularly in grading practices, this tends to show up with fairly uncomplimentary comments on the evaluation. Make sure your grading practices are consistent and that students understand how you are arriving at the grades you give. Take some class time to discuss, for example, the relative merits of learning something versus getting a diploma. Most students seem shocked when you tell them that a high grade point average will merely get them an initial job interview. It is helpful if they *hear* this rather than wait to experience it later.

Recommendation 7: Examine your own attitudes. Students are very perceptive about the teacher's attitude toward them. Ask yourself how you feel about students— are they your reason for being a teacher or a necessary, but unwelcome, impediment to your research agenda? Students are human beings too and it helps to treat them with respect. This does not imply that the professor should curry students' favor; it does imply that the Golden Rule works with students, too—treat them as you would like to have been treated when you were a student.

A number of other recommendations which could improve your evaluations might be listed, but, in fact, these items are really a list of things which will help you be a better teacher. Those techniques are covered elsewhere in this book.

CONCLUSION

With all their difficulties, student evaluations of instruction serve a very real purpose in the academic environment. They are the primary source of feedback from the learner to the teacher. Properly handled and interpreted, they can provide you with valuable information which can help you do your job better.

In economic terms, the student is the final consumer of the product "education." It behooves you as the "producer" to understand your customers, to listen to their complaints, to correct those things which can be corrected, and to explain why those things that cannot be changed *should* not be changed.

Student evaluations which provide input to personnel committees and administrators are likewise a valuable part of the academic environment. They can provide the supervisor evidence of the effectiveness of the teacher from the student's point of view. Certainly they should not be considered as the *sole* evidence of teaching performance; they *do* provide the evaluator with additional information on which to base a judgment. The more information those charged with evaluating performance have, the more likely the judgment they form is a reflection of reality. It is incumbent on administrators to practice caution in carefully interpreting the results of student evaluations, just as it is also important for them to carefully interpret the merit of a piece of research or the value of a service activity.

Avoid developing a negative attitude about evaluations, even though you may hear colleagues claim that they are unfair, biased, based on the opinions of people who have no knowledge of what should be done in the classroom, and a general waste of time. Accept them for what they are—additional evidence that needs interpretation. Very few of us *like* to have someone critically evaluate us, particularly if they might find less than perfection. However, evaluation is necessary and can help all of us, as a community of scholars, achieve our common goal of providing the best education possible to our students.

NOTES

1 This view is no longer widespread and has been fairly thoroughly discounted by educational research. While many good researchers are also good teachers, there is no justification for a *post hoc ergo propter hoc* leap of faith to impute causality. [See Yunker and Marlin (1984) for a review of the literature and an economic analysis of the relationship of teaching performance and research productivity.]

2 This procedure is not recommended if you are not willing to institute changes as a result of the student input. If you do not agree with students' recommendations, tell them so and tell them why. On the other hand, if you indicate even tacit agreement and then do not follow up, you will have lost the faith of the students and can get yourself into hot water in a hurry.

3 The question is "how large is too large?" I have conducted successful oral evaluations with seventy students, although I believe that I have had better results with fewer students. I know professors who have conducted oral evaluations in classes of over two hundred. The maximum size depends on the individual and the relationship of openness previously established.

4 "Importance" in this instance is indicated by seeing which individual attributes correlated most highly with the "overall" ranking for each teacher.

5 An example of a 50-item questionnaire that is clearly aimed at diagnosis and improvement of teaching rather than a single overall summary evaluation is the Teaching Analysis By Students (TABS) form available from the Clinic to Improve University Teaching at the University of Massachusetts at Amherst. This form has been used as the basis for teaching improvement consultations at several universities.

6 The major problems are centered around finding a reliable measurement for student performance. To compare various student groups, standardized tests must be used. Unfortunately, most standardized tests deal only with beginning courses (e.g., the Test of Understanding of College Economics), so conclusions about all students must be extrapolated from the performance of beginning students. There is also the problem that a teacher may perform in a highly competent manner, the student may recognize this outstanding performance by a "high" evaluation, yet still not perform well on a test. The difficulty is that the student utility function may be such that students prefer to use the time saved by "efficient" instruction in studying for other courses or other activities and not perform any better on the standardized test. (See Yunker and Marlin, 1984.)

7 Details of these tests and citations of the original sources can be found in Cashin (1988).

8 Likewise, Cashin (1988) provides details and citations on the studies which explain the variables that do not relate to the student evaluation scores.

9 Marsh's 1984 survey article has detailed discussion and complete citations on each of the variables listed as affecting student evaluation scores. In cases where there are important studies not included in Marsh's article, I have provided specific citations. Most of the variables listed in the text were also examined in Aigner and Thum (1986) in a study of economics students at the University of Southern California. The results of their study confirm those cited in Marsh.

10 Marsh has a comprehensive explanation of the original "Dr. Fox" studies and related follow-up studies (Marsh, 1984, pp. 742-746).

11   Aigner and Thum (1986) and De Canio (1986) discuss this relationship in *Journal of Economic Education* articles. Using different techniques, they both concluded that expected grades have little or no effect on student evaluation scores.

12   Perhaps conducting evaluations where students believe they could be identified might prejudice their evaluations. However, my own research on students' perception of the evaluation process indicates that if there are precautions taken to assure anonymity, students believe they are fair and unbiased. They do, however, indicate a real ignorance as to what is done with evaluations after they are completed (Marlin, 1987).

REFERENCES

Aigner, D. J., and F. D. Thum, 1986. "On Student Evaluation of Teaching Ability," *Journal of Economic Education*, 17, 107-118.

Cashin, W. E., 1988. "Student Ratings of Teaching: A Summary of the Research," *Exchange*, Center for Faculty Evaluation & Development, University of Kansas, Idea Paper No. 20.

Centra, J. A., 1980. *Determining Faculty Effectiveness*. San Francisco: Jossey-Bass.

De Canio, S. J., 1986. "Student Evaluations of Teaching—a Multinomial Logit Approach," *Journal of Economic Education*, 17, 165-176.

Feldman, K. A., 1988. "Effective College Teaching from the Students' and Faculty's View: Matched or Mismatched Priorities?" *Research in Higher Education*, 28, 291-344.

Marlin, J. W., 1987. "Student Perceptions of End-Of-Course Evaluations," *Journal of Higher Education*, 58, 704-754.

Marsh, H. W., 1986. "Students' Evaluations of University Teaching: Dimensionality, Reliability, Validity, Potential Biases, and Utility," *Journal of Educational Psychology*, 76, 707-754.

Yunker, J. A., and J. W. Marlin, 1984. "Performance Evaluation of College and University Faculty: An Economic Perspective," *Education Administration Quarterly*, 20, 9-37.

APPENDIX 18-1

USC EVALUATION QUESTIONNAIRE AND ECONOMICS SUPPLEMENTARY QUESTIONS

USC Evaluation Services

As a description of this course instructor, this statement is: (select the best response for each of the following statements, leaving a blank only if it is clearly not relevant)

	Very poor	Poor	Moderate (Average)	Good	Very good
LEARNING: You found the course intellectually challenging and stimulating.	1	2	3	4	5
You have learned something which you consider valuable.	1	2	3	4	5
Your interest in the subject has increased as a consequence of this course.	1	2	3	4	5
You have learned and understood the subject materials in this course.	1	2	3	4	5

	Very poor	Poor	Moderate (Average)	Good	Very good
ENTHUSIASM: Instructor was enthusiastic about teaching the course.	1	2	3	4	5
Instructor was dynamic and energetic in conducting the course.	1	2	3	4	5
Instructor enhanced presentations with the use of humor.	1	2	3	4	5
Instructor's style of presentation held your interest during class.	1	2	3	4	5
ORGANIZATION: Instructor's explanations were clear.	1	2	3	4	5
Course materials were well prepared and carefully explained.	1	2	3	4	5
Proposed objectives agreed with those actually taught so you knew where course was going.	1	2	3	4	5
Instructor gave lectures that facilitated taking notes.	1	2	3	4	5
GROUP INTERACTION: Students were encouraged to participate in class discussions.	1	2	3	4	5
Students were invited to share their ideas and knowledge.	1	2	3	4	5
Students were encouraged to ask questions and were given meaningful answers.	1	2	3	4	5
Students were encouraged to express their own ideas and/or question the instructor.	1	2	3	4	5
INDIVIDUAL RAPPORT: Instructor was friendly toward individual students.	1	2	3	4	5
Instructor made students feel welcome in seeking help/advice in or outside of class.	1	2	3	4	5
Instructor had a genuine interest in individual students.	1	2	3	4	5
Instructor was adequately accessible to students during office hours or after class.	1	2	3	4	5
BREADTH: Instructor contrasted the implications of various theories.	1	2	3	4	5
Instructor presented the background or origin of ideas/concepts developed in class.	1	2	3	4	5
Instructor presented points of view other than his/her own when appropriate.	1	2	3	4	5
Instructor adequately discussed current developments in the field.	1	2	3	4	5
EXAMINATIONS: Feedback on examinations/graded materials was available.	1	2	3	4	5
Methods of evaluating student work were fair and appropriate.	1	2	3	4	5
Examinations/graded materials tested course content as emphasized by the instructor.	1	2	3	4	5
ASSIGNMENTS: Required readings/texts were valuable.	1	2	3	4	5
Readings, homework, etc., contributed to appreciation and understanding of subject.	1	2	3	4	5
OVERALL: Compared with other courses you have taken at USC this course was:	1	2	3	4	5
OVERALL: Compared with other instructors you have had at USC, this instructor was:	1	2	3	4	5

	Very poor	Poor	Moderate (Average)	Good	Very good
STUDENT AND COURSE CHARACTERISTICS:					
(Leave blank if no response applies)					
Course difficulty, relative to other courses, was (1-Very easy...3-Medium...5-Very hard):	1	2	3	4	5
Course workload, relative to other courses, courses, was (1-Very easy...3-Medium...5-Very heavy):	1	2	3	4	5
Course pace was (1-Too slow... 3-About right...5-Too fast):	1	2	3	4	5
Hours per week required outside of class was (1-0 to 2, 2-2 to 5, 3-5 to 7, 4-8 to 12, 5-Over 12):	1	2	3	4	5
Level of interest in the subject prior to this course was (1-Very low ...3-Medium...5-Very high):	1	2	3	4	5
Overall GPA at USC is (1-Below 2.5, 2-2.5 to 3.0, 3-3.0 to 3.4, 4-3.4 to 3.7, 5-Above 3.7): Leave blank if not yet established at USC.	1	2	3	4	5
Expected grade in the course is (1-F, 2-D, 3-C, 4-B, 5-A):	1	2	3	4	5
Reason for taking the course is (1-Major require., 2-Major elective, 3-General ed. require., 4-Minor related field, 5-General interest only): Select the one which is best.	1	2	3	4	5
Year in school is (1-Fresh., 2-Soph., 3-Jr., 4-Sr., 5-Grad.):	1	2	3	4	5
Major department is (1-Soc. sci./Comm., 2-Nat. sci./Math, 3-Humanities, 4-Business, 5-Education, 6-Engineering, 7-Perf. arts, 8-Pub. Affairs, 9-Other, 10-Undeclared/Undecided):	1	2	3	4	5

APPENDIX 18-2

SAMPLE EVALUATION FORM

Read each statement carefully, circle your response on this sheet, and *USE A PENCIL* to mark your response on the separate answer sheet. Do *NOT* answer any questions for which you have insufficient information to make a meaningful response.

You are encouraged to add comments on this sheet. Please make a special effort to comment in the space following questions #11 and #12.

1 COMPARED TO OTHER 200-LEVEL COURSES YOU HAVE TAKEN AT THIS UNIVERSITY, HOW MUCH DO YOU THINK YOU LEARNED IN THIS COURSE?

Comment

A Much more
B A little more
C About the same
D A little less
E Much less

COMPARED TO OTHER 200-LEVEL INSTRUCTORS YOU HAVE HAD AT THIS UNIVERSITY, HOW WOULD YOU RATE YOUR INSTRUCTOR IN THIS COURSE WITH RESPECT TO:

2 Enthusiasm about teaching?

Comment

A One of the most enthusiastic
B Above average
C Average
D Below average
E One of the least enthusiastic

3 Preparation for class meetings?

Comment

A One of the most prepared
B Above average
C Average
D Blow average
E One of the least prepared

4 Availability for out-of-class consultation?

Comment

A One of the most available
B Above average
C Average
D Below average
E One of the least available

5 Making course objectives clear and giving students a good idea of what they are expected to learn?

Comment

A One of the most clear
B Above average
C Average
D Below average
E One of the least clear

6 Ability to construct exams and quizzes consistent with major learning objectives?

Comment

A One of the most able
B Above average
C Average
D Below average
E One of the least able

7 Providing helpful feedback on how well students are performing?

Comment

A One of the most helpful
B Above average
C Average
D Below average
E One of the least helpful

8 Ability to explain basic (textbook-type) material?

Comment

A One of the most able
B Above average
C Average
D Below average
E One of the least able

9 Ability to go beyond basic material and develop more sophisticated understanding?

Comment

A One of the most able
B Above average
C Average
D Below average
E One of the least able

10 Overall teaching effectiveness?

Comment

A One of the very best teachers
B Above average
C Average
D Below average
E One of the very worst teachers

11 WHAT *ONE* THING COULD YOUR INSTRUCTOR DO TO MOST IMPROVE HIS/HER EFFECTIVENESS AS A TEACHER? *PLEASE COMMENT*

12 WHAT *SPECIFIC* SUGGESTIONS DO YOU HAVE FOR IMPROVING THIS COURSE? *PLEASE COMMENT.*

APPENDIX 18-3

SAMPLE EVALUATION SUMMARY

INSTRUCTOR _____

Course		Econ 1 Fall 1987	Econ 1 Spring 1988	Econ 2 Fall 1988	Econ 2 Spring 1989
Term		Fall 1987	Spring 1988	Fall 1988	Spring 1989
No. & (%) of students completing evaluation questionnaire		54 (75%)	51 (67%)	54 (79%)	52 (68%)

*PERCENTAGE DISTRIBUTION OF RESPONSES, MEAN & (STD. DEV.) ON SELECTED QUESTIONS.

Question #1 Amount Learned		Fall 1987	Spring 1988	Fall 1988	Spring 1989
	MM (4)	22 %	22 %	19 %	44 %
	ALM (3)	32 %	37 %	50 %	40 %
	ATS (2)	32 %	33 %	28 %	14 %
	ALL (1)	9 %	6 %	4 %	2 %
	ML (0)	6 %	2 %	0 %	0 %
Mean and (Std. Dev.)		2.56 (1.10)	2.71 (.94)	2.83 (.76)	3.27 (.76)
Question #2 Enthusiasm	OOTME (4)	15 %	22 %	24 %	50 %
	AA (3)	50 %	65 %	65 %	44 %
	A (2)	22 %	14 %	9 %	6 %
	BA (1)	11 %	0 %	0 %	0 %
	OOTLE (0)	2 %	0 %	0 %	0 %
Mean and (Std. Dev.)		2.65 (.93)	3.08 (.59)	3.15 (.56)	3.44 (.60)
Question #3 Preparation	OOTMP (4)	28 %	43 %	57 %	67 %
	AA (3)	50 %	51 %	41 %	33 %
	A (2)	9 %	4 %	4 %	0 %
	BA (1)	13 %	0 %	0 %	0 %
	OOTLP (0)	0 %	2 %	0 %	0 %
Mean and (Std. Dev.)		2.93 (.94)	3.33 (.73)	3.52 (.57)	3.67 (.40)
Question #4 Availability	OOTMA (4)	11 %	8 %	15 %	42 %
	AA (3)	44 %	37 %	46 %	40 %
	A (2)	41 %	49 %	35 %	15 %
	BA (1)	0 %	2 %	0 %	0 %
	OOTLA (0)	0 %	0 %	0 %	0 %
Mean and (Std. Dev.)		2.69 (.67)	2.53 (.67)	2.79 (.69)	3.27 (.72)
Question #5 Clarity of Objectives	OOTMC (4)	28 %	33 %	39 %	58 %
	AA (3)	46 %	55 %	52 %	37 %
	A (2)	17 %	10 %	7 %	6 %
	BA (1)	9 %	2 %	0 %	0 %
	OOTLC (0)	0 %	0 %	0 %	0 %
Mean and (Std. Dev.)		2.93 (.90)	3.20 (.61)	3.32 (.61)	3.52 (.60)
Question #6 Exams & Quizzes	OOTMA (4)	20 %	24 %	33 %	48 %
	AA (3)	52 %	59 %	48 %	46 %
	A (2)	11 %	12 %	15 %	4 %
	BA (1)	11 %	6 %	4 %	2 %
	OOTLA (0)	6 %	0 %	0 %	0 %
Mean and (Std. Dev.)		2.70 (1.08)	3.00 (.77)	3.11 (.79)	3.40 (.66)
Question #7 Feedback	OOTMH (4)	19 %	28 %	39 %	40 %
	AA (3)	56 %	55 %	48 %	48 %
	A (2)	20 %	8 %	7 %	8 %
	BA (1)	4 %	10 %	4 %	2 %
	OOTLH (0)	2 %	0 %	0 %	0 %
Mean and (Std. Dev.)		2.85 (.83)	3.00 (.86)	3.25 (.75)	3.29 (.69)
Question #8 Basic Material	OOTMA (4)	32 %	47 %	52 %	65 %
	AA (3)	52 %	49 %	43 %	35 %
	A (2)	9 %	2 %	6 %	0 %
	BA (1)	4 %	2 %	0 %	0 %
	OOTLA (0)	4 %	0 %	0 %	0 %
Mean and (Std. Dev.)		3.04 (.94)	3.41 (.63)	3.46 (.60)	3.65 (.48)
Question #9 Beyond Basic Material	OOTMA (4)	11 %	24 %	39 %	54 %
	AA (3)	39 %	53 %	43 %	40 %
	A (2)	20 %	16 %	15 %	2 %
	BA (1)	22 %	8 %	4 %	4 %
	OOTLA (0)	7 %	0 %	0 %	0 %
Mean and (Std. Dev.)		2.24 (1.14)	2.92 (.84)	3.17 (.81)	3.44 (.72)
Question #10 Overall Effectiveness	OOTVB (4)	19 %	24 %	22 %	50 %
	AA (3)	26 %	61 %	57 %	42 %
	A (2)	35 %	16 %	20 %	8 %
	BA (1)	15 %	0 %	0 %	0 %
	OOTVW (0)	2 %	0 %	0 %	0 %
Mean and (Std. Dev.)		2.44 (1.01)	3.08 (.62)	3.02 (.65)	3.42 (.63)

* Some percentages may not total 100% due to rounding and some respondents not answering all questions. Nonresponses are omitted from the calculations of means and standard deviations.

CHAPTER 19

UTILIZING PEERS TO IMPROVE THE INSTRUCTIONAL PROCESS

James Niss

Peer evaluation has a long tradition in the academic setting. Scholarly publications are submitted to peer review prior to publication. Seminars and classes are expected to be times of critical analysis and critique. By training and by predisposition, faculty feel qualified to enter into the peer review process of scholarly activity. Peer review for publications in economics is but one aspect of the review process. Faculty regularly evaluate their colleagues for tenure, promotion, and merit pay increases. This evaluation process often requires that, in addition to an evaluation of scholarly output, data be collected to show evidence of the teacher inputs, to describe the process of instruction, and to measure the product or output of the instructional process.

Evaluation need not be a one-time event of great personal and economic import. Evaluation can and should be carried out with a view toward the improvement of both instruction and research. Evaluation processes are usually divided into two major types—summative and formative. Both review processes make use of the same types of supporting evidence; both are carried out by faculty, but the process, purposes, and end results are very different. Summative evaluation has as its major feature a highly structured process often carried out by peers and administrators for the purpose of making global decisions regarding the worth of the individual with respect to tenure, promotion, or merit pay—a predecision process. Formative evaluation is concerned with improving the level of instruction and research. This requires that the evaluation be carried out over a period of time with extensive feedback provided to assist the economics teacher with instructional and research capability improvement.

SUMMATIVE EVALUATION

Summative evaluation is concerned with levels of attainment at specific times such as at the tenure or promotion review periods. A summative peer review is designed to determine the worth or value of the activities in terms of some set of departmental or university criteria. In most instances the criteria include teaching and public service, as well as research and publication. However, the weight given to teaching and service is often very limited. How often have you heard the comment, "Teaching cannot be evaluated"? This view has led to a situation on many campuses that results in teaching receiving only modest consideration, whereas the publishing record is given extensive scrutiny.

Summative evaluation processes frequently do not allow for feedback, so improvement is less likely to take place and the process is often fraught with tension and controversy. The validity of peer reviews for the determination of recommendations for tenure and promotion has been called into question frequently. Peer ratings can be valid and reliable, but they are slightly more consistent for research than for teaching.

Cohen and McKeachie (1980, p. 149) point out that the correlation between faculty peer ratings of teaching and student ratings ranges between .87 and .62. They also reported " . . . correlations between sets of faculty juries of seven members in the range of .64 to .76 when instructors' overall evaluation of teaching was based on peer rankings." This suggests that observations by colleagues agree in large measure with student ratings and to a large extent with each other.

Research by Root (1987, p. 71) on the reliability of faculty evaluation of research, teaching and service showed that ". . . average intercorrelations. . . range from 0.63 for teaching to 0.85 for research" (p. 71). The ratings given by the six faculty raters were so consistent that Root suggested reducing the number to three. McIntosh (1986 p. 13) found that, "high scores in scholarly activity are the best predictor of overall merit ratings." On the other hand, Centra (1975) found in a study of 54 teachers that peer reviews based on classroom observation showed such an upward bias as to be virtually unusable. Ratings based on visits by three different colleagues resulted in 94 percent of the ratings being in the top two categories on a 5-point scale. These results are owing to the rather limited preparation of the observers prior to the observation. In most cases they had not planned and developed a procedure to allow them to do more than observe the presentation.

For the observations to be valid, the goals of the classroom observation session, the procedures and process of the session, and the outcomes of the session must be compared. Perhaps most importantly, this observation process cannot be limited to a single observation. Multiple visits conducted by well-trained observers are required to provide a valid measure of teaching classroom effectiveness.

Peers can be used with great confidence to evaluate the research and service output of a faculty member, and without training may be able to evaluate teaching for summative purposes based on impressions gained outside of the classroom. In order to obtain useful and valid measures of teaching, however, the evaluators must be trained to undertake the task of a total evaluation of the instructional process. The needs and demands of the summative evaluation process have not been discussed in great detail; however, the practices described below should provide much of the basic data required at the time of a summative evaluation. See Diamond et al. (1987) for a discussion of tenure and promotion evaluation procedures.

FORMATIVE EVALUATION

Formative evaluation includes extensive feedback mechanisms as one of the major components. Peers and consultants can and should consider the outputs of the classroom, research activities, and public service on a more-or-less continuing basis and offer advice, suggestions, and supportive comments for improvement. Formative evaluation has as its primary purpose the attainment of personal and institutional goals through a process of growth and development. These assessment processes are usually carried out in a nonthreatening, informal manner by a faculty peer or consultant in order to suggest new or innovative methods of improving and developing personally and professionally. It is of extreme importance that the processes of summative and formative evaluation be kept separate. If they are commingled, the openness and willingness to share with the peer may not be present. If this is the case, change and innovation may not take place. This is not to say that the evidence and fruits of the formative evaluation process in the form of teaching evaluations and research output will not be evident when the entire record is evaluated for tenure and promotion (Broskamp, 1984, p. 31). The focus of this chapter is on how peers can facilitate improved teaching utilizing the techniques of formative evaluation.

EVIDENCE OF GOOD TEACHING

To be in a position to assist in the improvement process, evidence must be collected and evaluated. In our professional roles, economists are concerned with inputs, outputs, and productivity. Therefore, as teachers of economics, we should be comfortable with a discussion of the inputs and outputs of the teaching process as well as with the process itself. The evidence to be collected is discussed under the heading of inputs, process, and outputs.

Teaching Inputs

The basic inputs are the capabilities and interests of the instructor and of the students. These inputs need to be refined into a set of evidence that can be used to suggest possible improvement strategies.

Course Materials   Items such as the course syllabus, reading lists, tests, and student handouts should be collected to provide insights into teacher inputs. The course syllabus should be organized in such a manner that there is a logical development of the economic ideas and concepts; the readings should reflect current thinking in economics; tests and other evaluation instruments should relate to the course goals and objectives, both in terms of cognitive learning and in terms of critical thinking and analytical skill development.

The course outline, reading list, and handouts should be examined in light of a set of specific criteria such as those listed below.

Course Outline

- Course objectives are clearly stated.
- Course objectives are appropriate for the course.
- Course material is current and up to date.
- Course material teaches to the course objective.
- Course requirements are appropriate for students and course level.
- Course, text, and reading materials are at an appropriate level.
- Evaluation procedures are clearly stated.
- Evaluation is keyed to course objectives.

Evaluation Instruments

- Evaluate attainment of course goals.
- Evaluate higher order skills.
  Analysis
  Application
  Synthesis
  Evaluation
- Avoid emphasis on recall and recognition.
- Show evidence of multiple-evaluation strategies.

Handouts, Simulations and Worksheets

- Stimulate students to think.
- Allow opportunities to practice skills.
  Economic analysis
  Writing
  Critical thinking
- Allow for self-evaluation or simple grading for prompt feedback.

Student Support

- Students are encouraged to request assistance.
- Office hours are held and utilized by students.
- Tutorial services are established.

Other Inputs Two other basic inputs are the teacher's knowledge and enthusiasm. Peers are in a good position to evaluate the subject matter expertise of a colleague. The objective material of the course outline and tests, publications, conversations and seminars are but a few of the many sources of information available to colleagues. Peers can add to these data an appreciation for the enthusiasm one has for teaching and for students. Enthusiasm is perhaps the most important factor in successful teaching and yet is the most intangible. We can obtain indications of enthusiasm when an economics teacher keeps regular office hours, and large numbers of students are waiting to discuss personal concerns as well as problems with economics. When a teacher keeps current in the field and wants to talk about successes and failures in the classroom, a high level of enthusiasm for teaching can be inferred. Enthusiasm is like charisma; it can be recognized and, in most cases, it can be enhanced.

The Teaching Process

Gathering data on the teaching process is much more difficult than gathering data on inputs. The inputs are frequently more tangible and perhaps more objective. The process can be inferred from some artifacts of teaching such as course outline, tests, and readings, but in other ways it must be observed. Questions must be asked to determine if:

- The teacher is motivating.
- The teacher is enthusiastic.
- The teacher is a good communicator.
- Multiple teaching techniques are used.
    Discussion
    Simulation
    Case studies
    Peer instruction
- Multiple evaluation techniques are used.
    Evaluation of knowledge
    Observation of skills
    Measures of attitudinal change

Students have many different learning styles. Some are visual, others auditory; others must learn by doing or experiencing. A teaching process that uses a single style of instruction will fail to meet the needs of many students. In addition to recognition of diverse talents and methods of learning, Chickering and Samson (1987) encourage six other "good practices."

- Student-faculty contact
- Cooperation among students in the learning process
- Active learning
- Prompt feedback
- Time on task
- Communicating high expectations

A teaching-learning process that incorporates these good practices will make use of efficient and varied teaching strategies. Evaluation strategies must be as varied as the teaching strategies. A multiple-choice test that tests only recall and recognition often falls far short of the high goals set forth in the course outline.

Evidences of the Teaching Process

Data can be collected on the process of instruction that can be used to convey information and ideas and to develop skills and attitudes. Classroom activities can include lectures, discussions, peer-group discussions, tutorials, self-paced instruction, and team teaching. These instructional techniques and procedures each have major benefits and major shortcomings. The efficacy of using any one method must be evaluated in terms of the course goals and objectives. The extent to which a student can be expected to learn and to develop critical thinking skills in a highly structured lecture class is significantly different from the expectation that would be derived from a problem-solving discussion activity or from other analytical teaching techniques.

To obtain a clear understanding of the process, classroom observation is almost a necessity. Readings, tests, and other printed items can be collected, but enthusiasm, organization of the class, eye contact, discussion methods and the myriad of other teaching techniques must be observed. The observation process can occur in many ways and at different times. It may involve a live observation, it may utilize video tape, or it may be a combination of the two methods. The discussion of video taping, team teaching, and other forms of peer observation that follows will explore ways of obtaining the data required to complete a valid peer observation.

Teaching Outputs

It is often said that teaching cannot be evaluated. If that is true, how can teachers evaluate and grade students? We do set out to measure what students learn from the teaching process. Therefore, we should also be able to evaluate the teaching process and to suggest improvements for ourselves. The outputs of the teaching process—measures of learning, skills acquired, and attitudinal changes—can be objectively measured and collected.

Evidences of Teacher Output

Items such as student learning, as measured by standardized tests, measures of student learning as exemplified by mastery of written activities, measures of student learning as reflected by the attainment of job-related skills, and the ability to market these skills in the wider world can be collected. Student learning can and should be evaluated from these many different dimensions in order to insure that the instructional process remains a multidimensional activity. Measures of student motivation and student attitudinal change can be collected as well as teacher output.

Student Learning   Economics educators have a long tradition of researching the learning output of an economics course. This is a natural outcome given our concern for efficiency. Learning by students is often measured on standardized and normed instruments such as the Test of Understanding of College Economics and, at the high school level, by the Test of Economic Literacy. These tests attempt to measure learning or additions to knowledge in terms of some "agreed upon" set of course objectives, concepts, and levels of difficulty.

Most classroom learning is measured by means of teacher-made tests that are too often derived from test banks and manuals that include questions of dubious validity which frequently test only recall and recognition. Teacher-made tests should also measure higher level analytical skills, writing skills and changes in student attitudes toward economic questions. Measuring the acquisition of content knowledge is not enough. Facts change rapidly, but the skill and ability to carry out economic analysis and present the results in a clear and concise manner are life-long skills. (See Chapter 15 on multiple choice tests, and Chapter 16 on essay tests.)

Student Evaluations   Teacher and course evaluations have been discussed above in Chapter 18 by Professor James Marlin. If the questions asked are specific to the teaching process, inferences can be drawn that suggest possible changes. Global items such as, "This is the best teacher I have ever had," are of little value. They do not suggest ways to modify the teaching process in order to achieve greater learning. However, questions regarding assignment length, teacher availability, test fairness, course organization, and so on, do provide data that can suggest course changes.

Alumni Reports   Reports of teacher effectiveness solicited from a representative sample of former students can be an important part of instructional assessment. These data are highly correlated with responses on student course evaluations and can provide information on the lasting impressions of the course and the instructional process. Letters can be solicited from alumni, questions can be included on alumni surveys, and data can be collected from students if graduating seniors are asked to participate in an exit interview prior to leaving campus. These data are a good example of information that can be used both in the formative and summative processes.

PEER ASSESSMENT PROCESSES

When peers or committees of peers evaluate data on teacher inputs, the instructional process, and the outputs of the instructional process for summative purposes, the process is often extremely stressful. The process often does not provide a great deal of constructive feedback and has high levels of costs associated with it. On the other hand, a process of formative consultation can avoid most of these costs and at the same time move the teacher to a higher level of productivity. Rather than being judgmental, this consultative process assures that constructive feedback is provided at the appropriate time. Appendix 19-1 offers a checklist that can be used either on an individual basis, with a consultant, or with a departmental peer to focus the formative evaluation process on the important issues of course development and instruction. Completion of this checklist encourages instructors to evaluate many aspects of their teaching on a more objective basis. The results will provide a starting point for self-improvement or for discussions with a peer.

Each of us is looking for the teachable moment, that time when the student is ready to learn and will make great strides toward the desired goal. In the same sense, this peer consultation process must also look for a moment when the teacher is open to suggestion and change. To find this moment requires that the peer consultant have information on the inputs, process, and outputs of the teaching activity.

Most of the evidences of the teaching process are already in the hands of the teacher. The course outline, tests, handouts, class notes and measures of student learning and evaluations are or should be available. One additional item of great value is a written self-analysis prepared by the faculty member. This analysis will focus on the strengths and weaknesses of the economics instructional process as perceived by the teaching economist as he/she attempts to achieve a set of instructional goals and objectives.

SELF-ANALYSIS OF COURSE ORGANIZATION AND OBJECTIVES

The instructor can provide a guide to the organization and objectives of the course or courses and how these objectives relate to the overall departmental and learning objectives. Also included in the self-evaluation and the statement of course organization is a discussion of the types of intellectual tasks that the students are expected to complete. Critical thinking skills, team-work skills, and enhanced skill in learning on one's own are examples of intellectual tasks that can be established by the classroom instructor. These tasks are significantly higher order tasks than the acquisition of information and knowledge that frequently receive high priority in our teaching activities. This self-analysis should be related to the discussion of the course goals and objectives found in the syllabus. In the self-evaluation the faculty member can point out the major goals and objectives that are being attained, can describe the process of attainment, and can include an enumeration of his/her strengths and weaknesses.

Peter Selden (1984, p. 13) offers a set of questions that can help focus the self-assessment process and also provide clues to possible areas of change or innovation. The following questions relate to the teaching function:

> In which area of your discipline do you consider yourself strongest?
> What is your greatest strength as a teacher? Your greatest weakness?
> If you could change one thing, what would you most like to change about your teaching?
> Compared to others in your department, how do you assess your teaching performance?

A consultative peer or course developer can, in conjunction with the teacher, consider the course inputs and the self-evaluation statement in terms of the criteria listed above to offer suggested alternatives and/or teaching techniques. The overall organization of a course in terms of the ordering of concepts, models discussed, and major emphasis are areas that fall well within the scope of expertise of a peer from one's own discipline or area of study. Who better than a fellow economist can offer advice and council on the ways a course can be organized and structured? Peers in our departments can address questions of sequencing and emphasis of concepts, such as the placement of international trade or the use of indifference curves, the extent of mathematical emphasis, the degree that policy questions are included. Our economics department colleagues can offer some of the best advice available on these issues.

It is important to solicit the information during a formative process of evaluation, since, in most cases, these same inputs will be considered during the summative process. It may be necessary to collect some data on the outputs such as student learning and alumni perception. Collection of data on method, enthusiasm, rapport, and other attributes of teaching can often only be accomplished by observation of the teaching process. Observation may be direct or by video or audio tape. However the observation is made, great care must be taken to ensure that it does not detract from the teaching process.

ASSESSING CLASSROOM TEACHING: PEER OR SELF-APPRAISAL

A great deal of information can be gathered by collecting the physical evidences of teaching. However, classroom observation may be the only method available for the collection of much of the evidence of the teaching process itself. The observation may be compiled by a person physically observing the economics class, or it may be accomplished by video or a combination of video and personal observation. Video has become a common means of instruction. It is also being used as an effective means of improving instruction. Many universities offer consultant services that make use of video as a means of collecting classroom data. The camera is un-obtrusive and easily scheduled, the teacher can view the tape alone or with a consultant, and the tapes can be compared over time. As a result of these positive features, the use of video as a means of assisting peer evaluation has received increased attention. A full discussion of the use of video taping for self-evaluation is presented in Chapter 17.

A clear statement of the desired goals and accomplishments should be established prior to the taping. This statement provides a basic frame of reference for the questions: "Were your goals accomplished?" "If they were not, what was the reason?" With these questions as a beginning, the consultant or peer can discuss the class session from a number of different aspects.

- Organization
- Observation skills
- Use and effectiveness of visual aids
- Variety of teaching techniques
- Use of effective discussion
- Relation to students
- Treatment of minorities and females
- Personal mannerisms
- Listening skills

If a teacher desires to view the tape alone, these same kinds of questions can be provided on a handout as a means of stimulating thought and raising awareness.

Feedback provided by means of video and audio cassettes is effective in improving presentation skills and organization. A program of taping followed by a two-hour critique of the lecture and completion of a self-assessment form resulted in ". . . significant improvement of lecture skills . . ." (Hendricson, 1983, p. 165). ". . . The organizational problems were reduced and delivery skills were improved in the spring over the fall presentations." This study suggests that organizational problems can be overcome by means of video taping and consultation. They may also eliminate the most obvious problems of delivery.

Peer evaluation itself, utilizing in-class observation or video tape, offers an instructor who desires improvement an objective set of data covering his/her teaching. Peers need not be judgmental but rather should highlight the goals, objectives, and processes in light of what actually occurred in the class. This allows teachers to compare goals with outcomes and assess his/her attainment of the predetermined goals. Given support and encouragement, the self-assessment process can be a powerful adjunct to peer assessment by means of in-class observation.

A less formal peer observation process is offered by Tobias (1986). She suggests that faculty lecturers in economics and the sciences need to invite nonscience colleagues to attend lectures to serve as a sounding board. They should concentrate on the questions, "What is making this subject difficult for me? What could I, as the instructor, do to make it come clear?" (p. 36). Concerns regarding pacing, examples, organization, and level of presentation could be addressed by competent, but nontechnical, class participants. Humanists, behaviorists, and physical scientists could be invited to actively participate in the presentation and offer insights and a critique of the course and lecture. Noneconomists who participate as observers in our classes will be in a position to provide feedback regarding the pace at which concepts are delivered and will be able to provide intelligent feedback regarding the value to them of the concepts and tools of analysis that we present in our lectures. She concludes that: "Without the insight and continuing feedback from those who might critique their courses, lecturers in science cannot improve their wares. Those students for whom the material doesn't make sense simply disappear from the rolls" (p. 41). Thus from these visitors who are "new" to economics an instructor can ". . . learn more precisely what facilitates understanding and what makes his subject hard" (p. 41).

One-to-One Faculty Development

One-to-one faculty development is described by Elbow (1980) as a peer visitation program that has received enthusiastic faculty support. In this program peers would visit one faculty person a week. Elbow indicated that, ". . . well before the week of visitation, I asked the faculty members . . . the changes that they wanted to produce in students through their teaching, and, more personally, the satisfactions and dissatisfactions that came to them from teaching. I also invited stories about good and bad moments not only as teacher but also as student." This information provided the basis for a long discussion of teaching and the personal joys and tribulations associated with teaching (p. 26).

Next, I would observe. That is, I would be a kind of companion for a good part of the week's activities: usually a couple of two- to three-hour seminars (our staple here), a lecture or class, an individual conference or two, and probably also the two- to three-hour faculty seminar, where the small faculty team discussed the week's book for their own edification.

Before the final, long conversation at the end of the week (or the beginning of the next), where I brought together my most important perceptions and made my recommendations, if I had any, I usually sat down a couple of times to play back my perceptions of what had happened in a seminar, class, or conference (p. 27).

This process allows for the comparison of goals and outputs—both personal and professional. It also allows for feedback from a compassionate observer on how well these goals are being achieved. Feedback is just as important for teachers as it is for students.

Team Teaching

Perhaps one of the best means of improving instruction is to team teach a class. Team teaching means planning and teaching the class as a team and not just presenting a series of guest lectures. Team members plan the course together and consider the questions of objectives, materials, teaching strategies, and assessment techniques. This process encourages more discussion on the issues of developing and improving the course. The result should be an increased awareness on the part of the teams of the factors and techniques that result in enhanced outputs. Ideally, all team members should be in all or most of the class sessions. This assures a clear understanding of the content that is taught and teaching techniques. The team members can provide immediate feedback on the effectiveness of the various teaching strategies. They also can provide suggestions for new or different approaches. Team teaching offers an opportunity to talk about teaching and to see other teachers in action on a level of intensity that rarely occurs in most universities.

It is not always possible or desirable to team teach courses. The cost to the institution is high in terms of salary, and the cost to the team is high in terms of the time and effort required to develop and teach the course. Peer observation offers many of the benefits of team teaching but also offers lower cost.

Rorschach and Whitney (1985) report on a peer evaluation project that approaches team teaching in its impact and magnitude. They developed a visitation plan that included observing each other's class three hours each week for a full semester. They recorded their observations of the classes and met once each week to discuss their courses and their observations. It is of interest to note that they did not begin to compare each other's classes until well into the semester. It required several weeks of discussion before they were comfortable and secure enough to make critical comparisons. Comparisons showed that, ". . . Right from the beginning we had noticed two things: On a philosophical level we were in almost complete agreement. Ideas of active learning, promoting the autonomy of students, forming a community in the classroom, and writing as the making of meaning shaped most of our planning and provided a framework in which we interpreted classroom events. Actually, we were a little surprised to find just how much in agreement we were philosophically" (p. 5).

Even though they agreed on goals, they were not operationalized. One class was more open, more dynamic, with larger amounts of student initiation. This became apparent to the authors, and, as a result, teaching techniques and course procedures were changed in order to encourage more ". . . autonomous behavior within a community of writers" (p. i). This project offered two people a real opportunity to explore better the expectations for and the results of the teaching process. It did, however, require a very real commitment.

Constructing Common Examinations in Multisection Courses

When peers work together to create an examination for a multisection principles of economics course, the goals and objectives of the course must be clearly set out in order to develop the specifications for the examination. The concepts to be evaluated, the weight given to each concept, and the level of analysis will be lively topics of discussion. This process will soon spill over into an opportunity to describe teaching techniques that will best allow students to achieve mastery of the subject. Questions such as the ordering of concepts, the extent of internationalization of the courses, the use of case studies, and the extent to active learning must be discussed. The team must consider questions that evaluate student ability to analyze and evaluate as opposed to those that measure recall recognition.

As a result of the process of creating common examinations, each member of the course staff will be in a better position to evaluate his or her own instruction in relation to the peer group. Insights will be gained and observations shared that will result in improvements in the instructional process. The end result will be much the same as those obtained in a team teaching situation. However, the time commitment will be much less, and the participants will not be required to give up as much personal control and personal identity.

CONCLUSIONS

Peers can be a vital force in the improvement of teaching. One can hope that the process of evaluation for tenure and promotion can evoke some change. However, given its summative, once-and-for-all nature, the impact might be slight. Team teaching, team evaluation, peer observation, self-assessment and the many other forms of analysis have a common feature—they cause teaching to be discussed and assessed in terms of a set of objectives or goals. The improvement process can be facilitated by providing opportunities to discuss good teaching practices and desired outputs. Department colloquia, seminars, professional meetings, and the coffee room all provide for the discussion of teaching. When we, as economists, express our concerns about the quality and quantity of the teaching process as often and strongly as we express concerns for our research output, then teaching will be an equal partner with research in terms of our perception of a professional economist and in terms of compensation.

REFERENCES

Aleamoni, L. M. (ed.), *Techniques for Evaluating and Improving Instruction*, San Francisco: Jossey-Bass Publishers, 1987.

Braskamp, L. A., D. C. Brandenburg, and J. C. Ory, *Evaluating Teaching Effectiveness*, Beverly Hills: Sage Publications, Inc., 1984.

Centra, J. A., "Colleagues as Raters of Classroom Effectiveness," *Journal of Higher Education*, 16:1975, 327-337.

Chickering, Arthur W., and Zelda F. Gamson, "Seven Principles for Good Practice in Undergraduate Education," *The Wingspread Journal*, 9:June, 1987: 1-4.

Cohen, P. A., and W. J. McKeachie, "The Role of Colleagues in the Evaluation of College Teaching," *Improving College and University Teaching*, 28: Fall, 1980, 147-154.

Diamond, R. M., ed., *A Guide to Evaluating Teaching for Promotion and Tenure*, Syracuse: Center for Instructional Development, 1987.

Elbow, P., "One-to-One Faculty Development," *New Directions for Teaching and Learning*, 4:1980, 25-40.

Hendricson, W. D., and others, "Effects of Providing Feedback to Lecturers Via Videotape Recordings and Observer Critiques," *American Journal of Pharmaceutical Education*, 47:Fall, 1983, 165-166.

McIntosh, T. N., and T. E. Van Koevering, "Six-Year Case Study of Faculty Peer Reviews, Merit Ratings, and Pay Awards in a Multidisciplinary Department," *Journal of the College and University Personnel Association*, 37:Spring, 1986, 5-14.

Root, L. S., "Faculty Evaluation: Reliability of Peer Assessments of Research, Teaching, and Service," *Research in Higher Education*, 26:1987, 71-84.

Rorschach, E., and R. Whitney, "Relearning to Teach: Peer Observation As a Means of Professional Development for Teachers," Paper presented at the Annual Meeting of the National Council of Teachers of English Spring Conference, 1985 (4th, Houston, TX).

Seldin, P., *Changing Practices in Faculty Evaluation*, San Francisco: Jossey-Bass Publishers, 1984.

Tobias, S., "Peer Perspectives on the Teaching of Science," *Change*, 18:March/April, 1986, 36-41.

APPENDIX 19-1

ASSESSING TEACHING EFFECTIVENESS

Each of the following areas are of importance to the teaching process. Either by yourself or with a faculty colleague evaluate your teaching in terms of the following items. Evaluate your effectiveness on a five-point scale (with 5 being high) in terms of the extent to which you have achieved the criteria.

INPUTS TO THE TEACHING PROCESS—COURSE ORGANIZATION

The course objectives are clearly stated. _____
The course objectives are appropriate for the course. _____
The course material is current and up to date. _____

The course material teaches to the course objectives. _____

The course requirements are appropriate for students and course level. _____

The course, text, and reading materials are at an appropriate level. _____

The evaluation procedures are clearly stated. _____

The evaluation is keyed to course objectives. _____

Evaluation of Student Learning

The evaluation instruments:

Evaluate attainment of course goals. _____

Evaluate higher order skills. _____

- Analysis _____
- Application _____
- Synthesis _____
- Evaluation _____

Avoid emphasis of recall and recognition. _____

Show evidence of multiple evaluation strategies. _____

Handouts, Simulations and Worksheets

These items:

Stimulate students to think critically. _____

Allow opportunities to practice skills. _____

Allow for self-evaluation or simple grading for prompt feedback. _____

Student Support

Students are encouraged to request assistance. _____

Regular office hours are held and utilized by students. _____

Tutorial services are established. _____

THE TEACHING PROCESS—THE TEACHER

In my teaching, I:

Am motivating. _____

Am enthusiastic. _____

Am a good communicator. _____

Encourage student-faculty contacts. _____

Use multiple teaching techniques. _____

Use multiple evaluation techniques. _____

Encourage cooperation among students in the learning process. _____

Utilize active learning techniques. _____

Provide prompt feedback. _____

Require adequate time on task. _____

Communicate high expectations. _____

OUTPUTS OF THE TEACHING PROCESS

The assessment of learning shows a high level of student mastery. _____

The students have developed the ability to evaluate economic policy critically and to communicate the results clearly. _____

The students show the ability to learn and to work on their own. _____

The students have developed a positive attitude toward economics. _____

The course evaluations reflect positive attitudes to the course. _____

Feedback from alumni is positive and constructive. _____

INSTRUCTIONAL INNOVATION

I often discuss teaching issues and concerns with my peers. _____

I am actively engaged in revising my courses. _____

I am engaged in curriculum revision in the economics department. _____

I often observe other teachers in action. _____

I have peers observe my teaching on a regular basis. _____

I am searching for innovative ways to improve my course. _____

CHAPTER 20

RESEARCH ON TEACHING COLLEGE ECONOMICS

John J. Siegfried[*]
William B. Walstad

This chapter is about research on economics instruction that has implications for the effective teaching of the principles of economics course. The purpose is not to conduct a laborious review of the literature in economics education but rather to provide a brief guide to research efforts and to report results that may improve teaching effectiveness and student learning of introductory economics. This discussion of the main research conclusions that have emerged over the past 30 years should also be of value to department chairs or faculty committees who are responsible for making decisions about how the course is taught and thus may use the research results in more effectively organizing economics instruction for students.

The chapter is organized into four sections. First, we review the history of research on teaching college economics in order to acquaint instructors with the major developments and sources of information on the subject since its origin in the 1960s. Next, we describe problems with the measurement of the educational product and how this challenge has been treated in the research literature. The majority of the chapter, however, is devoted to the final two sections in which we examine the relationship between student characteristics and economics teaching and then turn attention to the influence of course format on student learning. Here we identify from the research key findings that we hope will be of use to economics principles instructors and administrators.

A HISTORICAL OVERVIEW

In Rendigs Fels's (1969) Presidential address to the Southern Economic Association, "Hard Research on a Soft Subject: Hypothesis-Testing in Economic Education," he describes economics education as a new and exciting challenge for hard research. In Fels's view, hard research in economics education uses quantitative methods and at times economic theory to address questions about the teaching and learning of economics. He recommends this type of research over "soft research," or the casual empiricism that so many economists use when they discuss economics instruction with colleagues while they would demand hard findings in other areas of economics. He then reviews the eight studies that had been conducted by that time that provide hard evidence about effective economics instruction.

Research on economics education has progressed in the decades since Fels devoted his Presidential address to it. A key contribution to this development was the publication, in 1968, of the *Test of Understanding of College Economics* (TUCE). The original test was prepared by a distinguished committee of economists that included George Stigler, Paul Samuelson, and G. L. Bach. It was revised in 1980 by a committee chaired by Phillip Saunders of Indiana University. A third edition will be available for use beginning in 1990.

There have been over a hundred studies of teaching effectiveness in a variety of settings that have used the original and revised TUCE exams as a nationally normed and standardized measure of cognitive achievement. The creation of this examination was crucial to the expansion of research on effective teaching in economics, for without a reliable and valid test measure it is difficult to conduct quality empirical studies. Teacher-made tests constructed from textbook test banks simply are not acceptable for research work in economics education (Walstad, 1987a).

The second factor spurring the growth of economics education research was the establishment in the 1950s of an annual session at the American Economic Association convention devoted to economics education and the organization of the *Journal of Economic Education* in 1969. The annual session at the AEA meetings and publication of its proceedings in the May *Papers and Proceedings* issue of the *American Economic Review* and the new *Journal of Economic Education* gave economists and educators an opportunity to report research findings on economics instruction. After a decade of growth, the *Journal* gained a respectable ranking among scholarly economics journals; a recent cross-citation study ranked it at the median of all scholarly journals in economics (Liebowitz and Palmer, 1984). There is little doubt that the establishment of the *Journal* helped economists who wanted to conduct research in economics education obtain credit for their scholarly work when they were reviewed for promotion and tenure.

By 1979 there was sufficient published research for John Siegfried and Rendigs Fels (1979) to construct a survey of research on teaching college economics that appeared in the *Journal of Economic Literature*. Most of the 179 articles and books cited in that review came from the *Journal of Economic Education* or from the economics education section published annually in the May proceedings issue of the

American Economic Review. About half of the studies used the TUCE as the measure of cognitive achievement.

That survey embraced several goals. The most important were to expose more professional economists to the work of those conducting economics education research, to report substantive conclusions from the research, and to evaluate the methodological foundation of the research. Subsequently William Becker (1983a, 1983b, 1983c) contributed a three-part essay that extended the survey, emphasizing theoretical model building and sound statistical methodology. The purpose of the present essay is to reconsider the substantive conclusions about teaching and learning economics reported by Siegfried and Fels (1979) in light of another decade's research contributions, and to communicate research findings that a conscientious college economics teacher or administrator might find useful. Further consideration of methodological issues is omitted. Much progress has been made in this area, particularly with the use of limited dependent variables (Becker and Walstad, 1987). Our goal here, however, is to report research findings that might improve economics education if implemented. We will also, from time to time, find it impossible to resist identifying important questions for future research.

Since 1979 growth in published economics education research has slowed. A complete revision of the Siegfried-Fels *Journal of Economic Literature* article to bring it up to date in 1989 would expand the list of references from 179 to approximately 250. Relatively few of these additions could be called "classics." The increment in economics education research contributions over the last decade is less than a third of the earlier decade, and in the face of even more economists indicating economics education as their primary specialty.[1] Why has there been such a precipitous decline in reported research findings? Several possible explanations come to mind. First, the easy questions naturally were addressed first. As the most important questions are answered and as the remaining become ever more difficult, fewer potential research efforts yield a positive expected net present value. Second, most of the research of the 1970s focused on the principles courses. Subsequent attention has switched to other economics courses and other aspects of economics instruction, e.g., the "major." With no *Test of Understanding College Economics* to evaluate achievement, research on other courses or the entire economics major is considerably more difficult.[2]

THE MEASUREMENT OF EDUCATIONAL OUTPUTS

The diversity and ambiguity of the goals of teaching economics at the college level are well known (Siegfried and Fels, 1979, 926-937). There have been three important additions to these debates in the last decade. First, Becker (1982), using a rigorous model of student utility maximization, confirmed that changes in instructional technology which permit students to convert time into learning more efficiently need not result in any change in the students' learning of economics. Benefits from more efficient pedagogical techniques may be used by students to "purchase" increased learning in other subjects, or may simply be converted into more leisure time. Whether the effort to enhance learning efficiency is worthwhile then turns on the values assigned to learning different things and the value of leisure.

Becker also addressed the possibility that a substantial component of value added by colleges and universities is produced by their sifting and winnowing services. Taubman and Wales (1973), for example, argue that up to half of earnings differentials enjoyed by college graduates are due to such screening. If screening is a valued product of college education, and if colleges and universities accept the challenge to produce it, the task then is to accomplish it as efficiently as possible. Becker's results indicate that the learning effects resulting from a change in the accuracy of student screening will depend on each student's relative achievement position within a college. Students above the modal knowledge level at a college will find it in their interest to increase learning in the face of improved screening accuracy. But a similar behavioral response does not follow automatically for utility maximizing students below the modal knowledge level. Therefore, the desirability of improvements in screening accuracy will depend on the weights assigned to learning by students at different points in the achievement distribution.

The second important contribution is Lee Hansen's (1986) effort to focus more attention on the economics major. Hansen proposes a hierarchy of proficiencies that we might reasonably expect undergraduate economics majors to acquire and demonstrate by the time they graduate. These proficiencies are:

- gaining access to existing knowledge
- displaying command of existing knowledge
- displaying ability to draw out existing knowledge
- utilizing existing knowledge to explore issues
- creating new knowledge

The challenge, of course, is to devise valid instruments to measure these proficiencies. The question is timely. The American Association of Colleges is currently engaged in the second part of a significant project on "study-in-depth," i.e., the major. Further study of the major is also a priority on the agenda of the American Economic Association's Committee on Economic Education (CEE). The CEE cosponsored a study of the economics major in 1980, which revealed virtually unanimous agreement on a list of required courses in the major that include principles of micro and macro, intermediate micro theory, intermediate macro theory, and economic statistics, and that the remainder of the major (usually 10 courses in total) consist of economics electives (Siegfried and Wilkinson, 1982). The next step is to identify the outcomes we expect to achieve by offering an integrated "major" rather than simple access to courses. In what way and for what reasons might we expect the "major" to add up to more than the sum of the contributions of individual courses? Issues of course sequencing, students' development of a critical perspective on their discipline, acquisition of sophisticated proficiencies, capacity to deal with complexity, the interconnection between disciplines, and ways to strengthen study-in-depth are all part of the agenda.

Third, there is new evidence about the capacity of multiple choice examinations to measure output in the cognitive domain. Lumsden and Scott (1983) discovered much weaker correlations between students' performance on multiple choice examinations and essay examinations (in the range of .2 to .3) than had been found in earlier studies (Siegfried and Fels, 1979, 928-929). Such evidence does not eliminate the value of multiple choice examinations for measuring some elements of economic understanding (after all, they may capture best the proficiencies we value highest). In view of the popularity of both essay and multiple choice examinations in economics, however, it does suggest that different examination formats may measure different dimensions of output. Lumsden and Scott's (1983) evidence reinforces Hansen's (1986) call for the development of sample essay questions to measure higher level proficiencies.

The character of testing instruments influences the behavior of faculty and students. When screening on higher level proficiencies can be accomplished accurately, more effort will be devoted to teaching those proficiencies.

STUDENT CHARACTERISTICS AND ECONOMICS TEACHING

The student is the target of classroom instruction for the economics teacher and accordingly has been the main subject of research in economics education. The relationship between student characteristics and economics teaching is complex and difficult to decipher, but we see worthwhile conclusions from the research on students emerging in six areas: (1) evaluation of teaching; (2) attitudes and achievement; (3) effort and study time; (4) learning technology; (5) gender; and (6) other characteristics.

Evaluation of Teaching

It is now accepted practice to use students' opinions of instruction as one factor in the evaluation of teaching at most colleges, in spite of the controversies that continue to surround such evaluations (Siegfried and Fels, 1979, 930-934). Systematic determinants of effective teaching may be difficult to discern because different equally effective teachers may adopt different teaching styles due to different endowments of skills, differing perceptions of what constitutes good teaching, and different search paths to ascertain which of the available styles works best for them (Lima, 1981). Indeed, Lima may be correct in his prediction that "individuals doing research into the empirical determinants of teaching effectiveness are doomed to be searching through a haystack which simply contains no needle" (1981, 1059).

The same conclusion might be applied to weather prediction or interest rate forecasting, but, nevertheless, empirical work continues on these topics; and it will likely continue on the question of what specific characteristics constitute effective teaching. If student evaluations (SETs) are an acceptable measure of some dimensions of teaching effectiveness, then it is important to know what can be done to improve those ratings.

Research results can enhance our understanding of what generates more favorable student attitudes toward economics instruction. In an early study of almost 5,000 course evaluations at the Graduate School of Business at Stanford University, Lumsden (1974) discovered that clarity of presentation, enthusiasm, and respect for students' opinions had the largest positive effect on overall course evaluations. In a more recent analysis of over 2,500 British students at 19 universities, Lumsden and Scott (1983) found clarity of presentation and imparting enthusiasm to be the most important teacher characteristics in the view of students. Of particular interest for improving student evaluations is their discovery that economics instructors at the same institutions substantially underestimated the importance of these two factors and overestimated the importance of knowing the subject matter well (in the eyes of the students, who may or may not be good judges of that) and (perceived) preparation for class.

Using 1,300 SETs from the University of Southern California, Aigner and Thum (1986) found that characteristics of good teaching include clarity of exposition, organization, "signaling" (the use of oral statements to draw attention to an upcoming point), questioning and probing to maintain active student involvement, accepting student's ideas, and rapport with students. These instructor-specific characteristics explained more than twice the linear variation in overall course ratings than did course-specific (e.g., whether the course was required, enrollment) *and* student-specific (e.g., whether the student was foreign, class year) characteristics combined. This suggests that individual instructors retain considerable control over their course evaluation destiny if the important instructor-specific characteristics are under their control.

DeCanio (1986) applied multinominal logit analysis to 6,900 individual student course evaluations at the University of California, Santa Barbara, and obtained results comparable to Aigner and Thum (1986). He found that "organization and preparation" and "communication skills" (e.g., value of lectures, lecture preparation, ability to explain material, and ability to answer questions) were strongly and positively associated with favorable teaching evaluations.

Finally, in a clever attempt to discern whether SET responses can identify more effective teachers, Shmanske (1988) followed the students of 17 introductory economics professors into their second economics course. Using binary variables for the different faculty he found little difference among their students in cognitive achievement in the subsequent economics course. Students' ratings of their first semester instructor also proved ineffective in separating the more successful students from the less successful students in the second course. His results, tentative though they may be, are consistent with the view that the students recognized there was actually little difference in the teaching effectiveness among the various instructors who taught them in the first semester.

The most controversial aspect of SETs is their use for salary, promotion and tenure decisions. One accusation is that instructors can "buy" better student evaluations by awarding higher grades. Aigner and Thum (1986) found evidence to support the accusation, but DeCanio (1986) and Sevier (1983) did not. Whatever is the relationship between SET ratings and grades, it may be beside the point. Dilts (1980), Blackwell (1983), and Zangenehzadeh (1988) have each recently described a method to control for unwanted influences on SETs. If differences in grading practices (as well as other differences, for example in class size, whether a course is required or not, or whether course enrollment is mostly freshmen or mostly seniors) are deemed inappropriate influences when course ratings are used for personnel decisions, they can be (more or less) excised. The point is that SETs must be interpreted with care, in light of the purpose to which they are being applied, and in clear recognition that they measure students' opinions accurately, but may or may not measure teaching effectiveness.

Attitudes and Achievement

The conventional belief has long been that there is a simultaneous relationship between economics achievement and attitudes towards economics as a subject. That is, if students like economics they will learn more and if they learn more their attitude toward the subject will improve. Most of the research on this problem was originally conducted with single equation ordinary least squares models (Ramsett, Johnson and Adams, 1973; Karstensson and Vedder, 1974). When estimated with two-stage least squares in simultaneous equations models, however, the results suggest that there may be a one-way relationship. That is, if students learn more economics, over and above what they would have known before they took the course, then they will like that subject more. In contrast, if they like the subject more, that does not necessarily mean they will learn more economics (Walstad, 1987b).

The implication of these studies is that what instructors need to be most concerned about is finding ways to teach students the subject. Don't worry about what they think of the subject initially or even during the course. If the instructor can teach them, the students will develop a greater appreciation (liking) for economics. In other words, attitudes towards economics may be a product of what students learn rather than a determinant of what they learn.

Effort and Study Time

All of the recent research on student effort finds that it matters. Leppel (1984) discovered that students who reported spending greater effort on a course earned higher grades. Prince, Kipps, Wilheim and Wetzel (1981) also found that student effort affected achievement. Paul (1982) reports that time spent on outside employment leads to lower achievement levels, and Schmidt (1983) observes, with empirical support, that the intensity as well as the total quantity of study time matters for learning economics. There is, unfortunately, no research on the effectiveness of various techniques instructors might employ to induce greater study effort, and little is known about the opportunity cost of incremental economics study time (Gleason and Walstad, 1988).

Learning Technology

Research efforts of the 1970s focused on developing more effective methods for instructors to teach economics. However, the process is not complete unless students learn what is taught. A promising recent development is the increased attention to how students learn (vis-a-vis how instructors teach). In Chapter 8 Rendigs Fels (1989) reports on his work concerning different strategies for learning different types of knowledge. One might hope that teaching students how to select a learning strategy well adapted to their individual talents and the character of the material to be learned might be productive. This approach is yet to be tested.

There is growing evidence that Siegfried and Fels's (1979) first conclusion, namely that different students learn economics in different ways, is accurate and important. Becker agrees, arguing that "too little is known about how certain (teaching) methods interact with given (student) characteristics" (1983a, 12).

Subsequent research provides empirical support for this conclusion. Charkins, O'-Toole, and Wetzel (1985) discovered that student's learning style (dependent, independent, or collaborative) affected the amount of economics learned. Wetzel, Potter and O'Toole (1982) went a step further and found that matching instructors' teaching styles with students' learning styles further increased learning. Whether teachers' and students' styles matched explained up to 50 percent more of the variation in student learning than traditional factors like students' verbal and quantitative skills. Miller (1982), applying frontier production function techniques, discovered that the efficiency with which students convert inputs into outputs in the learning process varies. His finding that younger students and women are less efficient learners indicates where the marginal impact of resources devoted toward helping students understand how to learn would have the greatest initial impact.

Gender

MacDowell, Senn, and Soper (1977) posed the question: "Does sex really matter?" Most people would say yes, of course it does. From the perspective of economics instruction, the answer is yes and no. Yes, sex matters because it has been found that at any point in time, using a stock model of economics knowledge, males score better than females on economics tests (Siegfried, 1979). This finding holds true both in terms of simple mean comparisons of scores on the TUCE, and other tests, and in regression studies that control for other variables. The results are fairly consistent in studies with multiple choice tests at the elementary, secondary, and college levels; all other things equal, males appear to know more economics than females. The difference in test scores is usually small, but statistically significant; whether it is of practical significance is open to debate (see Ladd, 1977).[3] Because of self-selection bias, the observed difference in test scores likely understates the difference between economics understanding of all men and all women (Heath, 1989).

The no answer to the question comes from research which has used a flow model [but see Watts and Lynch (1989) for a yes answer in a well executed flow model with a large sample]. With the flow model the initial stock of economic knowledge is controlled and we try to explain performance at the end of the course. In studies that have used this formulation, there is usually no difference between the performance of men and women. In other words, males and females appear to *learn* economics at the same rate. While women may enter a principles class with slightly less understanding, they seem to learn the same amount as men over the course of the semester. Where the initial disadvantage comes from remains a mystery.

Recent research from Great Britain, however, suggests a different picture and a possible solution to the mystery. Lumsden and Scott (1987) found that males tend to show slight superiority on multiple choice exams, but that females do substantially better on essay exams. The psychological literature suggests that females mature earlier and have higher verbal skills than males. Since essay exams tap verbal skills more than do multiple choice exams, it is reasonable to expect females would do better on them. Therefore, it may be the type of exam that is producing the sex differential rather than any inherent difference between the sexes in economics learning or understanding. If this finding is robust, the format of economics exams may itself introduce a sex bias. Multiple choice exams may favor males and essay exams may favor females. The pattern discovered by Lumsden and Scott is consistent with an earlier exploratory study by Marianne Ferber and colleagues (1983) at the University of Illinois who found a significant difference in measured understanding economics between males and females on classroom multiple choice tests but no gender difference on essay tests.

Other Characteristics

It is well established that college entrance examination scores are positively and significantly associated with economics test performance. Verbal SAT scores seem to be more important than quantitative SAT scores for achievement on the TUCE. The TUCE, recall, is designed to measure achievement in the introductory economics course. Verbal and quantitative SAT scores are *both* important for achievement on the Economics component of the Graduate Record Examination taken during an undergraduate's senior year (Siegfried and Raymond, 1984). This pattern of results is consistent with the obvious fact that quantitative skills become relatively more important for learning economics as a student advances toward graduate study.

Siegfried and Fels (1979) reported that measures of student maturity, such as age and year in school, usually show no relationship to cognitive performance. Recent research on this subject casts some doubt on that conclusion. Manahan (1983), Hodgin (1984), and Reid (1983) all report that older students perform better than younger students, ceteris paribus. Leppel (1984) finds evidence that married students perform better. And two recent studies, Bonello, Schwartz, and Davisson (1984) and Watts and Lynch (1989) report that freshmen are at a distinct disadvantage in introductory economics, everything else the same. If these research results hold up under additional scrutiny, they have obvious implications for the scheduling of introductory economics courses in the curriculum.

Finally, there has been a national trend for more students to study economics in high school as more states mandate the subject or more students take economics as an elective. This development might have an effect on the content and pace of the college principles course if students arrive at the course demonstrating mastery of the basic subject matter. A recent study by Walstad and Soper (1988), however, indicates that students could correctly answer only 52 percent of the questions on the *Test of Economic Literacy* after taking an economics course in high school and showed only a 7.5 percent increase in knowledge during the course. The finding is consistent with earlier work by Saunders (1970). He concluded that having taken high school economics did not hurt students taking a college principles course, but it did not give students a significant advantage either. So, most college instructors can assume that students enter their principles course without much prior knowledge of the subject. For those students capable of learning college principles in high school, there is now an Advanced Placement course (Buckles and Morton, 1988).

COURSE FORMAT AND STUDENT LEARNING

Choices made by instructors, administrators, and faculty committees often influence student learning in the principles course. Decisions involve (1) the use of innovative teaching methods; (2) the selection of textbook; (3) the choice of class size; (4) the sequence of micro and macro; and (5) the use of graduate instructors. Each of these considerations merits brief discussion based on recent research findings.

Innovative Pedagogies

The emphasis of recent research in economics education has been on factors that matter for achievement in the context of traditional lecture and blackboard teaching. This appears to be the correct allocation of research efforts, since adoption of "innovative" teaching methods has been slow in spite of the verified effectiveness of some of them. Table 20-1 reports the percentage of institutions using different innovative teaching methods in *at least one* class of principles of economics during the 1979-80 academic year. Because all sections of principles at an institution may not use the special pedagogy, the reported figures overstate the proportion of students exposed to the special teaching methods. On the other hand, techniques such as computer managed instruction and television are specifically designed to improve learning in

TABLE 20-1   PERCENTAGE OF SCHOOLS USING INNOVATIVE TEACHING METHODS

Type of Innovative Teaching Method	All (n=538)	Research (n=56)	Doctorate (n=54)	Comprehensive (n=236)	Liberal Arts I (n=86)	Liberal Arts II (n=106)
			School Type			
Any Type	38%	43%	44%	37%	34%	38%
Computer-Assisted Methods (e.g., Games & Simulation)	17	14	20	14	23	16
Computer-Managed Instruction (or Personalized System of Instruction)	5	13	7	5	1	3
Self-Paced Instruction	9	13	6	11	5	9
Programmed Learning	7	5	9	8	5	8
Case Study Method	1	2	4	1	0	0
Television or Other Audio-Visual	19	11	28	18	12	22
Other	1	2	0	1	2	1

Source: Sweeney, Siegfried, Raymond and Wilkinson (1983)

large classes, and are more likely to be adopted where student enrollment pressures are greatest, in which case the reported figures, which count classes rather than students, would understate the proportion of students exposed to the special teaching methods. We have no insight concerning how the biases might balance.

Much of the research on economics education completed in the 1970s consisted of evaluations of new (to economics) teaching methods. Based on an extensive review of that literature Siegfried and Fels (1979) concluded (1) that games and computer assisted instruction generate about the same cognitive achievement, but probably cost more than conventional pedagogical methods; (2) that computerized study management systems seem to be more effective than computer games and simulation routines, particularly for low-achieving students; (3) that programmed instruction is efficient in the sense of bringing students to a given level of competence in less time, but generally students don't like it; (4) that students like self-paced instruction, and it increases learning in some circumstances; and (5) that television is about as effective as live lectures for student learning, but students do not like it either.

Additional research on these teaching methods since 1979 has been sparse. Almost all of the research on computer assisted instruction (games and simulations) is out of date as a result of a revolution in both computer hardware and software (Lewis, Dalgaard and Boyer, 1985). The conclusion with respect to the cost of computer games and simulations is particularly suspect as more publicly available packages replace the fixed costs of program writing previously incurred by individual instructors. Millerd and Robertson (1987) recently observed that the effectiveness of computer games may depend on the care with which they are integrated into a course. The conclusion that computer games and simulations are ineffective may be more an indictment of their implementation than of the concept as a teaching aid.

The innovative use of computers that continues to show the most substantial rewards is computer managed instruction (CMI). CMI systems usually administer periodic short quizzes and then provide rapid feedback to students. Marlin and Niss (1982) report further evidence that such systems help low achievers in economics courses, probably because they increase study discipline.

The latest study of programmed instruction (PI) (in which students fill in blanks in sentences in an economics book and are immediately informed whether their response is correct or incorrect) confirms the conclusion that PI reduces substantially the time required to master basic economic principles (Vredeveld, 1982). The problem with PI, however, is that instructors, in particular, do not like it, probably because it bores them. Vredeveld reports evidence that the attitude conveyed by the instructor about the PI book is important for determining what students get out of it, but conveying enthusiasm when one is bored may be difficult.

Textbook

In most studies of achievement in introductory economics, the choice of textbook does not appear to matter (Meinkoth, 1971; Saunders, 1973). There has been no research on this question in the past decade, however. As the leading texts in economics change, it is probably desirable to reevaluate this conclusion. In the only recent study of economics textbooks to come to our attention (Watts and Lynch, 1989) it was found that using a low level intermediate theory text in a principles of economics course was associated with statistically significantly lower revised TUCE examination scores than if a standard introductory text were adopted.

Class Size

Studies of introductory economics class size are almost unanimous in finding no influence on standardized examination test scores, which suggests that it might be taught cost effectively in the college auditorium (or gymnasium!). These studies, however, are mostly dated, and more needs to be learned about this important question since it is one of the few determinants of learning that is easy (but not cheap) to control. It is known that students do not *like* larger classes even if they do just as well in them (Levin, 1967; Mirus, 1973; McConnell and Sosin, 1984; DeCanio, 1986), and students' critical thinking skills appear to deteriorate with increasing class size (Lewis and Dahl, 1972). Average class sizes vary considerably in American higher education, even within a single course subject. Average enrollment per lecture section for micro, macro, and one-semester introductory courses by type of institution are reported for 1980 in Table 20-2.

The standard deviations around the mean class size in Table 20-2 are usually at least half of the course enrollment. The averages themselves vary from a low of 32 for the one-semester introductory course in Liberal Arts II colleges to 132 for the same course in research universities. There is clearly an enormous variety in the size of class to which principles of economics is taught, and perhaps that is appropriate in view of Levin's (1967) conclusion that class size does not matter. This is such an important question, however, that more sophisticated contemporary evidence would help department chairs decide whether to have all classes of, for example, 50 students each or a mixture of some with 75 and some with 25.

Course Sequence

There has been other work on the principles course that has some implications for effective instruction. A study by John Fizel and Jerry Johnson (1986) at the University of Wisconsin-Eau Claire provided some initial findings on principles course sequence. Students were randomly assigned to either a macro or a micro course during the fall semester. They then completed the principles course sequence in the spring semester. After controlling for student differences, the results indicated that students who took a micro first and macro second sequence performed significantly better than students who took a macro first and micro second sequence. Students, however, seem to like economics better when they took a macro to micro sequence. The majority of two-semester principles textbooks are organized with macro first, although with the expansion of book splits, it may not make much difference.

TABLE 20-2   AVERAGE ENROLLMENT PER LECTURE SECTION FOR MICRO, MACRO, AND ONE-SEMESTER INTRODUCTORY COURSES BY SCHOOL TYPE*

	School Classification					
Course	All	Research	Doctorate	Comprehensive	Liberal Arts I	Liberal Arts II
Micro	57	105	80	52	38	40
	(50)	(69)	(70)	(38)	(19)	(14)
	n=429	n=47	n=45	n=198	n=54	n=81
Macro	59	107	93	52	37	40
	(52)	(77)	(82)	(36)	(15)	(13)
	n=425	n=46	n=45	n=198	n=50	n=82
One-Semester	63	132	98	47	41	32
	(64)	(114)	(63)	(27)	(24)	(11)
	n=189	n=30	n=20	n=77	n=36	n=25

*Standard deviations are in parentheses.
Source: Sweeney, Siegfried, Raymond and Wilkinson (1983)

Graduate Student Instructors

The one study of graduate student instructors (GSIs) in the past decade (Watts and Lynch, 1989), adds further evidence that graduate students generally are just as good teachers as regular faculty even though, other things equal, experience results in better teaching and graduate students have less experience. The empirical evidence from studies done at Princeton, Hebrew University, Carnegie-Mellon, Indiana, Florida State, Nebraska, and (now) Purdue suggests that GSIs have compensating attributes that balance their lack of experience. Watts and Lynch (1989) did find, however, that the undergraduate students of non-native English speaking GSIs did significantly worse on a final examination than did the students of GSIs for whom English was their first language. This result is important in view of the fact that over thirty percent of Ph.D. students in economics in the United States now are foreign (Watts and Lynch, 1989). Of obvious further interest, in view of these findings, is whether the efforts of some departments and colleges to improve the pronunciation of English by non-native English speakers and to acclimate foreign students to U.S. college culture are effective.

CONCLUSION

Our knowledge of how to improve the effectiveness of instruction in principles of economics courses has improved substantially since the 1960s. Studies have been conducted on a variety of topics, in some cases using the best research techniques available to economists. Principles instructors and administrators no longer have to be satisfied with the casual observations of colleagues as answers to questions about the teaching and learning of economics. Instead they can rely on a body of research literature that is beginning to provide answers to many questions. In this chapter, we have identified some findings from the research literature on economics education that have direct and indirect implications for the teaching of college economics. More answers will come over the years because researchers are continuing to undertake scholarly studies that advance our understanding.

NOTES

*We acknowledge helpful comments by William E. Becker, Stephen Buckles, and Rendigs Fels.

1 In the 1978 Directory of the American Economic Association, 45 economists indicated economic education as their primary specialty. By 1985 this number had grown to 58.

2 For those instructors who want a source of current information on research articles, there exists a microcomputer file, *Research in Economic Education Database* (REED), available for purchase from the Joint Council on Economic Education (423 Park Avenue South, New York, New York 10016). REED contains detailed abstracts of most of the journal articles that have been published since 1970 and can be searched across key descriptors.

3 Many of the statistically significant findings in economics education research are subject to the same qualification. Much is often made of statistically significant differences in performance on the TUCE examination between an experimental and control group, when the magnitude of the difference is relatively small (e.g., under 10 percent). Whether such differences indicate a practically significant effect, however, will be known only when we can place a value on being able to answer one, two, or three additional questions on the TUCE.

REFERENCES

Aigner, Dennis J., and Frederick D. Thum, "On Student Evaluation of Teaching Ability," *Journal of Economic Education*, Fall 1986, *17*, 243-265.

American Economic Association, "Classification of Members by Fields of Specialization," *American Economic Review*, December 1978, *68*, 426-431.

_____, "Classification of Members by Fields of Specialization," *American Economic Review*, December 1985, *75*, 555-560.

Becker, William E., "The Educational Process and Student Achievement Given Uncertainty in Measurement," *American Economic Review*, March 1982, *72*, 229-236.

_____, "Economic Education Research: Part I, Issues and Questions," *Journal of Economic Education*, Winter 1983a, *14*, 10-17.

_____, "Economic Education Research: Part II, New Directions in Theoretical Model Building," *Journal of Economic Education*, Spring 1983b, *14*, 4-10.

_____, "Economic Education Research: Part III, Statistical Estimation Methods," *Journal of Economic Education*, Summer 1983c, *14*, 4-15.

Becker, William E., and William B. Walstad, *Econometric Modeling in Economic Education Research*, Boston: Kluwer-Nijhoff, 1987.

Blackwell, J. Lloyd, "A Statistical Interpretation of Student Evaluation Feedback: A Comment," *Journal of Economic Education*, Summer 1983, *14*, 28-31.

Bonello, Frank J., Thomas R. Swartz, and William I. Davisson, "Freshman-Sophomore Learning Differentials: A Comment," *Journal of Economic Education*, Summer 1984, *15*, 205-210.

Buckles, Stephen, and John Morton, "The Effects of Advanced Placement on College Introductory Economics Courses," *American Economic Review*, May 1988, *78*, 263-268.

Charkins, R. J., Dennis M. O'Toole, and James N. Wetzel, "Linking Teacher and Student Learning Styles with Student Achievement and Attitudes," *Journal of Economic Education*, Spring 1985, *16*, 111-120.

DeCanio, Stephen J., "Student Evaluations of Teaching—A Multinomial Logit Approach," *Journal of Economic Education*, Summer 1986, *17*, 165-175.

Dilts, David A., "A Statistical Interpretation of Student Evaluation Feedback," *Journal of Economic Education*, Spring 1980, *11*, 10-15.

Fels, Rendigs, "Hard Research on a Soft Subject: Hypothesis-Testing in Economic Education," *Southern Economic Journal*, July 1969, *36*, 1-9.

_____, "Student Study Methods in Economics," Chapter 8 in this volume (1989).

Ferber, Marianne A., Bonnie G. Birnbaum, and Carole A. Green, "Gender Differences in Economic Knowledge: A Reevaluation of the Evidence," *Journal of Economic Education*, Spring 1983, *14*, 24-37.

Fizel, John L., and Jerry D. Johnson, "The Effect of Macro/Micro Course Sequencing on Learning and Attitudes in Principles of Economics," *Journal of Economic Education*, Spring 1986, *17*, 87-98.

Gleason, Joyce P., and William B. Walstad, "An Empirical Test of an Inventory Model of Student Study Time," *Journal of Economic Education*, Fall 1988, *19*, 315-321.

Hansen, W. Lee, "What Knowledge is Most Worth Knowing—For Economics Majors," *American Economic Review*, May 1986, *76*, 149-152.

Heath, Julia, "An Econometric Model of the Role of Gender in Economic Education," *American Economic Review*, May 1989, *79*, 226-230.

Hodgin, Robert F., "Information Theory and Attitude Formation in Economic Education," *Journal of Economic Education*, Summer 1984, *15*, 191-196.

Karstensson, Lewis, and Richard K. Vedder, "A Note on Attitude as a Factor in Learning Economics," *Journal of Economic Education*, Spring 1974, *5*, 109-111.

Ladd, Helen F., "Male-Female Differences in Precollege Economic Education," in D. R. Wentworth et al., (eds.), *Perspectives on Economic Education*. New York: Joint Council on Economic Education, 1977.

Leppel, Karen, "The Academic Performance of Returning and Continuing College Students: An Economic Analysis," *Journal of Economic Education*, Winter 1984, *15*, 46-54.

Levin, Harry M., *Differences in Outcomes Between Large and Small Classes in Western Civilization and Economics*, Ph.D. dissertation, Rutgers University, 1967, UM Number 67-14, 428.

Lewis, Darrell R., and Tor Dahl, "Critical Thinking Skills in the Principles Course: An Experiment," in A. L. Welsh, ed., *Research Papers in Economic Education*, New York: Joint Council on Economic Education, 1972, 94-117.

_____, Bruce R. Dalgaard, and Carol M. Boyer, "Cost Effectiveness of Computer-Assisted Economics Instruction," *American Economic Review*, May 1985, *75*, 91-96.

Liebowitz, S. J., and J. P. Palmer, "Assessing the Relative Impacts of Economics Journals," *Journal of Economic Literature*, March 1984, *22*, 77-88.

Lima, Anthony K., "An Economic Model of Teaching Effectiveness," *American Economic Review*, December 1981, *71*, 1056-1059.

Lumsden, Keith, "The Information Content of Student Evaluation of Faculty and Courses," in K. Lumsden, ed., *Efficiency in Universities: The LaPaz Papers*, Amsterdam and New York: Elsevier Scientific, 1974, 175-204.

Lumsden, Keith G., and Alex Scott, "The Efficacy of Innovative Teaching Techniques in Economics: The U.K. Experience," *American Economic Review*, May 1983, *73*, 13-17.

———— and ————, "The Economics Student Reexamined: Male-Female Differences in Comprehension," *Journal of Economic Education*, Fall 1987, *18*, 365-375.

MacDowell, Michael A., Peter R. Senn, and John C. Soper, "Does Sex Really Matter?" *Journal of Economic Education*, Fall 1977, *9*, 28-33.

Manahan, Jerry, "An Educational Production Function for Principles of Economics," *Journal of Economic Education*, Spring 1983, *14*, 11-16.

Marlin, James W., and James F. Niss, "The Advanced Learning System, a Computer-Managed, Self-Paced System of Instruction: An Application in Principles of Economics," *Journal of Economic Education*, Summer 1982, *13*, 26-39.

McConnell, Campbell R., and Kim Sosin, "Some Determinants of Student Attitudes Toward Large Classes," *Journal of Economic Education*, Summer 1984, *15*, 181-190.

Meinkoth, Marian R., "Textbooks and the Teaching of Economic Principles," *Journal of Economic Education*, Spring 1971, *2*, 127-130.

Miller, Jimmie C., "Technical Efficiency in the Production of Economic Knowledge," *Journal of Economic Education*, Summer 1982, *13*, 3-13.

Millerd, Frank W., and Alastair R. Robertson, "Computer Simulations as an Integral Part of Intermediate Macroeconomics," *Journal of Economic Education*, Summer 1987, *18*, 269-286.

Mirus, Rolf, "Some Implications of Student Evaluation of Teachers," *Journal of Economic Education*, Fall 1973, *5*, 35-46.

Paul, Harvey, "The Impact of Outside Employment on Student Achievement in Macroeconomic Principles," *Journal of Economic Education*, Summer 1982, *13*, 51-56.

Prince, Raymond, Paul H. Kipps, Howard M. Wilhelm, and James N. Wetzel, "Scholastic Effort: An Empirical Test of Student Choice Models," *Journal of Economic Education*, Summer 1981, *12*, 15-25.

Ramsett, David E., Jerry D. Johnson, and Curtis Adams, "Some Evidence on the Value of Instructors in Teaching Economic Principles," *Journal of Economic Education*, Fall 1973, *5*, 57-62.

Reid, Roger, "A Note on the Environment as a Factor Affecting Student Performance in Principles of Economics," *Journal of Economic Education*, Fall 1983, *14*, 18-22.

Saunders, Phillip, "Does High School Economics Have a Lasting Impact?" *Journal of Economic Education*, Fall 1970, *1*, 39-55.

————, *The Lasting Effectiveness of Introductory Economics Courses*, final report, National Science Foundation Grant GY-7208, June 1973.

Schmidt, Robert, "Who Maximizes What? A Study in Student Time Allocation," *American Economic Review*, May 1983, *73*, 23-28.

Sevier, Daniel A., "Evaluations and Grades: A Simultaneous Framework," *Journal of Economic Education*, Summer 1983, *14*, 32-38.

Shmanske, Stephen, "On the Measurement of Teacher Effectiveness," *Journal of Economic Education*, Fall 1988, *19*, 307-314.

Siegfried, John, "Male-Female Differences in Economic Education: A Survey," *Journal of Economic Education*, Spring 1979, *10*, 1-11.

Siegfried, John, and Rendigs Fels, "Research on Teaching College Economics: A Survey," *Journal of Economic Literature*, September 1979, *17*, 923-969.

———— and James T. Wilkinson, "The Economics Curriculum in the United States: 1980," *American Economic Review: Proceedings*, May 1982, *72*, 125-142.

———— and Jennie Raymond, "A Profile of Senior Economics Majors in the United States," *American Economic Review: Proceedings*, May 1984, *74*, 19-25.

Sweeney, M. Jane Barr, John J. Siegfried, Jennie E. Raymond, and James T. Wilkinson, "The Structure of the Introductory Economics Course in the United States," *Journal of Economic Education* (Fall 1983), *14*, 68-75.

Taubman, Paul J., and Terence J. Wales, "Higher Education Mental Ability, and Screening," *Journal of Political Economy*, January/February 1973, *81*, 28-55.

Vredeveld, George, "Economics and Programmed Instruction," *Journal of Economic Education*, Summer 1982, *13*, 14-25.

Walstad, William B., "Measurement Instruments," in W. E. Becker and W. B. Walstad, eds., *Econometric Modeling in Economic Education Research*, Boston: Kluwer-Nijhoff, 1987a, 73-98.

———, "Applying Two Stage Least Squares," in W. E. Becker and W. B. Walstad, eds., *Econometric Modeling in Economic Education Research*, Boston: Kluwer-Nijhoff, 1987b, 111-134.

——— and John C. Soper, "A Report Card on the Economic Literacy of U.S. High School Students," *American Economic Review: Proceedings*, May 1988, *78*, 251-256.

Watts, Michael, and Gerald J. Lynch, "The Principles Courses Revisited," *American Economic Review*, May 1989, *79*, 236-241.

Wetzel, James N., W. James Potter, and Dennis M. O'Toole, "The Influence of Learning and Teaching Styles on Student Attitudes and Achievement in the Introductory Economics Course: A Case Study," *Journal of Economic Education*, Winter 1982, *13*, 33-39.

Zangenehzadeh, Hamid, "Grade Inflation: A Way Out," *Journal of Economic Education*, Summer 1983, *19*, 217-226.

ALPHABETICAL LIST OF AUTHORS

G. L. Bach, Frank E. Buck Professor of Economics and Public Policy, Emeritus, Stanford University. Former Chairman of the American Economic Association's Committee on Economic Education.

William E. Becker, Professor of Economics, Indiana University, Bloomington. Editor of the *Journal of Economic Education*.

Michael J. Boskin, Burnet C. and Mildred Finley Wohlford Professor of Economics, Stanford University. Currently on leave to serve as the Chairman of the President's Council of Economic Advisers.

Robert Eisner, William R. Kenan Professor of Economics, Northwestern University. President of the American Economic Association, 1988.

Rendigs Fels, Professor of Economics, Emeritus, Vanderbilt University. Former Secretary-Treasurer and Treasurer of the American Economic Association.

Marianne A. Ferber, Professor of Economics, University of Illinois at Urbana-Champaign. Former member of the American Economic Association's Committee on Economic Education.

W. Lee Hansen, Professor of Economics and of Education Policy Studies, University of Wisconsin-Madison. Former Chairman of the American Economic Association's Committee on Economic Education.

James W. Marlin, Jr., President of Nebraska Council on Economic Education. Former Chair of the Department of Economics at Appalachian State University.

Campbell R. McConnell, Carl Adolph Happold Professor of Economics, University of Nebraska-Lincoln. Former member of the American Economic Association's Committee on Economic Education.

James F. Niss, Professor of Economics and Director of Faculty Development, Western Illinois University. Director of the Western Illinois Center for Economic Education.

Jerry L. Petr, C. Wheaton Battey Professor of Economics, University of Nebraska-Lincoln. Former member of the Editorial Board of the *Journal of Economic Issues*.

Michael K. Salemi, Professor of Economics, University of North Carolina at Chapel Hill. Former member of the American Economic Association's Committee on Economic Education.

Paul A. Samuelson, Institute Professor of Economics, Emeritus, Massachusetts Institute of Technology. Nobel Laureate in Economic Science, 1970.

Phillip Saunders, Professor and Chair, Department of Economics, Indiana University-Bloomington. Director of the Indiana University Center for Economic Education.

John J. Siegfried, Professor of Economics, Vanderbilt University. Current Chairman of the American Economic Association's Committee on Economic Education.

William B. Walstad, Professor of Economics, University of Nebraska-Lincoln. Director of the National Center for Research in Economic Education.

Michael Watts, Associate Professor of Economics, Purdue University. Director of the Purdue Center for Economic Education.

Arthur L. Welsh, Professor of Economics, Pennsylvania State University. Former Vice President and Director of the College and University Program of the Joint Council on Economic Education.

DeVon L. Yoho, Associate Professor of Economics, Ball State University. Director of the Ball State Center for Economic Education.

INDEX